Financial Mathematics

A Practical Guide for Actuaries and other Business Professionals

Second Edition

Chris Ruckman

Fellow of the Society of Actuaries, Member of the American Academy of Actuaries

Joe Francis

Fellow of the Society of Actuaries, Member of the American Academy of Actuaries,
Chartered Financial Analyst

BPP

PROFESSIONAL
EDUCATION

BPP Professional Education
Farmington, CT

ISBN: 0-9753136-4-9

Preface

If you're not a close personal friend or a relative of the authors, why should you buy the second edition of this book? In other words, what makes this text different from other interest theory or financial mathematics textbooks?

As professional educators who have also worked in the actuarial and investment professions, the authors have had ample opportunity to observe the common stumbling blocks encountered by students. This text is a clear, practical and student-friendly guide in which theoretical derivations have been balanced with a practical, structured approach to the material. The intended audience is not only students learning about the mathematics of finance for the first time, but also those who, having learned the concepts some time ago, would like to have a practical reference guide.

This text has been written by financial professionals with financial professionals in mind, and it should be particularly helpful to students who wish to become actuaries or other investment professionals. For more information about an actuarial career, visit www.beanactuary.org or www.soa.org. Aspiring actuaries in the UK should visit www.actuaries.org.uk. For more information about the Chartered Financial Analyst®* designation, visit www.cfainstitute.org.

Selected illustrative end-of-chapter practice questions have been taken from relevant past actuarial exams. The abbreviation SOA/CAS refers to questions published by the Society of Actuaries and the Casualty Actuarial Society. The abbreviation IOA/FOA refers to questions published by the Institute of Actuaries and the Faculty of Actuaries in the United Kingdom.

The numerical solutions to all of the end-of-chapter practice questions can be found at the end of the book. Detailed worked solutions to these practice questions can be downloaded free of charge from the BPP Professional Education website at **www.bpptraining.com** (go to any page and look for Text Question Solutions in the "About our Products" menu). Other useful study resources can also be found in our online store, including an extensive supplemental FM Question and Answer Bank with hundreds of exam-style questions as well as online lectures and online multiple choice tests, to name just a few. For students preparing for the SOA FM/CAS 2 exam, it is critically important to work as many exam-style questions as possible. Our supplemental FM Q&A Bank should be very helpful in this regard.

The second edition of this text includes some new material, such as variable perpetuity factors and continuously decreasing annuity factors in Chapter 3. We've also added 40 review questions at the end of the book, which are modeled after the SOA FM / CAS 2 Exam. Throughout the text, other revisions have also been made to help explain the concepts even more clearly.

Students may prefer to work interest theory problems with a financial calculator, but we find that students generally gain a better understanding with a scientific calculator. A scientific calculator forces the student to develop a good understanding of interest theory concepts. Relying on a financial calculator instead of learning the basic concepts often results in a superficial understanding of the material. Nonetheless, sometimes a financial calculator is the best tool to solve a certain problem, such as determining the interest rate embedded in an annuity factor. Where helpful, we've illustrated how to use a financial calculator in our solutions.

Finally, a note on rounding. Our policy in this text has been to keep full accuracy within intermediate calculations even though an intermediate result may be shown as a rounded value.

* Chartered Financial Analyst® is a trademark owned by the CFA institute.

Acknowledgements

This text could not have been completed without the helpful contributions of many outstanding individuals. David Carr has been instrumental in conceptualizing and reviewing the first drafts of each chapter. Beverly Butler's superb technical review greatly improved the grammatical and numerical accuracy of each chapter. Any errors in this text are solely our own. Denise Rosengrant took the final chapters and produced the physical book that is now in your hands. Being able to work with such a brilliant set of coworkers not only improved the quality of this text, but it also made writing this text much more enjoyable than it otherwise would have been.

We are also grateful to our colleagues who taught us many valuable lessons over the course of our careers. We have been fortunate to work with many exceptional people, including several actuaries and investment professionals, who were instrumental in guiding our respective career paths.

Past exam questions are reprinted with permission from the Society of Actuaries, the Casualty Actuarial Society, the Institute of Actuaries and the Faculty of Actuaries.

Last, but by no means least, we are very appreciative of the support and guidance from each of our parents that have both directly and indirectly made this book possible.

Chris Ruckman and Joe Francis

October, 2005

This book is dedicated to our family and friends who have enriched our lives. It is impossible to list each person individually, but you know who you are!

Table of contents

1

Interest rates

In addition to being a medium of exchange, money can also be thought of as a cash amount that is invested to earn even more cash as **interest**. The word interest can be translated from the Greek language as the birth of money from money.

Interest is defined as the payment by one party (the borrower) for the use of an asset that belongs to another party (the lender) over a period of time. This asset is also known as **capital**. In this sense, capital is just money that earns interest. Other forms of productive capital exist, but with interest theory, we are primarily interested in monetary capital, which we also refer to as the **principal** amount.

When interest is expressed as a percent of the capital amount, it is referred to as an **interest rate**. Interest rates are most often computed on an annual basis, but they can be determined for non-annual time periods as well.

We have two perspectives to consider. The first is the perspective of the owner of the capital who would like to be compensated for lending it. The second is the perspective of the borrower of the capital who is willing to pay the lender for the right to borrow it.

The borrower pays interest to the lender for the use of the money. The lender may require additional compensation for the risk of **default**, which is the risk that the borrower will not be able to repay the loan principal. If some risk of default exits, the lender will typically demand a higher interest rate to compensate for assuming this risk of default.

Lenders typically require **collateral**, *ie* something of value pledged as security against the risk of default, to help guarantee the loan will be repaid. The comedian Bob Hope once observed that "A bank is a place that will lend you money if you can prove you don't need it."

In this first chapter, we consider interest earned over annual time periods, but in later chapters we consider non-annual time periods as well. We look at five ways to express interest: **simple interest**, **compound interest**, **simple discount**, **compound discount**, and **continuous interest**. We can break these methods down into two classes: simplistic and realistic.

The simple interest and simple discount methods, as their names imply, belong to the simplistic class. These methods are impractical for large, complicated financial transactions. They may be used, however, for small, simple transactions.

The compound interest, compound discount, and continuous interest methods belong to the realistic class. Compound interest is generally used for financial transactions. Compound discount is less common, but it isn't difficult to grasp once we become comfortable with compound interest. Continuous interest appears frequently in academic and theoretical discussions of valuation.

All three of the realistic methods are consistent with one another. Just as distance can be measured in miles or kilometers, interest can be measured using compound interest, compound discount, or continuous interest rates. And just as a European visiting America could insist on converting all distance measurements into metric, a finance professor working at a bank could insist on converting compound interest rates into continuous interest rates. The professor's calculations would produce the correct values regardless of which type of rate was used.

Compound interest, which allows interest to grow on previously earned interest, has amazing accumulation powers when compared to simple interest, which does not allow interest to grow on previously earned interest. Albert Einstein is said to have noted that the most powerful force in the universe is compound interest.

In this chapter, we also develop methods for **accumulating** payments to a future point in time and **discounting** payments to a previous point in time.

When a payment is accumulated to a future point in time, its **future value** is calculated, taking into account any interest that will be earned during the investment period. When a payment is discounted to a previous point in time, its **present value** is calculated, taking into account any interest that will be earned during the investment period. In order to value a cash flow, we need to know the exact amount of the cash flow and the exact timing of the cash flow. This chapter illustrates the **time value of money**, *ie* a \$1 payment now is worth more than \$1 payable in one year's time.

1.1   Interest

Interest on savings accounts

When money is deposited into a bank account, it typically earns interest. The depositor can be thought of as the **lender** and the bank can be thought of as the **borrower**. The borrower pays interest to the lender to compensate for the use of the money and any risk of default.

Let's say a person deposits \$1,000 into a bank account. One year later, the account has accumulated to \$1,050. This amount consists of \$1,000, representing the initial deposit or **capital**, and \$50, representing the **interest** earned on the deposit over the year. The amount of interest earned over a period of time is simply the difference between the accumulated account value at the end of the period and the accumulated account value at the beginning of the period.

For any amount of interest earned over a given period, we can also calculate the associated **interest rate**. The interest rate in effect for a one-year period is the amount of interest earned over the year divided by the initial accumulated value.

In this example, the interest rate for the year is:

$$\frac{1,050 - 1,000}{1,000} = \frac{50}{1,000} = 0.05 \quad \text{or} \quad 5\%$$

At this point, let's keep things simple by considering annual time periods only, but in later chapters we will consider non-annual time periods.

Interest

The amount of interest earned from time t to time $t+s$ is:

$$AV_{t+s} - AV_t$$

where AV_t is the accumulated value at time t.

Interest rate

The annual interest rate i in effect from time t to time $t+1$ is:

$$i = \frac{AV_{t+1} - AV_t}{AV_t}$$

where t is measured in years.

For example, Bob invests \$3,200 in a savings account on January 1, 2004. On December 31, 2004, the account balance has grown to \$3,294.08.

The total interest earned during 2004 is:

$$3,294.08 - 3,200.00 = \$94.08$$

The annual interest rate during 2004 is:

$$\frac{3,294.08 - 3,200.00}{3,200.00} = \frac{94.08}{3,200.00} = 0.0294 \quad \text{or} \quad 2.94\%$$

Interest on loans

The same theory and definitions can be applied to a loan.

A person may borrow money from a bank, *eg* to buy a car. In this case, the bank is the lender, and the individual is the borrower. As before, the borrower pays interest to the lender to compensate for the use of the money and any risk of default.

Let's say a person borrows \$12,000 from a bank. The loan is to be repaid in full in one year's time with a payment to the bank of \$12,780. This amount consists of \$12,000, representing the initial amount of the loan, and \$780, representing the interest paid on the loan over the year.

The annual interest rate in this example is:

$$\frac{12,780 - 12,000}{12,000} = \frac{780}{12,000} = 0.065 \quad \text{or} \quad 6.5\%$$

When we use interest rates in the context of a loan, two important points should be kept in mind:

1.   The **principal amount** of the loan is the amount provided to the borrower when the loan is originated. (In the example above, the principal amount is $12,000.)

2.   Interest begins to accrue when the loan is originated and continues to accrue until the loan is repaid in full.

The second point is analogous to a savings account: interest begins to accrue when the money is deposited and continues to accrue until the deposit is repaid (withdrawn) in full.

1.2 *Simple interest*

When money is invested in an account paying **simple interest**, interest is only earned on the initial deposit. Interest is not earned on the interest that has previously accrued.

Simple interest

If X is invested in an account that pays simple interest at a rate of i per year, then the accumulated value of the investment after t years is:

$$AV_t = X(1+ti)$$

The accumulated value is composed of the initial investment of X and t years of simple interest at the rate of i per year, Xti. The interest earned each year is Xi.

For example, let's assume a bank account is opened with a deposit of $100. The account pays simple interest of 8% per year. We have $i = 0.08$ and $X = 100$.

The accumulated value of the account at the end of one year is:

$$AV_1 = 100(1+1\times 0.08) = \$108.00$$

The accumulated value of the account at the end of ten years is:

$$AV_{10} = 100(1+10\times 0.08) = \$180.00$$

The accumulated value of the account at the end of twenty years is:

$$AV_{20} = 100(1+20\times 0.08) = \$260.00$$

With simple interest, the account value increases linearly over time. This is shown in the following graph.

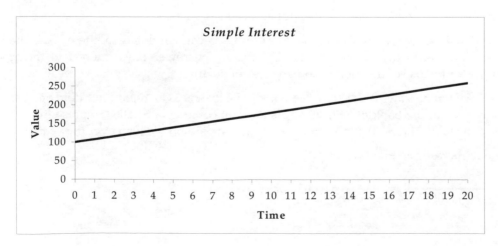

As the continuous nature of the graph implies, the formula for the accumulated value of a deposit under simple interest still applies if t is not an integer. When t is not an integer, interest is paid on a pro-rata (proportional) basis.

For example, a bank account that pays simple interest of 6% per year is opened with a deposit of $100. What is the accumulated value of the account at the end of 9 months?

Since we're working with an annual simple interest rate, t should be expressed in terms of the number of years on deposit. So we have $X = 100$, $t = 9/12 = 0.75$ years, and $i = 0.06$.

Hence, the accumulated value after 9 months is:

$$AV_{0.75} = 100(1 + 0.75 \times 0.06) = \$104.50$$

Example 1.1

A bank accounts pays 3.6% simple interest. Anna deposits $10,000 on January 1, 2004 and leaves her funds to earn interest.

Calculate the accumulated value of Anna's account on April 1, 2006 and January 1, 2007.

Solution

On April 1, 2006, we have $t = 2$ years 3 months $= 2.25$ years, so the accumulated value is:

$$AV_{2.25} = 10,000(1 + 2.25 \times 0.036) = \$10,810.00$$

On January 1, 2007, we have $t = 3$ years, so the accumulated value is:

$$AV_3 = 10,000(1 + 3 \times 0.036) = \$11,080.00 \qquad\qquad ♦♦$$

Banks don't typically use simple interest because it is just too, well, simplistic. If banks actually paid simple interest, then depositors could earn more interest by pursuing the following simple strategy: as soon as interest is credited to the account, withdraw the total account value and immediately re-deposit it, using the interest paid-to date to increase the size of the deposit. This is illustrated in the following example.

Example 1.2

A bank accounts pays 6% simple interest. Randy deposits $100 and leaves his funds to earn interest for 2 years. Leonard also deposits $100, but Leonard withdraws his accumulated value at the end of 1 year, and he then immediately returns the money to the bank, depositing it in a new account.

Who has the greater accumulated value at the end of 2 years: Randy or Leonard?

Solution

At the end of two years, Randy has $112:

$$AV_2 = 100(1 + 2 \times 0.06) = \$112.00$$

At the end of 1 year, Leonard has $106:

$$AV_1 = 100(1 + 1 \times 0.06) = \$106.00$$

But Leonard then withdraws the $106 at the end of 1 year and deposits the $106 in a new account, which also earns a simple interest rate of 6% per year. At the end of the second year, Leonard's accumulated value is $112.36:

$$AV_2 = 106(1 + 1 \times 0.06) = \$112.36$$

Leonard has the greater accumulated value at the end of two years.   ♦♦

In the example above, Leonard found a way to earn interest on the interest he earned in the first year. As we'll see in the next section, when interest is earned on interest, the interest is **compounding**.

If banks used simple interest, then depositors who withdrew and re-deposited their funds would have higher account values than the depositors who simply left their funds in their accounts. Since it doesn't make sense to reward depositors for withdrawing and re-depositing their funds, banks and other financial institutions don't actually use simple interest when calculating accumulated values.

However, simple interest is sometimes used in circumstances where accuracy is not very important. For example, if the time period is short or if the amount of money involved is small, then simple interest might be considered sufficiently accurate.

1.3   Compound interest

When money is deposited into an account paying **compound interest**, interest is earned on the initial deposit *and* the interest that has previously accrued. This is analogous to using simple interest, but periodically the interest is credited to the account and the interest rate then applies to the new, larger balance.

We examine annual compounding in this chapter, which means that interest is credited to the account annually. It is also possible to compound more or less frequently than annually, and we will learn more about non-annual compounding in Chapter 4.

Compound interest

If X is invested in an account that pays compound interest at a rate of i per year, then the accumulated value of the investment after t years is:

$$AV_t = X(1+i)^t$$

Consider another bank account that is opened with a deposit of $100. This account pays compound interest of 8% per year. Let's compare this compound interest account to the simple interest account that we examined earlier that paid simple interest of 8% per year.

Under both compound and simple interest, the accumulated value at the end of one year is $108:

$$\text{Compound interest account:} \quad AV_1 = 100(1+0.08)^1 = \$108.00$$
$$\text{Simple interest account:} \quad AV_1 = 100(1+1\times0.08) = \$108.00$$

With compound interest, the entire accumulated value, not just the original principal, earns interest. This causes the accumulated value in the second year to grow more quickly under compound interest than under simple interest. The accumulated value of the account under compound interest is $0.64 greater at the end of two years than the accumulated value under simple interest:

$$\text{Compound interest account:} \quad AV_2 = 100(1+0.08)(1+0.08) = \$116.64$$
$$\text{Simple interest account:} \quad AV_2 = 100(1+2\times0.08) = \$116.00$$

The $0.64 difference is due to the fact that under compound interest, the $8 of interest that was earned in the first year earns $0.64 in interest over the second year:

$$8(0.08) = \$0.64$$

Instead of calculating the accumulated value year by year, we can use the formula from the box above to obtain the same accumulated value at the end of two years under compound interest:

$$AV_2 = 100(1+0.08)^2 = \$116.64$$

The accumulated value of the compound interest account at the end of ten years is:

$$AV_{10} = 100(1+0.08)^{10} = \$215.89$$

Notice that at the end of the tenth year, the accumulated value under compound interest exceeds the $180 accumulated value that we calculated under simple interest.

The accumulated value of the compound interest account at the end of the twentieth year is:

$$AV_{20} = 100(1+0.08)^{20} = \$466.10$$

At the end of the twentieth year, the accumulated value under compound interest is much greater than the $260 accumulated value under simple interest. This illustrates the power of compound interest. As time passes, an account paying compound interest exhibits geometric (or exponential) growth, while an account paying simple interest exhibits linear growth.

The following graph shows how the value of the account using compound interest increases over time. The dotted line shows the linear progression of the deposit earning simple interest.

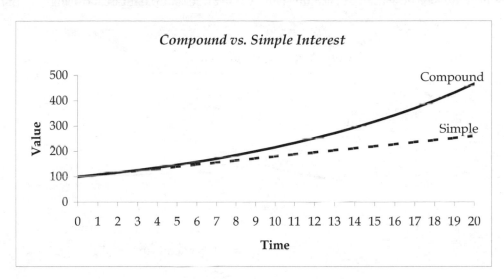

As the graph implies, the formula for the accumulated value of a deposit under compound interest still applies if t is not an integer, assuming that interest is paid on a pro-rata basis.

For example, after 2.5 years the accumulated value of the compound interest account in the current example is:

$$AV_{2.5} = 100(1+0.08)^{2.5} = \$121.22$$

Example 1.3

Drew invests $100 on January 1, 2004 in a bank account that pays compound interest of 5% per year. What is the accumulated value of the account on October 1, 2005?

Solution

We have $X = 100$, $i = 0.05$, and $t = 1$ year 9 months $= 1.75$ years.

So, the accumulated value of the account on October 1, 2005 is:

$$AV_{1.75} = 100(1+0.05)^{1.75} = \$108.91$$

◆ ◆

Example 1.4

Helen borrows $1,000 for 3 years at a compound interest rate of 11.65%. What will the total payment be in 3 years to repay both the loan principal and interest due on the loan?

Solution

We have $X = 1,000$, $i = 0.1165$, and $t = 3$.

So, the total payment required in 3 years is:

$$AV_3 = 1,000(1.1165)^3 = \$1,391.80 \qquad \blacklozenge\blacklozenge$$

Based on the discussion so far, one might think that the accumulated value of an account earning compound interest always exceeds the accumulated value of an account earning the same simple interest rate. But this is only true when the period is greater than one year. When the investment period is less than one year, the accumulated account value under simple interest actually exceeds the accumulated account value under the same compound interest rate.

Since the difference between the accumulated values is small when the elapsed time is less than one year, this effect is not easily observed in the previous chart. So, let's magnify the portion of the chart from time 0 to 1 year. The graph below illustrates that the accumulated value under compound interest is less than the accumulated value under simple interest during the first year.

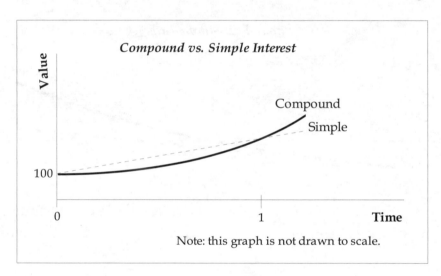

For example, if the simple interest rate and the compound interest rate are each 5%, let's determine the accumulated amount of a $100 deposit after 6 months.

Under simple interest and compound interest, the deposit accumulates to:

$$\text{Compound interest account:} \quad AV_{0.5} = 100(1 + 0.05)^{0.5} = \$102.47$$
$$\text{Simple interest account:} \quad AV_{0.5} = 100(1 + 0.5 \times 0.05) = \$102.50$$

This may not seem like a big difference, but consider a large pension fund deposit of $100,000,000. Instead of a $0.03 difference between account values, we have a $30,000 difference!

We can also state the relationship between simple and compound interest mathematically.

For $i > 0$, we have:

$$1 + ti > (1+i)^t \quad \text{for } 0 < t < 1 \qquad ie \text{ simple interest greater before one year}$$
$$1 + ti = (1+i)^t \quad \text{for } t = 1 \qquad ie \text{ simple and compound interest equal over one year}$$
$$1 + ti < (1+i)^t \quad \text{for } t > 1 \qquad ie \text{ compound interest greater after more than one year}$$

Let's take another look at Example 1.2. This time, the bank credits interest to Leonard and Randy at a compound interest rate, and the resulting treatment is more equitable.

Example 1.5

A bank accounts pays 6% compound interest. Randy deposits $100 and leaves his funds to earn interest for 2 years. Leonard also deposits $100, but Leonard withdraws his accumulated value at the end of 1 year, and he then immediately returns the money to the bank, depositing it in a new account. Who has the greater accumulated value at the end of 2 years: Randy or Leonard?

Solution

At the end of two years, Randy has $112.36:

$$AV_2 = 100(1+0.06)^2 = \$112.36$$

At the end of 1 year, Leonard has $106:

$$AV_1 = 100(1+0.06) = \$106.00$$

Leonard withdraws the $106 at the end of 1 year and then deposits the $106 in a new account, which also earns a compound interest rate of 6% per year. At the end of the second year, Leonard's accumulated value is $112.36:

$$AV_2 = 106(1+0.06) = \$112.36$$

Leonard and Randy each have $112.36 at the end of two years.   ♦♦

If the type of interest is not specified, the convention is to use compound interest, especially if a period longer than one year is being considered. From now on, a compound interest rate of $x\%$ per year compounded annually will be referred to as an **annual effective interest rate** of $x\%$.

We discuss this in more detail later, but for now we should understand that the effective interest rate is effective over the time period in question, which is one year in the case of an annual effective interest rate.

Example 1.6

Carmen borrows $1,000 for 90 days at an annual effective interest rate of 8.25%. What will the total payment be in 90 days to repay both the loan principal and interest due on the loan?

Solution

The term of the loan is 3 months, so $t = 3/12 = 0.25$. The total payment is:

$$AV_{0.25} = 1,000(1.0825)^{0.25} = \$1,020.02$$ ♦♦

Example 1.7

Sam borrows $20,000. He repays the loan 4 years later with a payment of $26,709.38. What is the annual effective interest rate on the loan?

Solution

We have $X = 20,000$, $t = 4$, and $AV_4 = 26,709.38$. Solving for i we have:

$$26,709.38 = 20,000(1+i)^4$$
$$\Rightarrow 1+i = \left(\frac{26,709.38}{20,000}\right)^{1/4}$$
$$\Rightarrow i = 7.5\%$$ ♦♦

1.4 Accumulated value

We have already learned how to accumulate a single payment into the future. The same can be done for several payments. In later chapters, we'll develop useful notation and formulas to do this, but for now we'll just use the basic principles that we've learned so far.

Compound interest accumulated value factor

Under compound interest, the accumulated value after t years of a deposit of $1 is the compound interest accumulated value factor:

$$AVF_t = (1+i)^t$$

Simple interest accumulated value factor

Under simple interest, the accumulated value after t years of a deposit of $1 is the simple interest accumulated value factor:

$$AVF_t = (1+ti)$$

Let's consider the situation when there is more than one deposit. For example, a deposit of $100 is invested today and another $100 deposit is invested at the end of 5 years. Using an annual effective interest rate of 6%, how much is this investment worth at the end of 10 years?

The initial deposit of $100 is invested for 10 years. The accumulated value at time 10 years is:

$$100(1.06)^{10}$$

The second deposit is invested for $10 - 5 = 5$ years. The accumulated value at time 10 years is:

$$100(1.06)^5$$

So, the total accumulated value at time 10 years is:

$$100(1.06)^{10} + 100(1.06)^5 = 179.085 + 133.823 = \$312.91$$

These cash flows can be illustrated on a timeline.

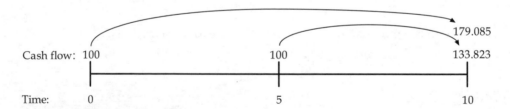

Timelines such as this are particularly useful when the cash flows are complicated.

Example 1.8

A deposit of $100 is invested today. Another $100 is invested at the end of 5 years. Using an annual simple interest rate of 6%, how much is this investment worth at the end of 10 years?

Solution

Under simple interest, the total investment at time 10 years is worth:

$$100(1 + 10 \times 0.06) + 100(1 + 5 \times 0.06) = \$290.00$$

♦♦

Example 1.9

A deposit of $\$X$ is invested at time 6 years at an annual effective interest rate of 8%. A second deposit of $\$X$ is invested at time 8 years at the same interest rate. At time 11 years, the accumulated amount of the investment is $976. Calculate X.

Solution

The first deposit is invested for $11-6=5$ years, and the second deposit is invested for $11-8=3$ years. The timeline is as follows:

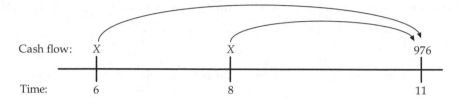

The accumulated amount at time 11 years is:

$$X(1.08)^5 + X(1.08)^3 = 976.00$$

Solving this, we have:

$$2.72904X = 976.00$$
$$\Rightarrow \quad X = \$357.63$$

◆◆

Example 1.10

Jim invests $500 at the beginning of 2002, 2003, and 2004 in a bank account that pays simple interest. At the end of 2004, the accumulated value of the account is $1,635. Calculate the rate of interest paid by the bank.

Solution

The first deposit is invested for 3 full years; the second deposit for 2 full years; and the final deposit for just one year.

Under simple interest, the total accumulated value at the end of 2004 is:

$$500(1+3i) + 500(1+2i) + 500(1+i) = 500(3+6i)$$

Solving for i, we have:

$$500(3+6i) = 1,635$$
$$\Rightarrow i = 4.5\%$$

◆◆

1.5 *Present value*

Not only can we determine the accumulated value of investments at a future point in time, but we can also find the value now, at time 0, of a payment to be made in the future, taking into account any interest that will be earned during the investment period. This is known as the **present value** of a future payment. The process of allowing for future interest in determining a present value is also known as **discounting** a payment.

The present value of $\$X$ payable in t years is the amount that, if invested now at an annual effective interest rate i, will accumulate to $\$X$ at time t years.

For example, suppose that the annual effective interest rate is 5%, and we need to make a payment of $100 in one year's time. What is the present value of the $100 payable in one year?

Clearly the answer must be less than $100. If we have $100 now, we can invest it at 5% to obtain $105 in one year. So, how much do we need to invest now at 5% in order to have $100 in 1 year? If we denote this unknown quantity as PV, then PV can be found by solving:

$$PV \times 1.05 = 100$$

$$\Rightarrow PV = \frac{100}{1.05} = 95.238095$$

Since $95.24 would accumulate to $100 in 1 year, the present value of $100 in 1 year is $95.24.

Present value

Assuming an annual compound interest rate of i, the present value of a payment of $\$X$ to be made in t years is:

$$PV_t = \frac{X}{(1+i)^t} = X(1+i)^{-t}$$

In interest theory applications, many present values are calculated. Notation has been developed to assist with expressing present values.

General one-year present value factor

The one-year present value factor, which is also known as the one-year discount factor, is:

$$v = \frac{1}{1+i} = (1+i)^{-1}$$

Compound interest present value factor

Under compound interest, the present value of a payment of $1 to be made in t years is the compound interest present value factor:

$$PVF_t = v^t = (1+i)^{-t}$$

Simple interest present value factor

Under simple interest, the present value of a payment of $1 to be made in t years is the simple interest present value factor:

$$PVF_t = (1+ti)^{-1}$$

A payment's present value can be determined as of any point in time. If the valuation date is not specified, we usually assume that we are at time 0 when we calculate present values. However, we can also imagine ourselves to be at a later point in time. So it is also valid to refer to a "present value at time n".

Notice that we have introduced a new variable, v, which is the present value factor for one year. When we study annuities in Chapter 2, we'll find it convenient to write v instead of $(1+i)^{-1}$. The present value factor is simply the inverse of the accumulated value factor. We should also notice that the present value factors for both compound and simple interest are equivalent only when $t = 1$.

Let's derive a formula for i in terms of v. We have:

$$v = \frac{1}{1+i}$$

Rearranging, we have:

$$1+i = \frac{1}{v} \quad \Rightarrow \quad i = \frac{1}{v} - 1 \quad \text{or} \quad i = \frac{1-v}{v}$$

Example 1.11

A payment of \$10 is to be made at time 7 years. Determine the present value of this payment at time 0 and at time 4 years. The annual effective interest rate is 6%.

Solution

The investment is discounted for $7 - 0 = 7$ years to determine the present value at time 0:

$$PV_7 = 10v^7 = \frac{10}{(1.06)^7} = \$6.65$$

The present value of an investment at time 4 years of \$10 made at time 7 years is the amount of money that would need to be set aside at time 4 years so that the accumulated value at time 7 is \$10. The investment is discounted for $7 - 4 = 3$ years to determine the present value at time 4:

$$PV_3 = 10v^3 = \frac{10}{(1.06)^3} = \$8.40$$

◆◆

Example 1.12

A payment of \$10 is made at time 7 years. Determine the present value of this payment at time 0 and at time 4 years. The annual simple interest rate is 6%.

Solution

The present value at time 0 under simple interest is:

$$PV_7 = \frac{10}{(1+7\times0.06)} = \$7.04$$

The present value at time 4 under simple interest is:

$$PV_3 = \frac{10}{(1+3\times0.06)} = \$8.47$$

◆◆

1.6 Rate of discount

So far we have considered simple and compound interest rates. Given an annual interest rate i, if an investor deposits or loans \$1 at time 0, a payment of $(1+i)$ is returned at time 1 year. The interest of i is paid at the *end* of the time period.

Another valid approach is to view the interest as being paid at the *beginning* of the time period. When interest is paid at the beginning of the time period, interest is paid in advance, and it is known as **discount**.

Just as with interest, the amount of discount earned is simply the difference between the accumulated account value at the end of the period and the accumulated account value at the beginning of the period.

For any amount of discount earned over a period, we can also calculate an associated discount rate. The discount rate in effect for a one-year period is the amount of discount earned over the year divided by the *ending* accumulated value.

Discount

The amount of discount earned from time t to time $t+s$ is:

$$AV_{t+s} - AV_t$$

where AV_t is the accumulated value at time t.

Discount rate

The annual discount rate d in effect for the year from time t to time $t+1$ is:

$$d = \frac{AV_{t+1} - AV_t}{AV_{t+1}}$$

where t is measured in years.

Let's work through a simple example to explain this. Consider the case of a one-year loan of $1. The lender loans $1 at time 0. The borrower pays discount (*ie* interest) to the lender at time 0, and returns a payment of $1 at time 1 year. The interest is paid at the beginning of the time period.

If interest were payable on the loan at the end of year, the amount of interest payable at that time would be i. But the discount is payable at the beginning of the year, so we must find the present value of the payment of i. Hence, the discount payable at time 0 is:

$$iv = \frac{i}{1+i}$$

The net amount that the borrower receives at time 0 from the loan is the amount of the loan ($1) less the discount ($iv$):

$$\text{Loan amount} - \text{discount} = 1 - iv = 1 - \frac{i}{1+i} = \frac{1}{1+i} = v$$

So, the borrower receives a net payment of v now in exchange for a promise to repay $1 in one year. In other words, the present value at the beginning of the year is v, and the accumulated value at the end of the year is $1. This is consistent with the fact that the present value of $1 payable one year from now is v.

The rate of discount, which is denoted by d, is defined as the amount of the discount (iv) divided by the accumulated value at the end of the year ($1).

Hence, the discount rate is:

$$d = iv$$

We can derive an alternative expression for d:

$$d = iv = \frac{i}{1+i} = 1 - \frac{1}{1+i} = 1 - v$$

This is consistent with the fact that the borrower effectively pays interest of $(1-v)$ at the beginning of the year.

Rate of discount

The annual rate of discount, d, is the amount of interest payable at the start of the year, on a loan of $1 for one year.

$$d = (1-v) = \frac{i}{1+i} = iv$$

It is very useful to become comfortable converting between these variables. Given that i represents the interest paid at the end of a year, and d represents the discount paid at the start of the year, this relationship makes sense. We can think of d as the present value of a payment of i payable at the end of the year.

We can rearrange the definition to obtain a relationship between the variables i and d:

$$i = \frac{d}{1-d}$$

As we've seen in the previous sections, interest rates can be used to accumulate and discount cash flows. We can also accumulate and discount payments using the rate of discount. (Don't be confused by the fact that discount rates bear the adjective "discount" – in this respect, the terminology can be a little confusing.)

Since $d = (1-v)$, we have $v = 1-d$. We already know that v is the one-year discount factor. We also know that the accumulation factor is the inverse of the discount factor. Using this, we can determine the present value and accumulated value factors for compound rates of discount.

Compound rate of discount present value factor

Assuming an annual compound rate of discount of d, the present value of a payment of $1 to be made in t years is the compound rate of discount present value factor:

$$PVF_t = (1-d)^t$$

Compound rate of discount accumulated value factor

Assuming an annual compound rate of discount of d, the accumulated value after t years of a deposit of $1 is the compound rate of discount accumulated value factor:

$$AVF_t = (1-d)^{-t}$$

Example 1.13

An investor would like to have $5,000 at the end of 20 years. The annual compound rate of discount is 5%. How much should the investor deposit today to reach that goal?

Solution

The present value factor for compound discount is $(1-d)^t$.

The investor should set aside:

$$5,000(1-d)^t = 5,000(1-0.05)^{20} = 5,000(0.95)^{20} = \$1,792.43$$

◆◆

Example 1.14

An investor deposits $1,000 today. The annual compound rate of discount is 6%. What is the accumulated value of the investment at the end of 10 years?

Solution

The accumulated value factor for compound discount is $(1-d)^{-t}$.

The accumulated value at the end of 10 years is:

$$AV_{10} = 1,000(1-d)^{-t} = 1,000(1-0.06)^{-10} = \$1,856.61$$ ◆◆

We can also have a simple rate of discount instead of a compound rate of discount. Recall that with simple interest, the interest itself does not earn interest.

Simple rate of discount present value factor

Assuming an annual simple rate of discount of d, the present value of a payment of $1 to be made in t years is the simple rate of discount present value factor:

$$PVF_t = (1-td)$$

Simple rate of discount accumulated value factor

Assuming an annual simple rate of discount of d, the accumulated value after t years of a deposit of $1 is the simple rate of discount accumulated value factor:

$$AVF_t = (1-td)^{-1}$$

Example 1.15

An investor would like to have $10,000 at the end of 5 years. The annual simple rate of discount is 3%. How much should the investor deposit today to reach that goal?

Solution

The present value factor for simple discount is $(1-td)$.

The investor should set aside:

$$10,000(1-td) = 10,000(1-5\times0.03) = \$8,500.00$$ ◆◆

Example 1.16

An investor deposits $5,000 today. The annual simple rate of discount is 5%. What is the accumulated value of the investment at the end of 7 months?

Solution

The accumulated value factor for simple discount is $(1-td)^{-1}$. Since we're working with an annual discount rate, the variable t should be expressed in terms of years. So, $t = 7/12$ years.

The accumulated value at the end of 7 months is:

$$AV_{\frac{7}{12}} = 5,000(1-td)^{-1} = 5,000(1-\frac{7}{12}\times0.05)^{-1} = \$5,150.21$$ ◆◆

Simple rates of interest and discount are not used very often, and when they are used, it is generally over short periods of time. The next example illustrates why simple discount is suitable only for short periods of time.

Example 1.17

An investor would like to have $5,000 at the end of 20 years. The simple rate of discount is 5%. How much should the investor deposit today to reach that goal?

Solution

The present value factor for simple discount is $(1-td)$. The investor should set aside:

$$PV_{20} = 5,000(1-td) = 5,000(1-20 \times 0.05) = 5,000(0) = \$0$$

This seems a little silly, but it is the correct answer if we use a simple rate of discount. The lender would lend $5,000 now. Each year's interest is:

$$\$5,000(0.05) = \$250$$

Therefore, 20 years of interest is $5,000:

$$\$250(20) = \$5,000$$

Subtracting the interest received of $5,000 from the principal of $5,000, the investor's net payment is zero. Since all of the interest is paid up front, the borrower is left with nothing at time 0, but has an obligation to pay $5,000 at time 20 years. This is an excellent deal for the lender, but the reality is that the lender will not find anyone willing to agree to these terms.   ♦♦

Simple discount and simple interest are simply unrealistic for use over longer periods of time, so it is usually best to assume that any rate of interest or rate of discount is a compound rate unless otherwise stated.

1.7   Constant force of interest

We have considered the discrete cases where interest is payable at the start or at the end of the year. An annual compound interest rate is the change in the account value over one year, expressed as a percentage of the beginning-of-year value. An annual compound discount rate is the change in the account value over one year, expressed as a percentage of the end-of-year value.

We now consider the case of interest that is **compounded continuously**. A continuously compounded interest rate is called the **force of interest**. The force of interest at time t is denoted δ_t. Non-annual compounding is covered in more detail in Chapter 4.

The force of interest is the *instantaneous* change in the account value, expressed as an annualized percentage of the *current value*.

If the annual effective interest rate is constant, then the force of interest is also constant. When the force of interest is constant, the subscript t is omitted from δ_t since the force of interest does not vary over time. We can derive the value of δ as follows.

In terms of calculus, the force of interest is the derivative of the accumulated value with respect to time expressed as a percentage of the accumulated value at time t:

$$\delta = \frac{AV_t'}{AV_t}$$

where AV_t' is the first derivative of AV_t with respect to t.

Using the standard calculus result:

$$\frac{d}{dx}a^x = a^x \ln a$$

We have:

$$AV_t' = \frac{d}{dt}X(1+i)^t = X(1+i)^t \ln(1+i)$$

Hence we can solve for the force of interest:

$$\delta = \frac{AV_t'}{AV_t} = \frac{X(1+i)^t \ln(1+i)}{X(1+i)^t} = \ln(1+i)$$

Constant force of interest rate

When the force of interest is constant, the force of interest can be expressed in terms of the annual effective interest rate i:

$$\delta = \ln(1+i)$$

For example, if the annual effective interest rate is 5%, then the force of interest is:

$$\delta = \ln(1+i) = \ln(1.05) = 0.048790$$

Let's derive expressions for i and v in terms of δ. Rearranging $\delta = \ln(1+i)$, we have:

$$1+i = e^\delta \quad \Rightarrow \quad i = e^\delta - 1$$

We also have:

$$v = (1+i)^{-1} = e^{-\delta}$$

We recognize $(1+i)$ as the one-year accumulated value factor and v as the one-year present value factor, so we can now express accumulated values and present values in terms of the constant force of interest.

Constant force of interest accumulated value factor

Assuming a constant force of interest of δ, the accumulated value after t years of a payment of $1 is the constant force of interest accumulated value factor:

$$AVF_t = e^{\delta t}$$

Constant force of interest present value factor

Assuming a constant force of interest of δ, the present value of a payment of $1 to be made in t years is the constant force of interest present value factor:

$$PVF_t = e^{-\delta t}$$

Example 1.18

If the constant force of interest is 6%, what is the corresponding annual effective rate of interest?

Solution

The corresponding annual effective rate of interest is calculated as follows:

$$i = e^{\delta} - 1 = e^{0.06} - 1 = 0.06184 \text{ or } 6.184\%$$

Example 1.19

Using a constant force of interest of 4.2%, calculate the present value of a payment of $1,000 to be made in 8 years' time.

Solution

The present value is:

$$1,000e^{-8\delta} = 1,000e^{-8\times0.042} = \$714.62$$

Example 1.20

A deposit of $500 is invested at time 5 years. The constant force of interest is 6% per year. Determine the accumulated value of the investment at the end of 10 years.

Solution

The money is invested for $10 - 5 - 5$ years.

The accumulated amount is:

$$500e^{5\delta} = 500e^{5\times0.06} = \$674.93$$

1.8 Varying force of interest

In the previous section, the force of interest was constant over time. The force of interest can vary over time, in which case we write it as δ_t. It is defined as:

$$\delta_t = \frac{AV'_t}{AV_t}$$

Using the standard calculus result:

$$\frac{d}{dx}\ln\big(f(x)\big) = \frac{f'(x)}{f(x)}$$

We can write:

$$\frac{d}{dt}\ln(AV_t) = \frac{AV'_t}{AV_t}$$

Hence we have:

$$\delta_t = \frac{d}{dt}\ln(AV_t)$$

Integrating both sides of the equation from t_1 to t_2, where $t_1 < t_2$:

$$\int_{t_1}^{t_2} \delta_t \, dt = \int_{t_1}^{t_2} \frac{d}{dt}\ln[AV_t]dt = \ln[AV_{t_2}] - \ln[AV_{t_1}] = \ln\left[\frac{AV_{t_2}}{AV_{t_1}}\right]$$

Hence:

$$\exp\left[\int_{t_1}^{t_2} \delta_t dt\right] = \frac{AV_{t_2}}{AV_{t_1}}$$

Let's consider the meaning of this important result.

The accumulated value at time t_2 divided by the accumulated value at time t_1 is equal to 1 plus the percentage increase in the accumulated value from time t_1 to time t_2.

Hence the accumulated value at time t_2 of $1 invested at time t_1 is given by:

$$\exp\left[\int_{t_1}^{t_2} \delta_t dt\right]$$

Before, we only used one subscript of t to simplify the notation when we have a deposit at time 0 that is accumulated to a later time t. When the deposit is made at a time other than time 0, the following notation is more useful.

Varying force of interest accumulated value factor

The varying force of interest accumulated value factor at time t_2 of an investment of $1 made at time t_1 is:

$$AVF_{t_1,t_2} = \exp\left[\int_{t_1}^{t_2} \delta_t dt\right]$$

Example 1.21

A deposit of $10 is invested at time 2 years. Using a force of interest of $\delta_t = 0.2 - 0.02t$, find the accumulated value of this payment at the end of 5 years.

Solution

The accumulated value is:

$$AV_{2,5} = 10\exp\left[\int_2^5 (0.2 - 0.02t)\, dt\right] = 10\exp\left[\left(0.2t - 0.01t^2\right)\Big|_2^5\right]$$

$$= 10e^{0.75-0.36} = 10e^{0.39} = \$14.77 \qquad\qquad \blacklozenge\blacklozenge$$

In a similar manner, we can determine the present value of a payment using a varying force of interest. We recall that the present value is the inverse of the accumulated value.

Varying force of interest present value factor

The varying force of interest present value factor at time t_1 of a payment of $1 to be made at time t_2 is:

$$PVF_{t_1,t_2} = \exp\left[-\int_{t_1}^{t_2} \delta_t\, dt\right]$$

Notice that the only difference between the present value and the accumulated value using a non-constant force of interest is the negative sign in the exponent of the present value equation.

Example 1.22

A deposit of \$200 is invested at time 8 years. Using a force of interest of $\delta_t = 0.1 - 0.002t$, find the present value of this payment at the end of 3 years.

Solution

The present value is:

$$PV_{3,8} = 200\exp\left[-\int_3^8 (0.1-0.002t)\,dt\right] = 200\exp\left[-\left(0.1t-0.001t^2\right)\Big|_3^8\right]$$

$$= 200e^{-(0.736-0.291)} = 200e^{-0.445} = \$128.16 \qquad \blacklozenge\blacklozenge$$

1.9   *Discrete changes in interest rates*

The results and techniques used so far in this chapter can be applied to other situations. This section looks at some examples where the interest rate changes at specific points in time. For example, the annual effective interest rate might be $x\%$ for the first m years and then $y\%$ for the next n years.

Example 1.23

A deposit of \$100 is invested at time 0. The annual effective interest rate is 5% from time 0 to time 7 years and thereafter is 6%. Calculate the accumulated value of the investment at time 10 years.

Solution

At time 7 years, the accumulated value of the investment is:

$$AV_7 = 100(1.05)^7$$

This amount is then accumulated for a further 3 years at a rate of 6% per year. The accumulated value at time 10 is:

$$AV_{10} = 100(1.05)^7(1.06)^3 = \$167.59 \qquad \blacklozenge\blacklozenge$$

Example 1.24

A deposit of \$2,500 is invested at time 0. The annual effective rate of interest is 2.5% from time 0 to time 6 years. The annual effective rate of discount is 2.5% from time 6 to time 10 years and the annual force of interest is 2.5% thereafter. Find the accumulated value of the investment at time 13 years.

Solution

The accumulation factor from time 0 to time 6 years is:

$$AVF_{0,6} = 1.025^6$$

The accumulation factor from time 6 to time 10 years is:

$$AVF_{6,10} = (1-0.025)^{-4} = 0.975^{-4}$$

The accumulation factor from time 10 to time 13 years is:

$$AVF_{10,13} = e^{3 \times 0.025}$$

The accumulated value of the investment from time 0 to time 13 years is therefore:

$$
\begin{aligned}
AV_{0,13} &= 2,500 \times AVF_{0,6} \times AVF_{6,10} \times AVF_{10,13} \\
&= 2,500 \times 1.025^6 \times 0.975^{-4} \times e^{3 \times 0.025} \\
&= \$3,458.09
\end{aligned}
$$

♦ ♦

Chapter 1 Practice Questions

Question guide

- Questions 1.1 – 1.10 test material from Sections 1.1 – 1.6.
- Questions 1.11 – 1.16 test material from Sections 1.7 – 1.9.
- Questions 1.17 – 1.20 are from the SOA/CAS Course 2 exam or the IOA/FOA 102 exam.

Question 1.1

$300 is deposited in a bank account, which pays simple interest of 3.5% a year. Calculate the accumulated value of the deposit after 6 years.

Question 1.2

Fund P earns interest at a simple rate of 4% a year. Fund Q earns interest at a simple rate of $i\%$ a year. $100 is invested in fund P and $118.50 is invested in fund Q. The accumulated amount in the two funds will be equal after 5 years. Determine the simple rate of interest i.

Question 1.3

$800 is deposited in a bank account, which pays compound interest of 5.25% a year. Calculate the accumulated value of the deposit after 15 years.

Question 1.4

Fund P earns interest at a compound rate of 4% a year. Fund Q earns interest at a compound rate of $i\%$ a year. $100 is invested in fund P and $118.50 is invested in fund Q. The accumulated amount in the two funds will be equal after 5 years. Determine the compound rate of interest i.

Question 1.5

Using an annual effective rate of interest of 5%, find the present value of an investment of $5,000 at time 20 years.

Question 1.6

Your great-great-great grandfather set aside $10 on July 1, 1876 in an account paying 5% annual effective interest. Assuming no additional deposits or withdrawals were made, what is the account balance on January 1, 2004? What would the account balance have been if the account had been paying an annual effective interest rate of 10% instead of 5% all of these years?

Question 1.7

Larry has a credit card balance of $10,000. The annual effective interest rate on the credit card is 15%. Larry takes out a home equity loan to pay off his credit card balance. The interest rate on the home equity loan is 5%. Ignoring taxes, how much does this strategy save Larry, assuming he pays off the loan in full 18 months from now?

Question 1.8

Using an annual effective rate of discount of 5% per year, find the accumulated value at time 20 years of an investment of $5,000 at time 0.

Question 1.9

Using a simple rate of discount of 4% per year, find the present value of a payment of $5,000 at time 3 months.

Question 1.10

A $15,000 car loan is repaid with one payment of $18,375.65 after 36 months. What is the annual effective discount rate?

Question 1.11

$500 is paid at time 8 years at a constant force of interest of 10%. Determine the present value of the investment at time 0.

Question 1.12

$1,000 is paid at time 6 years. Find the present value at time 4 years using a force of interest of $\delta_t = 0.05 + 0.002t$.

Question 1.13

Find the accumulated value at time 5 years of $30 that is invested at time 0. Use a force of interest of $\delta_t = 0.02t + 0.01$.

Question 1.14

A payment of $1,000 is due at time 15 years. Between times 0 to 5 years, the annual effective rate of interest is 7%. Between times 5 and 10 years it is 9% and between times 10 and 15 years it is 4%. Calculate the present value of the payment at time 0.

Question 1.15

$100 is invested at time 0. The constant force of interest is 7% from time 0 to time 5 years and 5% from time 5 to time 8 years. Determine the accumulated value of the investment at time 8 years.

Question 1.16

The effective annual rate of discount has been 4% for the last 5 years. Prior to that, it was 5%. A bank account has a balance of $457 today. A single deposit of $X was placed in the account 8 years ago. Calculate the value of X.

Question 1.17 *SOA/CAS*

Bruce and Robbie each open up new bank accounts at time 0. Bruce deposits $100 into his bank account, and Robbie deposits $50 into his. Each account earns an annual effective discount rate of d. The amount of interest earned in Bruce's account during the 11th year is equal to X. The amount of interest earned in Robbie's account during the 17th year is also equal to X. Calculate X.

Question 1.18 *SOA/CAS*

Ernie makes deposits of $100 at time 0, and X at time 3. The fund grows at a force of interest $\delta_t = 0.01t^2$, $t > 0$. The amount of interest earned from time 3 to time 6 is X.

Calculate X.

Question 1.19 *SOA/CAS*

David can receive one of the following two payment streams:

(i) $100 at time 0, $200 at time n, and $300 at time $2n$
(ii) $600 at time 10.

At an annual effective interest rate of i, the present values of the two streams are equal.

Given $v^n = 0.75941$, determine i.

Question 1.20 *IOA/FOA*

The force of interest, δ_t is:

$$\delta_t = \begin{cases} 0.04 & 0 < t \le 5 \\ 0.01(t^2 - t) & t > 5 \end{cases}$$

Calculate the present value of $100 payable at time 10.

2

Level annuities

In this chapter, we apply the principles that we learned in Chapter 1 to find the present and accumulated values of a regular series of payments. We also look at equations of value that involve equating the values of different series of payments, often the cash inflows and cash outflows of transactions, and solving for the unknown variable.

We first consider a *regular* series of *level* payments, which is called a **level annuity**. Regular means that the payments are made at uniform periodic intervals (such as annually or monthly), and level means that the periodic payments are all the same amount.

In this chapter, we restrict our attention to level annuities with annual payments, and to annual rates of interest and discount. In Chapter 3 we'll study annuities with payments that are not level, and in Chapter 4 we'll study non-annual payments and non-annual rates of interest and discount.

A **period-certain annuity** is an annuity where the payments continue for a certain period, such as 25 years. A **contingent annuity** is an annuity where the payments continue for an uncertain period, such as the duration of the recipient's life. Actuarial mathematics examines contingent annuities. In interest theory, we focus on period-certain annuities.

2.1 *Annuity-immediate*

Consider a series of n payments of \$1 to be made at annual intervals, with the first payment to be made 1 year from now and the last payment to be made n years from now:

This is an example of an **annuity-immediate**. The first payment is at time 1 and the last payment is at time n years. The payments occur at the end of each time period.

For a given interest rate, we can calculate the present value of these payments at time 0. The present value of the first payment at time 1 year is $1 \times v$. The present value of the second payment at time 2 years is $1 \times v^2$. The present value of the nth payment at time n years is $1 \times v^n$. So, the present value of the series of payments at time 0 is:

$$v + v^2 + \cdots + v^n$$

This is a geometric series and can be simplified using the generic geometric series summation formula:

$$a + ar + ar^2 + \cdots + ar^{n-1} = \frac{a(1 - r^n)}{1 - r}$$

Setting $a = v$ and $r = v$, we have:

$$v + v^2 + \cdots + v^n = \frac{v(1 - v^n)}{1 - v} = \frac{(1 - v^n)}{(1 + i)(1 - v)} = \frac{1 - v^n}{1 + i - 1} = \frac{1 - v^n}{i}$$

The present value of this simple annuity-immediate is represented by the actuarial symbol $a_{\overline{n}|}$, which is pronounced **a-angle-n**. It is valued at time 0, which is one year before the first payment is made.

If there is any possible ambiguity about the interest rate being used, then the present value of an annuity-immediate may be written as $a_{\overline{n}|i}$.

Annuity-immediate present value factor

Assuming an annual effective interest rate i, the annuity-immediate present value factor is the present value at time 0 of a series of payments of \$1 at time 1 year, \$1 at time 2 years, and so on, up to \$1 at time n years:

$$a_{\overline{n}|i} = \frac{1 - v^n}{i} = \frac{1 - (1 + i)^{-n}}{i}$$

For example, the present value of a 5-year annuity-immediate using an annual effective interest rate of 7% is:

$$a_{\overline{5}|7\%} = \frac{1 - 1.07^{-5}}{0.07} = 4.100197$$

In the unlikely event that the interest rate is zero, the present value of the series of payments is just n. Algebraically:

$$a_{\overline{n}|0\%} = n$$

Of course, if $n = 0$, then there are no payments, hence:

$$a_{\overline{0}|i} = 0 \quad \text{for any interest rate } i$$

The present value of a series of payments of $\$X$ at time 1 year, $\$X$ at time 2 years, and so on, up to $\$X$ at time n years is $Xa_{\overline{n}|}$.

As an example, let's say that payments of $\$100$ are expected at times 1 year, 2 years, and so on, up to and including 10 years. The annual effective interest rate is 4%. What is the present value of these payments at time 0?

To determine the answer, it's often useful to draw a timeline diagram:

The present value of the payments at time 0 is:

$$100a_{\overline{10}|4\%} = 100\frac{1-v^{10}}{i} = 100\frac{1-1.04^{-10}}{0.04} = \$811.09$$

Example 2.1

Determine the present value of regular payments of $\$50$ to be made at the end of each of the next 15 years. The annual effective interest rate is 10%.

Solution

The present value at time 0 is:

$$50a_{\overline{15}|10\%} = 50\frac{1-1.1^{-15}}{0.1} = \$380.30 \qquad\qquad \blacklozenge\blacklozenge$$

We can also calculate the accumulated value of an annuity-immediate at time n. Let's develop an expression for the accumulated value at time n years of the payments of $\$1$ at time 1 year, $\$1$ at time 2 years, and so on, up to $\$1$ at time n.

Looking at the timeline, the payments for the annuity-immediate occur as before:

To determine the accumulated value, each payment is accumulated to time n years. The first payment is accumulated for $n-1$ years, so its accumulated value at time n is $1 \times (1+i)^{n-1}$. The second payment is accumulated for $n-2$ years, so it accumulated value at time n is $1 \times (1+i)^{n-2}$. The last payment is accumulated for 0 years since it occurs at time n, so its accumulated value is simply 1.

Putting all of these accumulated value terms together, we get the accumulated value of the series of payments at time n years:

$$(1+i)^{n-1} + (1+i)^{n-2} + \cdots + 1$$

Using the generic geometric series summation formula again with $a = 1$ and $r = 1 + i$, we have:

$$1 + (1+i) + \cdots + (1+i)^{n-2} + (1+i)^{n-1} = \frac{1-(1+i)^n}{1-(1+i)} = \frac{(1+i)^n - 1}{i}$$

The accumulated value of this simple annuity-immediate is represented by the actuarial symbol $s_{\overline{n}|}$, which is pronounced **s-angle-n**. It is valued at the time the last payment is made, which is at time n years.

Annuity-immediate accumulated value factor

Assuming an annual effective interest rate i, the annuity-immediate accumulated value factor is the accumulated value at time n years of a series of payments of \$1 at time 1 year, \$1 at time 2 years, and so on, up to \$1 at time n years:

$$s_{\overline{n}|i} = \frac{(1+i)^n - 1}{i}$$

As for the present value factor, we have $s_{\overline{n}|0\%} = n$. Also, $s_{\overline{0}|i} = 0$ for any interest rate i.

For example, suppose that payments of \$100 are expected at times 1 year, 2 years, and so on, with the last payment at time 10 years. The annual effective interest rate is 4%. What is the accumulated value of these payments at time 10 years?

First, let's draw a timeline diagram:

The accumulated value of the payments at time 10 years is:

$$100 s_{\overline{10}|4\%} = 100 \frac{1.04^{10} - 1}{0.04} = \$1,200.61$$

Example 2.2

Determine the accumulated value at time 15 years of regular payments of \$50 to be made at the end of each of the next 15 years. The annual effective interest rate is 10%.

Solution

The accumulated value at time 15 years is:

$$50 s_{\overline{15}|10\%} = 50 \frac{1.1^{15} - 1}{0.1} = \$1,588.62 \qquad \blacklozenge\blacklozenge$$

Let's consider the relationship between the present value of an annuity-immediate and the accumulated value of an annuity-immediate. Since $s_{\overline{n}|}$ is the accumulated value factor (at time n years) and $a_{\overline{n}|}$ is the present value factor (at time 0), the accumulated value factor is equivalent to the present value factor accumulated for n years:

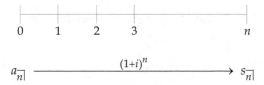

So, we have:

$$s_{\overline{n}|} = (1+i)^n \, a_{\overline{n}|}$$

Thus, the annuity-immediate accumulated value factor equals the n-year accumulated value factor multiplied by the annuity-immediate present value factor.

When the accumulated value factor is discounted for n years, the result is the present value factor:

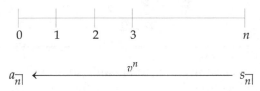

And we have:

$$a_{\overline{n}|} = v^n s_{\overline{n}|}$$

Thus, the annuity-immediate present value factor equals the n-year present value factor multiplied by the annuity-immediate accumulated value factor.

2.2 *Annuity-due*

Consider a series of n payments of \$1 to be made at annual intervals, with the first payment to be made now and the last payment is to be made at time $n-1$ years:

This is an example of an **annuity-due**. The first payment is a time 0 and the last payment is at time $n-1$ years. The payments occur at the start of each time period.

Notice that there are still n payments, just as is the case for an annuity-immediate. The only difference is that each payment has been shifted one year earlier.

For a given interest rate, we can calculate the present value of these payments at time 0. The present value of the first payment that occurs now is 1. The present value of the second payment at time 1 year is $1 \times v$. The present value of the nth payment at time $n-1$ years is $1 \times v^{n-1}$. So, the present value of the series of payments at time 0 is:

$$1 + v + v^2 + \cdots + v^{n-1}$$

This is a geometric series and it can be simplified. Using the generic geometric series summation formula with $a = 1$ and $r = v$, we have:

$$1 + v + v^2 + \cdots + v^{n-1} = \frac{1(1 - v^n)}{1 - v} = \frac{1 - v^n}{d}$$

The present value of this simple annuity-due is represented by the actuarial symbol $\ddot{a}_{\overline{n}|}$, which is pronounced **a-double-dot-angle-n**. It is valued at time 0, when the first payment is made.

Annuity-due present value factor

Assuming an annual effective interest rate i, the annuity-due present value factor is the present value at time 0 of a series of payments of \$1 at time 0, \$1 at time 1 year, \$1 at time 2 years, and so on, up to \$1 at time $n-1$ years:

$$\ddot{a}_{\overline{n}|i} = \frac{1 - v^n}{d}$$

Notice the similarity between the notation for an annuity-immediate and an annuity-due. Also notice the similarities between the formulas, since the denominator of the annuity-immediate factor has just changed from i to d for the annuity-due factor. It's easy to remember this difference, since the annuity-**d**ue factor has a d in the denominator, whereas the annuity-**i**mmediate factor has an i in the denominator.

As an example, let's consider payments of \$100 that are received at times 0, 1 year, 2 years, and so on, with the last payment at time 15 years. The annual effective interest rate is 5%. What is the present value of these payments at time 0?

First, let's draw a timeline diagram:

Notice that there are 16 payments in total: the first is at time 0, the second at time 1, and so on, up to the 16th at time 15. It is a common mistake to assume that there are only 15 payments in a situation like this, *ie* the first payment is often forgotten.

One method to count the payments correctly is to count the number of time periods between the first and last payments, and then add 1 to this number. In this case, there are $15 - 0 + 1 = 16$ payments.

The present value of the 16 payments at time 0 is given by:

$$100\ddot{a}_{\overline{16}|5\%} = 100\frac{1 - v^{16}}{d}$$

Using the fact that $d = 1 - v$, the present value is:

$$100 \frac{1 - 1.05^{-16}}{1 - 1.05^{-1}} = \$1,137.97$$

This could also be evaluated using $d = \dfrac{i}{1+i}$ instead. We get the same present value either way:

$$100 \frac{1 - 1.05^{-16}}{0.05 / 1.05} = \$1,137.97$$

Example 2.3

Find the present value of 25 regular annual payments of \$3,500 at the beginning of each year, starting now. The annual effective interest rate is 9%.

Solution

The present value at time 0 is:

$$3,500 \ddot{a}_{\overline{25}|9\%} = 3,500 \frac{1 - 1.09^{-25}}{0.09 / 1.09} = \$37,473.14 \qquad \blacklozenge\blacklozenge$$

We can also calculate the accumulated value of an annuity-due at time n years. Let's develop an expression for the accumulated value at time n years of the payments of \$1 at time 0, \$1 at time 1 year, \$1 at time 2 years, and so on, up to \$1 at time $n-1$ years.

Let's remind ourselves of the annuity-due timeline:

1	1	1	1	$\cdots$	1		payment

|---|---|---|---|---|---|---|---|
| 0 | 1 | 2 | 3 | $\cdots$ | $n-1$ | n | time |

To determine the accumulated value, each payment is accumulated to time n years. The first payment at time 0 is accumulated for n years, the second payment at time 1 is accumulated for $n-1$ years, and the last payment at time $n-1$ is accumulated for 1 year. The accumulated value of these payments is:

$$(1+i)^n + (1+i)^{n-1} + \cdots + (1+i)$$

Using the generic geometric series formula again with $a = (1+i)^n$ and $r = (1+i)^{-1}$, we have:

$$(1+i)^n + (1+i)^{n-1} + \cdots + (1+i) = \frac{(1+i)^n (1 - (1+i)^{-n})}{1 - (1+i)^{-1}} = \frac{(1+i)^n - 1}{d}$$

The accumulated value of this simple annuity-due is represented by the symbol $\ddot{s}_{\overline{n}|}$, which is pronounced **s-double-dot-angle-n**. It is valued at time n years, which is 1 year after the last payment is made.

Annuity-due accumulated value factor

Assuming an annual effective interest rate i, the annuity-due accumulated value factor is the accumulated value at time n years of a series of payments of \$1 at time 0, \$1 at time 1 year, \$1 at time 2 years, and so on, up to \$1 at time $n-1$ years:

$$\ddot{s}_{\overline{n}|i} = \frac{(1+i)^n - 1}{d}$$

Note the similarity between the formula for $\ddot{s}_{\overline{n}|}$, with a denominator of d, and the formula for $s_{\overline{n}|}$, with a denominator of i.

For example, suppose that payments of \$100 are received at times 0, 1 year, 2 years, and so on, with the last payment at time 12 years. The annual effective interest rate is 7%. What is the accumulated value of these payments at time 13 years?

Once again, we can draw a timeline diagram of the cash flows:

Notice that there are $12 - 0 + 1 = 13$ payments. The accumulated value of the payments at time 13 years is given by:

$$100\ddot{s}_{\overline{13}|7\%} = 100\frac{(1.07)^{13} - 1}{0.07/1.07} = \$2,155.05$$

Example 2.4

Find the accumulated value at time 8 years of 8 regular annual payments of \$34.50 made at the beginning of each year, starting now. The annual effective interest rate is 9.5%.

Solution

The accumulated value at time 8 years is:

$$34.50\ddot{s}_{\overline{8}|9.5\%} = 34.50\frac{1.095^8 - 1}{0.095/1.095} = \$424.25 \qquad\qquad \blacklozenge\blacklozenge$$

Let's consider the relationship between the present value of an annuity-due and the accumulated value of an annuity-due. Since $\ddot{s}_{\overline{n}|}$ is the accumulated value factor (at time n years) and $\ddot{a}_{\overline{n}|}$ is the present value factor (at time 0), the accumulated value factor is equivalent to the present value factor accumulated for n years.

So we have:

$$\ddot{s}_{\overline{n}|} = (1+i)^n \ddot{a}_{\overline{n}|}$$

$$\ddot{a}_{\overline{n}|} = v^n \ddot{s}_{\overline{n}|}$$

In other words, just as we saw before with the relationship between the present value factor and the accumulated value factor for the annuity-immediate, the annuity-due accumulated value factor equals the n-year accumulated value factor multiplied by the annuity-due present value factor. Also, the annuity-due present value factor equals the n-year present value factor multiplied by the annuity-due accumulated value factor.

We conclude this section by considering the relationship between the present value of an n-year annuity-due with that of an n-year annuity-immediate, *ie* the relationship between $\ddot{a}_{\overline{n}|}$ and $a_{\overline{n}|}$.

We have:

$$\ddot{a}_{\overline{n}|} = 1 + v + v^2 + \cdots + v^{n-1}$$

$$a_{\overline{n}|} = v + v^2 + v^3 + \cdots + v^n$$

From these equations, it is simple to see that:

$$a_{\overline{n}|} = v\ddot{a}_{\overline{n}|}$$

$$\ddot{a}_{\overline{n}|} = (1+i)a_{\overline{n}|}$$

The payments for $\ddot{a}_{\overline{n}|}$ correspond with those of $a_{\overline{n}|}$, except that each payment of the annuity-due is made exactly one year earlier than the corresponding payment of the annuity-immediate. The present value of each payment of the annuity-due is greater than the present value of the corresponding payment of the annuity-immediate by a factor of $(1+i)$.

Let's also consider the relationship between the present value of an n-year annuity-due with that of an $(n-1)$-year annuity-immediate. We have:

$$\ddot{a}_{\overline{n}|} = 1 + v + v^2 + \cdots + v^{n-1}$$

$$a_{\overline{n-1}|} = v + v^2 + \cdots + v^{n-1}$$

From these equations, it is simple to see that:

$$\ddot{a}_{\overline{n}|} = 1 + a_{\overline{n-1}|}$$

These simple relationships are useful to know because they can often reduce the number of calculations required in a given situation.

Keep in mind that a payment that occurs at the beginning of year t is the same as a payment that occurs at time $t-1$ years since the beginning of the first year is actually time 0. A payment that occurs at the end of year t is the same as a payment that occurs at time t years.

2.3   Deferred annuities

An annuity that starts at some point after the first time period is known as a **deferred annuity**. A deferred annuity can be either an annuity-immediate or an annuity-due.

Present values and accumulated values of deferred annuities can be evaluated by combining the present value and accumulated value factors from Chapter 1 with the annuity factors from this chapter.

For example, let's say that payments of \$100 are received at times 12 years, 13 years, and so on, with the last payment at time 20 years. The annual effective interest rate is 4%. What is the present value of these payments at time 0?

Let's first draw a timeline diagram:

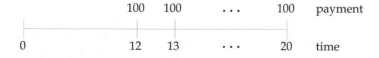

Notice that this series has $20 - 12 + 1 = 9$ payments. The present value of these 9 payments at time 11 years is given by $100a_{\overline{9}|4\%}$. This is because if we are at time 11 years, we value a series of 9 annual payments, starting in one year, with the annuity-immediate present value factor.

However, we need the value at time 0. We can find this by discounting the above amount, $100a_{\overline{9}|}$, by 11 years from time 11 years to time 0.

So the present value at time 0 is given by:

$$100a_{\overline{9}|4\%}\,v^{11} = 100\frac{1-1.04^{-9}}{0.04}1.04^{-11} = \$482.98$$

Alternatively, the present value of these 9 payments at time 12 years is $100\ddot{a}_{\overline{9}|4\%}$. This is because if we are at time 12 years, we value a series of 9 annual payments, starting right away, with the annuity-due present value factor.

So the present value at time 0 can also be determined by:

$$100\ddot{a}_{\overline{9}|4\%}\,v^{12} = 100\frac{1-1.04^{-9}}{0.04/1.04}1.04^{-12} = \$482.98$$

In general, to value a deferred annuity that starts in m years, we simply multiply the appropriate annuity factor by the m-year present value factor.

Deferred annuity-immediate present value

The present value at time 0 of an n-year annuity-immediate that starts in m years where the first payment of \$1 occurs at time $m+1$ years and the last payment occurs at time $m+n$ years is:

$$_{m|}a_{\overline{n}|i} = v^m a_{\overline{n}|i}$$

Deferred annuity-due present value

The present value at time 0 of an n-year annuity-due that starts in m years where the first payment of \$1 occurs at time m years and the last payment occurs at time $m+n-1$ years is:

$$_{m|}\ddot{a}_{\overline{n}|i} = v^m \ddot{a}_{\overline{n}|i}$$

As we have seen, many problems can be solved using either an annuity-immediate factor or an annuity-due factor. For example, if we need to determine the present value at time 0 of payments of \$10 at the end of years 5 to 11 inclusive, there are many different expressions we could use for the present value. We first note that there are $11-5+1=7$ payments in this series.

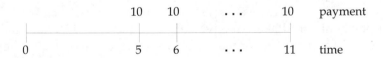

Two equivalent present value expressions for this series are:

$$10\times_{4|}a_{\overline{7}|} = 10v^4 a_{\overline{7}|}$$

and:

$$10\times_{5|}\ddot{a}_{\overline{7}|} = 10v^5 \ddot{a}_{\overline{7}|}$$

When faced with problems similar to this, use whichever method you prefer, or the one that is most appropriate given the information available. It is often helpful to set up the problem in a diagram and work from there, using the given values as the framework to set up the problem.

 ### Example 2.5

Find the present value at time 5 years of regular payments of \$500 at times 15 years, 16 years, and so on, with the last payment at time 30 years. The annual effective discount rate is 4%.

Solution

First, note that the question gives the effective rate of discount, not the effective rate of interest. There are $30 - 15 + 1 = 16$ payments. The timeline is:

The present value at time 15 years is:

$$500\ddot{a}_{\overline{16}|}$$

Discounting the time 15-year present value by 10 years, the present value at time 5 years is:

$$500\ddot{a}_{\overline{16}|}v^{10} = 500\frac{1-v^{16}}{d}v^{10} = 500\frac{1-0.96^{16}}{0.04}0.96^{10} = \$3,985.65$$

Alternatively, the present value at time 14 years is:

$$500a_{\overline{16}|}$$

So, the present value at time 5 years (9 years earlier) is:

$$500a_{\overline{16}|}v^{9}$$

Since we were given $d = 0.04$, we can calculate $v = 1 - d = 0.96$ and $i = v^{-1} - 1 = 0.96^{-1} - 1$, so the present value at time 5 years is:

$$500\frac{1-v^{16}}{i}v^{9} = 500\frac{1-0.96^{16}}{0.96^{-1}-1}0.96^{9} = \$3,985.65 \qquad \blacklozenge\blacklozenge$$

In the following example, we calculate the accumulated value of a deferred annuity.

Example 2.6

Payments of \$400 are received at times 12 years, 13 years, and so on, with the last payment at time 20 years. The annual effective interest rate is 5%. Find the accumulated value of these payments at time 30 years.

Solution

Let's draw a timeline of the cash flows. Note that there are $20 - 12 + 1 = 9$ payments.

We can calculate the accumulated value of these payments at time 30 years in several ways.

First, we can calculate the present value at time 0, and then accumulate this value to time 30 years. Using the deferred annuity-due factor, the present value at time 0 is:

$$400\,_{12|}\ddot{a}_{\overline{9}|5\%} = 400\ddot{a}_{\overline{9}|5\%}v^{12} = 400\frac{1-1.05^{-9}}{0.05/1.05}(1.05)^{-12} = \$1,662.32$$

Hence, the accumulated value at time 30 years is:

$$400_{\,12|}\ddot{a}_{\overline{9}|5\%}(1.05)^{30} = (1,662.32)(1.05)^{30} = \$7,184.44$$

Note that our policy in this text is to keep full accuracy in the intermediate calculations (even though we may show an intermediate result that is rounded to the penny) in order that the final answer is accurate to the penny.

Secondly, we can calculate the accumulated value at the time of last payment (at time 20 years), and then accumulate this value to time 30 years. The accumulated value of the payments at time 20 years is given by $400s_{\overline{9}|}$. This is because if we are at time 20 years, we accumulate a series of 9 annual payments made at the end of each of the preceding 9 years with the annuity-immediate accumulated value factor.

Using the accumulated value of an annuity-immediate, the value at 20 years is:

$$400s_{\overline{9}|5\%} = 400\frac{1.05^9 - 1}{0.05} = \$4,410.63$$

Hence, the accumulated value at time 30 years is:

$$400s_{\overline{9}|5\%}(1.05)^{10} = (4,410.63)(1.05)^{10} = \$7,184.44$$

We can calculate this answer in other ways too, *eg* by calculating the present value at time 0 of a deferred annuity-immediate, and accumulating this value to time 30 years:

$$400_{\,11|}a_{\overline{9}|5\%}(1.05)^{30}$$

Or, we can calculate the accumulated value at time 21 years of a 9-year annuity-due, and accumulate this value to time 30 years:

$$400\ddot{s}_{\overline{9}|5\%}(1.05)^9$$

We leave you to verify that these formulas give the same numerical answer.   ◆◆

2.4   *Continuously payable annuities*

So far we have considered payments that are received at the start or end of each annual time period. Payments can also be made *continuously* over the year, in which case the annuity is called a **continuously paid annuity**.

An analogy might help to explain the concept of a continuously payable level payment stream. Imagine a water faucet that produces a steady stream of water when the valve is set to a certain open position at time 0. Let's say that in this case, the faucet produces 1,000 gallons of water per year. As long as the valve is not adjusted, the faucet continues to produce 1,000 gallons of water each year.

The timeline diagram for a continuously paid annuity of $1 per year from time 0 to n years is:

The present value at time 0 of a payment of \$1 per year received continuously over the period from time 0 to time n years is written as $\bar{a}_{\overline{n}|}$. It is pronounced **a-bar-angle-n** and it is valued at time 0.

Previously, in order to find the present value of a series of payments, we have been able to sum the present value of each payment. When we are dealing with continuous payments, we adopt an analogous approach, using calculus.

The amount paid in a very small time interval of length dt starting at time t is $1\,dt$. The present value of this payment is $v^t\,dt$. To find the present value of the continuous annuity, we integrate all such payments since we are working with the continuous case.

If the force of interest is constant over the period, *ie* $\delta = \ln(1+i)$, we have:

$$\bar{a}_{\overline{n}|} = \int_0^n 1\,v^t\,dt = \left[\frac{v^t}{\ln v}\right]_0^n = \frac{v^n - 1}{\ln v} = \frac{1 - v^n}{\ln(1+i)} = \frac{1 - v^n}{\delta}$$

Continuously payable annuity present value factor

The continuously payable annuity present value factor is the present value at time 0 of the continuously payable annuity, where the rate of payment is \$1 per year paid continuously from time 0 to time n years:

$$\bar{a}_{\overline{n}|i} = \frac{1 - v^n}{\delta}$$

For example, let's say that payments of \$600 a year are received continuously for 5 years from time 0 to time 5 years. The annual effective interest rate is 6%. What is the present value of these payments at time 0?

The present value at time 0 is:

$$600\bar{a}_{\overline{5}|6\%} = 600\frac{1 - v^n}{\delta} = 600\frac{1 - 1.06^{-5}}{\ln(1.06)} = \$2,602.50$$

Example 2.7

A bank makes payments continuously at a rate of \$400 per year. The payments are made between times 5 and 7 years. Find the present value of these payments at time 2 years using an annual effective rate of discount of 4%.

Solution

We have $d = 0.04$. This means that $v = 1 - d = 0.96$, $1 + i = \dfrac{1}{0.96}$ and $\delta = \ln(1+i) = \ln(1/0.96)$.

The present value at time 5 years is:

$$400\bar{a}_{\overline{2}|}$$

The present value at time 2 years is:

$$400\bar{a}_{\overline{2}|}v^3 = 400\frac{1 - v^2}{\delta}v^3 = 400\frac{1 - 0.96^2}{\ln(1/0.96)}0.96^3 = \$679.67 \qquad \blacklozenge\blacklozenge$$

We can, as usual, also calculate the accumulated value of a continuously paid annuity.

The accumulated value at time n of a payment of \$1 per year received continuously over the period from time 0 to time n years is written as $\bar{s}_{\overline{n}|}$. It is pronounced **s-bar-angle-n** and it is valued at time n years.

Multiplying the continuously payable annuity present value factor by the n-year accumulated value factor, we have:

$$\bar{s}_{\overline{n}|} = (1+i)^n \bar{a}_{\overline{n}|} = (1+i)^n \frac{1-v^n}{\delta} = \frac{(1+i)^n - 1}{\delta}$$

Note that we also have:

$$\bar{a}_{\overline{n}|} = v^n \bar{s}_{\overline{n}|}$$

Continuously payable annuity accumulated value factor

The continuously payable annuity accumulated value factor is the accumulated value at time n years of a continuously payable annuity, where the rate of payment is \$1 per year payable continuously from time 0 to time n years:

$$\bar{s}_{\overline{n}|i} = \frac{(1+i)^n - 1}{\delta}$$

As an example, let's say that payments of \$600 a year are received continuously for 5 years from time 0 to time 5 years. The annual effective interest rate is 6%. What is the accumulated value at time 5 years of these payments?

The accumulated value at time 5 years is:

$$600\bar{s}_{\overline{5}|6\%} = 600\frac{(1+i)^n - 1}{\delta} = 600\frac{1.06^5 - 1}{\ln(1.06)} = \$3,482.74$$

Example 2.8

A company makes payments continuously at a rate of \$200 per year. The payments are made between times 2 and 7 years. Find the accumulated value of these payments at time 10 years using an annual effective interest rate of 6.5%.

Solution

The present value at time 2 years is:

$$200\bar{a}_{\overline{5}|6.5\%} = 200\frac{1-v^5}{\delta} = 200\frac{1-1.065^{-5}}{\ln(1.065)} = \$857.86$$

Accumulating the present value for 8 years, the accumulated value at time 10 years is:

$$857.86(1.065)^8 = \$1,419.76$$

Alternatively, the accumulated value at time 7 years is:

$$200\bar{s}_{\overline{5}|6.5\%} = 200\frac{(1+i)^5 - 1}{\delta} = 200\frac{1.065^5 - 1}{\ln(1.065)} = \$1,175.35$$

Accumulating this amount for 3 years, the accumulated value at time 10 years is:

$$1,175.35(1.065)^3 = \$1,419.76$$

◆◆

We conclude this section by considering the relationship between the present value factors of a continuously payable annuity ($\bar{a}_{\overline{n}|}$), an annuity-due ($\ddot{a}_{\overline{n}|}$), and an annuity-immediate ($a_{\overline{n}|}$), all with the same payment term (n). We have:

$$\bar{a}_{\overline{n}|} = \frac{1 - v^n}{\delta} \qquad\qquad \ddot{a}_{\overline{n}|} = \frac{1 - v^n}{d} \qquad\qquad a_{\overline{n}|} = \frac{1 - v^n}{i}$$

Hence:

$$\bar{a}_{\overline{n}|} = \frac{d}{\delta}\ddot{a}_{\overline{n}|} \qquad\qquad\qquad \ddot{a}_{\overline{n}|} = \frac{\delta}{d}\bar{a}_{\overline{n}|}$$

and:

$$\bar{a}_{\overline{n}|} = \frac{i}{\delta}a_{\overline{n}|} \qquad\qquad\qquad a_{\overline{n}|} = \frac{\delta}{i}\bar{a}_{\overline{n}|}$$

Similarly, for the accumulated value factors $\bar{s}_{\overline{n}|}$, $\ddot{s}_{\overline{n}|}$, and $s_{\overline{n}|}$, we have:

$$\bar{s}_{\overline{n}|} = \frac{d}{\delta}\ddot{s}_{\overline{n}|} \qquad\qquad\qquad \ddot{s}_{\overline{n}|} = \frac{\delta}{d}\bar{s}_{\overline{n}|}$$

and:

$$\bar{s}_{\overline{n}|} = \frac{i}{\delta}s_{\overline{n}|} \qquad\qquad\qquad s_{\overline{n}|} = \frac{\delta}{i}\bar{s}_{\overline{n}|}$$

For example, if we know that $a_{\overline{25}|7.2\%} = 11.4466$, then we can easily calculate $\bar{a}_{\overline{25}|7.2\%}$ as:

$$\bar{a}_{\overline{25}|7.2\%} = \frac{i}{\delta}a_{\overline{25}|7.2\%} = \frac{0.072}{\ln(1.072)}11.4466 = 11.8539$$

2.5 Perpetuities

A **perpetuity** is an annuity with payments that continue forever. In other words, a perpetuity is an annuity where $n = \infty$.

Consider an infinite series of payments of \$1 made at time intervals of 1 year, where the first payment occurs 1 year from now:

This is an example of a **perpetuity-immediate**. The first payment occurs in 1 year and the annual payments continue indefinitely.

The present value at time 0 of this infinite series of payments is:

$$v + v^2 + v^3 + \cdots$$

This is an infinite geometric series and can be simplified using the generic summation formula:

$$a + ar + ar^2 + \cdots = \frac{a}{1-r} \qquad \text{for } |r| < 1$$

Setting $a = v$ and $r = v$, we have:

$$v + v^2 + v^3 + \cdots = \frac{v}{1-v} = \frac{1}{1+i-1} = \frac{1}{i}$$

Notice that for positive rates of interest, the value of v will be between 0 and 1, satisfying the condition for the convergence of the geometric series. This formula can be remembered by letting $n \to \infty$ (so that $v^n \to 0$) in the formula for the present value of an annuity-immediate.

The present value of this simple perpetuity-immediate is represented by the symbol $a_{\overline{\infty}|}$. It is pronounced **a-angle-infinity**. It is valued at time 0, which is 1 year before the first payment is made.

Perpetuity-immediate present value factor

Assuming an annual effective interest rate i, the perpetuity-immediate present value factor is the present value at time 0 of a series of payments where the payments are \$1 at time 1 year, \$1 at time 2 years, and so on, to infinity:

$$a_{\overline{\infty}|i} = \frac{1}{i}$$

Example 2.9

Determine the present value of payments of \$5 to be made at the end of each year starting this year. The payments continue forever. The annual effective interest rate is 8%.

Solution

The present value at time 0 is:

$$5a_{\overline{\infty}|8\%} = \frac{5}{i} = \frac{5}{0.08} = \$62.50 \qquad\qquad \blacklozenge\blacklozenge$$

We can also define a **perpetuity-due.** The first payment occurs now and the annual payments continue indefinitely.

The timeline diagram is:

```
    1     1     1     1    ...            payment
    |     |     |     |
    +-----+-----+-----+-------->
    0     1     2     3    ...            time
```

The present value at time 0 of the perpetuity-due is:

$$1 + v + v^2 + \cdots$$

Using the generic geometric series formula again with $a = 1$ and $r = v$, we have:

$$1 + v + v^2 + \cdots = \frac{1}{1-v} = \frac{1}{d}$$

The present value of this simple perpetuity-due is represented by the symbol $\ddot{a}_{\overline{\infty}|}$, which is pronounced **a-double-dot-angle-infinity**. It is valued at time 0, when the first payment is made.

Perpetuity-due present value factor

Assuming an annual effective interest rate i, the perpetuity-due present value factor is the present value at time 0 of a series of payments where the payments are \$1 at time 0, \$1 at time 1 year, and so on, to infinity:

$$\ddot{a}_{\overline{\infty}|i} = \frac{1}{d}$$

Example 2.10

Determine the present value of payments of \$100 to be made at the beginning of each year, starting now. The payments continue forever. The annual effective interest rate is 4%.

Solution

The present value at time 0 is:

$$100\ddot{a}_{\overline{\infty}|4\%} = \frac{100}{d} = \frac{100}{0.04/1.04} = \$2,600.00 \qquad\qquad \blacklozenge\blacklozenge$$

There is a simple relationship between the present value of a perpetuity-immediate, $a_{\overline{\infty}|}$, and the present value of a perpetuity-due, $\ddot{a}_{\overline{\infty}|}$.

We have:

$$a_{\overline{\infty}|} = v + v^2 + v^3 + \cdots$$

$$\ddot{a}_{\overline{\infty}|} = 1 + v + v^2 + \cdots$$

Hence:

$$\ddot{a}_{\overline{\infty}|} = 1 + a_{\overline{\infty}|}$$

We can also define a **continuously payable perpetuity**, where the payments are made as a continuous payment stream. We now have continuous payments, so instead of summing discrete payments, we integrate the discounted value of the payments. The present value at time 0 is:

$$\int_0^\infty 1 v^t \, dt = \left[\frac{v^t}{\ln v} \right]_0^\infty = \frac{v^\infty - 1}{\ln v} = \frac{1}{\ln(1+i)} = \frac{1}{\delta}$$

The present value of this simple continuously payable perpetuity is represented by the symbol $\bar{a}_{\overline{\infty}|}$, which is pronounced **a-bar-angle-infinity**. It is valued at time 0.

Continuously payable perpetuity present value factor

Assuming an annual effective interest rate i, the continuously payable perpetuity present value factor is the present value at time 0 of a series of payments where the payments are paid continuously at a rate of \$1 per year forever:

$$\bar{a}_{\overline{\infty}|i} = \frac{1}{\delta}$$

Example 2.11

Determine the present value of payments of $25 payable continuously each year, starting now and continuing indefinitely. The annual effective interest rate is 7%.

Solution

The present value at time 0 is:

$$25\bar{a}_{\overline{\infty}|7\%} = \frac{25}{\delta} = \frac{25}{\ln(1.07)} = \$369.50 \qquad \blacklozenge\blacklozenge$$

The same relationships that we saw for n-year annuities also hold for perpetuities, *ie*:

$$\bar{a}_{\overline{\infty}|} = \frac{d}{\delta}\ddot{a}_{\overline{\infty}|} \qquad\qquad \bar{a}_{\overline{\infty}|} = \frac{i}{\delta}a_{\overline{\infty}|}$$

$$\ddot{a}_{\overline{\infty}|} = \frac{\delta}{d}\bar{a}_{\overline{\infty}|} \qquad\qquad \ddot{a}_{\overline{\infty}|} = \frac{i}{d}a_{\overline{\infty}|}$$

$$a_{\overline{\infty}|} = \frac{\delta}{i}\bar{a}_{\overline{\infty}|} \qquad\qquad a_{\overline{\infty}|} = \frac{d}{i}\ddot{a}_{\overline{\infty}|}$$

Finally, note that we do not consider the accumulated values of perpetuities. The payments continue indefinitely, so the accumulated value would be infinite.

2.6   Equations of value

For an individual person or a financial institution such as a bank, cash flows come in and cash flows go out. Let's consider a simple financial transaction between two parties. From each party's perspective, the transaction involves cash inflows and cash outflows, depending upon whether the cash flow is positive or negative. The present value of the cash inflows to one party equals the present value of the cash outflows to the other party.

For example, if a bank lends Jack $5,000 at time 0, Jack has a positive cash flow (inflow) of $5,000 at time 0, whereas the bank has a negative cash flow (outflow) of −$5,000 at time 0. When Jack repays the loan to the bank in installments, he has negative cash flows whereas the bank has positive cash flows.

An **equation of value** helps to solve problems by providing a relationship between cash inflows and cash outflows, which we can use to solve for an unknown variable. To set up the equation of value, we simply equate two equivalent expressions and simplify them until we can solve for the unknown variable.

Equation of value

The equation of value that governs cash flows is:

   Present value of inflows = present value of outflows

We use this equation of value in a variety of contexts. We may solve an equation of value to find an unknown amount of money, a number of years or an interest rate. Let's look at some examples of equations of value with a variety of unknown parameters.

Example 2.12

A bank loans $4,000 to Joe. In 5 years, Joe will pay the bank a lump sum of $4,750 as repayment of the loan and interest. What is the annual effective interest rate that the bank has charged on the loan?

Solution

The present value of Joe's inflow is 4,000.

The present value of Joe's outflow is $4,750v^5$.

Equating these, the equation of value is:

$$4,750v^5 = 4,000$$

Solving for i, we have:

$$v^5 = \frac{4,000}{4,750} = 0.842105$$

$$\Rightarrow v = 0.966214$$

$$\Rightarrow 1+i = \frac{1}{v} = 1.035$$

Hence, the annual effective interest rate is 3.5%.   ♦ ♦

Example 2.13

Connie buys an annuity-immediate from an insurance company. Connie pays $300,000 and in return receives level payments of X at the end of each year for the next 15 years. The annual effective interest rate is 6%. Calculate X.

Solution

The present value of Connie's outflow is 300,000.

The present value of Connie's inflow is $Xa_{\overline{15}|6\%}$.

Equating these, the equation of value is:

$$Xa_{\overline{15}|6\%} = 300,000$$

Solving for X, we have:

$$X\frac{1-1.06^{-15}}{0.06} = 300,000$$

$$\Rightarrow X = \frac{300,000}{9.712249} = \$30,888.83$$

Hence, Connie receives an annual payment of $30,888.83.   ♦ ♦

Example 2.14

Karen invests $36,370 now in order to receive $4,500 at the end of each year for n years, with the first payment at time 5 years. Using an annual effective interest rate of 7%, calculate n.

Solution

The present value of Karen's outflow is 36,370.

The present value of Karen's inflow is $4,500v^4 a_{\overline{n}|7\%}$.

Equating these, the equation of value is:

$$4,500v^4 a_{\overline{n}|7\%} = 36,370$$

Rewriting this equation, we have:

$$4,500(1.07)^{-4} \frac{1-1.07^{-n}}{0.07} = 36,370$$

$$\Rightarrow \quad 1-1.07^{-n} = 0.74159$$

This can be solved by rearranging the terms and then taking logs of both sides:

$$1.07^{-n} = 0.25841$$

$$\Rightarrow \quad -n\ln 1.07 = \ln 0.25841$$

$$\Rightarrow \quad n = 20$$

Karen receives the payments for 20 years.   ◆◆

Example 2.15

David borrows $\$X$ at time 0 and must repay the loan with payments of \$45,000 at times 3, 4, 5 and 6 years. Using an annual effective interest rate of 9%, determine X .

Solution

The present value of David's inflow is X .

The present value of David's outflow is $45,000v^2 a_{\overline{4}|9\%}$.

Equating these, the equation of value is:

$$X = 45,000v^2 a_{\overline{4}|9\%}$$

Hence:

$$X = 45,000v^2 a_{\overline{4}|9\%} = 45,000(1.09)^{-2} \frac{1-1.09^{-4}}{0.09} = \$122,706.33$$ ◆◆

At times we may need to solve an equation of value using a numerical method, such as linear interpolation. This is illustrated in the following example.

Example 2.16

Marilyn invests \$3,500 at time 0 in order to receive payments of \$450 at times 1 year, 2 years, 3 years, and so on, with the last payment at time 10 years. Determine the annual effective interest rate that Marilyn earns.

Solution

If we represent the outflow as a negative payment, the timeline diagram looks like this:

-3,500	450	450	...	450	payment
0	1	2	...	10	time

The present value of Marilyn's inflow is $450a_{\overline{10}|i}$.

The present value of Marilyn's outflow is $3,500$.

Equating these, the equation of value is:

$$450a_{\overline{10}|i} = 3,500$$

To calculate i , we need to use a numerical method. Many modern financial calculators are capable of solving problems such as this, but we can also use an iterative method or simply trial and error.

A quick calculation using an interest rate of 5% shows that:

$$450a_{\overline{10}|5\%} = 450\frac{1-(1.05)^{-10}}{0.05} = \$3,474.78$$

We require a higher present value, so we need to try a *lower* interest rate. Let's try 4.9%.

$$450a_{\overline{10}|4.9\%} = 450\frac{1-(1.049)^{-10}}{0.049} = \$3,491.72$$

Again, we require a higher present value, so we need to try a lower interest rate. Let's try 4.8%.

$$450a_{\overline{10}|4.8\%} = 450\frac{1-(1.048)^{-10}}{0.048} = \$3,508.78$$

Now that we know that the correct answer lies between 4.8% and 4.9%, we can estimate the unknown interest rate using linear interpolation.

In general, if the present values calculated at interest rates i_1 and i_2 are P_1 and P_2 respectively, then the interest rate i corresponding to a present value of P can be approximated by:

$$i \approx i_1 + \frac{P_1 - P}{P_1 - P_2} \times (i_2 - i_1)$$

where $i_1 < i < i_2$ and $P_2 < P < P_1$.

In this case, we have $i_1 = 4.8\%$, $i_2 = 4.9\%$, $P_1 = 3,508.78$, $P_2 = 3,491.72$, and $P = 3,500$.

Interpolating, we have:

$$i \approx 4.8 + \frac{3,508.78 - 3,500.00}{3,508.78 - 3,491.72} \times (4.9 - 4.8) = 4.8515\%$$

Hence, the interest rate is approximately equal to 4.85%.   ◆ ◆

Note that linear interpolation does not give exactly the right answer in Example 2.16, because an annuity-immediate is not a linear function of i. The correct answer (found using a financial calculator) is $i = 4.85136\%$. So, our answer using linear interpolation was good, but not perfect.

The accuracy of the linear interpolation formula depends on the range of values over which we interpolate. The farther apart P_1 and P_2 are, the less accurate the approximation will be.

For example, suppose that we interpolate between $i_1 = 4\%$ and $i_2 = 5\%$. We have:

$$P_1 = 450 a_{\overline{10}|4\%} = 450 \frac{1-(1.04)^{-10}}{0.04} = \$3,649.90$$

$$P_2 = 450 a_{\overline{10}|5\%} = 450 \frac{1-(1.05)^{-10}}{0.05} = \$3,474.78$$

And our estimate of i is:

$$i \approx 4.0 + \frac{3,649.90 - 3,500.00}{3,649.90 - 3,474.78} \times (5.0 - 4.0) = 4.8560\%$$

This second estimated value is considerably less accurate than our initial calculation.

Chapter 2 Practice Questions

Question guide

- Questions 2.1 – 2.9 test material from Sections 2.1 – 2.4.

- Questions 2.10 – 2.17 test material from Sections 2.5 – 2.6.

- Questions 2.18 – 2.20 are from the SOA/CAS Course 2 exam.

Question 2.1

Tyler graduates from college today and turns 22 years old. Starting one year from today, Tyler makes level annual deposits into a savings account that pays 4% per year. How much would Tyler need to deposit at the end of each year to have $1,000,000 on his 65th birthday?

Question 2.2

Paul expects to receive payments of $1,000 at the end of each year for 5 years, with payments to start one year from now. Howard expects to receive payments of X at the end of each year for 10 years, with payments to start one year from now. At an annual effective interest rate of 5%, the present values of their cash flows are the same. Determine X.

Question 2.3

Starting today, Matt receives payments of $20 at the beginning of each of the next three years. Starting three years from now, Matt receives payments of $10 at the beginning of each of the next three years. The annual effective interest rate is 8%. Calculate the present value of these payments.

Question 2.4

Starting today, Sandy sets aside $10,000 at the beginning of each year into a bank account that pays an annual effective interest rate of 5.5%. She makes 25 such deposits. Thirty years from today, Sandy uses the accumulated value in the account to purchase an annuity that pays X at the beginning of each year for 25 years. Determine X.

Question 2.5

Find the present value at time 0 of regular payments of $50 at times 25 years, 26 years, and so on, with the last payment at time 40 years. Use an annual effective interest rate of 12%.

Question 2.6

Find the accumulated value at time 15 years of payments of $300 at times 5 years, 6 years, and so on, with the last payment at time 10 years. Use an annual effective interest rate of 3% and an annuity-immediate.

Question 2.7

Find the accumulated value at time 15 years of regular payments of $50 made at times 5 years, 6 years, and so on, with the last payment at time 10 years. Use an annual effective interest rate of 16% and an annuity-due.

Question 2.8

Find the present value at time 2 years of payments of $400 at times 8 years, 9 years, and so on, with the last payment at time 15 years. Use an annual effective interest rate of 9%.

Question 2.9

$100 per year is received continuously from time 5 years to time 8 years. Assuming an annual effective interest rate of 4.5%, what is the accumulated value at time 10 years?

Question 2.10

Mary receives payments of $100 at the beginning of each year, including today, forever. Virginia receives payments of X at the end of each year, starting 5 years from today, forever. The present values of their payments are the same at an annual effective interest rate of 10%. Calculate X.

Question 2.11

Payments of $5,000 are received at the end of each year for 10 years, after which payments of $1,000 are received at the end of each year forever. The annual effective interest rate is 9%. Determine the present value of these payments.

Question 2.12

Jim invests X at time 7 years in order to receive $500 at the end of each year for 15 years starting at the end of the 10th year. Using an annual effective rate of interest of 4%, find X.

Question 2.13

Alan pays $4,000 at time n years in order to receive $438.52 at the end of each year for n years, starting at time $(n+1)$ years. The annual effective rate of interest is 8%. Find n.

Question 2.14

Martha pays $1,500 at time 10 years in order to receive $1,000 at time 11 years and $1,000 at time 12 years. Find the annual effective rate of interest that she earns on her money.

Question 2.15

Michael pays $2,500 at time 0 in order to receive $400 at the end of each year for 7 years with the first payment at the end of the first year. He also receives a lump sum of $1,000 at time 8 years. Find the annual effective rate of interest that he earns on his money.

Question 2.16

You invest $320.74 now in order to receive $40 at the start of each year for n years, with the first payment in exactly 5 years. Using an annual effective rate of interest of 5.6%, find n.

Question 2.17

You invest $50,000 at time 0 in order to receive payments of $$X$ at times 15 years, 16 years, and so on, with the last payment at time 25 years. Using an annual effective rate of interest of 7%, find X.

Question 2.18   *SOA/CAS*

A perpetuity-immediate pays $$X$ per year. Brian receives the first n payments, Colleen receives the next n payments, and Jeff receives the remaining payments. Brian's share of the present value of the original perpetuity is 40%, and Jeff's share is K. Calculate K.

Question 2.19   *SOA/CAS*

The present values of the following three annuities are equal:

(i)   Perpetuity-immediate paying $1 each year, calculated at an annual effective interest rate of 7.25%

(ii)   50-year annuity-immediate paying $1 each year, calculated at an annual effective interest rate of j %

(iii) n-year annuity-immediate paying $1 each year, calculated at an annual effective interest rate of $j-1$ %.

Calculate n.

Question 2.20   *SOA/CAS*

To accumulate $8,000 at the end of $3n$ years, deposits of $98 are made at the end of each of the first n years and $196 at the end of each of the next $2n$ years.

The annual effective rate of interest is i. You are given $(1+i)^n = 2.0$.

Determine i.

3

Varying annuities

Overview

So far we have considered level annuities, which provide a series of level of payments over a defined period, such as $400 at the end of each year for 12 years.

We may also need to evaluate the present value or accumulated value of payments that increase each period (such as payments of $50, $55, $60, $65, *etc*) or decrease each period (such as payments of $105, $95, $85, $75, *etc*). A series of payments that increase or decrease predictably each period is known as a **varying annuity**.

This chapter explains how to calculate present values and accumulated values of varying annuities both from first principles and using shortcut formulas. We then develop the idea that the amount of payment can change continuously, that is, the payment stream received at any time t is a function of t. Once again, we learn how to evaluate the present value and accumulated value of such payment streams.

3.1 Increasing annuity-immediate

Consider a stream of annual payments where the first payment occurs in 1 year, and each payment is higher than the previous one by a constant amount, such as payments of $55, $60, $65, and so on. This is an example of an **increasing annuity-immediate**.

The simplest case of an increasing annuity-immediate is one that has payments of $1 at time 1 year, $2 at time 2 years, $3 at time 3 years, and so on, up to n at time n years.

Let's develop the present value of this series of payments. The present value of the first payment occurring at time 1 year is $1 \times v^1$. The present value of the second payment occurring at time 2 years is $2 \times v^2$. The present value of the last payment of n occurring at time n years is $n \times v^n$.

The present value of the series of payments is written as $(Ia)_{\overline{n}|}$:

$$(Ia)_{\overline{n}|} = v + 2v^2 + 3v^3 + \cdots + nv^n$$

In words, $(Ia)_{\overline{n}|}$ is called the present value of an increasing annuity-immediate. It is pronounced **i-a-angle-n**, and it is valued at time 0.

This expression can be simplified into a formula for the present value factor for an increasing annuity-immediate. Multiplying both sides of the equation by $1+i$, we have:

$$(1+i)(Ia)_{\overline{n}|} = 1 + 2v + 3v^2 + \cdots + nv^{n-1}$$

Subtracting the first equation from the second, we get:

$$(1+i)(Ia)_{\overline{n}|} - (Ia)_{\overline{n}|} = 1 + 2v - v + 3v^2 - 2v^2 + \cdots + nv^{n-1} - (n-1)v^{n-1} - nv^n$$

$$\Rightarrow \quad i(Ia)_{\overline{n}|} = 1 + v + v^2 + \cdots + v^{n-1} - nv^n = \ddot{a}_{\overline{n}|} - nv^n$$

$$\Rightarrow \quad (Ia)_{\overline{n}|} = \frac{\ddot{a}_{\overline{n}|} - nv^n}{i}$$

Increasing annuity-immediate present value factor

Assuming an annual effective interest rate i, the increasing annuity-immediate present value factor is the present value of a series of payments of $1 at time 1 year, $2 at time 2 years, and so on, up to n at time n years:

$$(Ia)_{\overline{n}|i} = \frac{\ddot{a}_{\overline{n}|i} - nv^n}{i}$$

This formula is used to calculate the present value of various payments that fit this pattern. For example, let's determine an expression for the present value at time 0 of payments of $5 at time 1 year, $10 at time 2 years, $15 at time 3 years, and so on, up to $100 at time 20 years.

The timeline diagram of the payments is:

The present value of the payments at time 0 is:

$$5v + 10v^2 + \cdots + 100v^{20} = 5\left(v + 2v^2 + \cdots + 20v^{20}\right) = 5(Ia)_{\overline{20}|}$$

Of course, the present value is just 5 times the present value factor of the increasing annuity-immediate. Given a set of cash flows, we extract a factor so that the remaining cash flows fit the pattern of an increasing annuity-immediate.

Example 3.1

Dan receives $400 in 1 year, $800 in two years, $1,200 in three years and so on until the final payment of $4,000. Using an annual effective interest rate of 6%, determine the present value of these payments at time 0.

Solution

The present value at time 0 is:

$$400v + 800v^2 + 1,200v^3 + \cdots + 4,000v^{10} = 400(Ia)_{\overline{10}|6\%}$$

Calculating the required values, we have:

$$\ddot{a}_{\overline{10}|6\%} = \frac{1 - 1.06^{-10}}{0.06 / 1.06} = 7.801692$$

$$\Rightarrow \quad (Ia)_{\overline{10}|6\%} = \frac{7.801692 - 10 \times 1.06^{-10}}{0.06} = 36.962408$$

So the present value is $400 \times 36.962408 = \$14,784.96$. ◆◆

In the examples so far, the payments have started with the amount by which the payments change from one period to the next. We might also want to evaluate the present value of payments that follow a pattern such as $100, $110, $120, \cdots, $200. This can be done by representing the present value of the payments as the present value of a level annuity plus the present value of an increasing annuity.

In this simple example, we can represent payments of $100, $110, $120, \cdots, $200 as the sum of a level annuity-immediate of $90 and an increasing annuity-immediate of $10, $20, $30, \cdots, $110.

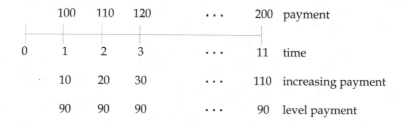

Example 3.2

Determine an expression for the present value at time 0 of payments of $55 at time 1 year, $60 at time 2 years, $65 at time 3 years and so on, up to the last payment at time 20 years.

Solution

The last payment must be \$55 plus 19 increases of \$5, which gives \$150. From first principles, the present value is:

$$55v + 60v^2 + 65v^3 + \cdots + 150v^{20}$$

This can be separated into two series:

55	60	65	$\cdots$	150	payment
0	1	2	3	$\cdots$	20	time
	5	10	15	$\cdots$	100	increasing payment
	50	50	50	$\cdots$	50	level payment

The present value of which is:

$$\left(50v + 50v^2 + 50v^3 + \cdots + 50v^{20}\right) + \left(5v + 10v^2 + 15v^3 + \cdots + 100v^{20}\right)$$

This is a level annuity-immediate plus an increasing annuity-immediate, so an expression for the present value at time 0 is:

$$50a_{\overline{20}|} + 5(Ia)_{\overline{20}|}$$

Notice that there are other ways to express the same present value. For example, we could separate the payments into the following series:

55	60	65	$\cdots$	150	payment
0	1	2	3	$\cdots$	20	time
		5	10	$\cdots$	95	increasing payment
	55	55	55	$\cdots$	55	level payment

The present value of which is:

$$\left(55v + 55v^2 + 55v^3 + \cdots + 55v^{20}\right) + \left(5v^2 + 10v^3 + 15v^4 + \cdots + 95v^{20}\right)$$

$$= 55\left(v + v^2 + v^3 + \cdots + v^{20}\right) + 5v\left(v + 2v^2 + 3v^3 + \cdots + 19v^{19}\right)$$

Hence, an alternative expression for the present value at time 0 is:

$$55a_{\overline{20}|} + 5v(Ia)_{\overline{19}|}$$ $\blacklozenge\ \blacklozenge$

Now that we can determine the present value of an increasing annuity-immediate, we can also find the accumulated value of an increasing annuity-immediate.

The accumulated value at time n of payments of \$1 at time 1 year, \$2 at time 2 years, \$3 at time 3 years, and so on up to \$$n$ at time n, is written as $(Is)_{\overline{n}|}$. It is called the accumulated value of an increasing annuity-immediate. It is pronounced **i-s-angle-n**, and it is valued at time n.

The accumulated value can be found most easily by accumulating the present value:

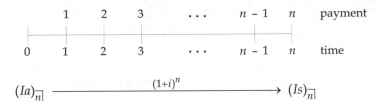

So, we have:

$$(Is)_{\overline{n}|} = (1+i)^n (Ia)_{\overline{n}|}$$

We can algebraically manipulate this expression to find an alternative expression for the accumulated value of an increasing annuity-immediate:

$$(Is)_{\overline{n}|} = (1+i)^n (Ia)_{\overline{n}|} = (1+i)^n \frac{\ddot{a}_{\overline{n}|} - nv^n}{i} = \frac{(1+i)^n \ddot{a}_{\overline{n}|} - n(1+i)^n v^n}{i} = \frac{\ddot{s}_{\overline{n}|} - n}{i}$$

Increasing annuity-immediate accumulated value factor

Assuming an annual effective interest rate i, the increasing annuity-immediate accumulated value factor is the accumulated value at time n years of a series of payments of $1 at time 1 year, $2 at time 2 years, and so on, up to n at time n years:

$$(Is)_{\overline{n}|i} = (1+i)^n (Ia)_{\overline{n}|i} = \frac{\ddot{s}_{\overline{n}|i} - n}{i}$$

For example, let's determine the accumulated value at time 20 years of payments of $5 at time 1 year, $10 at time 2 years, $15 at time 3 years, and so on, up to $100 at time 20 years.

The timeline diagram of the payments is:

The accumulated value of the payments at time 20 years is:

$$5(1+i)^{19} + 10(1+i)^{18} + \cdots + 100 = 5(1+i)^{20} (Ia)_{\overline{20}|} = 5(Is)_{\overline{20}|}$$

The accumulated value is 5 times the accumulated value of the increasing annuity-immediate.

Example 3.3

The following payments are to be received: $500 in 1 year, $520 in 2 years, $540 in 3 years and so on, until the final payment of $800. Using an annual effective interest rate of 2%, determine the accumulated value of these payments at the time of the last payment.

Solution

With increases of $20, there are $15+1=16$ payments in total, since $800 = 500 + 15 \times 20$. The last payment is at time 16 years, since the first payment occurred at time 1 year.

The timeline diagram of the cash flows is:

The accumulated value at 16 years is:

$$500(1.02)^{15} + 520(1.02)^{14} + 540(1.02)^{13} + \cdots + 800 = 480s_{\overline{16}|2\%} + 20(Is)_{\overline{16}|2\%}$$

Calculating the required values, we have:

$$s_{\overline{16}|2\%} = \frac{1.02^{16} - 1}{0.02} = 18.639285$$

$$\ddot{s}_{\overline{16}|2\%} = (1.02)18.639285 = 19.012071$$

$$\Rightarrow \quad (Is)_{\overline{16}|2\%} = \frac{19.012071 - 16}{0.02} = 150.603548$$

So the accumulated value at time 16 years is:

$$480 \times 18.639285 + 20 \times 150.603548 = \$11,958.93$$

Alternatively, we could calculate the present value and accumulate it for 16 years. The present value at time 0 is:

$$500v + 520v^2 + 540v^3 + \cdots + 800v^{16} = 480a_{\overline{16}|2\%} + 20(Ia)_{\overline{16}|2\%}$$

The accumulated value at time 16 years is:

$$(1+i)^{16}\left(480a_{\overline{16}|2\%} + 20(Ia)_{\overline{16}|2\%}\right)$$

Calculating the required values, we have:

$$a_{\overline{16}|2\%} = \frac{1 - 1.02^{-16}}{0.02} = 13.577709$$

$$\ddot{a}_{\overline{16}|2\%} = \frac{1 - 1.02^{-16}}{0.02 / 1.02} = 13.849264$$

$$\Rightarrow \quad (Ia)_{\overline{16}|2\%} = \frac{13.849264 - 16 \times 1.02^{-16}}{0.02} = 109.706524$$

So the accumulated value at time 16 years is:

$$(1.02)^{16}\left(480 \times 13.577709 + 20 \times 109.706524\right) = \$11,958.93 \qquad \blacklozenge\blacklozenge$$

Increasing perpetuity-immediate

Thus far in this section, we have examined the increasing annuity-immediate in which the number of payments is finite. Relaxing this restriction, we can allow an infinite number of payments and consider the **increasing perpetuity-immediate**. In this case, there are payments of $1 at time 1 year, $2 at time 2 years, $3 at time 3 years, and so on, continuing indefinitely.

Let's develop the present value of this series of payments. The present value of this series of payments is $(Ia)_{\overline{\infty}|}$:

$$(Ia)_{\overline{\infty}|} = v + 2v^2 + 3v^3 + \cdots$$

In words, $(Ia)_{\overline{\infty}|}$ is called the present value of an increasing perpetuity-immediate. It is pronounced **i-a-angle-infinity**, and it is valued at time 0.

This expression can be simplified into a formula for the present value factor for an increasing perpetuity-immediate. Multiplying both sides of the equation by v, we have:

$$v(Ia)_{\overline{\infty}|} = v^2 + 2v^3 + 3v^4 + \cdots$$

Subtracting the second equation from the first, we get:

$$(Ia)_{\overline{\infty}|} - v(Ia)_{\overline{\infty}|} = v + v^2 + v^3 + \cdots$$

$$\Rightarrow \quad (1-v)(Ia)_{\overline{\infty}|} = a_{\overline{\infty}|}$$

$$\Rightarrow \quad (Ia)_{\overline{\infty}|} = \frac{1}{i(1-v)} = \frac{1}{id} = \frac{1+i}{i^2}$$

Increasing perpetuity-immediate present value factor

Assuming an annual effective interest rate i, the increasing perpetuity-immediate present value factor is the present value of a series of payments of $1 at time 1 year, $2 at time 2 years, and so on, continuing without end:

$$(Ia)_{\overline{\infty}|i} = \frac{1+i}{i^2}$$

This formula is used to calculate the present value of various payments that fit this pattern. For example, let's determine the present value at time 0 of payments of $5 at time 1 year, $10 at time 2 years, $15 at time 3 years, and so on, assuming the annual effective interest rate is 5%.

The present value of the payments at time 0 is:

$$5v + 10v^2 + 15v^3 + \cdots = 5(Ia)_{\overline{\infty}|} = \frac{5(1.05)}{(0.05)^2} = \$2,100.00$$

3.2 *Increasing annuity-due*

Consider a stream of annual payments where the first payment is made now, and each payment is higher than the previous one by a constant amount, such as payments of $55, $60, $65, and so on. This is an example of an **increasing annuity-due**.

The simplest case of an increasing annuity-due is one that has payments of $1 at time 0, $2 at time 1 years, $3 at time 2 years, and so on, up to n at time $n-1$ years.

Let's develop the present value of this series of payments. The present value of the first payment occurring at time 0 is just 1. The present value of the second payment occurring at time 1 year is $2 \times v$. The present value of the last payment of n occurring at time $n-1$ years is $n \times v^{n-1}$.

The present value of the series of payments is written as $(I\ddot{a})_{\overline{n}|}$:

$$(I\ddot{a})_{\overline{n}|} = 1 + 2v + 3v^2 + \cdots + nv^{n-1}$$

In words, $(I\ddot{a})_{\overline{n}|}$ is called the present value of an increasing annuity-due. It is pronounced **i-a-double-dot-angle-n**, and it is valued at time 0.

This expression can be simplified into a formula for the present value factor of an increasing annuity-due. Multiplying both sides of the equation by v, we get:

$$v(I\ddot{a})_{\overline{n}|} = v + 2v^2 + 3v^3 + \cdots + nv^n$$

Subtracting the second equation from the first, we get:

$$(I\ddot{a})_{\overline{n}|} - v(I\ddot{a})_{\overline{n}|} = 1 + v + v^2 + \cdots + v^{n-1} - nv^n$$

$$\Rightarrow (1-v)(I\ddot{a})_{\overline{n}|} = \ddot{a}_{\overline{n}|} - nv^n$$

$$\Rightarrow (I\ddot{a})_{\overline{n}|} = \frac{\ddot{a}_{\overline{n}|} - nv^n}{1-v} = \frac{\ddot{a}_{\overline{n}|} - nv^n}{d}$$

Increasing annuity-due present value factor

Assuming an annual effective interest rate i, the increasing annuity-due present value factor is the present value of a series of payments of \$1 at time 0, \$2 at time 1 years, and so on, up to \$$n$ at time $n-1$ years:

$$(I\ddot{a})_{\overline{n}|i} = \frac{\ddot{a}_{\overline{n}|i} - nv^n}{d}$$

Notice that this formula is similar to the formula for the increasing annuity-immediate present value factor, but the i in the denominator has been replaced by a d. This is a convenient way to remember the formulas. This formula can be used to evaluate the present value of various payments that fit this pattern.

For example, let's determine an expression for the present value at time 0 of payments of \$10 paid at time 0, \$20 paid at time 1 year, \$30 paid at time 2 years, and so on, up to \$200 paid at time 19 years.

The timeline diagram of the payments is:

The present value of the payments at time 0 is:

$$10 + 20v + 30v^2 + \cdots + 200v^{19} = 10\left(1 + 2v + 3v^2 + \cdots + 20v^{19}\right) = 10(I\ddot{a})_{\overline{20}|}$$

Of course, the present value is just 10 times the present value factor of the increasing annuity-due. Given a set of cash flows, we try to extract a factor so that the remaining cash flows fit the pattern of an increasing annuity-due.

Example 3.4

Determine the present value at time 0 of payments of $75 at time 0, $80 at time 1 year, $85 at time 2 years, and so on, up to $175 at time 20 years. The annual effective interest rate is 4%.

Solution

The timeline diagram of the payment stream is:

75	80	85	90	$\cdots$	175	payment
0	1	2	3	$\cdots$	20	time
5	10	15	20	$\cdots$	105	increasing payment
70	70	70	70	$\cdots$	70	level payment

Notice that we have 21 payments in total, so an expression for the present value at time 0 is:

$$70\ddot{a}_{\overline{21}|} + 5(I\ddot{a})_{\overline{21}|}$$

Calculating the required values, we have:

$$\ddot{a}_{\overline{21}|4\%} = \frac{1 - 1.04^{-21}}{0.04/1.04} = 14.590326$$

$$\Rightarrow \quad (I\ddot{a})_{\overline{21}|4\%} = \frac{14.590326 - 21 \times 1.04^{-21}}{0.04/1.04} = 139.745338$$

So the present value at time 0 is:

$$70 \times 14.590326 + 5 \times 139.745338 = \$1,720.05$$

Notice that we could have used other equivalent expressions to determine the same present value.

For example, we could have split the payments as follows:

75	80	85	90	$\cdots$	175	payment
0	1	2	3	$\cdots$	20	time
	5	10	15	$\cdots$	100	increasing payment
75	75	75	75	$\cdots$	75	level payment

This would have lead to an equivalent expression:

$$75\ddot{a}_{\overline{21}|} + 5(Ia)_{\overline{20}|}$$

$\blacklozenge\blacklozenge$

Now that we can determine the present value of an increasing annuity-due, we can also calculate the accumulated value of an increasing annuity-due by accumulating the present value.

The accumulated value at time n of payments of $1 at time 0, $2 at time 1 year, $3 at time 2 years, and so on, up to n at time $n-1$, is written as $(I\ddot{s})_{\overline{n}|}$. It is called the accumulated value of an increasing annuity-due. It is pronounced **i-s-double-dot-angle-n**, and it is valued at time n.

The accumulated value can be found most easily by accumulating the present value:

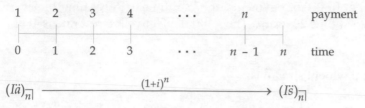

So, we have:

$$(I\ddot{s})_{\overline{n}|} = (1+i)^n (I\ddot{a})_{\overline{n}|}$$

We can algebraically manipulate this expression to find an alternative expression for the accumulated value of an increasing annuity-due:

$$(I\ddot{s})_{\overline{n}|} = (1+i)^n (I\ddot{a})_{\overline{n}|} = (1+i)^n \frac{\ddot{a}_{\overline{n}|} - nv^n}{d}$$

$$= \frac{(1+i)^n \ddot{a}_{\overline{n}|} - n(1+i)^n v^n}{d} = \frac{\ddot{s}_{\overline{n}|} - n}{d}$$

Increasing annuity-due accumulated value factor

Assuming an annual effective interest rate i, the increasing annuity-due accumulated value factor is the accumulated value at time n years of a series of payments of \$1 at time 0, \$2 at time 1 year, and so on, up to \$$n$ at time $n-1$ years:

$$(I\ddot{s})_{\overline{n}|i} = (1+i)^n (I\ddot{a})_{\overline{n}|i} = \frac{\ddot{s}_{\overline{n}|i} - n}{d}$$

For example, let's determine the accumulated value at time 20 years of payments of \$10 at time 0, \$20 at time 1 year, \$30 at time 2 years, and so on, up to \$200 at time 19 years. The annual effective interest rate is 4%.

The timeline diagram of the payments is:

The accumulated value of the payments at time 20 years is:

$$10(1+i)^{20} + 20(1+i)^{19} + 30(1+i)^{18} + \cdots + 200(1+i) = 10(1+i)^{20} (I\ddot{a})_{\overline{20}|} = 10(I\ddot{s})_{\overline{20}|}$$

Calculating the required values:

$$\ddot{s}_{\overline{20}|4\%} = \frac{(1.04)^{20} - 1}{0.04 / 1.04} = 30.969202$$

$$10(I\ddot{s})_{\overline{20}|4\%} = 10 \times \frac{30.969202 - 20}{0.04 / 1.04} = \$2,851.99$$

Increasing perpetuity-due

Building upon the concept of the increasing annuity-due, we can also consider the **increasing perpetuity-due** in which the payments are $1 at time 0, $2 at time 1 year, $3 at time 2 years, and so on, continuing indefinitely.

Let's develop the present value of this series of payments. The present value of the series of payments is written as $(I\ddot{a})_{\overline{\infty}|}$:

$$(I\ddot{a})_{\overline{\infty}|} = 1 + 2v + 3v^2 + \cdots$$

In words, $(I\ddot{a})_{\overline{\infty}|}$ is called the present value of an increasing perpetuity-due. It is pronounced **i-a-double-dot-angle-infinity**, and it is valued at time 0.

This expression can be simplified into a formula for the present value factor of an increasing perpetuity-due. Multiplying both sides of the equation by v, we get:

$$v(I\ddot{a})_{\overline{\infty}|} = v + 2v^2 + 3v^3 + \cdots$$

Subtracting the second equation from the first, we get:

$$(I\ddot{a})_{\overline{\infty}|} - v(I\ddot{a})_{\overline{\infty}|} = 1 + v + v^2 + \cdots$$

$$\Rightarrow (1-v)(I\ddot{a})_{\overline{\infty}|} = \ddot{a}_{\overline{\infty}|}$$

$$\Rightarrow (I\ddot{a})_{\overline{\infty}|} = \frac{1}{d(1-v)} = \frac{1}{d^2}$$

Increasing perpetuity-due present value factor

Assuming an annual effective interest rate i, the increasing perpetuity-due present value factor is the present value of a series of payments of $1 at time 0, $2 at time 1 years, and so on, continuing indefinitely:

$$(I\ddot{a})_{\overline{\infty}|i} = \frac{1}{d^2}$$

As an example, let's determine the present value at time 0 of payments of $10 paid at time 0, $20 paid at time 1 year, $30 paid at time 2 years, and so on, assuming the annual effective interest rate is 5%.

The present value of the payments at time 0 is:

$$10 + 20v + 30v^2 + \cdots = 10(I\ddot{a})_{\overline{\infty}|} = \frac{10}{(0.05/1.05)^2} = \$4,410.00$$

3.3 Decreasing annuity-immediate

Consider a stream of annual payments where the first payment occurs in 1 year, and each subsequent payment is less than the previous one by a constant amount, such as payments of $55, $50, $45, and so on. This is an example of a **decreasing annuity-immediate**.

The simplest case of a decreasing annuity-immediate is one that has payments of $\$n$ at time 1 year, $\$(n-1)$ at time 2 years, $\$(n-2)$ at time 3 years, and so on, down to \$1 at time n years.

Let's develop the present value of this series of payments.

The present value of the first payment occurring at time 1 year is $n \times v$. The present value of the second payment occurring at time 2 years is $(n-1) \times v^2$. The present value of the last payment of \$1 occurring at time n years is $1 \times v^n$.

The present value of the series of payments is written as $(Da)_{\overline{n}|}$:

$$(Da)_{\overline{n}|} = nv + (n-1)v^2 + (n-2)v^3 + \cdots + v^n$$

In words, $(Da)_{\overline{n}|}$ is called the present value of a decreasing annuity-immediate. It is pronounced **d-a-angle-n**, and it is valued at time 0.

This expression can be simplified into a formula for the present value factor of a decreasing annuity-immediate. Multiplying both sides of the equation by $1+i$, we get:

$$(1+i)(Da)_{\overline{n}|} = n + (n-1)v + (n-2)v^2 + \cdots + v^{n-1}$$

Subtracting the first equation from the second, we get:

$$i(Da)_{\overline{n}|} = n - v - v^2 - \cdots - v^n = n - \left(v + v^2 + \cdots + v^n\right) = n - a_{\overline{n}|}$$

$$\Rightarrow (Da)_{\overline{n}|} = \frac{n - a_{\overline{n}|}}{i}$$

Decreasing annuity-immediate present value factor

Assuming an annual effective interest rate i, the decreasing annuity-immediate present value factor is the present value of a series of payments of $\$n$ at time 1 year, $\$(n-1)$ at time 2 years, and so on, down to \$1 at time n years:

$$(Da)_{\overline{n}|i} = \frac{n - a_{\overline{n}|i}}{i}$$

This can be used to evaluate the present value of various payments that fit the pattern of a decreasing annuity-immediate.

It is important to note that the first payment of $(Da)_{\overline{n}|}$ is n. Hence, the first payment of $(Da)_{\overline{20}|}$ is \$20 and the first payment of $10(Da)_{\overline{6}|}$ is $10 \times 6 = \$60$. This is useful to remember when determining the appropriate factor to apply to the decreasing annuity-immediate present value factor when matching the pattern of payments.

For example, let's determine the present value at time 0 of payments of \$55 at time 1 year, \$50 at time 2 years, \$45 at time 3 years, and so on, down to \$5 at time 11 years. The annual effective interest rate is 4%.

Drawing the timeline diagram, we have:

The present value at time 0 is:

$$5(Da)_{\overline{11}|4\%}$$

This present value is calculated as follows:

$$a_{\overline{11}|4\%} = 8.760477$$

$$5(Da)_{\overline{11}|4\%} = 5 \times \frac{11 - 8.760477}{0.04} = \$279.94$$

We can also express $(Da)_{\overline{n}|}$ in terms of $a_{\overline{n}|}$ and $(Ia)_{\overline{n}|}$. To do this, we consider the expression:

$$(Da)_{\overline{n}|} + (Ia)_{\overline{n}|}$$

The payments under the decreasing annuity-immediate decrease by \$1 each year and the payments under the increasing annuity-immediate increase by \$1 each year. The increase and decrease combine to produce a level payment.

This level payment is \$$(n+1)$ each year because the sum of the individual payments under the increasing and decreasing annuity will always give $n+1$. The timeline is:

So, we have:

$$(Da)_{\overline{n}|} + (Ia)_{\overline{n}|} = (n+1)a_{\overline{n}|}$$

$$\Rightarrow (Da)_{\overline{n}|} = (n+1)a_{\overline{n}|} - (Ia)_{\overline{n}|}$$

In our previous example, we could have calculated $5(Da)_{\overline{11}|4\%}$ as:

$$5(Da)_{\overline{11}|4\%} = 5\left(12a_{\overline{11}|4\%} - (Ia)_{\overline{11}|4\%}\right) = 60a_{\overline{11}|4\%} - 5(Ia)_{\overline{11}|4\%}$$

Calculating the required values, we find that:

$$5(Da)_{\overline{11}|4\%} = 60a_{\overline{11}|4\%} - 5(Ia)_{\overline{11}|4\%} = 60 \times 8.760477 - 5 \times 49.137638 = \$279.94$$

Example 3.5

Amelia receives \$400 in 1 year, \$350 in 2 years, \$300 in 3 years, and so on, until the final payment of \$50. Using an annual effective interest rate of 3.5%, calculate the present value of these payments at time 0.

Solution

The last payment is $400 less 7 decrements of $50. So the last payment is at time 8 years since the first payment was at time 1 year.

The present value at time 0 is:

$$400v + 350v^2 + 300v^3 + \cdots + 50v^8 = 50(Da)_{\overline{8}|3.5\%}$$

Calculating the required values:

$$a_{\overline{8}|3.5\%} = \frac{1 - 1.035^{-8}}{0.035} = 6.873956$$

$$\Rightarrow \quad (Da)_{\overline{8}|3.5\%} = \frac{8 - 6.873956}{0.035} = 32.172699$$

So the present value is:

$$50 \times 32.172699 = \$1,608.63$$

Alternatively, we could use:

$$50(Da)_{\overline{8}|3.5\%} = 50\left(9a_{\overline{8}|3.5\%} - (Ia)_{\overline{8}|3.5\%}\right) = 450a_{\overline{8}|3.5\%} - 50(Ia)_{\overline{8}|3.5\%} \qquad \blacklozenge\blacklozenge$$

So far the payments that we have considered have ended with the amount by which the payments are decreasing from one period to the next. We also need to evaluate the present value of payments that follow a pattern such as $40, $38, $36, \cdots, $30, *ie* payments that don't end with the amount by which the payments are changing from one period to the next.

This can be done by considering the present value of the payments to be the present value of a decreasing annuity plus the present value of a level annuity.

Example 3.6

Determine the present value at time 0 of payments of $5,000 at time 1 year, $4,950 at 2 years, $4,900 at 3 years, and so on, down to the last payment at time 10 years. The annual effective interest rate is 5%.

Solution

The last payment must be $5,000 less 9 decreases of $50, which gives $4,550. From first principles, the present value at time 0 is:

$$5,000v + 4,950v^2 + 4,900v^3 + \cdots + 4,550v^{10}$$

This can be separated into two series:

5,000	4,950	4,900	$\cdots$	4,550	payment
0	1	2	3	$\cdots$	10	time
	500	450	400	$\cdots$	50	decreasing payment
	4,500	4,500	4,500	$\cdots$	4,500	level payment

The present value can be expressed as:

$$\left(4,500v + 4,500v^2 + 4,500v^3 + \cdots + 4,500v^{10}\right) + \left(500v + 450v^2 + 400v^3 + \cdots + 50v^{10}\right)$$

This is a level annuity-immediate plus a decreasing annuity-immediate, so an expression for the present value is simplified to:

$$4,500a_{\overline{10}|5\%} + 50(Da)_{\overline{10}|5\%}$$

Calculating the required values:

$$a_{\overline{10}|5\%} = \frac{1 - 1.05^{-10}}{0.05} = 7.721735$$

$$\Rightarrow \quad (Da)_{\overline{10}|5\%} = \frac{10 - 7.7217349}{0.05} = 45.565301$$

So the present value is:

$$4,500 \times 7.721735 + 50 \times 45.565301 = \$37,026.07$$

The expression for the present value could alternatively be expressed as:

$$\left(5,050v + 5,050v^2 + 5,050v^3 + \cdots + 5,050v^{10}\right) - \left(50v + 100v^2 + 150v^3 + \cdots + 500v^{10}\right)$$

This is a level annuity-immediate less an increasing annuity-immediate, so an expression for the same present value could also be:

$$5,050a_{\overline{10}|5\%} - 50(Ia)_{\overline{10}|5\%}$$

Calculating the required values:

$$\ddot{a}_{\overline{10}|5\%} = \frac{1 - 1.05^{-10}}{0.05/1.05} = 8.107822$$

$$\Rightarrow \quad (Ia)_{\overline{10}|5\%} = \frac{8.107822 - 10 \times 1.05^{-10}}{0.05} = 39.373783$$

And the present value is:

$$5,050 \times 7.721735 - 50 \times 39.373873 = \$37,026.07 \qquad \blacklozenge\blacklozenge$$

Now that we can determine the present value of a decreasing annuity-immediate, we can calculate the accumulated value of a decreasing annuity-immediate by accumulating the present value.

The accumulated value at time n of payments of $\$n$ at time 1 year, $\$(n-1)$ at time 2 years, $\$(n-2)$ at time 3 years, and so on, down to $\$1$ at time n years, is written $(Ds)_{\overline{n}|}$. It is called the accumulated value of a decreasing annuity-immediate. It is pronounced **d-s-angle-n**, and it is valued at time n.

Drawing the timeline for a decreasing annuity-immediate once again, we have:

	n	$n-1$	$n-2$	$\cdots$	2	1	payment
0	1	2	3	$\cdots$	$n-1$	n	time

$$(Da)_{\overline{n}|} \xrightarrow{\quad (1+i)^n \quad} (Ds)_{\overline{n}|}$$

So, the accumulated value of a decreasing annuity-immediate is equal to the present value of a decreasing annuity-immediate accumulated for n years:

$$(Ds)_{\overline{n}|} = (1+i)^n (Da)_{\overline{n}|}$$

$$= (1+i)^n \left(\frac{n - a_{\overline{n}|}}{i} \right) = \frac{n(1+i)^n - s_{\overline{n}|}}{i}$$

Decreasing annuity-immediate accumulated value factor

Assuming an annual effective interest rate i, the decreasing annuity-immediate accumulated value factor is the accumulated value at time n years of a series of payments of \$$n$ at time 1 year, \$$(n-1)$ at time 2 years, \$$(n-2)$ at time 3 years, down to \$1 at time n years:

$$(Ds)_{\overline{n}|i} = (1+i)^n (Da)_{\overline{n}|i} = \frac{n(1+i)^n - s_{\overline{n}|i}}{i}$$

As an example, let's calculate the accumulated value at time 8 years of the series of payments from Example 3.5.

The present value at time 0 was \$1,608.63. This present value is accumulated for 8 years to get the accumulated value at time 8 years:

$$50(Ds)_{\overline{8}|3.5\%} = 50(1.035)^8 (Da)_{\overline{8}|3.5\%} = 50 \times 1.316809 \times 32.172699 = \$2,118.26$$

3.4   *Decreasing annuity-due*

Consider a stream of annual payments where the first payment occurs now, and each subsequent payment is less than the previous one by a constant amount, such as payments of \$55, \$50, \$45, and so on. This is an example of a **decreasing annuity-due**.

The simplest case of a decreasing annuity-due is one that has payments of \$$n$ at time 0, \$$(n-1)$ at time 1 year, \$$(n-2)$ at time 2 years, down to \$1 at time $n-1$ years. The timeline diagram of these cash flows is:

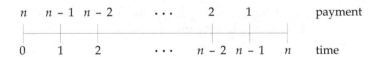

The symbol for the present value of this pattern of cash flows is $(D\ddot{a})_{\overline{n}|}$. It is called the present value of a decreasing annuity-due. It is pronounced **d-a-double-dot-angle-n**, and it is valued at time 0.

Working from first principles to calculate this present value at time 0, we have:

$$(D\ddot{a})_{\overline{n}|} = n + (n-1)v + (n-2)v^2 + \cdots + v^{n-1}$$

Multiplying both sides of the equation by v, we get:

$$v(D\ddot{a})_{\overline{n}|} = nv + (n-1)v^2 + (n-2)v^3 + \cdots + v^n$$

Subtracting the second equation from the first, we get:

$$(1-v)(D\ddot{a})_{\overline{n}|} = n - v - v^2 - \cdots - v^n = n - a_{\overline{n}|}$$

$$\Rightarrow (D\ddot{a})_{\overline{n}|} = \frac{n - a_{\overline{n}|}}{1-v} = \frac{n - a_{\overline{n}|}}{d}$$

Decreasing annuity-due present value factor

Assuming an annual effective interest rate i, the decreasing annuity-due present value factor is the present value at time 0 of payments of \$n at time 0, \$(n-1) at time 1 year, \$(n-2) at time 2 years, down to \$1 at time $n-1$ years:

$$(D\ddot{a})_{\overline{n}|i} = \frac{n - a_{\overline{n}|i}}{d}$$

As an example, let's calculate the present value of a series of payments of \$100 now, \$90 in 1 year, \$80 in 2 years, and so on, down to \$10 at time 9 years using an annual effective interest rate of 3%.

The present value at time 0 is:

$$100 + 90v + 80v^2 + \cdots + 10v^9 = 10(D\ddot{a})_{\overline{10}|3\%}$$

Calculating the required values:

$$a_{\overline{10}|3\%} = \frac{1 - 1.03^{-10}}{0.03} = 8.530203$$

$$\Rightarrow (D\ddot{a})_{\overline{10}|3\%} = \frac{10 - 8.530203}{0.03 / 1.03}$$
$$= 50.463036$$

So the present value is:

$$10 \times 50.463036 = \$504.63$$

Now that we can determine the present value of a decreasing annuity-due, we can also calculate the accumulated value of a decreasing annuity-due by accumulating the present value.

The accumulated value at time n of payments of \$n at time 0, \$(n-1) at time 1 year, \$(n-2) at time 2 years, down to \$1 at time $n-1$ years is written as $(D\ddot{s})_{\overline{n}|}$. It is called the accumulated value of a decreasing annuity-due. It is pronounced **i-s-double-dot-angle-n**, and it is valued at time n.

The accumulated value can be found most easily by accumulating the present value:

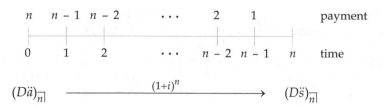

So, the accumulated value of a decreasing annuity-due is equal to the present value of a decreasing annuity-due accumulated for n years:

$$(D\ddot{s})_{\overline{n}|} = (1+i)^n (D\ddot{a})_{\overline{n}|}$$

$$= (1+i)^n \left(\frac{n - a_{\overline{n}|}}{d} \right) = \frac{n(1+i)^n - s_{\overline{n}|}}{d}$$

Decreasing annuity-due accumulated value factor

Assuming an annual effective interest rate i, the decreasing annuity-due accumulated value factor is the accumulated value at time n years of a series of payments of \$$n$ at time 0, \$$(n-1)$ at time 1 year, \$$(n-2)$ at time 2 years, down to \$1 at time $n-1$ years:

$$(D\ddot{s})_{\overline{n}|} = (1+i)^n (D\ddot{a})_{\overline{n}|} = \frac{n(1+i)^n - s_{\overline{n}|i}}{d}$$

Returning to our previous example, let's calculate the accumulated value at time 10 years of a series of payments of \$100 now, \$90 in 1 year, \$80 in 2 years, and so on, down to \$10 at time 9 years using an annual effective interest rate of 3%.

The accumulated value at 10 years is:

$$100(1.03)^{10} + 90(1.03)^9 + 80(1.03)^8 + \cdots + 10(1.03)^1 = 10(D\ddot{s})_{\overline{10}|3\%}$$

Calculating the required values, we have:

$$s_{\overline{10}|3\%} = \frac{1.03^{10} - 1}{0.03} = 11.463879$$

$$\Rightarrow (D\ddot{s})_{\overline{10}|3\%} = \frac{10(1.03)^{10} - 11.463879}{0.03/1.03} = 67.818101$$

So the accumulated value at time 10 years is:

$$10 \times 67.818101 = \$678.18$$

Alternatively, we could calculate the present value and accumulate it for 10 years. We calculated the present value at time 0 before as:

$$10(D\ddot{a})_{\overline{10}|3\%} = \$504.63$$

So we accumulate this value for 10 years to get the accumulated value at 10 years:

$$10(D\ddot{s})_{\overline{10}|3\%} = (1.03)^{10} 504.63 = \$678.18$$

We end this section by considering the relationship between the decreasing annuity-immediate present value factor, $(Da)_{\overline{n}|}$, and the decreasing annuity-due present value factor, $(D\ddot{a})_{\overline{n}|}$.

Since the annuity-immediate has the annual effective interest rate in the denominator and the annuity-due has the annual effective rate of discount in the denominator, we can apply the factor i/d to convert from the annuity-immediate to the annuity-due:

$$(D\ddot{a})_{\overline{n}|} = \frac{i}{d}(Da)_{\overline{n}|}$$

As we have seen, we can also convert the annuity-immediate into an annuity-due by accumulating the annuity-immediate for 1 year:

$$(D\ddot{a})_{\overline{n}|} = (1+i)(Da)_{\overline{n}|}$$

Alternatively, we can convert the annuity-due into an annuity-immediate by discounting the annuity-due for 1 year:

$$(Da)_{\overline{n}|} = v(D\ddot{a})_{\overline{n}|}$$

3.5 *Continuously payable varying annuities*

Continuously payable increasing annuities

Consider a payment stream where the payments are made at a continuous rate but increase at discrete times. A payment stream of $100 continuously in year 1, $200 continuously in year 2, $300 continuously in year 3, up to $1,000 continuously in year 10 is an example of a **continuously payable increasing annuity**.

An analogy might help to understand to concept of a continuously payable varying payment stream. Imagine a water faucet that produces a steady stream of water when the valve is set to a certain open position at time 0. Let's say that in this case the faucet produces 1,000 gallons of water per year. At time 1 year, the valve is adjusted so that the faucet produces 2,000 gallons of water per year. At time 2 years, the valve is again adjusted so that the faucet produces 3,000 gallons of water per year, and so on.

The simplest case of a continuously payable increasing annuity is one that pays $1 continuously in the first year, $2 continuously in the second year, and so on, up to n continuously in the nth year.

The symbol for the present value of this pattern of cash flows is $(I\bar{a})_{\overline{n}|}$. It is called the present value of a continuously payable increasing annuity. It is pronounced **i-a-bar-angle-n**, and it is valued at time 0.

Recall from Chapter 2 that $\bar{a}_{\overline{1}|}$ is the present value, at the beginning of the year, of $1 paid continuously for 1 year. We can then write the present value of these payments as:

$$(I\bar{a})_{\overline{n}|} = \bar{a}_{\overline{1}|} + 2\bar{a}_{\overline{1}|}v + 3\bar{a}_{\overline{1}|}v^2 + \cdots + n\bar{a}_{\overline{1}|}v^{n-1}$$

$$= \bar{a}_{\overline{1}|}\left(1 + 2v + 3v^2 + \cdots + nv^{n-1}\right)$$

$$= \bar{a}_{\overline{1}|}(I\ddot{a})_{\overline{n}|} = \frac{1-v}{\delta} \times \frac{\ddot{a}_{\overline{n}|} - nv^n}{d} = \frac{\ddot{a}_{\overline{n}|} - nv^n}{\delta}$$

This is the same type of formula that we have seen for the other increasing annuity functions, but with δ as the denominator rather than i or d.

Continuously payable increasing annuity present value factor

Assuming an annual effective interest rate i, the continuously payable increasing annuity present value factor is the present value of payments of $1 continuously in the first year, $2 continuously in the second year, and so on, up to $n continuously in the nth year:

$$(I\bar{a})_{\overline{n}|i} = \frac{\ddot{a}_{\overline{n}|i} - nv^n}{\delta}$$

For example, let's determine the present value of a series of payments of $10 continuously in year 1, $20 continuously in year 2, $30 continuously in year 3, and so on, up to $100 continuously in year 10, assuming the annual effective interest rate is 5%.

The present value is:

$$10(I\bar{a})_{\overline{10}|5\%}$$

Calculating the required values, we have:

$$\ddot{a}_{\overline{10}|5\%} = \frac{1 - 1.05^{-10}}{0.05/1.05} = 8.107822$$

$$\Rightarrow \quad (I\bar{a})_{\overline{10}|5\%} = \frac{8.107822 - 10(1.05)^{-10}}{\ln(1.05)} = 40.350123$$

So the present value is:

$$10 \times 40.350123 = \$403.50$$

Example 3.7

Determine the present value of payments of $50 continuously in year 1, $60 continuously in year 2, $70 continuously in year 3, and so on, up to $140 continuously in year 10. The annual effective interest rate is 6%.

Solution

These payments are equivalent to a level, continuously payable annuity with a payment of $40 each year, plus a continuously payable increasing annuity with payments of $10 continuously in year 1, $20 continuously in year 2, $30 continuously in year 3, up to $100 continuously in year 10.

```
      50     60     70                  140
    <---><-----><----->   . . .      <------>      payment

    |----|------|------|----. . .----|-------|
    0    1      2      3     . . .    9     10      time

      10     20     30                 100
    <---><-----><----->   . . .      <------>      increasing payment

      40     40     40                  40
    <---><-----><----->   . . .      <------>      level payment
```

The present value is:

$$40\bar{a}_{\overline{10}|6\%} + 10(I\bar{a})_{\overline{10}|6\%}$$

Calculating the required values, we have:

$$\ddot{a}_{\overline{10}|6\%} = \frac{1 - 1.06^{-10}}{0.06 / 1.06} = 7.801692$$

$$\overline{a}_{\overline{10}|6\%} = \frac{1 - 1.06^{-10}}{\ln(1.06)} = 7.578745$$

$$(I\,\overline{a})_{\overline{10}|6\%} = \frac{7.801692 - 10(1.06)^{-10}}{\ln(1.06)} = 38.060512$$

So the present value is:

$$40 \times 7.578745 + 10 \times 38.060512 = \$683.75 \qquad \blacklozenge\blacklozenge$$

Now that we can determine the present value of a continuously payable increasing annuity, we can also calculate the accumulated value of a continuously payable increasing annuity by accumulating the present value for n years, as we have seen.

The symbol for the accumulated value of a continuously payable increasing annuity is $(I\,\overline{s})_{\overline{n}|}$. It is pronounced **i-s-bar-angle-n**, and it is valued at time n years.

We have:

$$(I\,\overline{s})_{\overline{n}|} = (1+i)^n (I\,\overline{a})_{\overline{n}|} = (1+i)^n \left(\frac{\ddot{a}_{\overline{n}|} - nv^n}{\delta} \right) = \frac{\ddot{s}_{\overline{n}|} - n}{\delta}$$

Continuously payable increasing annuity accumulated value factor

Assuming an annual effective interest rate i, the continuously payable increasing annuity accumulated value factor is the accumulated value at time n years of payments of $1 continuously in the first year, $2 continuously in the second year, and so on, up to $n continuously in the nth year:

$$(I\,\overline{s})_{\overline{n}|i} = \frac{\ddot{s}_{\overline{n}|i} - n}{\delta}$$

For example, using the figures in Example 3.7 we can calculate the accumulated value of the payments at time 10 by accumulating the present value for 10 years:

$$(1.06)^{10} \times 683.75 = \$1,224.49$$

Continuously payable increasing perpetuities

The **continuously payable increasing perpetuity** pays $1 continuously over the first year, $2 continuously over the second year, $3 continuously over the third year, and so on, forever.

The symbol for the present value of this pattern of cash flows is $(I\,\overline{a})_{\overline{\infty}|}$. It is called the present value of a continuously payable increasing perpetuity. It is pronounced **i-a-bar-angle-infinity**, and it is valued at time 0.

Note that the bar over the a means that the payments are continuous. The absence of a bar over the I indicates that the increases occur at discrete periodic intervals.

Just as we did with the present value factor of the continuously payable increasing annuity, we can write the present value of these payments as:

$$(I\bar{a})_{\overline{\infty}|} = \bar{a}_{\overline{1}|} + 2\bar{a}_{\overline{1}|}v + 3\bar{a}_{\overline{1}|}v^2 + \cdots$$

$$= \bar{a}_{\overline{1}|}\left(1 + 2v + 3v^2 + \cdots\right)$$

$$= \bar{a}_{\overline{1}|}(I\ddot{a})_{\overline{\infty}|} = \frac{1-v}{\delta} \times \frac{1}{d^2} = \frac{1}{\delta d}$$

Continuously payable increasing perpetuity present value factor

Assuming an annual effective interest rate i, the continuously payable increasing perpetuity present value factor is the present value of payments of \$1 continuously in the first year, \$2 continuously in the second year, and so on, forever:

$$(I\bar{a})_{\overline{\infty}|i} = \frac{1}{\delta d} = \frac{1+i}{\delta i}$$

For example, let's determine the present value of a series of payments of \$10 paid continuously in year 1, \$20 paid continuously in year 2, \$30 paid continuously in year 3, and so on, assuming the annual effective interest rate is 5%.

The present value at time 0 is:

$$10(I\bar{a})_{\overline{\infty}|5\%} = \frac{10(1.05)}{\ln(1.05) \times 0.05} = \$4,304.15$$

Continuously payable decreasing annuities

Consider a payment stream where the payments are made at a continuous rate but decrease at discrete times. A payment stream of \$1,000 continuously in year 1, \$900 continuously in year 2, \$800 continuously in year 3, down to \$100 continuously in year 10 is an example of a **continuously payable decreasing annuity**.

The simplest case of a continuously payable decreasing annuity is one that pays \$$n$ continuously in the first year, \$$(n-1)$ continuously in the second year, and so on, down to \$1 continuously in the nth year.

The symbol for the present value of this pattern of cash flows is $(D\bar{a})_{\overline{n}|}$. It is called the present value of a continuously payable decreasing annuity. It is pronounced **d-a-bar-angle-n**, and it is valued at time 0.

We can write the present value of these payments as:

$$(D\bar{a})_{\overline{n}|} = n\bar{a}_{\overline{1}|} + (n-1)\bar{a}_{\overline{1}|}v + (n-2)\bar{a}_{\overline{1}|}v^2 + \cdots + \bar{a}_{\overline{1}|}v^{n-1}$$

$$= \bar{a}_{\overline{1}|}\left(n + (n-1)v + (n-2)v^2 + \cdots + v^{n-1}\right)$$

$$= \bar{a}_{\overline{1}|}(D\ddot{a})_{\overline{n}|} = \frac{1-v}{\delta} \times \frac{n - a_{\overline{n}|}}{d} = \frac{n - a_{\overline{n}|}}{\delta}$$

Continuously payable decreasing annuity present value factor

Assuming an annual effective interest rate i, the continuously payable decreasing annuity present value factor is the present value at time 0 of payments of $\$n$ continuously in the first year, $\$(n-1)$ continuously in the second year, and so on, down to $\$1$ continuously in the nth year:

$$(D\bar{a})_{\overline{n}|i} = \frac{n - a_{\overline{n}|i}}{\delta}$$

Example 3.8

Determine the present value of a series of payments of $\$100$ continuously in year 1, $\$90$ continuously in year 2, $\$80$ continuously in year 3, and so on, down to $\$10$ continuously in year 10, assuming the annual effective interest rate is 5%.

Solution

The present value is:

$$10(D\bar{a})_{\overline{10}|5\%}$$

Calculating the required values, we have:

$$a_{\overline{10}|5\%} = \frac{1 - 1.05^{-10}}{0.05} = 7.721735$$

$$\Rightarrow \quad (D\bar{a})_{\overline{10}|5\%} = \frac{10 - 7.721735}{\ln(1.05)} = 46.695171$$

So the present value is:

$$10 \times 46.695171 = \$466.95$$

◆◆

Now that we can determine the present value of a continuously payable decreasing annuity, we can also calculate the accumulated value of a continuously payable decreasing annuity by accumulating the present value for n years, as we have seen.

The symbol for the accumulated value of a continuously payable decreasing annuity is $(D\bar{s})_{\overline{n}|}$. It is pronounced **d-s-bar-angle-n**, and it is valued at time n years.

We have:

$$(D\bar{s})_{\overline{n}|} = (1+i)^n (D\bar{a})_{\overline{n}|} = (1+i)^n \left(\frac{n - a_{\overline{n}|}}{\delta} \right) = \frac{n(1+i)^n - s_{\overline{n}|}}{\delta}$$

Continuously payable decreasing annuity accumulated value factor

Assuming an annual effective interest rate i, the continuously payable decreasing annuity accumulated value factor is the accumulated value at time n years of payments of $\$n$ continuously in the first year, $\$(n-1)$ continuously in the second year, and so on, down to $\$1$ continuously in the nth year:

$$(D\bar{s})_{\overline{n}|i} = \frac{n(1+i)^n - s_{\overline{n}|i}}{\delta}$$

3.6 Compound increasing annuities

Consider an annuity where each payment is greater than the previous one by a constant factor, such as payments of $100, $110, $121, and so on, *ie* the payments increase by 10% each period. This is an example of a **compound increasing annuity**.

There is no standard notation for the present value of such an annuity but these annuities are very useful in finance since, for example, we may need to work with payments that increase in line with inflation. Let's work through a general example and then work some specific examples.

Consider payments made at the end of each year for n years. The first payment of $1 is made at time 1 year. The remaining payments increase at a compound rate of e each year.

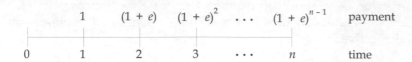

These payments fit the pattern of a **compound increasing annuity-immediate**.

Working from first principles, the present value is:

$$v + (1+e)v^2 + (1+e)^2 v^3 + \cdots + (1+e)^{n-1} v^n$$

We can rewrite the present value as:

$$\frac{1}{1+e}\left((1+e)v + (1+e)^2 v^2 + (1+e)^3 v^3 + \cdots + (1+e)^n v^n\right)$$

Now let $u = (1+e)v$. This gives the present value as:

$$\frac{1}{1+e}\left(u + u^2 + u^3 + \cdots + u^n\right)$$

Notice that the expression in the bracket is the same as an annuity-immediate, so we can rewrite the present value as:

$$\frac{1}{1+e}a_{\overline{n}|j}$$

where the annuity-immediate is calculated at a different rate of interest, j, such that:

$$u = \frac{1}{1+j}$$

We can calculate the value of j as follows:

$$j = \frac{1}{u} - 1$$
$$= \frac{1}{v(1+e)} - 1$$
$$= \frac{1+i}{1+e} - 1$$
$$= \frac{1+i-(1+e)}{1+e} = \frac{i-e}{1+e}$$

Thus the compound increasing annuity-immediate can be evaluated as a level annuity-immediate calculated at a different effective rate of interest, j, which depends on i and e.

Compound increasing annuity-immediate present value factor

The compound increasing annuity-immediate present value factor is the present value at time 0 of a series of payments of $1 at the end of the first year, with subsequent annual payments increasing by a factor of e each year, up to the last payment of $\$(1+e)^{n-1}$ at time n years:

$$\frac{1}{1+e}a_{\overline{n}|j} = \frac{1}{1+e}\left[\frac{1-(1+j)^{-n}}{j}\right] \qquad \text{where } j = \frac{i-e}{1+e}$$

Let's work through a numerical example.

Example 3.9

Jack receives a payment at the end of each year for 10 years. The first payment is $1,500. The remaining payments increase by 6%, compounded each time. Calculate the present value of the payments at time 0, using an annual effective rate of interest of 10.24%.

Solution

The timeline diagram is:

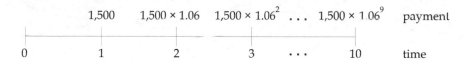

From first principles, the present value of the payments is:

$$1,500v + 1,500(1.06)v^2 + 1,500(1.06)^2 v^3 + \cdots + 1,500(1.06)^9 v^{10}$$

This can be written as:

$$\frac{1}{1.06}\left(1,500(1.06)v + 1,500(1.06)^2 v^2 + 1,500(1.06)^3 v^3 + \cdots + 1,500(1.06)^{10} v^{10}\right)$$

This is equivalent to:

$$\frac{1,500}{1.06}a_{\overline{10}|j}$$

using an interest rate of $j = \dfrac{0.1024 - 0.06}{1.06} = 0.04$, *ie* 4%.

So the present value is:

$$\frac{1,500}{1.06}a_{\overline{10}|4\%} = \frac{1,500}{1.06}\left[\frac{1-1.04^{-10}}{0.04}\right] = \$11,477.68 \qquad\qquad \blacklozenge\blacklozenge$$

The rate of interest j is sometimes called the **net interest rate**. We calculate j by reducing the original interest rate i by the rate of increase e. Mathematically:

$$1+j = \frac{1+i}{1+e}$$

In Example 3.9, we saw that:

$$1+j = \frac{1+i}{1+e} = \frac{1.1024}{1.06} = 1.04 \quad \Rightarrow \quad j = 4\%$$

Consider payments made at the beginning of each year for n years. The first payment of \$1 is made at time 0. The remaining payments increase at a compound rate of e each year.

1	$(1 + e)$	$(1 + e)^2$	$\cdots$	$(1 + e)^{n-1}$		payment
0	1	2	$\cdots$	$n - 1$	n	time

These payments fit the pattern of a **compound increasing annuity-due**.

Working from first principles, the present value is:

$$1 + (1+e)v + (1+e)^2 v^2 + \cdots + (1+e)^{n-1} v^{n-1}$$

Now let $u = (1+e)v$. This gives the present value as:

$$1 + u + u^2 + \cdots + u^{n-1}$$

This expression is equal to an annuity-due, so we can rewrite the present value as:

$$\ddot{a}_{\overline{n}|j}$$

where the annuity-due is calculated using an interest rate of j such that:

$$u = \frac{1}{1+j} \quad \Rightarrow \quad j = \frac{i-e}{1+e}$$

Thus the compound increasing annuity-due can be evaluated as a level annuity-due calculated at a different effective rate of interest, j, which depends on i and e.

Compound increasing annuity-due present value factor

The compound increasing annuity-due present value factor is the present value at time 0 of a series of payments of \$1 at time 0, with subsequent annual payments increasing by a factor of e each year, up to the last payment of $\$(1+e)^{n-1}$ at time $n-1$ years:

$$\ddot{a}_{\overline{n}|j} = \frac{1-(1+j)^{-n}}{j/(1+j)} \qquad \text{where } j = \frac{i-e}{1+e}$$

Note that the present value of the compound increasing annuity-due does not include the factor $1/(1+e)$, which was needed to value a compound increasing annuity-immediate.

Example 3.10

Jill receives payments at the start of each of the next 20 years. The first payment is \$400, which is paid now. The payments from then on increase at a rate of 15% each year. Using an annual effective rate of interest of 23.05%, find the present value of these payments at time 0.

Solution

The timeline diagram is:

400	400×1.15	400×1.15^2	400×1.15^3	$\cdots$	400×1.15^{19}	payment
0	1	2	3	$\cdots$	19	time

The present value is:

$$400 + 400(1.15)v + 400(1.15)^2 v^2 + \cdots + 400(1.15)^{19} v^{19}$$

If $u = 1.15v$, then the present value is:

$$400 + 400u + 400u^2 + \cdots + 400u^{19} = 400\ddot{a}_{\overline{20}|j}$$

where the interest rate j is equal to:

$$j = \frac{i-e}{1+e} = \frac{0.2305 - 0.15}{1.15} = 0.07, \ ie\ 7\%$$

So the present value is:

$$400\ddot{a}_{\overline{20}|7\%} = 400\frac{1 - 1.07^{-20}}{0.07/1.07} = \$4,534.24$$

Alternatively, using the standard result for a finite geometric series with $a = 400$ and $r = 1.15v$, we have:

$$\frac{a(1-r^n)}{1-r} = \frac{400\left(1 - 1.15^{20} v^{20}\right)}{1 - 1.15v} = \frac{400\left(1 - 1.15^{20} \times 1.2305^{-20}\right)}{1 - 1.15(1.2305)^{-1}} = \$4,534.24 \qquad \blacklozenge\blacklozenge$$

We can also calculate the accumulated value of a compound increasing annuity at time n years by multiplying the present value at time 0 by the n-year accumulation factor. We see this in the next example.

Example 3.11

Using the information in Example 3.10, calculate the accumulated value of the payments received by Jill at time 20 years.

Solution

The present value at time 0 is $4,534.24.

Hence, the accumulated value at time 20 years is:

$$(1.2305)^{20} \times 4,534.24 = \$287,168.42$$

Note that we have kept full accuracy in the intermediate calculations (even though we may show an intermediate result that is rounded to the penny) in order that the final answer is accurate to the penny.

Alternatively, from first principles, the accumulated value at time 20 years is:

$$400(1.2305)^{20} + 400(1.15)(1.2305)^{19} + 400(1.15)^2(1.2305)^{18} + \cdots + 400(1.15)^{19}(1.2305)^1$$

$$= 400(1.2305)^{20}\left[1 + \frac{1.15}{1.2305} + \left(\frac{1.15}{1.2305}\right)^2 + \left(\frac{1.15}{1.2305}\right)^3 + \cdots + \left(\frac{1.15}{1.2305}\right)^{19}\right]$$

We can value the term in the square brackets using the standard result for a finite geometric series with $a = 1$ and $r = 1.15/1.2305$.

Hence, the accumulated value at time 20 years is:

$$400(1.2305)^{20}\left[\frac{1 - (1.15/1.2305)^{20}}{1 - 1.15/1.2305}\right] = \$287,168.42 \qquad \blacklozenge\blacklozenge$$

3.7 *Continuously varying payment streams*

For all the annuities that we have looked at so far in this chapter, changes in the payments have taken place at discrete times, *ie* at the end (or start) of each year. We now consider annuities for which the amount of payment changes continuously. In doing so, we extend the theory that we studied in Chapter 2 in order to calculate present values and accumulated values of more complicated payment streams.

Let's start by considering a payment stream where the payments are made at a periodic rate ρ_t at any point in time, t. This periodic payment rate is a function of time. The payments are received from time $t = a$ to $t = b$. The force of interest during the time period is δ_t.

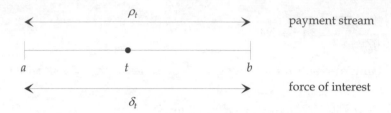

Our first goal is to determine the present value of the payment stream at time $t = a$.

Recall from Chapter 1 that the present value at time a of a payment of \$1 made at time t, using a force of interest δ_t is:

$$\exp\left[-\int_a^t \delta_s \, ds\right]$$

Hence, to calculate the total present value of all the payments from time a to time b we need to sum the present values of the payments (that is, integrate them in the continuous case) between time a and time b.

Therefore, the total present value at time a of the payment stream from $t = a$ to $t = b$ is:

$$\int_a^b \rho_t \exp\left[-\int_a^t \delta_s \, ds\right] dt$$

Continuously varying payment stream present value

The continuously varying payment stream present value is the present value at time a of a payment stream ρ_t from $t = a$ to $t = b$ with a force of interest during the time period of δ_t:

$$\int_a^b \rho_t \exp\left[-\int_a^t \delta_s \, ds\right] dt$$

Note that the lower limit in the integral of the force of interest is a, which is the starting time and the time at which we require the present value.

It can be helpful to think of this as a three-step process:

Step 1. Write the payment at time t.

Step 2. Multiply the payment by the discount factor from time t back to time a.

Step 3. Integrate from the start time to the end time of the payment stream to get the total present value of all the payments.

For example, consider a payment stream at a constant rate of $5 per year from time 2 to 6 years. The force of interest is given by $\delta_t = 0.03 + 0.01t$. Let's write an expression for the present value at time 2 years.

Step 1.   The payment at time t is made at the rate of $5 per year.
Step 2.   The discount factor from time t back to time 2 years is:

$$\exp\left[-\int_2^t (0.03 + 0.01s)\ ds\right]$$

Step 3.   So, the present value at time 2 years of all the payments from time 2 to 6 years is:

$$\int_2^6 5\exp\left[-\int_2^t (0.03 + 0.01s)\ ds\right] dt$$

Let's work through a couple of numerical examples.

Example 3.12

Calculate the present value at $t = 0$ of a continuous payment stream made at the constant rate of $\rho_t = \$25$ per year from time 0 to time 10 years. The force of interest is given by $\delta_t = 0.04$.

Solution

The present value at $t = 0$ is:

$$\int_a^b \rho_t \exp\left[-\int_a^t \delta_s\ ds\right] dt = \int_0^{10} 25\exp\left[-\int_0^t 0.04\ ds\right] dt$$

$$= \int_0^{10} 25\exp[-0.04s]_0^t\ dt$$

$$= \int_0^{10} 25 e^{-0.04t}\ dt$$

$$= \frac{25}{0.04}\left[-e^{-0.04t}\right]_0^{10}$$

$$= \frac{25}{0.04}\left[-e^{-0.40} + e^0\right]$$

$$= \$206.05$$

Note that we could have calculated the present value in this example using the theory we learned in Chapter 2. The present value of $25 payable continuously for 10 years with a constant force of interest is simply:

$$25\bar{a}_{\overline{10}|}$$

Since $\delta = 0.04$, we have $v = e^{-0.04}$, hence:

$$25\bar{a}_{\overline{10}|} = 25\frac{1 - v^{10}}{\delta} = 25\frac{1 - e^{-0.4}}{0.04} = \$206.05 \qquad \blacklozenge\blacklozenge$$

Example 3.13

A continuous payment stream is received from time 0 to time 0.5 years, where the annual rate of payment at time t is $\rho_t = 5t + 2$. The force of interest is given by $\delta_t = 0.1t + 0.04$. Find the present value of this payment stream at time 0.

Solution

The present value is:

$$\int_a^b \rho_t \exp\left[-\int_a^t \delta_s \, ds\right] dt = \int_0^{0.5} (5t+2)\exp\left[-\int_0^t (0.1s+0.04) \, ds\right] dt$$

$$= \int_0^{0.5} (5t+2)\exp\left[-(0.05s^2+0.04s)\Big]_0^t\right] dt$$

$$= \int_0^{0.5} (5t+2)\exp\left[-(0.05t^2+0.04t)\right] dt$$

We can use substitution to evaluate this integral:

$$u = -0.05t^2 - 0.04t$$

$$\frac{du}{dt} = -0.1t - 0.04$$

$$du = (-0.1t - 0.04)dt$$

Hence, the present value is:

$$-50 \int_0^{0.5} (-0.1t-0.04)\exp\left[-0.05t^2 - 0.04t\right] dt = -50 \int_0^{0.5} e^u \, du$$

$$= -50 e^u\Big|_0^{0.5}$$

$$= -50\left[\exp\left[-0.05t^2 - 0.04t)\right]\right]_0^{0.5}$$

$$= -50\left[\exp(-0.0325) - \exp(0)\right] = \$1.60 \qquad \blacklozenge \blacklozenge$$

We may also need to calculate the present value of a continuously varying payment stream that does not start immediately, *eg* the present value at time 0 of a payment stream that starts at time $a > 0$ and ends at time b. We can approach this problem in two ways.

First, we can calculate the present value at time a using the approach described above, and then apply a discount factor to discount the present value from time a to time 0.

Alternatively, we can determine the present value at time 0 by changing the lower limit of integration in the integral of the force of interest to 0, *ie*:

$$\int_a^b \rho_t \exp\left[-\int_0^t \delta_s \, ds\right] dt$$

This is illustrated in the next example.

Example 3.14

Calculate the present value at $t = 0$ of a continuous payment stream made at the constant rate of $\rho_t = \$5$ a year from time 2 to 6 years. The force of interest is given by $\delta_t = 0.03$.

Solution

Changing the lower limit in the integral of the force of interest, the present value at time 0 is:

$$\int_2^6 5\exp\left[-\int_0^t 0.03\ ds\right] dt = \int_2^6 5\exp\left[-0.03s\right]_0^t\ dt = \int_2^6 5e^{-0.03t}\ dt$$

$$= \frac{5}{0.03}\left[-e^{-0.03t}\right]_2^6 = \frac{5}{0.03}\left[-e^{-0.18}+e^{-0.06}\right]$$

$$= \$17.75$$

Alternatively, we see that the present value at time 2 is simply:

$$5\bar{a}_{\overline{4}|} = 5\frac{1-v^4}{\delta} = 5\frac{1-e^{-4\delta}}{\delta} = 5\frac{1-e^{-0.12}}{0.03} = \$18.85$$

The present value factor from time 2 to time 0 is:

$$\exp\left[-\int_0^2 \delta_s\ ds\right] = e^{-2\delta} = e^{-0.06} = 0.941765$$

Hence the present value at time 0 is:

$$18.85 \times 0.941765 = \$17.75 \qquad\qquad \blacklozenge\blacklozenge$$

We can also calculate the accumulated value of a continuously varying payment stream. Let's start by reminding ourselves of the timeline:

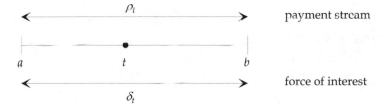

We first determine the accumulated value of the payment stream at time $t = b$. Recall from Chapter 1 that the accumulated value at time b of a payment of \$1 made at time t using a force of interest δ_t is:

$$\exp\left[\int_t^b \delta_s\ ds\right]$$

Hence, to calculate the total accumulated value of all the payments from time a to time b we need to sum the accumulated values of the payments (that is, integrate them in the continuous case) between time a and time b, which gives:

$$\int_a^b \rho_t \exp\left[\int_t^b \delta_t\ ds\right] dt$$

Continuously varying payment stream accumulated value

The continuously varying payment stream accumulated value is the accumulated value at time b of a payment stream ρ_t from $t = a$ to $t = b$ with a force of interest during the time period of δ_t:

$$\int_a^b \rho_t \exp\left[\int_t^b \delta_s \; ds\right] dt$$

Note that the upper limit in the integral of the force of interest is b, the finishing time, which is the time at which we require the accumulated value.

Again, it can be helpful to think of this as a three-step process:

Step 1. Write the payment at time t.

Step 2. Multiply the payment by the accumulation factor from time t to time b.

Step 3. Integrate from the start time to the end time of the payment stream to get the total accumulated value of all the payments.

For example, consider a payment stream at a constant rate of \$100 per year from time 5 to 15 years. The force of interest is given by $\delta_t = 0.005t - 0.01$. Let's write an expression for the accumulated value at time 15 years.

Step 1. The payment at time t is made at the rate of \$100 per year.

Step 2. The accumulation factor from time t to time 15 years is:

$$\exp\left[\int_t^{15}(0.005s - 0.01) \; ds\right]$$

Step 3. So, the accumulated value at time 15 years of all the payments from time 5 to 15 years is:

$$\int_5^{15} 100 \exp\left[\int_t^{15}(0.005s - 0.01) \; ds\right] dt$$

Example 3.15

Calculate the accumulated value at time 6 years of a continuous payment stream paid at a rate of $\rho_t = \$500$ per year from time 1 to 6 years. The force of interest is given by $\delta_t = 0.045$.

Solution

The accumulated value at time 6 years is:

$$\int_a^b \rho_t \exp\left[\int_t^b \delta_s \; ds\right] dt = \int_1^6 500 \exp\left[\int_t^6 0.045 \; ds\right] dt = \int_1^6 500 e^{0.045(6-t)} \; dt$$

$$= 500\left[-\frac{1}{0.045}e^{0.045(6-t)}\right]_1^6 = \frac{500}{0.045}\left[e^{0.045\times5} - e^0\right]$$

$$= \frac{500}{0.045}\left[e^{0.225} - 1\right] = \$2,803.59$$

Note that we can calculate this answer more simply as $500\overline{s}_{\overline{5}|}$ at an interest rate of $i = e^{0.045} - 1$.

We may also need to calculate the accumulated value of a continuously varying payment stream at some time after the payments cease, *eg* the accumulated value at time c of a payment stream that starts at time a and ends at time $b < c$. We can approach this problem in two ways.

First, we can calculate the accumulated value at time b using the approach described above, and then apply an accumulated value factor to accumulate the present value from time b to time c.

Alternatively, we can determine the accumulated value at time c by changing the upper limit of integration in the integral of the force of interest to c, ie:

$$\int_a^b \rho_t \exp\left[\int_t^c \delta_s \, ds\right] dt$$

This is illustrated in the next example.

Example 3.16

Calculate the accumulated value at $t = 8$ years of a continuous payment stream paid at an annual rate of $\rho_t = 100e^{-0.04t}$ from time $t = 1$ to $t = 5$ years. The force of interest is given by $\delta_t = 0.02$.

Solution

The accumulated value at $t = 8$ years is:

$$\int_a^b \rho_t \exp\left[\int_t^c \delta_s \, ds\right] dt = \int_1^5 100e^{-0.04t} \exp\left[\int_t^8 0.02 \, ds\right] dt = \int_1^5 100e^{-0.04t} \exp[0.02s]_t^8 \, dt$$

$$= 100 \int_1^5 e^{-0.04t} e^{0.16 - 0.02t} \, dt = 100 \int_1^5 e^{0.16 - 0.06t} \, dt$$

$$= \frac{100}{0.06}\left[-e^{0.16 - 0.06t}\right]_1^5 = \frac{100}{0.06}\left[e^{-0.14} + e^{0.1}\right]$$

$$= \$393.02$$

Alternatively, we can calculate the accumulated value at time 5 years as:

$$\int_a^b \rho_t \exp\left[\int_t^b \delta_s \, ds\right] dt = \int_1^5 100e^{-0.04t} \exp\left[\int_t^5 0.02 \, ds\right] dt = \int_1^5 100e^{-0.04t} \exp[0.02s]_t^5 \, dt$$

$$= 100 \int_1^5 e^{-0.04t} e^{0.1 - 0.02t} \, dt = 100 \int_1^5 e^{0.1 - 0.06t} \, dt$$

$$= \frac{100}{0.06}\left[-e^{0.1 - 0.06t}\right]_1^5 = \frac{100}{0.06}\left[-e^{-0.2} + e^{0.04}\right]$$

$$= \$370.13$$

And the accumulation factor from time 5 to time 8 years as:

$$\exp\left[\int_5^8 \delta_s \, ds\right] = e^{3\delta} = e^{0.06} = 1.061837$$

Hence the accumulated value at time 8 years is:

$$370.13 \times 1.061837 = \$393.02$$

◆◆

3.8 *Continuously increasing annuities*

Let's consider the special case of a continuously increasing continuously payable payment stream in which a continuous payment is received from time 0 to time n years. The payment rate at time t is $\rho_t = t$, and the force of interest is constant at δ.

The present value of this payment stream at time 0 is:

$$\int_0^n t \exp\left[-\int_0^t \delta \; ds\right] dt = \int_0^n t e^{-\delta t} \; dt$$

This can be integrated by parts. From calculus, the formula for integrating by parts is:

$$\int u \, dv = uv - \int v \, du$$

In this case, using $u = t$, $v = -\dfrac{\exp(-\delta t)}{\delta}$ and $dv = \exp(-\delta t)dt$:

$$\int_0^n t \exp(-\delta t) \; dt = \left[-\frac{t}{\delta}\exp(-\delta t)\right]_0^n - \int_0^n \frac{\exp(-\delta t)}{-\delta} \; dt$$

$$= -\frac{n\exp(-\delta n)}{\delta} - \left[\frac{1}{\delta^2}\exp(-\delta t)\right]_0^n$$

$$= -\frac{n\exp(-\delta n)}{\delta} - \frac{\exp(-\delta n)}{\delta^2} + \frac{1}{\delta^2}$$

$$= \frac{\left(\dfrac{1-\exp(-\delta n)}{\delta}\right) - n\exp(-\delta n)}{\delta}$$

Since $v = e^{-\delta}$, we have $v^n = e^{-\delta n}$. Therefore:

$$\int_0^n t \exp(-\delta t) \; dt = \frac{\left(\dfrac{1-\exp(-\delta n)}{\delta}\right) - n\exp(-\delta n)}{\delta}$$

$$= \frac{\dfrac{1-v^n}{\delta} - nv^n}{\delta} = \frac{\overline{a}_{\overline{n}|} - nv^n}{\delta}$$

The present value of this continuously payable, continuously increasing annuity with a payment at time t of $\rho_t = t$ is written $(\overline{Ia})_{\overline{n}|}$. It is pronounced **i-bar-a-bar-angle-n** and is valued a time 0.

Present value factor for a rate of payment of *t* at time *t*

Assuming a constant force of interest δ, the present value factor for a rate of payment of t at time t is the present value at time 0 of a payment of t at time t, received from time 0 to time n:

$$(\overline{Ia})_{\overline{n}|i} = \frac{\overline{a}_{\overline{n}|i} - nv^n}{\delta}$$

Notice that the payments are continuously increasing as well as being continuously paid, so a bar is placed above both the I and the a.

Example 3.17

Sam receives continuous payments at an annual rate of $8t+5$ from time 0 to 10 years. The continuously compounded interest rate is 9%. Determine the present value at time 0.

Solution

The payment stream can be split into two parts so that the present value is:

$$8(\overline{Ia})_{\overline{10}|} + 5\overline{a}_{\overline{10}|}$$

Calculating the required values:

$$i = e^{0.09} - 1 = 9.4174\%$$

$$\overline{a}_{\overline{10}|} = \frac{1-(1.094174)^{-10}}{0.09} = 6.593670$$

$$(\overline{Ia})_{\overline{10}|} = \frac{6.593670 - 10(1.094174)^{-10}}{0.09} = 28.088592$$

The present value is:

$$8 \times 28.088592 + 5 \times 6.593670 = \$257.68 \qquad \blacklozenge\blacklozenge$$

Now that we can determine the present value of a payment of t at time t, we can also calculate the accumulated value of a payment of t at time t by accumulating the present value for n years. The symbol for the accumulated value of a payment of t at time t is $(\overline{Is})_{\overline{n}|}$. It is pronounced **i-bar-s-bar-angle-n**, and it is valued at time n years.

Accumulated value factor for a rate of payment of t at time t

Assuming a constant force of interest δ, the accumulated value factor for a rate of payment of t at time t is the accumulated value at time n years of a payment of t at time t, received from time 0 to time n years:

$$(\overline{Is})_{\overline{n}|i} = (1+i)^n (\overline{Ia})_{\overline{n}|i} = \frac{\overline{s}_{\overline{n}|i} - n}{\delta}$$

Example 3.18

Using the information in Example 3.17, calculate the accumulated value at time 10 years of the payments received by Sam.

Solution

The accumulated value at 10 years is:

$$8(\overline{Is})_{\overline{10}|} + 5\overline{s}_{\overline{10}|}$$

Calculating the required values:

$$\overline{s}_{\overline{10}|} = \frac{(1.094174)^{10} - 1}{0.09} = 16.217811$$

$$(\overline{Is})_{\overline{10}|} = \frac{16.217811 - 10}{0.09} = 69.086789$$

The accumulated value is:

$$8 \times 69.086789 + 5 \times 16.217811 = \$633.78 \qquad \blacklozenge\blacklozenge$$

Example 3.19

Nancy receives a payment stream from time 2 to time 7 years that pays an annual rate of $2t-3$ at time t. The force of interest is constant at 6% over the period. Calculate the accumulated amount of the payment stream at time 7 years.

Solution

We can calculate the accumulated value at time 7 years of a payment stream rate of $2t-3$ from time 0 to time 7 years as:

$$2(\overline{Is})_{\overline{7}|} - 3\overline{s}_{\overline{7}|}$$

However, we need to subtract the accumulated value at time 7 years of a payment stream rate of $2t-3$ from time 0 to time 2 years in order to solve this problem. The accumulated value at time 2 years of a payment stream rate of $2t-3$ from time 0 to time 2 years is:

$$2(\overline{Is})_{\overline{2}|} - 3\overline{s}_{\overline{2}|}$$

Accumulating this amount to time 7 years, we have:

$$\left(2(\overline{Is})_{\overline{2}|} - 3\overline{s}_{\overline{2}|}\right)e^{0.06\times(7-2)} = \left(2(\overline{Is})_{\overline{2}|} - 3\overline{s}_{\overline{2}|}\right)e^{0.3}$$

Hence, the required accumulated value at 7 years can be expressed as:

$$2(\overline{Is})_{\overline{7}|} - 3\overline{s}_{\overline{7}|} - \left(2(\overline{Is})_{\overline{2}|} - 3\overline{s}_{\overline{2}|}\right)e^{0.3}$$

Calculating the required values:

$$i = e^{0.06} - 1 = 6.1837\%$$

$$\overline{s}_{\overline{7}|} = \frac{(1.061837)^7 - 1}{0.06} = 8.699360$$

$$\overline{s}_{\overline{2}|} = \frac{(1.061837)^2 - 1}{0.06} = 2.124948$$

$$(\overline{Is})_{\overline{7}|} = \frac{8.699360 - 7}{0.06} = 28.322667$$

$$(\overline{Is})_{\overline{2}|} = \frac{2.124948 - 2}{0.06} = 2.082467$$

Hence, the accumulated value at 7 years is:

$$2\times 28.322667 - 3\times 8.699360 - (2\times 2.082467 - 3\times 2.124948)e^{0.3} = \$33.53 \qquad\qquad \blacklozenge\,\blacklozenge$$

Note that we can also solve Example 3.19 using first principles by solving the integral:

$$\int_{2}^{7}(2t-3)\exp\left[\int_{t}^{7}0.06\ ds\right]dt$$

This alternative approach requires integration by parts and is left as an exercise. If you work through the algebra, you should calculate a final answer of \$33.53 and learn a valuable lesson that the standard results introduced in this chapter can save a great deal of hard work!

Continuously payable continuously increasing perpetuity

Extending the concept of the continuously payable continuously increasing annuity in which the payment stream ends at time n, we can allow the payments to continue indefinitely. The payment rate at time t is once again $\rho_t = t$, and the force of interest is constant at δ.

We can develop the present value of this **continuously payable continuously increasing perpetuity** by allowing n to extend to infinity in the present value factor $(\overline{I}\overline{a})_{\overline{n}|}$:

$$(\overline{I}\overline{a})_{\overline{\infty}|} = \lim_{n \to \infty} (\overline{I}\overline{a})_{\overline{n}|} = \lim_{n \to \infty} \frac{\overline{a}_{\overline{n}|i} - nv^n}{\delta} = \lim_{n \to \infty} \frac{\frac{1-(1+i)^{-n}}{\delta} - n(1+i)^{-n}}{\delta} = \frac{\frac{1-0}{\delta} - 0}{\delta} = \frac{1}{\delta^2}$$

In words, $(\overline{I}\overline{a})_{\overline{\infty}|}$ is the present value factor of a continuously payable continuously increasing perpetuity. It is pronounced **i-bar-a-bar-angle-infinity**, and it is valued at time 0.

Present value factor for a perpetual rate of payment of t at time t

Assuming a constant force of interest δ, the present value factor for a rate of payment of t at time t is the present value at time 0 of a rate of payment of t at time t, received from time 0 and continuing indefinitely:

$$(\overline{I}\overline{a})_{\overline{\infty}|} = \frac{1}{\delta^2}$$

Notice that the payments are continuously increasing as well as being continuously paid, so a bar is placed above both the I and the a.

As an example, let's determine the present value of a payment stream that pays a rate of $5t$ at time t. The payments start at time 0 and they continue indefinitely. The annual effective interest rate is 7%. The present value is:

$$5(\overline{I}\overline{a})_{\overline{\infty}|} = 5 \frac{1}{[\ln(1.07)]^2} = \$1,092.25$$

3.9   Continuously decreasing annuities

We conclude this chapter by considering the case of a continuously decreasing continuously payable payment stream in which a continuous payment is received from time 0 to time n years. The rate of payment at time t is $\rho_t = n - t$, and the force of interest is constant at δ.

The present value of this **continuously payable continuously decreasing annuity** with a rate of payment at time t of $\rho_t = n - t$ from time 0 to time n years is written $(\overline{D}\overline{a})_{\overline{n}|}$. It is pronounced **d-bar-a-bar-angle-n** and is valued a time 0.

This present value can be expressed in terms of the present value of a continuously paid level annuity and the present value of an increasing annuity. We can use this relationship to derive the present value factor for the continuously decreasing annuity:

$$(\overline{D}\overline{a})_{\overline{n}|i} = n\overline{a}_{\overline{n}|} - (\overline{I}\overline{a})_{\overline{n}|} = n\overline{a}_{\overline{n}|} - \frac{\overline{a}_{\overline{n}|} - nv^n}{\delta} = \frac{n(1-v^n) - \overline{a}_{\overline{n}|} + nv^n}{\delta} = \frac{n - \overline{a}_{\overline{n}|}}{\delta}$$

Present value factor for a rate of payment of $n - t$ at time t

Assuming a constant force of interest δ, the present value factor valued at time 0 for a rate of payment at time t of $n - t$ received from time 0 to time n is:

$$(\overline{D}\overline{a})_{\overline{n}|i} = \frac{n - \overline{a}_{\overline{n}|i}}{\delta}$$

Notice that the payments are continuously decreasing as well as being continuously paid, so a bar is placed above both the D and the a.

Example 3.20

Otto receives a payment at an annual rate of $10 - t$ from time 0 to time 10 years. The force of interest is 6%. Determine the present value of these payments at time 0.

Solution

Calculating the required values, we can then determine the present value:

$$i = e^{0.06} - 1 = 6.184\%$$

$$\overline{a}_{\overline{10}|} = \frac{1 - (1.06184)^{-10}}{0.06} = 7.51981$$

$$(\overline{D}\overline{a})_{\overline{10}|} = \frac{10 - 7.51981}{0.06} = \$41.34 \qquad\qquad \blacklozenge\blacklozenge$$

Now that we can calculate the present value of a rate of payment of $n - t$ occurring at time t, we can also calculate the accumulated value of a rate of payment of $n - t$ occurring at time t by accumulating the present value for n years. The symbol for the accumulated value of a rate of payment of t at time t is $(\overline{D}\overline{s})_{\overline{n}|}$. It is pronounced **d-bar-s-bar-angle-n**, and it is valued at time n years.

Accumulated value factor for a rate of payment of $n - t$ at time t

Assuming a constant force of interest δ, the accumulated value factor valued at time n years for a continuous payment stream paid at a rate of $n - t$ at time t, received from time 0 to time n years, is:

$$(\overline{D}\overline{s})_{\overline{n}|i} = (1+i)^n (\overline{D}\overline{a})_{\overline{n}|i} = \frac{n(1+i)^n - \overline{s}_{\overline{n}|i}}{\delta}$$

Example 3.21

Using the information from the previous example, determine the accumulated value at time 10 years of the payments received by Otto.

Solution

We can determine the accumulated value by accumulating the present value for 10 years. The accumulated value at time 10 years is:

$$(\overline{D}\overline{s})_{\overline{10}|} = 41.33657 e^{10 \times 0.06} = \$75.32$$

Alternatively, we can calculate the accumulated value directly. Calculating the required values, we can then determine the accumulated value:

$$i = e^{0.06} - 1 = 6.184\%$$

$$\overline{s}_{\overline{10}|} = \frac{(1.06184)^{10} - 1}{0.06} = 13.70198$$

$$(\overline{Ds})_{\overline{10}|} = \frac{10(1.06184)^{10} - 13.70198}{0.06} = \$75.32 \qquad\qquad \blacklozenge\,\blacklozenge$$

Chapter 3 Practice Questions

Question guide

- Questions 3.1 – 3.10 test material from Sections 3.1 – 3.4.

- Questions 3.11 – 3.16 test material from Sections 3.5 – 3.9.

- Questions 3.17 – 3.20 are from the SOA/CAS Course 2 exam or the IOA/FOA 102 exam.

Question 3.1

Max receives $300 in 1 year, $350 in 2 years, $400 in 3 years, and so on until the final payment of $800. Using an annual effective rate of interest of 4%, find the present value of these payments at time 0.

Question 3.2

Using the information from Question 3.1, determine the accumulated value of the payments at time 12 years.

Question 3.3

Kendra receives $900 now, $970 in 1 year, $1,040 in 2 years, $1,110 in 3 years, and so on, until the final payment of $1,600. Using an annual effective rate of interest of 9%, find the present value of these payments at time 0.

Question 3.4

Using the information from Question 3.3, determine the accumulated value of these payments at time 11 years.

Question 3.5

Alex receives $600 in 1 year, $580 in 2 years, $560 in 3 years, and so on, until the final payment of $400. Using an annual effective rate of interest of 4%, find the present value of these payments at time 0.

Question 3.6

Using the information from Question 3.5, calculate the accumulated value of the payments at time 20 years.

Question 3.7

Rhonda receives annual payments that begin with the first payment of $50 today. Each subsequent payment decreases by $10 per year until time 4 years, and then each subsequent payment increases by $10 per year until the last payment at time 8 years. The annual effective interest rate is 5%. Determine the present value of the payments at time 0.

Question 3.8

Mary is saving money for her retirement. She needs $750,000 in 10 years to purchase a retirement apartment in Florida. She invests X now, $X - 5,000$ in 1 year, $X - 10,000$ in 2 years, and so on, down to $X - 45,000$ in 9 years. Using an annual effective rate of interest of 5%, find X.

Question 3.9

A bank is offering a special deal. If you invest X now, the bank will give you $15,000 at time 7 years, $14,000 at time 8 years, $13,000 at time 9 years, and so on, with the last payment being at time 14 years. Using an annual effective rate of interest of 8%, determine X.

Question 3.10

You invest $500 at time 8 years, $1,000 at time 9 years, $1,500 at time 10 years, and so on, up to the last payment at time 20 years. What is the accumulated value of these payments at time 25 years using an annual effective rate of interest of 4.5%?

Question 3.11

Determine the accumulated value at time 10 years of payments that are received continuously over each year. The payment is $100 during the first year, $105 during the second year, $110 during the third year, and so on, up to the last payment of $145 in year 10. The annual effective interest rate is 7%.

Question 3.12

Calculate the accumulated value at time 10 years of payments that are received continuously over each year. The payment is $200 during the first year, and each subsequent payment decreases by $15 per year, until the last payment of $80 is received in the ninth year. The annual effective interest rate is 4%.

Question 3.13

Brian turns 25 years old today and would like to receive inflation-adjusted retirement payments on each of his birthdays from age 65 to 95, inclusive. The first payment at age 65 will be $100,000. The inflation rate is assumed to be 0% until age 65, and then it is assumed to be 2% per year. The annual effective interest rate is 6%. How much money should Brian set aside today to fund these future payments? Use an annuity-immediate to determine the answer.

Question 3.14

Using the same information as Question 3.13, verify the answer using an annuity-due.

Question 3.15

Calculate the present value at time 0 of a payment stream that pays a continuous rate of $5t + 1$ at time t from time 0 to 10 years. The force of interest during this time is $\delta_t = 0.01 + 0.05t$.

Question 3.16

A payment stream that pays a continuous rate of $1.8t^2 + 6t$ at time t is received from time 5 to time 10 years. The force of interest from time 0 to time 5 years is $\delta_t = 0.008t + 0.03$, and the force of interest from time 5 to time 10 years is $\delta_t = 0.0003t^2 + 0.001t$. Determine the present value of the payment stream at time 0.

Question 3.17   *SOA/CAS*

Susan invests $Z at the end of each year for seven years at an annual effective interest rate of 5%. The interest credited at the end of each year is reinvested at an annual effective rate of 6%. The accumulated value at the end of seven years is $X.

Lori invests $Z at the end of each year for 14 years at an annual effective interest rate of 2.5%. The interest credited at the end of each year is reinvested at an annual effective rate of 3%. The accumulated value at the end of 14 years is $Y.

Calculate $\dfrac{Y}{X}$.

Question 3.18   *SOA/CAS*

Mike buys a perpetuity-immediate with varying annual payments. During the first 5 years, the payment is constant and equal to $10. Beginning in year 6, the payments start to increase. For year 6 and all future years, the current year's payment is k% larger than the previous year's payment.

At an annual effective interest rate of 9.2%, the perpetuity has a present value of $167.50.

Calculate k, given $k < 9.2$.

Question 3.19   *SOA/CAS*

Payments are made to an account at a continuous rate of $(8k + tk)$, where $0 \le t \le 10$. Interest is credited at a force of interest $\delta_t = \dfrac{1}{8+t}$.

After 10 years, the account is worth $20,000.

Calculate k.

Question 3.20   *FOA/IOA*

A 20-year annuity certain provides payments annually of $200 at time 1 year, $180 at time 2 years, $160 at time 3 years, and so on, until the payments have reduced to $60. Payments then continue at $60 per year until the 20th payment has been made. The annual effective interest rate is 4%. Determine the present value of the annuity.

4

Non-annual interest rates and annuities

Overview

So far we have focused on annual effective rates of interest or discount. This has been fine for calculating present and accumulated values of annual payments. However, payments can occur with any frequency, such as monthly, quarterly or even every other year, and annual effective interest rates are not always the most convenient way to value these payments.

We can evaluate the present and accumulated amounts of payments that occur more or less frequently than once a year by using an effective rate of interest with a compounding frequency that matches the payment frequency, such as monthly, quarterly or every other year. We study this method in the first part of this chapter.

We then look at a different way of expressing interest rates, namely **nominal interest rates**. Nominal interest rates can be used to determine present and accumulated values of payments that occur more or less frequently than once per year.

Throughout this chapter, we refer back to the level, increasing and decreasing annuities that we have studied in earlier chapters, so it is helpful to keep these definitions and formulas in mind.

Students sometimes confuse the terms **biannual** and **biennial**, perhaps because they sound somewhat alike. Biannual and semiannual mean twice per year, that is, every 6 months. Biennial means every other year.

4.1 Non-annual interest and discount rates

In many real-life situations, payments are made more frequently than annually. For example, payments on consumer loans are usually made on a monthly basis. The interest rate on a loan with monthly payments may be expressed as an annual effective rate or a monthly effective interest rate. To determine the present value or accumulated value of such a loan, it is more convenient to use the monthly effective interest rate.

Let's start by considering a payment frequency of p payments per year. The length of the period between each payment is $1/p$ years. The annual effective interest rate is i. If an investment of $1 is made at the start of a period, then at the end of the period this amount will have grown to:

$$(1+i)^{\frac{1}{p}}$$

This is equivalent to saying that the effective interest rate over the period is:

$$(1+i)^{\frac{1}{p}} - 1$$

Non-annual $p$thly effective interest rates

Assuming an annual effective interest rate i and p time periods per year, the corresponding $p$thly effective interest rate for a $p$thly period is:

$$(1+i)^{\frac{1}{p}} - 1$$

For example, let's determine the monthly effective interest rate that corresponds to an annual effective interest rate of 7%. So, our time period is one month, and we have $p = 12$.

The monthly effective interest rate is:

$$(1+i)^{\frac{1}{p}} - 1 = 1.07^{\frac{1}{12}} - 1 = 0.005654 \quad \text{or} \quad 0.5654\%$$

We can check this answer by considering the accumulated value of a deposit of $1 that is invested for 12 time periods (*ie* one year). Using the monthly effective interest rate, the accumulated value is:

$$1.005654^{12} = \$1.07$$

This is clearly consistent with the annual effective interest rate of 7%.

Example 4.1

Determine the biannual (twice a year) effective interest rate that corresponds to an annual effective interest rate of 8%.

Solution

The time period is six months, and we have $p = 2$. The biannual effective rate of interest is:

$$1.08^{\frac{1}{2}} - 1 = 0.039230 \quad \text{or} \quad 3.9230\%$$

♦♦

A similar conversion can be made for annual effective discount rates.

Suppose there are p time periods per year. The annual effective discount rate is d. If \$1 is borrowed for one time period, the net amount payable at the start of the period (*ie* the amount of the loan less the amount of the discount) is:

$$(1-d)^{\frac{1}{p}}$$

This is equivalent to saying that the effective discount rate over the period is:

$$1-(1-d)^{\frac{1}{p}}$$

Using the relationship $d = 1-(1+i)^{-1}$, we can also express the effective discount rate over the period as:

$$1-(1+i)^{-\frac{1}{p}}$$

Non-annual *p*thly effective discount rates

Assuming an annual effective discount rate d and p time periods per year, the corresponding *p*thly effective discount rate for a *p*thly period is:

$$1-(1-d)^{\frac{1}{p}} = 1-(1+i)^{-\frac{1}{p}}$$

For example, let's determine the monthly effective discount rate that corresponds to an annual effective discount rate of 7%.

The monthly effective discount rate is:

$$1-(1-d)^{\frac{1}{p}} = 1-(1-0.07)^{\frac{1}{12}} = 0.006029 \quad \text{or} \quad 0.6029\%$$

We can check this answer by considering the discount payable at time 0 on a loan of \$1 for 12 time periods (*ie* one year). Using the monthly effective discount rate, the discount is:

$$1-(1-0.006029)^{12} = \$0.07$$

This is clearly consistent with the annual effective discount rate of 7%.

Example 4.2

Calculate the biannual effective discount rate that corresponds to an annual effective discount rate of 8%.

Solution

The biannual effective rate of discount is:

$$1-(1-0.08)^{\frac{1}{2}} = 0.040834 \quad \text{or} \quad 4.0834\%$$

◆ ◆

The *p*thly effective interest and discount rates can be used to calculate the present value and the accumulated value of payments that occur p times per year.

Example 4.3

Find the present value of payments of $35 at the end of each month for the next 24 months. The annual effective rate of interest is 5%.

Solution

The timeline diagram of the cash flows is:

The monthly effective rate of interest is:

$$1.05^{\frac{1}{12}} - 1 = 0.004074 \quad \text{or} \quad 0.4074\%$$

Working in months, the present value is:

$$\frac{35}{1.004074} + \frac{35}{(1.004074)^2} + \cdots + \frac{35}{(1.004074)^{24}}$$

This pattern should be familiar. It matches the pattern of the annuity-immediate present value factor, with n expressed in months instead of years and i expressed as the monthly effective interest rate instead of the annual effective interest rate.

Using the number of months and the monthly effective interest rate, the present value can be expressed as:

$$35a_{\overline{24}|0.4074\%}$$

The present value is then:

$$35a_{\overline{24}|0.4074\%} = 35 \times \frac{1 - 1.004074^{-24}}{0.004074} = \$798.69$$

♦♦

Example 4.4

Find the accumulated value of payments of $540 per year paid in equal installments at the start of each quarter for 5 years. The annual effective rate of discount is 6%.

Solution

There are $5 \times 4 = 20$ quarters in 5 years and the quarterly payment is $540 / 4 = \$135$.

The timeline diagram of the cash flows is:

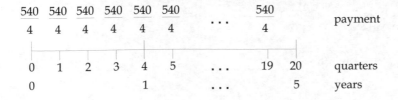

The quarterly effective rate of discount is:

$$1 - 0.94^{\frac{1}{4}} = 0.015350 \quad \text{or} \quad 1.5350\%$$

Using the relationship $i = d / (1 - d)$, the quarterly effective interest rate is:

$$\frac{0.015350}{1 - 0.015350} = 0.015589 \quad \text{or} \quad 1.5589\%$$

Working in quarters, the accumulated value at 5 years is:

$$135(1.015589)^{20} + 135(1.015589)^{19} + \cdots + 135(1.015589)$$

This pattern fits the annuity-due accumulated value factor if we work in quarters instead of years. Using the number of quarters and the quarterly effective interest and discount rates, the accumulated value at 5 years can be written as:

$$135\ddot{s}_{\overline{20}|1.5589\%} = 135 \times \frac{1.015589^{20} - 1}{0.015350} = \$3,188.82 \qquad \blacklozenge\blacklozenge$$

Note that the factor applied to the annuity-due accumulated value factor is the payment for the corresponding time period. The time units and the payments must be consistent with each other.

The notation for $p$thly effective rates is potentially confusing.

A $p$thly effective interest rate is written $\dfrac{i^{(p)}}{p}$. It can be pronounced as **i-upper-p-over-p**.

Hence, we have:

$$\frac{i^{(p)}}{p} = (1 + i)^{\frac{1}{p}} - 1$$

For example, using the information in Example 4.1, we have:

$$\frac{i^{(2)}}{2} = (1 + i)^{\frac{1}{2}} - 1 = 1.08^{\frac{1}{2}} - 1 = 0.039230$$

Similarly, a $p$thly effective discount rate is written $\dfrac{d^{(p)}}{p}$. It can be pronounced as **d-upper-p-over-p**.

Hence, we have:

$$\frac{d^{(p)}}{p} = 1 - (1 - d)^{\frac{1}{p}}$$

For example, using the information in Example 4.2, we have:

$$\frac{d^{(2)}}{2} = 1 - (1 - d)^{\frac{1}{2}} = 1 - (1 - 0.08)^{\frac{1}{2}} = 0.040834$$

The symbols $i^{(p)}$ and $d^{(p)}$ represent a **nominal $p$thly interest rate** and a **nominal $p$thly discount rate** respectively, and this is what we study in the next two sections of this chapter.

4.2 *Nominal pthly interest rates*

As we have seen, an interest rate can be quoted as an annual effective rate or as a *pthly* effective rate, where there are p time periods per year. We can also quote an interest rate as a **nominal *pthly* interest rate**.

A nominal interest rate is expressed as an annualized rate by multiplying the effective *pthly* rate of interest by the number of time periods, p. For example, if the effective monthly rate of interest is 0.3%, then the nominal interest rate based on monthly compounding of interest is $0.3\% \times 12 = 3.6\%$.

In order to define a nominal *pthly* interest rate fully, we must state the frequency with which the interest is compounded annually, *ie* the value of p. In general, if an interest rate is compounded p times a year then we say that the nominal rate is **convertible *pthly***. The word nominal may be stated explicitly or this type of rate may be referred to as a **convertible rate.**

A nominal *pthly* interest rate is denoted $i^{(p)}$, which is pronounced **i-upper-p**. For example, an effective monthly rate of interest of 0.3% would be described as an interest rate of 3.6% a year convertible monthly. This is written in the notation as:

$$i^{(12)} = 0.036 \quad \text{or} \quad 3.6\%$$

A nominal rate of interest convertible *pthly* can be converted to an effective *pthly* rate of interest by dividing it by p, since the effective *pthly* rate of interest is:

$$\frac{i^{(p)}}{p}$$

Nominal rate of interest convertible *pthly*

Assuming an annual effective interest rate i and p time periods per year, the corresponding nominal annual interest rate convertible *pthly* is:

$$i^{(p)} = p \times \frac{i^{(p)}}{p} = p\left[(1+i)^{\frac{1}{p}} - 1\right]$$

For example, let's determine the monthly effective interest rate that corresponds to an interest rate of 6% a year convertible monthly.

The nominal interest rate convertible monthly is:

$$i^{(12)} = 0.06$$

This interest rate is divided by 12 to determine the monthly effective interest rate:

$$\frac{i^{(12)}}{12} = \frac{0.06}{12} = 0.5\%$$

As we'll see, it is important to be able to convert between nominal interest rates and effective interest rates so that either can be used to calculate present values and accumulated values.

Relationship between nominal interest rates

Two equivalent nominal interest rates compounded at different frequencies, $p$thly and $m$thly, are related by:

$$\left(1+\frac{i^{(p)}}{p}\right)^{p} = \left(1+\frac{i^{(m)}}{m}\right)^{m}$$

If we let $m=1$, we can relate the annual effective interest rate to a nominal interest rate convertible $p$thly:

$$\left(1+\frac{i^{(p)}}{p}\right)^{p} = 1+i$$

This relationship is a rearrangement of the formula that relates nominal interest rates and effective interest rates.

Example 4.5

Find the value of the nominal interest rate convertible quarterly when the annual effective interest rate is 5%.

Solution

When the annual effective interest rate is i, the nominal interest rate convertible quarterly is:

$$i^{(4)} = 4\left((1.05)^{\frac{1}{4}} - 1\right) = 0.049089$$

So the nominal interest rate convertible quarterly is about 4.91%.   ♦♦

Example 4.6

The nominal interest rate convertible biannually is 7%. Calculate the annual effective interest rate and the nominal interest rate convertible monthly.

Solution

The annual effective interest rate is calculated as:

$$1+i = \left(1+\frac{i^{(2)}}{2}\right)^{2} = \left(1+\frac{0.07}{2}\right)^{2} = 1.035^2 = 1.071225$$

$$\Rightarrow i = 7.12\%$$

The nominal interest rate convertible monthly is calculated as:

$$\left(1+\frac{i^{(12)}}{12}\right)^{12} = 1.071225$$

$$\Rightarrow i^{(12)} = 12\left[(1.071225)^{\frac{1}{12}} - 1\right] = 6.90\%$$ ♦♦

Consider $100 invested in an account that pays an effective interest rate of 5% a year. Suppose that after each quarter of a year the interest earned is withdrawn.

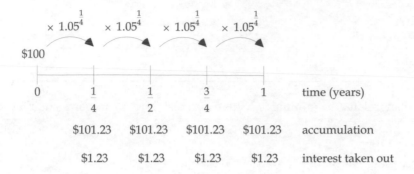

The accumulated value of $100 will be $100 \times 1.05^{\frac{1}{4}} = \$101.23$ at the end of the first quarter and so interest of $1.23 will be taken out at that time. This leaves $100 in the bank. Suppose after another quarter of a year the interest is again withdrawn. Again, the accumulated value will be $101.23 and the interest will be $1.23. Repeating this means that the total interest earned in this way is $4 \times \$1.23 = \$4.92$. Since $100 was originally invested, this means that the interest earned over a year is 4.92%. This is the nominal rate of interest convertible quarterly. The slight difference from Example 4.5 is due to rounding.

Notice how the value of $i^{(4)}$ is slightly less than the annual effective rate of i. This is as expected. The interest of $1.23 is taken out every quarter, so no interest is earned on this $1.23 and the overall rate is lower.

Similarly, the nominal interest rate convertible monthly, $i^{(12)}$, is even lower than $i^{(4)}$.

Equivalent interest rates must produce equivalent present values and accumulated values. If an interest rate is compounded more frequently, it would produce a higher accumulated value. To produce the same accumulated value, the rate that is compounded more frequently must be less than the rate that is compounded less frequently.

This example provides an intuitive way of thinking about nominal rates of interest. A rate of interest convertible *p*thly can be thought of as the total amount of interest earned over a year, if the interest earned every *p*th of a year is withdrawn.

So an interest rate of 12% convertible monthly is equivalent to a monthly effective interest rate of 1%. It is convenient and easy to express interest rates in this way.

The present and accumulated values using nominal interest rates and non-annual payments can now be calculated.

Example 4.7

Determine the accumulated value at time 7 years of a payment of $30 at time 0. The nominal interest rate is 6% a year convertible quarterly.

Solution

The annual effective rate of interest is:

$$i = \left(1 + \frac{i^{(4)}}{4}\right)^4 - 1 = \left(1 + \frac{0.06}{4}\right)^4 - 1 = (1.015)^4 - 1 = 6.1364\%$$

The accumulated value is:

$$30(1.061364)^7 = \$45.52$$

This could also be calculated working in quarters. There are $4 \times 7 = 28$ quarters in 7 years. The quarterly effective rate of interest is:

$$\frac{i^{(4)}}{4} = \frac{0.06}{4} = 1.5\%$$

The accumulated value is then:

$$30(1.015)^{28} = \$45.52 \qquad \qquad \blacklozenge\blacklozenge$$

Example 4.8

Calculate the present value at time 0 years of a payment of \$5,000 at time 12 years. The nominal interest rate of 8% a year is convertible biannually.

Solution

If i is the annual effective rate of interest, the present value is:

$$5,000v^{12} = 5,000(1+i)^{-12}$$

Since $i^{(2)} = 0.08$, we have:

$$i = \left(1 + \frac{i^{(2)}}{2}\right)^2 - 1 = \left(1 + \frac{0.08}{2}\right)^2 - 1 = (1.04)^2 - 1 = 8.16\%$$

So the present value is:

$$5,000(1.0816)^{12} = \$1,950.61$$

Alternatively, this could be calculated working in half-years. There are $12 \times 2 = 24$ half-year periods in 12 years. The biannual effective rate of interest is:

$$\frac{i^{(2)}}{2} = \frac{0.08}{2} = 4\%$$

The present value is then:

$$5,000(1.04)^{-24} = \$1,950.61 \qquad \qquad \blacklozenge\blacklozenge$$

4.3   Nominal pthly discount rates

Discount rates can also be quoted as either effective or nominal rates. Once again, the word nominal may be stated explicitly or this type of rate may be referred to as a convertible rate, such as a discount rate of 6% a year convertible monthly.

The notation for a nominal discount rate convertible $p$thly is $d^{(p)}$, which is pronounced as **d-upper-p**.

A nominal rate of discount convertible $p$thly can be converted to an effective $p$thly rate of discount by dividing it by p, since the effective $p$thly rate of discount is:

$$\frac{d^{(p)}}{p}$$

Nominal rate of discount convertible *p*thly

Assuming an annual effective discount rate d and p time periods per year, the corresponding nominal annual discount rate convertible *p*thly is:

$$d^{(p)} = p \times \frac{d^{(p)}}{p} = p\left[1 - (1-d)^{\frac{1}{p}}\right]$$

For example, let's determine the monthly effective discount rate that corresponds to a discount rate of 12% a year convertible monthly.

The nominal discount rate convertible monthly is:

$$d^{(12)} = 0.12$$

This rate is divided by 12 to determine the monthly effective discount rate:

$$\frac{d^{(12)}}{12} = \frac{0.12}{12} = 1.0\%$$

As before, it is important to be able to convert between nominal discount rates and effective discount rates.

Relationship between nominal discount rates

Two equivalent nominal discount rates compounded at different frequencies, *p*thly and *m*thly, are related by:

$$\left(1 - \frac{d^{(p)}}{p}\right)^p = \left(1 - \frac{d^{(m)}}{m}\right)^m$$

If we let $m = 1$, we can relate the annual effective discount rate to a nominal discount rate convertible *p*thly:

$$\left(1 - \frac{d^{(p)}}{p}\right)^p = 1 - d$$

This relationship is a rearrangement of the formula that relates nominal discount rates and effective discount rates.

Example 4.9

Determine the annual effective rate of discount that corresponds to a nominal rate of discount of 4% a year convertible monthly.

Solution

We have $d^{(12)} = 0.04$, so:

$$d = 1 - \left(1 - \frac{d^{(12)}}{12}\right)^{12} = 1 - \left(1 - \frac{0.04}{12}\right)^{12} = 3.9275\%$$

♦♦

It is also useful to be able to convert between nominal interest rates convertible *p*thly and nominal discount rates convertible *m*thly.

Relationship between nominal interest rates and nominal discount rates

A nominal interest rate convertible *p*thly and a nominal discount rate convertible *m*thly are related by:

$$\left(1+\frac{i^{(p)}}{p}\right)^{p} = \left(1-\frac{d^{(m)}}{m}\right)^{-m}$$

For example, we can convert between the annual effective interest rate and the nominal discount rate convertible m times per year by setting $p=1$ in the definition above. This gives:

$$1+i = \left(1-\frac{d^{(m)}}{m}\right)^{-m} \quad \Rightarrow \quad i = \left(1-\frac{d^{(m)}}{m}\right)^{-m} - 1$$

Example 4.10

Determine the discount rate convertible monthly that corresponds to an interest rate of 4% convertible quarterly.

Solution

We have $i^{(4)} = 0.04$, so:

$$\left(1-\frac{d^{(12)}}{12}\right)^{-12} = \left(1+\frac{i^{(4)}}{4}\right)^{4} = \left(1+\frac{0.04}{4}\right)^{4} = 1.01^{4} = 1.040604$$

$$\Rightarrow d^{(12)} = 12\left(1-1.040604^{-\frac{1}{12}}\right) = 3.9735\%$$

Alternatively, this can be calculated more directly:

$$d^{(12)} = 12\left[1-\left(\left(1+\frac{i^{(4)}}{4}\right)^{4}\right)^{-\frac{1}{12}}\right] = 12\left[1-(1.01)^{-\frac{1}{3}}\right] = 3.9735\%$$

◆◆

Present values and accumulated values can be calculated using nominal discount rates and non-annual payments.

Example 4.11

Find the accumulated value at time 10 years of a payment of $1,000 at time 5 years. The nominal rate of discount is 5% a year convertible every other month.

Solution

We have $d^{(6)} = 0.05$, so the annual effective rate of discount is:

$$d = 1-\left(1-\frac{d^{(6)}}{6}\right)^{6} = 1-\left(1-\frac{0.05}{6}\right)^{6} = 4.8970\%$$

The accumulated value at 10 years (after 5 years of investment) is:

$$1,000(1-d)^{-5} = 1,000(1-0.048970)^{-5} = \$1,285.37$$

Alternatively, we could work in two-month periods directly. There are 6 two-month periods in each year, so there are $6 \times 5 = 30$ such periods in 5 years.

Hence, the accumulated value at 10 years is then:

$$1{,}000\left(1 - \frac{0.05}{6}\right)^{-30} = \$1{,}285.37$$

     ◆◆

Example 4.12

Calculate the present value at time 0 of a payment of \$250 at time 10 years. The nominal rate of discount is 12% a year convertible biannually.

Solution

We have $d^{(2)} = 0.12$, so the annual effective rate of discount is:

$$d = 1 - \left(1 - \frac{d^{(2)}}{2}\right)^2 = 1 - \left(1 - \frac{0.12}{2}\right)^2 = 11.64\%$$

The present value at time 0 is:

$$250(1-d)^{10} = 250(1 - 0.1164)^{10} = \$72.53$$

Alternatively, we could work in half-years directly. There are 20 half-years in 10 years, so the present value at time 0 is:

$$250\left(1 - \frac{0.12}{2}\right)^{20} = \$72.53$$

    ◆◆

Let's now turn our attention to annuities with non-annual payments.

4.4 *Annuities-immediate payable pthly*

In Example 4.3, we calculated the present value of an annuity-immediate with non-annual payments using a non-annual effective interest rate. Let's consider another approach by looking at the general case and deriving some useful results.

Consider payments at the rate of \$1 per year that are payable $p$thly for n years at the end of each period. Each $p$thly payment is $1/p$, and there are np payments in total.

The timeline diagram is:

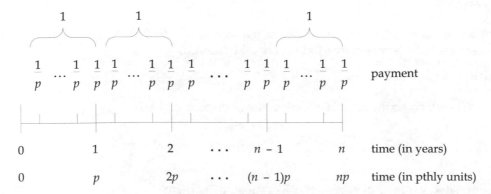

This set of cash flows is known as a ***pthly annuity-immediate***, and its present value is denoted $a_{\overline{n}|}^{(p)}$.

The present value of this $p$thly annuity-immediate is:

$$a_{\overline{n}|}^{(p)} = \frac{1}{p}v^{\frac{1}{p}} + \frac{1}{p}v^{\frac{2}{p}} + \frac{1}{p}v^{\frac{3}{p}} + \cdots + \frac{1}{p}v^{\frac{np}{p}}$$

The sum of a geometric series of np terms, with $a = \frac{1}{p}v^{\frac{1}{p}}$ and $r = v^{\frac{1}{p}}$, is:

$$a_{\overline{n}|}^{(p)} = \frac{\frac{1}{p}v^{\frac{1}{p}}\left(1 - v^{\frac{np}{p}}\right)}{1 - v^{\frac{1}{p}}} = \frac{(1 - v^n)}{p(1+i)^{\frac{1}{p}}\left(1 - v^{\frac{1}{p}}\right)} = \frac{1 - v^n}{p\left[(1+i)^{\frac{1}{p}} - 1\right]} = \frac{1 - v^n}{i^{(p)}}$$

The last step uses the expression for $i^{(p)}$, the nominal interest rate convertible p times per year. Notice the similarity between this annuity formula and the formulas we saw in Chapter 2.

Present value factor for a $p$thly annuity-immediate

The present value of payments of \$1 per year payable $p$thly for n years at the end of each period, using an annual effective interest rate of i is:

$$a_{\overline{n}|i}^{(p)} = \frac{1 - v^n}{i^{(p)}} = \frac{1 - (1+i)^{-n}}{i^{(p)}}$$

This is valued at time 0 and is pronounced **a-upper-p-angle-n**.

For example, consider payments of \$3,600 a year paid in equal installments at the end of each month for 7 years. The nominal rate of interest is 5% a year convertible quarterly.

We could work with monthly time periods to calculate the present value of the payments since the payments occur monthly. There are payments of $3,600 / 12 = \$300$ at the end of each month for $7 \times 12 = 84$ months. The rate of interest should be consistent, so we should use a monthly effective rate.

We can calculate the monthly effective rate directly from the quarterly effective rate:

$$\frac{i^{(12)}}{12} = \left[\left(1 + \frac{0.05}{4}\right)^4\right]^{\frac{1}{12}} - 1 = \left(1 + \frac{0.05}{4}\right)^{\frac{1}{3}} - 1 = 0.4149\%$$

Working in months, the present value of these payments is:

$$\frac{300}{1.004149} + \frac{300}{(1.004149)^2} + \cdots + \frac{300}{(1.004149)^{84}}$$

As we have seen, this expression can be written using the annuity-immediate present value factor in terms of the number of months and the monthly effective interest rate:

$$300 a_{\overline{84}|0.4149\%} = 300 \times \frac{1 - 1.004149^{-84}}{0.004149} = \$21,240.16$$

Alternatively, the present value can also be found using a $p$thly annuity-immediate present value factor. Working in years, the annual effective interest rate is:

$$i = \left(1 + \frac{0.05}{4}\right)^4 - 1 = 5.0945\%$$

Since the monthly effective interest rate is 0.4149%, we have:

$$i^{(12)} = 12 \times 0.004149$$

Hence, the present value is:

$$3{,}600 a_{\overline{7}|}^{(12)} = 3{,}600 \times \frac{1-(1+i)^{-7}}{i^{(12)}} = 3{,}600 \times \frac{1-1.050945^{-7}}{12 \times 0.004149} = \$21{,}240.16$$

Notice that we use the number of years and the amount paid over a year with the *p*thly annuity-immediate present value factor.

The expression $X a_{\overline{n}|}^{(p)}$ represents the present value of payments of X per year for n years, paid p times in each year at the end of each sub-period. Each payment of the annuity $X a_{\overline{n}|}^{(p)}$ is X/p.

For example, the present value of payments of $600 a year for 20 years, paid monthly at the end of each month is represented by $600 a_{\overline{20}|}^{(12)}$. The annual payment is $600 and the number of years is 20. Each monthly payment is $600/12 = \$50$.

Example 4.13

Find the present value at time 0 of payments of $30 at the end of each quarter for 8 years. The nominal rate of interest is 5% a year convertible monthly.

Solution

The timeline diagram is:

The annual payment is four times the quarterly payment, which is $4 \times 30 = \$120$. So, working in years, the present value is:

$$120 a_{\overline{8}|}^{(4)}$$

The annual effective rate of interest is:

$$i = \left(1 + \frac{0.05}{12}\right)^{12} - 1 = 5.1162\%$$

We also need $i^{(4)}$ in order to evaluate the present value.

$$i^{(4)} = 4\left((1.051162)^{\frac{1}{4}} - 1\right) = 5.0209\%$$

The present value is:

$$120 a_{\overline{8}|5.1162\%}^{(4)} = 120 \times \frac{1-(1+i)^{-8}}{i^{(4)}} = 120 \times \frac{1-1.051162^{-8}}{0.050209} = \$786.61$$

Alternatively, working in quarters, the quarterly effective rate is:

$$\frac{i^{(4)}}{4} = 1.051162^{\frac{1}{4}} - 1 = 1.2552\% .$$

Hence, the present value is:

$$30a_{\overline{32}|1.2552\%} = 30 \times \frac{1 - 1.012552^{-32}}{0.012552} = \$786.61$$

◆◆

There are often several different ways to write an expression for a present value. Depending upon the information available, one approach may be significantly easier than another approach. Some people prefer to use an effective interest rate with the same compounding frequency as the payment frequency.

As we see from Example 4.13, a couple of alternative expressions for the present value of a *p*thly annuity-immediate are:

$$a_{\overline{n}|i}^{(p)} = \frac{1 - \left(1 + \frac{i^{(p)}}{p}\right)^{-np}}{i^{(p)}} \quad \text{and} \quad a_{\overline{n}|i}^{(p)} = \frac{1}{p} a_{\overline{np}|\frac{i^{(p)}}{p}}$$

Example 4.14

Determine the present value at time 0 of payments of \$480 at the end of each quarter for 8 years. The annual effective interest rate is 6%. Use an effective rate of interest expressed:

(i)   annually

(ii)   quarterly

(iii)   every other year.

Solution

Part (i)

The total annual payment is $4 \times 480 = \$1,920$. There are 4 payments per year for 8 years, so the present value is:

$$1,920a_{\overline{8}|}^{(4)}$$

The nominal annual interest rate convertible quarterly is:

$$i^{(4)} = 4\left((1+i)^{\frac{1}{4}} - 1\right) = 4\left(1.06^{0.25} - 1\right) = 0.058695$$

So, the present value is:

$$1,920a_{\overline{8}|6\%}^{(4)} = 1,920 \times \frac{1 - 1.06^{-8}}{0.058695} = \$12,187.81$$

Part (ii)

The quarterly payment is 480. There is only one payment per quarter and payments are made for $8 \times 4 = 32$ quarters, so the present value is:

$$480a_{\overline{32}|}$$

where the annuity is valued at the quarterly effective rate of interest.

The quarterly effective rate of interest is:

$$\frac{i^{(4)}}{4} = 1.06^{0.25} - 1 = 0.014674$$

So, the present value is:

$$480a_{\overline{32}|1.4674\%} = 480 \times \frac{1-1.014674^{-32}}{0.014674} = \$12,187.81$$

Part (iii)

The two-yearly effective rate of interest is:

$$\frac{i^{\left(\frac{1}{2}\right)}}{\frac{1}{2}} = 1.06^2 - 1 = 0.123600$$

The payment every two years is $8 \times 480 = \$3,840$. There 8 payments in every two-year period, and there are 4 two-year periods in 8 years, so the present value is:

$$3,840a^{(8)}_{\overline{4}|12.36\%} = 3,840 \times \frac{1-1.1236^{-4}}{8\left[(1.1236)^{\frac{1}{8}} - 1\right]} = \$12,187.81 \qquad \blacklozenge\blacklozenge$$

This example illustrates that there usually are several ways to solve an interest theory question, depending on how you look at it. It is frequently easier to convert the interest rate into an effective interest rate for the time period between payments, as in part (ii) above.

An expression for the accumulated value of a *p*thly annuity-immediate can be obtained by accumulating the present value:

$$(1+i)^n a^{(p)}_{\overline{n}|} = (1+i)^n \frac{1-v^n}{i^{(p)}} = \frac{(1+i)^n - 1}{i^{(p)}}$$

This accumulated value is denoted $s^{(p)}_{\overline{n}|}$, which is pronounced **s-upper-p-angle-n**. It is valued at time *n* years.

Accumulated value factor for a *p*thly annuity-immediate

The accumulated value at time *n* years of payments of \$1 per year payable *p*thly for *n* years at the end of each period, using an annual effective interest rate of *i* is:

$$s^{(p)}_{\overline{n}|i} = \frac{(1+i)^n - 1}{i^{(p)}} = (1+i)^n a^{(p)}_{\overline{n}|i}$$

Alternative expressions for the accumulated value of a *p*thly annuity-immediate include:

$$s^{(p)}_{\overline{n}|i} = \frac{\left(1+\frac{i^{(p)}}{p}\right)^{np} - 1}{i^{(p)}} \quad \text{and} \quad s^{(p)}_{\overline{n}|i} = \left(1+\frac{i^{(p)}}{p}\right)^{np} \times a^{(p)}_{\overline{n}|i} \quad \text{and} \quad s^{(p)}_{\overline{n}|i} = \frac{1}{p} s_{\overline{np}|\frac{i^{(p)}}{p}}$$

Example 4.15

Find the accumulated value at time 10 years of payments of \$200 at the end of every other month for 10 years. Use a nominal rate of interest of 12% a year convertible quarterly.

Solution

Working in years, the annual payment is $6 \times 200 = \$1,200$, and the accumulated value is:

$$1,200 s^{(6)}_{\overline{10}|} = 1,200 \frac{(1+i)^{10}-1}{i^{(6)}}$$

The annual effective interest rate is:

$$i = \left(1+\frac{0.12}{4}\right)^4 - 1 = 12.5509\%$$

The nominal interest rate convertible two-monthly is:

$$i^{(6)} = 6\left(1.125509^{\frac{1}{6}} - 1\right) = 11.9408\%$$

Hence, the accumulated value is:

$$1,200 s^{(6)}_{\overline{10}|12.5509\%} = 1,200 \times \frac{1.125509^{10}-1}{0.119408} = \$22,732.55 \qquad \blacklozenge\blacklozenge$$

It is useful to be able to convert the annual annuity-immediate present value factor into a $p$thly annuity-immediate present value factor. The former has the annual effective interest rate in the denominator, and the latter has the nominal interest rate convertible $p$thly in the denominator, so we have:

$$a^{(p)}_{\overline{n}|} = \frac{i}{i^{(p)}} a_{\overline{n}|} \qquad \text{and} \qquad a_{\overline{n}|} = \frac{i^{(p)}}{i} a^{(p)}_{\overline{n}|}$$

Following similar logic, we can convert between $s^{(p)}_{\overline{n}|}$ and $s_{\overline{n}|}$ using:

$$s^{(p)}_{\overline{n}|} = \frac{i}{i^{(p)}} s_{\overline{n}|} \qquad \text{and} \qquad s_{\overline{n}|} = \frac{i^{(p)}}{i} s^{(p)}_{\overline{n}|}$$

4.5 Annuities-due payable pthly

Consider payments at the rate of \$1 per year that are payable $p$thly for n years at the start of each period. Each $p$thly payment is $1/p$, and there are np payments in total.

The timeline diagram is:

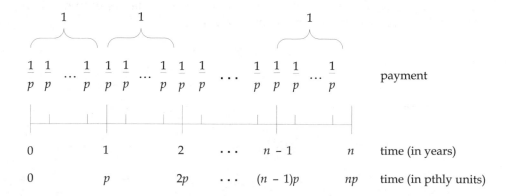

This set of cash flows is known as a **pthly annuity-due**. Its present value is denoted $\ddot{a}^{(p)}_{\overline{n}|}$, which is pronounced **a-double-dot-upper-p-angle-n**. It is valued at time 0.

The present value of this *pthly* annuity-due is:

$$\ddot{a}^{(p)}_{\overline{n}|} = \frac{1}{p} + \frac{1}{p}v^{\frac{1}{p}} + \frac{1}{p}v^{\frac{2}{p}} + \frac{1}{p}v^{\frac{3}{p}} + \cdots + \frac{1}{p}v^{\frac{np-1}{p}}$$

The sum of a geometric series of np terms, with $a = \frac{1}{p}$ and $r = v^{\frac{1}{p}}$, is:

$$\ddot{a}^{(p)}_{\overline{n}|} = \frac{\frac{1}{p}\left(1 - v^{\frac{np}{p}}\right)}{1 - v^{\frac{1}{p}}} = \frac{(1 - v^n)}{p\left(1 - v^{\frac{1}{p}}\right)} = \frac{1 - v^n}{p\left[1 - (1-d)^{\frac{1}{p}}\right]} = \frac{1 - v^n}{d^{(p)}}$$

The last step uses the expression for $d^{(p)}$, the nominal discount rate convertible p times per year.

Present value factor of a *pthly* annuity-due

The present value of payments of \$1 a year payable *pthly* for n years at the start of each period, beginning at time 0, is:

$$\ddot{a}^{(p)}_{\overline{n}|i} = \frac{1 - v^n}{d^{(p)}} = \frac{1 - (1+i)^{-n}}{d^{(p)}}$$

Alternative expressions for the present value of a *pthly* annuity-due include:

$$\ddot{a}^{(p)}_{\overline{n}|i} = \frac{1 - \left(1 + \frac{i^{(p)}}{p}\right)^{-np}}{d^{(p)}} \qquad \text{and} \qquad \ddot{a}^{(p)}_{\overline{n}|i} = \frac{1}{p}\ddot{a}_{\overline{np}|\frac{i^{(p)}}{p}}$$

In general, $X\ddot{a}^{(p)}_{\overline{n}|}$ represents the present value of payments of X per year for n years, paid p times in each year at the start of each sub-period.

Example 4.16

Determine the present value at time 0 of payments of \$1,000 at the start of each month for 5 years, starting at time 0. The nominal interest rate convertible quarterly is 4%.

Solution

The timeline diagram is:

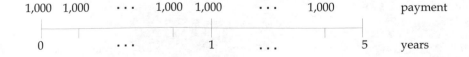

Working in years with an annual payment of $12 \times 1,000 = \$12,000$, the present value is:

$$12,000\ddot{a}^{(12)}_{\overline{5}|} = 12,000 \times \frac{1-(1+i)^{-5}}{d^{(12)}}$$

The annual effective rate of interest is:

$$i = \left(1 + \frac{0.04}{4}\right)^4 - 1 = 4.0604\%$$

The discount rate convertible monthly is:

$$d^{(12)} = 12\left(1-(1-d)^{\frac{1}{12}}\right) = 12\left(1-v^{\frac{1}{12}}\right) = 12\left(1-1.040604^{-\frac{1}{12}}\right) = 3.9735\%$$

The present value is:

$$12,000\ddot{a}^{(12)}_{\overline{5}|4.0604\%} = 12,000 \times \frac{1-1.040604^{-5}}{0.039735} = \$54,497.17 \qquad \blacklozenge\blacklozenge$$

An expression for the accumulated value of a $p$thly annuity-due can be obtained by accumulating the present value:

$$(1+i)^n \ddot{a}^{(p)}_{\overline{n}|} = (1+i)^n \frac{1-v^n}{d^{(p)}} = \frac{(1+i)^n-1}{d^{(p)}}$$

This accumulated value is denoted $\ddot{s}^{(p)}_{\overline{n}|}$, and is pronounced **s-double-dot-upper-p-angle-n**. It is valued at time n years.

Accumulated value factor of a $p$thly annuity-due

The accumulated value at time n years of payments of \$1 a year payable $p$thly for n years at the start of each period, beginning at time 0, is:

$$\ddot{s}^{(p)}_{\overline{n}|i} = (1+i)^n \ddot{a}^{(p)}_{\overline{n}|i} = \frac{(1+i)^n-1}{d^{(p)}}$$

Alternative expressions for the accumulated value of a $p$thly annuity-due include:

$$\ddot{s}^{(p)}_{\overline{n}|i} = \frac{\left(1+\dfrac{i^{(p)}}{p}\right)^{np}-1}{d^{(p)}} \quad \text{and} \quad \ddot{s}^{(p)}_{\overline{n}|i} = \left(1+\frac{i^{(p)}}{p}\right)^{np} \times \ddot{a}^{(p)}_{\overline{n}|i} \quad \text{and} \quad \ddot{s}^{(p)}_{\overline{n}|} = \frac{1}{p}\ddot{s}_{\overline{np}|\frac{i^{(p)}}{p}}$$

Example 4.17

Determine the accumulated value at time 9 years of payments of \$775 at the start of every month for 9 years, starting at time 0. The nominal interest rate convertible monthly is 12%.

Solution

The timeline diagram is:

Working in years with an annual payment of $12 \times 775 = \$9,300$, the accumulated value is:

$$9,300\ddot{s}^{(12)}_{\overline{9}|} = 9,300 \times \frac{(1+i)^9 - 1}{d^{(12)}}$$

Calculating i and $d^{(12)}$, we have:

$$i = \left(1 + \frac{0.12}{12}\right)^{12} - 1 = 12.6825\%$$

$$d^{(12)} = 12\left(1 - (1-d)^{\frac{1}{12}}\right) = 12\left(1 - v^{\frac{1}{12}}\right) = 12\left(1 - 1.126825^{-\frac{1}{12}}\right) = 11.8812\%$$

The accumulated value is:

$$9,300\ddot{s}^{(12)}_{\overline{9}|12.6825\%} = 9,300 \times \frac{1.126825^9 - 1}{0.118812} = \$150,986.67$$

◆◆

4.6 *Increasing pthly annuities*

There are two different types of increasing $p$thly annuities. The first is the **increasing *p*thly annuity** where the increase occurs once per year. The second is the ***p*thly increasing *p*thly annuity** where the increase takes place with each $p$thly payment. The former is discussed in this section, and the latter is discussed in the next section.

Increasing pthly annuity-immediate

Consider payments of $1/p$ at the end of each $p$thly time period in the first year, $2/p$ at the end of each $p$thly time period in the second year and so on for n years:

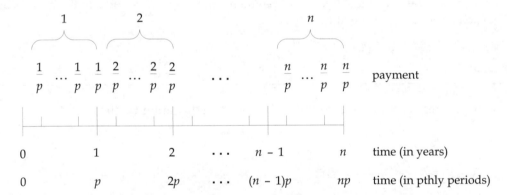

This pattern of cash flows is known as an **increasing *p*thly annuity-immediate**. Its present value is denoted $(Ia)^{(p)}_{\overline{n}|}$, which is pronounced **i-a-upper-p-angle-n**. It is valued at time 0.

Using first principles, the present value of these payments is:

$$(Ia)^{(p)}_{\overline{n}|} = \frac{1}{p}v^{\frac{1}{p}} + \frac{1}{p}v^{\frac{2}{p}} + \cdots + \frac{1}{p}v^{\frac{p}{p}} + \frac{2}{p}v^{\frac{p+1}{p}} + \frac{2}{p}v^{\frac{p+2}{p}} + \cdots + \frac{2}{p}v^{\frac{2p}{p}} + \cdots + \frac{n}{p}v^{\frac{(n-1)p+1}{p}} + \cdots + \frac{n}{p}v^{\frac{np}{p}}$$

$$= \frac{1}{p}\left(v^{\frac{1}{p}} + v^{\frac{2}{p}} + \cdots + v^{\frac{p}{p}}\right)\left(1 + 2v + 3v^2 + \cdots + nv^{n-1}\right)$$

This can be simplified by noting:

$$\frac{1}{p}\left(v^{\frac{1}{p}} + v^{\frac{2}{p}} + \cdots + v^{\frac{p}{p}}\right) = a^{(p)}_{\overline{1}|}$$

and:

$$1 + 2v + 3v^2 + \cdots + nv^{n-1} = (I\ddot{a})_{\overline{n}|}$$

Finally, the present value is:

$$(Ia)^{(p)}_{\overline{n}|} = a^{(p)}_{\overline{1}|}(I\ddot{a})_{\overline{n}|} = \frac{1-v}{i^{(p)}} \times \frac{\ddot{a}_{\overline{n}|} - nv^n}{d} = \frac{\ddot{a}_{\overline{n}|} - nv^n}{i^{(p)}}$$

So, the present value of these payments can be determined by adjusting the formula for the present value of an increasing annuity.

Present value factor of an increasing $p$thly annuity-immediate

The present value of payments of $1/p$ at the end of each $p$thly time period in the first year, $2/p$ at the end of each $p$thly time period in the second year and so on for n years is:

$$(Ia)^{(p)}_{\overline{n}|i} = \frac{\ddot{a}_{\overline{n}|i} - nv^n}{i^{(p)}}$$

Example 4.18

Determine the present value of $1 at the end of each quarter in the first year, $2 at the end of each quarter in the second year, $3 at the end of each quarter in the third year, and so on for 5 years. The annual effective interest rate is 4%.

Solution

Let's first draw the timeline diagram:

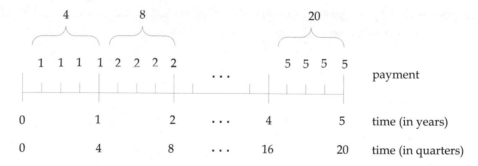

The factor $(Ia)^{(4)}_{\overline{5}|}$ values a payment of $1/4$ at the end of each quarter during the first year, $2/4$ at the end of each quarter during the second year, and so on.

So, the present value is 4 times greater, *ie*:

$$4(Ia)^{(4)}_{\overline{5}|} = 4 \times \frac{\ddot{a}_{\overline{5}|} - 5v^5}{i^{(4)}}$$

Calculating the required values:

$$i^{(4)} = 4\left[(1.04)^{\frac{1}{4}} - 1\right] = 3.9414\%$$

$$\ddot{a}_{\overline{5}|} = \frac{1 - (1.04)^{-5}}{0.04/1.04} = 4.629895$$

$$(Ia)_{\overline{5}|}^{(4)} = \frac{4.629895 - 5(1.04)^{-5}}{0.039414} = 13.199996$$

The present value of the payments is:

$$4(Ia)_{\overline{5}|}^{(4)} = 4 \times 13.199996 = \$52.80$$ 　　　　　　　　　　　◆◆

The accumulated value of an increasing *p*thly annuity-immediate can be determined by accumulating the present value of the increasing *p*thly annuity-immediate for n years.

It is written $(Is)_{\overline{n}|}^{(p)}$, which is pronounced **i-s-upper-p-angle-n**. It is valued at time n years.

Accumulated value factor of an increasing *p*thly annuity-immediate

The accumulated value of payments of $1/p$ at the end of each *p*thly time period in the first year, $2/p$ at the end of each *p*thly time period in the second year and so on for n years is:

$$(Is)_{\overline{n}|i}^{(p)} = (1+i)^n (Ia)_{\overline{n}|i}^{(p)} = \frac{\ddot{s}_{\overline{n}|i} - n}{i^{(p)}}$$

For example, the accumulated value at time 5 years of the cash flows in Example 4.18 is:

$$(Is)_{\overline{5}|}^{(4)} = (1+i)^5 (Ia)_{\overline{5}|}^{(4)} = 1.04^5 \times 52.80 = \$64.24$$

Increasing pthly annuity-due

Consider payments of $1/p$ at the start of each *p*thly time period in the first year, $2/p$ at the start of each *p*thly time period in the second year and so on for n years:

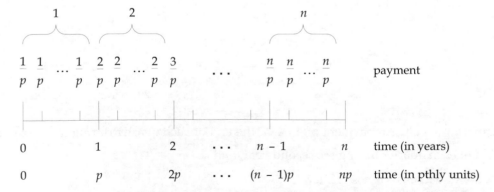

This pattern of cash flows is known as an **increasing *p*thly annuity-due**. Its present value is denoted $(I\ddot{a})_{\overline{n}|}^{(p)}$, which is pronounced **i-a-double-dot-upper-p-angle-n**. It is valued at time 0.

As you might suspect, the present value of these payments is obtained by replacing the $i^{(p)}$ in the denominator of $(Ia)_{\overline{n}|}^{(p)}$ with $d^{(p)}$.

Present value factor of an increasing *p*thly annuity-due

The present value of payments of $1/p$ at the start of each *p*thly time period in the first year, $2/p$ at the start of each *p*thly time period in the second year and so on for n years is:

$$(I\ddot{a})_{\overline{n}|i}^{(p)} = \frac{\ddot{a}_{\overline{n}|i} - nv^n}{d^{(p)}}$$

Example 4.19

Determine the present value of $10 at the start of each quarter in the first year, $20 at the start of each quarter in the second year, $30 at the start of each quarter in the third year, and so on for 5 years. The annual effective interest rate is 4%.

Solution

The present value is:

$$40(I\ddot{a})_{\overline{5}|}^{(4)} = 40 \times \frac{\ddot{a}_{\overline{5}|} - 5v^5}{d^{(4)}}$$

Calculating the required values:

$$d^{(4)} = 4\left[1 - (1.04)^{-\frac{1}{4}}\right] = 3.9029\%$$

$$\ddot{a}_{\overline{5}|} = \frac{1 - (1.04)^{-5}}{0.04/1.04} = 4.629895$$

$$(I\ddot{a})_{\overline{5}|}^{(4)} = \frac{4.629895 - 5(1.04)^{-5}}{0.039029} = 13.330060$$

The present value of the payments is:

$$40(I\ddot{a})_{\overline{5}|}^{(4)} = 40 \times 13.330060 = \$533.20$$

       ◆◆

As before, the accumulated value of an increasing *p*thly annuity-due can be determined by accumulating the present value of the increasing *p*thly annuity-due for n years.

It is written $(I\ddot{s})_{\overline{n}|}^{(p)}$, which is pronounced **i-s-double-dot-upper-p-angle-n**. It is valued at time n years.

Accumulated value factor of an increasing *p*thly annuity-due

The accumulated value of payments of $1/p$ at the start of each *p*thly time period in the first year, $2/p$ at the start of each *p*thly time period in the second year and so on for n years is:

$$(I\ddot{s})_{\overline{n}|i}^{(p)} = (1+i)^n (I\ddot{a})_{\overline{n}|i}^{(p)} = \frac{\ddot{s}_{\overline{n}|i} - n}{d^{(p)}}$$

For example, the accumulated value at time 5 years of the cash flows in Example 4.19 is:

$$(I\ddot{s})^{(4)}_{\overline{5}|} = (1+i)^5 (I\ddot{a})^{(4)}_{\overline{5}|} = 1.04^5 \times 533.20 = \$678.72$$

4.7 Pthly increasing pthly annuities

The other type of increasing *p*thly annuity is one in which the payments increase each *p*thly period. This is called a **pthly increasing pthly annuity**. We consider immediate and due versions of these annuities.

Pthly increasing pthly annuity-immediate

The first point to note is that the first payment is not $1/p$. Instead, consider payments of $1/p^2$ at the end of the first *p*thly time period, $2/p^2$ at the end of the second *p*thly time and so on for n years:

Also, note that the final payment of the first year is $1/p$, the final payment of the second year is $2/p$, and the final payment of the nth year is n/p.

Using first principles, let's derive the present value of these payments, which we denote as PV:

$$PV = \frac{1}{p^2}v^{\frac{1}{p}} + \frac{2}{p^2}v^{\frac{2}{p}} + \cdots + \frac{np}{p^2}v^{\frac{np}{p}}$$

Multiplying this by $v^{\frac{1}{p}}$, we have:

$$PVv^{\frac{1}{p}} = \frac{1}{p^2}v^{\frac{2}{p}} + \frac{2}{p^2}v^{\frac{3}{p}} + \cdots + \frac{np}{p^2}v^{\frac{np+1}{p}}$$

Subtracting the second series from the first, we have:

$$PV\left(1 - v^{\frac{1}{p}}\right) = \left[\frac{1}{p^2}v^{\frac{1}{p}} + \frac{1}{p^2}v^{\frac{2}{p}} + \cdots + \frac{1}{p^2}v^{\frac{np}{p}}\right] - \frac{np}{p^2}v^{\frac{np+1}{p}}$$

The term in square brackets is a geometric series.

Summing this geometric series with $a = \frac{1}{p^2}v^{\frac{1}{p}}$, $r = v^{\frac{1}{p}}$, we have:

$$PV\left(1 - v^{\frac{1}{p}}\right) = \frac{1}{p^2}v^{\frac{1}{p}} \times \frac{1 - (v^{\frac{1}{p}})^{np}}{1 - v^{\frac{1}{p}}} - \frac{np}{p^2}v^{\frac{np+1}{p}} = \frac{1}{p^2}v^{\frac{1}{p}} \times \frac{1 - v^n}{1 - v^{\frac{1}{p}}} - \frac{np}{p^2}v^{\frac{np+1}{p}}$$

We can further simplify this algebraically:

$$PV\left(1-v^{\frac{1}{p}}\right) = \frac{1}{p}v^{\frac{1}{p}} \times \frac{1-v^n}{p\left(1-(1-d)^{\frac{1}{p}}\right)} - \frac{n}{p}v^{\frac{np+1}{p}} = \frac{1}{p}v^{\frac{1}{p}} \times \frac{1-v^n}{d^{(p)}} - \frac{n}{p}v^{\frac{np+1}{p}} = \frac{1}{p}v^{\frac{1}{p}}\left(\ddot{a}_{\overline{n}|}^{(p)} - nv^n\right)$$

$$\Rightarrow \quad PV = \frac{\ddot{a}_{\overline{n}|}^{(p)} - nv^n}{p\left(v^{-\frac{1}{p}}-1\right)} = \frac{\ddot{a}_{\overline{n}|}^{(p)} - nv^n}{p\left((1+i)^{\frac{1}{p}}-1\right)} = \frac{\ddot{a}_{\overline{n}|}^{(p)} - nv^n}{i^{(p)}}$$

After all that algebra, we see that the present value of these payments can be calculated simply by adjusting the formula for the present value of an increasing *pthly* annuity.

This set of cash flows is known as a ***pthly increasing pthly annuity-immediate***. Its present value is denoted $(I^{(p)}a)_{\overline{n}|}^{(p)}$, which is pronounced **i-upper-p-a-upper-p-angle-n**. It is valued at time 0.

Present value factor of a *pthly* increasing *pthly* annuity-immediate

The present value of payments of $1/p^2$ at the end of the first *pthly* time period, $2/p^2$ at the end of the second *pthly* time period and so on for n years is:

$$(I^{(p)}a)_{\overline{n}|i}^{(p)} = \frac{\ddot{a}_{\overline{n}|i}^{(p)} - nv^n}{i^{(p)}}$$

Note that the first superscript (p) after the I signifies that the increases occur each *pthly* period, and that the second superscript (p) above the angle signifies that the payments are made *pthly*.

Also notice the similarities between this formula and the definition of $(Ia)_{\overline{n}|}^{(p)}$:

$$(Ia)_{\overline{n}|i}^{(p)} = \frac{\ddot{a}_{\overline{n}|i} - nv^n}{i^{(p)}}$$

Example 4.20

Determine the present value of $1 at the end of the first quarter, $2 at the end of the second quarter, $3 at the end of the third quarter, and so on for 5 years. The annual effective interest rate is 4%.

Solution

The timeline diagram is:

The factor $(I^{(4)}a)^{(4)}_{\overline{5|}}$ values a payment of $1/16$ at the end of the first quarter, $2/16$ at the end of the second quarter, and so on.

This payment series is $4^2 = 16$ times greater than that. So, the present value of the payments is:

$$16(I^{(4)}a)^{(4)}_{\overline{5|}} = 16 \times \frac{\ddot{a}^{(4)}_{\overline{5|}} - 5v^5}{i^{(4)}}$$

Calculating the required values:

$$i^{(4)} = 4\left[(1.04)^{\frac{1}{4}} - 1\right] = 3.9414\%$$

$$d^{(4)} = 4\left[1 - (1.04)^{-\frac{1}{4}}\right] = 3.9029\%$$

$$\ddot{a}^{(4)}_{\overline{5|}} = \frac{1 - (1.04)^{-5}}{0.039029} = 4.562572$$

$$(I^{(4)}a)^{(4)}_{\overline{5|}} = \frac{4.562572 - 5(1.04)^{-5}}{0.039414} = 11.491882$$

The present value is:

$$16(I^{(4)}a)^{(4)}_{\overline{5|}} = 16 \times 11.491882 = \$183.87$$

Many students find it easier to solve a problem like this by calculating a *p*thly increasing *p*thly annuity using the number of *p*thly periods and the *p*thly effective interest rate in the formula for the increasing annuity. Let's work through this alternative approach too.

In this case, there are 20 quarterly periods and the quarterly effective interest rate is:

$$\frac{i^{(4)}}{4} = (1.04)^{0.25} - 1 = 0.9853\%$$

Using a quarterly effective interest rate, the factor $(Ia)_{\overline{20|}}$ values a payment of 1 at the end of the first quarter, 2 at the end of the second quarter, and so on. This is identical to the payment series in this question. So, the present value is:

$$(Ia)_{\overline{20|}0.9853\%}$$

Calculating the present value of the annuity-due using the quarterly effective interest rate:

$$\ddot{a}_{\overline{20|}0.9853\%} = \frac{1 - (1.009853)^{-20}}{0.009853 / 1.009853} = 18.250289$$

Hence, the total present value of the payment series is:

$$(Ia)_{\overline{20|}} = \frac{18.250289 - 20(1.009853)^{-20}}{0.009853} = \$183.87 \qquad \blacklozenge\blacklozenge$$

As we see from this example, an alternative expression for the present value of a *p*thly increasing *p*thly annuity-immediate is:

$$(I^{(p)}a)^{(p)}_{\overline{n|}i} = \frac{1}{p^2}(Ia)_{\overline{np|}\frac{i^{(p)}}{p}}$$

The accumulated value of the *p*thly increasing *p*thly annuity-immediate can be determined by accumulating the present value of the *p*thly increasing *p*thly annuity-immediate for n years.

It is written $(I^{(p)}s)^{(p)}_{\overline{n}|}$, which is pronounced **i-upper-p-s-upper-p-angle-n**. It is valued at time n years.

Accumulated value factor of a *p*thly increasing *p*thly annuity-immediate

The accumulated value of payments of $1/p^2$ at the end of the first *p*thly time period, $2/p^2$ at the end of the second *p*thly time period and so on for n years is:

$$(I^{(p)}s)^{(p)}_{\overline{n}|i} = (1+i)^n (I^{(p)}a)^{(p)}_{\overline{n}|i} = \frac{\ddot{s}^{(p)}_{\overline{n}|i} - n}{i^{(p)}}$$

For example, the accumulated value at time 5 of the payments described in Example 4.20 is:

$$16(I^{(4)}s)^{(4)}_{\overline{5}|} = (1+i)^5 16(I^{(4)}a)^{(4)}_{\overline{5}|} = 1.04^5 \times 183.87 = \$223.71$$

Pthly increasing pthly annuity-due

To calculate the present value of a **pthly increasing pthly annuity-due** in which payments are made at the start of each quarter, we make the standard adjustment to the formula for the *p*thly increasing *p*thly annuity-immediate, *ie* we replace the term $i^{(p)}$ in the denominator with the term $d^{(p)}$.

The present value of a *p*thly increasing *p*thly annuity-due is denoted $(I^{(p)}\ddot{a})^{(p)}_{\overline{n}|}$, which is pronounced **i-upper-p-a-double-dot-upper-p-angle-n**. It is valued at time 0.

Present value factor of a *p*thly increasing *p*thly annuity-due

The present value of payments of $\dfrac{1}{p^2}$ at the start of the first *p*thly time period, $\dfrac{2}{p^2}$ at the start of the second *p*thly time period and so on for n years is:

$$(I^{(p)}\ddot{a})^{(p)}_{\overline{n}|i} = \frac{\ddot{a}^{(p)}_{\overline{n}|i} - nv^n}{d^{(p)}}$$

Example 4.21

Determine the present value of $1 at the start of the first quarter, $2 at the start of the second quarter, $3 at the start of the third quarter, and so on for 5 years. The annual effective interest rate is 4%.

Solution

The present value of the payments is:

$$16(I^{(4)}\ddot{a})^{(4)}_{\overline{5}|} = 16 \times \frac{\ddot{a}^{(4)}_{\overline{5}|} - 5v^5}{d^{(4)}}$$

From Example 4.20, we have:

$$i^{(4)} = 3.9414\% \qquad d^{(4)} = 3.9029\% \qquad \ddot{a}_{\overline{5}|}^{(4)} = 4.562572$$

$$\Rightarrow (I^{(4)}\ddot{a})_{\overline{5}|}^{(4)} = \frac{4.562572 - 5(1.04)^{-5}}{0.039029} = 11.605116$$

The present value is:

$$16(I^{(4)}\ddot{a})_{\overline{5}|}^{(4)} = 16 \times 11.605116 = \$185.68$$

Alternatively, working in quarters, there are $4 \times 5 = 20$ quarterly periods in the 5 years, and the quarterly effective interest rate is:

$$\frac{i^{(4)}}{4} = (1.04)^{0.25} - 1 = 0.9853\%$$

So, the present value is:

$$(I\ddot{a})_{\overline{20}|0.9853\%} = \frac{\ddot{a}_{\overline{20}|0.9853\%} - 20v^{20}}{d}$$

Calculating the present value of the annual annuity-due:

$$\ddot{a}_{\overline{20}|} = \frac{1 - (1.009853)^{-20}}{0.009853 / 1.009853} = 18.250289$$

Hence, the present value is:

$$(I\ddot{a})_{\overline{20}|0.9853\%} = \frac{18.250289 - 20(1.009853)^{-20}}{0.009853 / 1.009853} = \$185.68 \qquad\qquad \blacklozenge\blacklozenge$$

Finally, the accumulated value of the *p*thly increasing *p*thly annuity-due can be determined by accumulating the present value of the *p*thly increasing *p*thly annuity-due for n years.

It is written $(I^{(p)}\ddot{s})_{\overline{n}|}^{(p)}$, which is pronounced **i-upper-p-s-double-dot-upper-p-angle-n**. It is valued at time n years.

Accumulated value factor of a *p*thly increasing *p*thly annuity-due

The accumulated value of payments of $1/p^2$ at the start of the first *p*thly time period, $2/p^2$ at the start of the second *p*thly time period and so on for n years is:

$$(I^{(p)}\ddot{s})_{\overline{n}|i}^{(p)} = (1+i)^n (I^{(p)}\ddot{a})_{\overline{n}|i}^{(p)} = \frac{\ddot{s}_{\overline{n}|i}^{(p)} - n}{d^{(p)}}$$

For example, the accumulated value at time 5 of the payments described in Example 4.21 is:

$$16(I^{(4)}\ddot{s})_{\overline{5}|}^{(4)} = (1+i)^5 16(I^{(4)}\ddot{a})_{\overline{5}|}^{(4)} = 1.04^5 \times 185.68 = \$225.91$$

Chapter 4 Practice Questions

> ## Question guide
>
> - Questions 4.1 – 4.11 test material from Sections 4.1 – 4.5.
> - Questions 4.12 – 4.16 test material from Sections 4.6 – 4.7.
> - Questions 4.17 – 4.20 are from the SOA/CAS Course 2 exam or the IOA/FOA 102 exam.

Question 4.1

Calculate the accumulated value, at the end of 8 years, of payments of $4,000 a year which are paid monthly at the start of each month. The annual effective rate of interest is 9%.

Question 4.2

Find the annual effective rate of interest equivalent to a nominal rate of interest of 8% a year convertible biannually.

Question 4.3

Determine the present value of payments of $500 at the end of each year for the next 20 years. The nominal rate of interest is 5% a year convertible monthly.

Question 4.4

Find the accumulated value at time 20 years of payments of $35 at times 0, 1, 2, and so on, with the last payment at 19 years. The nominal rate of interest is 7% a year convertible biannually.

Question 4.5

Determine the annual effective interest rate that corresponds to a nominal rate of discount of 6% a year convertible quarterly.

Question 4.6

Calculate the present value of payments of $1,000 at the end of each year for the next 5 years. The nominal rate of discount is 10% a year convertible biannually.

Question 4.7

Find the accumulated value at time 15 years of payments of $455 at times 0, 1, 2, and so on, until the last payment at 14 years. The nominal rate of discount is 3.5% a year convertible monthly.

Question 4.8

Determine the present value at time 0 of payments of $4,800 a year paid at the end of each month for 7 years. The nominal rate of interest is 9% a year convertible every 4 months.

Question 4.9

Money is received at a rate of $6,880 a year. Find the accumulated value at time 16 years of the money received, given that payments are received at the end of every other year. The nominal rate of interest is 10% a year convertible every 6 months.

Question 4.10

Calculate the present value at time 0 of payments of $50 paid at the start of each month for 7 years, starting at time 0. The nominal rate of interest is 4% a year convertible quarterly.

Question 4.11

Find the accumulated value at time 20 years of payments of $50,000 a year paid at the start of every half-year, starting at time 0. The nominal rate of interest is 6% a year convertible monthly.

Question 4.12

Determine the present value of payments of $10 at the end of every month during the first year, $20 at the end of every month during the second year, $30 at the end of every month during the third year, and so on for 10 years. The nominal interest rate is 12% convertible monthly.

Question 4.13

Calculate the accumulated value at time 15 years of payments of $35 at the start of every quarter during the first year, $70 at the start of every quarter in the second year, $105 at the start of every quarter during the third·year, and so on for 15 years. The nominal interest rate is 12% convertible monthly.

Question 4.14

Find the present value of payments of $5 now, $10 in 6 months, $15 in one year, $20 in 18 months, and so on for 6 years. The nominal discount rate is 12% convertible every 6 months.

Question 4.15

Determine the accumulated value at time 5 years of payments of $50 at the end of the first quarter, $55 at the end of the second quarter, $60 at the end of the third quarter, and so on for 5 years. The annual effective interest rate is 6%.

Question 4.16

Marlene invests X now in order to receive $5 in 2 months, $10 in 4 months, $15 in 6 months, and so on. The payments continue for 10 years. The annual effective rate of interest is 8%. Determine X.

Question 4.17   *SOA/CAS*

At an annual effective interest rate of i, $i > 0\%$, the present value of a perpetuity paying $10 at the end of each 3-year period, with the first payment at the end of year 6, is $32.

At the same annual effective rate of i, the present value of a perpetuity-immediate paying $1 at the end of each 4-month period is X.

Calculate X.

Question 4.18   *SOA/CAS*

Tawny makes a deposit into a bank account which credits interest at a nominal interest rate of 10% per annum, convertible semiannually.

At the same time, Fabio deposits $1,000 into a different bank account, which is credited with simple interest.

At the end of 5 years, the forces of interest on the two accounts are equal, and Fabio's account has accumulated to Z.

Determine Z.

Question 4.19   *SOA/CAS*

Olga buys a 5-year increasing annuity for X. Olga will receive $2 at the end of the first month, $4 at the end of the second month, and for each month thereafter the payment increases by $2.

The nominal interest rate is 9% convertible quarterly. Calculate X.

Question 4.20   *FOA/IOA*

A sum of $100 is accumulated at a nominal rate of discount of 7.5% per year convertible quarterly for 1 year, and then at a nominal rate of interest of 7.5% per year convertible quarterly for 1 year. What is the accumulated amount of the investment after 2 years?

5

Project appraisal and loans

Overview

So far, we have been studying the background material necessary to tackle situations involving selected practical examples of interest theory, such as assessing business projects, investment funds and loans using mathematical measures of investment performance.

In the first section of this chapter, we consider how to compare different business projects to determine which is best. We start with a description of **discounted cash flow analysis**, and then proceed to the **net present value** model. Along the way, we consider **internal rate of return** and **inflation**.

We then look at investment funds and develop methods to assess the performance of fund managers. We consider both **time-weighted** interest rates and **dollar-weighted** interest rates. We also look at two ways of allocating investment income: the **calendar year** method and the **portfolio year** method.

Finally, we study **loans** and consider two ways in which they can be repaid – the **amortization** method and the **sinking fund** method. Among other things, we calculate the payments on a loan, the interest and principal components of a particular payment and how to determine the amount of the loan balance outstanding at a given point during the loan.

5.1 Discounted cash flow analysis

We start this section by considering business projects where money is coming in to the investor (cash inflows) and money is being paid out by the investor (cash outflows). We look at the present value of project cash flows using **discounted cash flow (DCF)** analysis. We specifically examine two DCF measures for assessing a project: **net present value** and **internal rate of return**.

Why should a corporation invest in a particular project? Since a corporation is owned by its shareholders, a firm should invest in a project if it creates additional value for its shareholders above and beyond all relevant costs associated with the project. A company should therefore invest in a project that is worth more to its owners on a present value basis than the project costs. But how does a company make that determination?

The company is on a quest to identify the best project from a group of alternative projects. The best project is defined as the one that maximizes shareholder wealth for the company. The best measure of value created for the shareholders is the net present value model. Consequently, the net present value model is preferred for selecting the best project.

Net present value is not a difficult concept, but it can be somewhat tricky to calculate in practice. To determine a project's net present value, we forecast all relevant net cash flows from the project over its life and then discount them back at an appropriate risk-adjusted interest rate, which we denote as r.

Net present value (NPV)

The net present value of a series of cash flows is the present value of cash inflows minus the present value of cash outflows:

$$\text{NPV} = \sum_{t=0}^{n} \frac{\text{cash inflow}_t}{(1+r)^t} - \sum_{t=0}^{n} \frac{\text{cash outflow}_t}{(1+r)^t}$$

Expressed another way, NPV is the sum of the present values of all *net* cash flows over n years:

$$\text{NPV} = \sum_{t=0}^{n} \frac{\text{net CF}_t}{(1+r)^t}$$

where $\text{net CF}_t = \text{cash inflow}_t - \text{cash outflow}_t$.

In the above equation, the time period t and the interest rate r need to be consistent. If the time periods are semiannual, for example, then the interest rate r should be a semiannual effective interest rate.

The interest rate is referred to as r since it is the **required return** of the project considering the level of risk inherent in the projected cash flows. This interest rate is also referred to as the **cost of capital**.

The net present value depends on the interest rate r used to calculate the discounted value of the payments. A riskier project should be discounted at a higher required return since the future cash flows are less likely to occur as expected. A higher interest rate produces a lower net present value.

The interest rate r is also known as the **opportunity cost of capital** for the project. The opportunity cost is the return on a similarly risky asset that the company could have earned if it did not invest in the project. Usually investors have a benchmark interest rate that they target for a particular type of investment, and they use this rate in their calculations.

NPV is an estimate that is based on many assumptions, and it is only as good as those assumptions. Cash flows are often projected many years into the future, and the accuracy of these estimates is not known for many years.

For example, let's assume a company pays $120,000 to purchase a property. The company pays $3,000 at the end of each of the next 6 months to renovate the property. At the end of the eighth month the company sells the property for $150,000. The project's cost of capital is an annual effective interest rate is 8%. What is the net present value of this project for the company?

Let's work in annual periods first. The nominal interest rate convertible monthly is:

$$i^{(12)} = 12\left[1.08^{\frac{1}{12}} - 1\right] = 0.077208$$

The present value of the cash inflows is:

$$150,000v^{\frac{8}{12}} = 150,000(1.08)^{-\frac{8}{12}} = 142,497.9956$$

The present value of the cash outflows is:

$$120,000 + (12 \times 3,000)a_{\overline{0.5}|}^{(12)} = 120,000 + 36,000\frac{1 - 1.08^{-0.5}}{0.077208} = 137,601.5114$$

So the net present value is $142,497.9956 - 137,601.5114 = \$4,896.48$.

Alternatively we could work in months, using an effective monthly rate of interest of:

$$\frac{i^{(12)}}{12} = 1.08^{\frac{1}{12}} - 1 = 0.006434$$

An equivalent expression for the net present value of the cash flows is then:

$$150,000v^8 - \left(120,000 + 3,000a_{\overline{6}|0.6434\%}\right)$$

The project adds value to the corporation if its net present value is greater than zero, but the project reduces shareholder wealth if its net present value is less than zero. When choosing between two projects, the company should choose the project that creates the most shareholder wealth, that is, the one that has the greater NPV. If a project's net present value equals zero, its return exactly matches the required return and the project should be accepted as long as there are no positive NPV projects also under consideration.

Example 5.1

A project requires an initial investment of $50,000. The project will generate net cash flows of $15,000 at the end of the first year, $40,000 at the end of the second year, and $10,000 at the end of the third year. The project's cost of capital is 13%. According to the NPV model, should you invest in the project?

Solution

We calculate the project's net present value using the formula:

$$\begin{aligned}\text{NPV} &= \sum_{t=0}^{n} \frac{\text{net } CF_t}{(1+r)^t} \\ &= \frac{-50,000}{(1.13)^0} + \frac{15,000}{(1.13)^1} + \frac{40,000}{(1.13)^2} + \frac{10,000}{(1.13)^3} \\ &= \$1,530.71\end{aligned}$$

Since the project's net present value is greater than zero, it is a worthwhile investment.   ◆◆

If we think of NPV as a function of the interest rate and set the NPV equal to zero, we get an equation of value. The interest rate that satisfies this equation of value is called the **yield** or **internal rate of return**.

Internal rate of return (IRR)

The IRR is the interest rate that equates the present value of cash inflows with the present value of cash outflows:

$$\sum_{t=0}^{n} \frac{\text{cash inflow}_t}{(1+IRR)^t} = \sum_{t=0}^{n} \frac{\text{cash outflow}_t}{(1+IRR)^t}$$

In other words, the IRR is the interest rate that causes the net present value to equal zero:

$$NPV = \sum_{t=0}^{n} \frac{\text{net CF}_t}{(1+IRR)^t} = 0$$

It is customary to express the IRR as an annual effective interest rate. The IRR can be thought of as the interest rate that causes the project to break even on a time-value-of-money basis.

The IRR is often difficult to calculate unless a spreadsheet or a modern financial calculator is used. If a spreadsheet is not handy, the IRR may be determined by trial and error.

Once again, let's assume a company pays $120,000 to purchase a property. The company pays $3,000 at the end of each of the next 6 months to renovate the property. At the end of the eighth month the company sells the property for $150,000. What is the project's internal rate of return?

Let's work in monthly periods and denote the *monthly* effective interest rate as j. If the net present value is zero, the equation of value to determine the IRR is:

$$150,000v^8 - (120,000 + 3,000a_{\overline{6}|j}) = 0$$

$$150,000(1+j)^{-8} - 3,000 \times \frac{1-(1+j)^{-6}}{j} - 120,000 = 0$$

We can determine j after a few steps by trial and error. At an annual effective interest rate of 15.0%, $j = 1.1715\%$ and the net present value is $-\$629.26$. At an annual effective interest rate of 14.0%, $j = 1.0979\%$ and the net present value is $\$125.06$. Using linear interpolation, we determine the annual effective interest rate (and the corresponding monthly effective interest rate) that causes the net present value to be zero:

$$(1+j)^{12} - 1 = 14.0\% + \frac{125.06 - 0}{125.06 - (-629.26)}(15.0\% - 14.0\%) = 14.1658\%$$

$$j = 1.141658^{\frac{1}{12}} - 1 = 1.1101\%$$

The actual answer is an annual effective interest rate of 14.1648%, so the approximation is pretty good.

This process to determine the IRR can be illustrated graphically. To draw this graph, we determine the net present values at various selected interest rates. If we plot NPV along the y-axis against various interest rates along the x-axis and then draw a line between those points, the IRR is at the point where the NPV crosses the x-axis (*ie* where the net present value equals zero). This graph is not linear, even though it appears to be. Determining the IRR in this fashion using linear interpolation produces an approximation for the actual IRR.

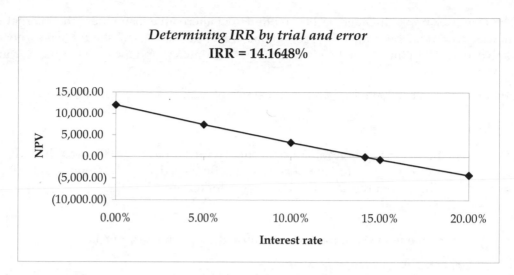

Consider once again a bank making a loan to an individual. In this case the bank acts as a lender or investor, and the individual acts as the borrower. Payments that are received by the investor (cash inflows) are taken to be positive cash flows. Payments that are made by the investor (cash outflows) are taken to be negative cash flows. For the borrower, the cash flows will be of the opposite sign. We'll cover loans in more detail soon, but for now let's apply the DCF techniques in an example to determine the IRR of a loan.

Example 5.2

A bank lends Diane $8,000 now. She repays $600 at the end of each quarter for 5 years. Find the annual effective internal rate of return.

Solution

Working in years, the equation of value is:

$$8,000 = 4 \times 600 a_{\overline{5}|}^{(4)}$$

$$8,000 = 2,400 \times \frac{1-(1+i)^{-5}}{4\left((1+i)^{\frac{1}{4}}-1\right)}$$

$$\Rightarrow \quad 13.33 = \frac{1-(1+i)^{-5}}{(1+i)^{\frac{1}{4}}-1}$$

It is fairly quick to try one value for the annual effective interest rate, and then use trial and error to home in on the correct answer. With a choice of 16.0%, the right-hand side of the above equation works out to be 13.86, which is higher than 13.33. So we must increase the value of i. With a choice of 17.0%, the right-hand side is 13.59, which is still too high. With a choice of 18.0%, the right-hand side is 13.32, which is just lower than 13.33. So the value of i is just less than 18.0%. Using linear interpolation, we have:

$$i = 17.0\% + \frac{13.59-13.33}{13.59-13.32}(18.0\%-17.0\%) = 17.96\%$$

♦♦

When working with the internal rate of return, it is important to remember what the rate means to both parties of the transaction. The borrower would like to have a low internal rate of return, since the IRR is the borrower's cost to borrow, while the lender would like to have a high internal rate of return, since the IRR is the lender's rate of return on the loan.

In the previous example, if Diane had been offered an alternative loan where the internal rate of return was 7% and where all other conditions were the same, she should have chosen the alternative loan. With the alternative loan, she pays less interest and the loan has a lower internal rate of return.

Note that it is possible to have a *negative* internal rate of return, as we see in the next example.

Example 5.3

John is offered the following investment opportunity. If he pays $30,000 now, he will receive $2,270 at the end of each year for the next 8 years. By considering the internal rate of return, comment on whether or not this is a wise investment for John.

Solution

Assuming an annual effective internal rate of return, the equation of value is:

$$30,000 = 2,270a_{\overline{8}|i}$$

The annuity-immediate present value factor is:

$$a_{\overline{8}|i} = \frac{30,000}{2,270} = 13.215859$$

Since $a_{\overline{8}|}$ represents the present value of 8 payments of $1, it has a value of less than 8 if it is evaluated at any positive interest rate. So, i is negative in this case.

This is verified by solving the equation:

$$a_{\overline{8}|i} = \frac{1-(1+i)^{-8}}{i} = 13.215859$$

The internal rate of return that satisfies this equation of value is approximately –10% a year, which implies the net present value of this investment is less than zero. John would be unwise to participate in this investment.   ♦ ♦

In a typical investment project, money is invested in the early stages, and then profits are generated later. In other words, negative net cash flows are usually followed by positive net cash flows. For a typical loan, money is received at the start (a positive cash flow initially), and then payments are made afterwards (negative cash flows later). In these situations, it can be shown that the equation of value has only one root, that is, the internal rate of return is unique. If the cash flows alternate back and forth between positive and negative, there might be more than one solution according to Descartes' rule of signs. According to this rule, the maximum number of solutions is equal to the number of sign changes in the equation of value polynomial. In some cases, there might even be no (sensible) solution. However, simple investment situations generally have a unique internal rate of return.

Interest reinvested at a different rate

Sometimes, interest that is earned may be reinvested at a different interest rate. Consider a deposit in which interest is earned at a certain rate, but the interest itself is then reinvested at a different interest rate. In this case, it is useful to employ increasing annuity factors.

Example 5.4

Vanessa invests $5,000 at the end of each of the next 15 years and her investment earns interest at an annual effective rate of 10%. The interest that she receives at the end of each year is reinvested and earns interest at an annual effective rate of 5%. Calculate the accumulated amount of the total investment at time 15 years.

Solution

At the end of the investment, the 15 payments of $5,000 she has invested will total $75,000 without considering interest. All interest payments she receives accumulate separately. So we need to calculate how much the interest payments will have accumulated to by time 15 years.

At the end of the second and subsequent years, Vanessa will receive $0.1 \times 5,000 = \$500$ interest on her first investment of $5,000. Similarly at the end of the third and subsequent years, she will receive $500 interest on her second investment of $5,000. So at time 2, she will have $500 to invest at 5%; at time 3, she will have $2 \times \$500$ to invest at 5%; and so on, until finally at time 15 years, she will have $14 \times \$500$.

The timeline diagram of the cash flows is:

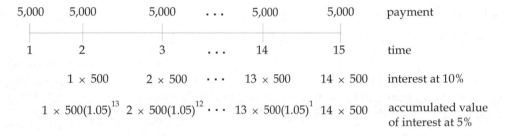

By time 15 years, she will have a total of:

$$75,000 + 500(1.05)^{13} + 2 \times 500(1.05)^{12} + \cdots + 14 \times 500$$

$$= 75,000 + 500(Is)_{\overline{14}|5\%}$$

$$= 75,000 + 500 \times \frac{\ddot{s}_{\overline{14}|5\%} - 14}{0.05}$$

$$- \$140,785.64 \qquad\qquad \blacklozenge\blacklozenge$$

We'll soon consider how this situation relates to the repayment of loans.

5.2   Nominal vs. real interest rates

The **inflation rate** is the rate at which prices have increased and is usually expressed as an annual rate. The Consumer Price Index is one measure of inflation in the economy. Inflation diminishes the value of money over time, so it is useful to determine the **real rate of interest** that is earned, net of inflation.

A **nominal interest rate** is a rate that has not been adjusted for inflation. A **real interest rate** is calculated by removing inflation from the nominal interest rate. This is done by adjusting the nominal rate for the changes in price due to inflation.

There are two meanings of the word nominal when describing interest rates. The one used here is to distinguish between nominal and real rates. Nominal rates have not been adjusted for inflation, while real rates have inflation stripped out. The other type of nominal rate is with respect to compounding frequency, which was discussed in Chapter 4. This type of nominal rate, which is convertible p times per year, is distinguished from effective $p$thly rates.

Nominal interest rates vs. real interest rates

The nominal interest rate, i, is made up of the real interest rate, i_{real}, and the inflation rate, π.

$$(1+i) = (1+i_{\text{real}})(1+\pi)$$

The real interest rate can be found by deflating the nominal interest rate.

$$i_{\text{real}} = \frac{(1+i)}{(1+\pi)} - 1$$

Solving for the nominal interest rate, we have:

$$(1+i) = (1+i_{\text{real}})(1+\pi)$$
$$\Rightarrow i = i_{\text{real}} + \pi + (i_{\text{real}})(\pi)$$

The nominal interest rate is not just the real rate plus the inflation rate. There is an interaction effect term of the real rate times the inflation rate. Sometimes we can use the real rate plus the inflation rate as an approximation of the nominal rate. If more precision is needed, we use the formula above including the interaction effect.

If inflation changes, then either the real interest rate or the nominal interest rate must change correspondingly. For example, if inflation is 2% and the nominal interest rate is 5%, then the real interest rate is:

$$\frac{1.05}{1.02} - 1 = 2.9\%$$

If inflation increases to 3% and the nominal interest rate does not change from 5%, then the real interest rate decreases to:

$$\frac{1.05}{1.03} - 1 = 1.9\%$$

If inflation increases to 3% and the real interest rate does not change from 2.9%, then the nominal interest rate increases to:

$$(1.029)(1.03) - 1 = 6.0\%$$

 Example 5.5

The nominal interest rate is 8% and the inflation rate is 2%. Determine the real interest rate.

Solution

The real interest rate is:

$$i_{\text{real}} = \frac{(1+i)}{(1+\pi)} - 1 = \frac{1.08}{1.02} - 1 = 0.058824 \quad \text{or} \quad 5.8824\%$$
       ◆◆

To remove the effects of inflation from nominal cash flows, we simply deflate the cash flows so they become real cash flows and then discount them using the real interest rate. But first, we must be careful to determine whether we are working with nominal cash flows or real cash flows. We do not want to deflate already deflated real cash flows. Alternatively, we can adjust the real interest rate for inflation and then discount the resulting nominal cash flows at the nominal interest rate.

Nominal cash flows are already inflated and real cash flows are already deflated. The relationship between real cash flows, nominal cash flows and the inflation rate is:

$$\text{real CF}_t = \frac{\text{nominal CF}_t}{(1+\pi)^t}$$

Hence, nominal cash flows are expressed in terms of future (less valuable) dollars, while real cash flows are expressed in terms of current dollars.

Present value formulas using nominal and real interest rates

Nominal cash flows are discounted with nominal interest rates and real cash flows are discounted with real interest rates.

$$PV = \sum_{t=0}^{n} \frac{\text{nominal CF}_t}{(1+i)^t} = \sum_{t=0}^{n} \frac{\text{nominal CF}_t}{(1+\pi)^t (1+i_{\text{real}})^t} = \sum_{t=0}^{n} \frac{\text{real CF}_t}{(1+i_{\text{real}})^t}$$

Use whichever formula is easiest to solve with the given information. For example, let's determine the present value of payments of $1,000 at the end of each year for 5 years. The real interest rate is 5% and the inflation rate is 2%.

It would be inappropriate to discount the cash flows at the real interest rate of 5% since the cash flows are nominal cash flows. Cash flows are assumed to be nominal unless we are told they are real cash flows. We could convert the nominal cash flows to real cash flows and discount those real cash flows using the real interest rate. The first real cash flow (stripped of inflation) at time 1 year is:

$$\frac{1,000}{1.02}$$

The second real cash flow at time 2 years is:

$$\frac{1,000}{(1.02)^2}$$

This process continues until the last real cash flow at time 5 years is:

$$\frac{1,000}{(1.02)^5}$$

These real cash flows could then be discounted at the real interest rate. However, it is usually easier to discount the nominal cash flows at the nominal interest rate. The nominal interest rate is:

$$i = (1.05)(1.02) - 1 = 7.1\%$$

The present value is then:

$$PV = 1,000 a_{\overline{5}|7.1\%} = 1,000 \times \frac{1 - (1.071)^{-5}}{0.071} = \$4,089.24$$

Example 5.6

A bond pays $50 in one year and $1,050 in two years. The real interest rate is 4% and the inflation rate is 2%. Determine the present value of the bond's cash flows.

Solution

The bondholder receives $50 at time 1 year and $1,050 at time 2 years. The nominal interest rate is $(1.04)(1.02)-1=6.08\%$ using the real rate of 4% and the inflation rate of 2%. The nominal cash flows are discounted with the nominal interest rate to find the present value.

$$PV = \sum_{t=0}^{2} \frac{\text{nominal CF}_t}{(1+i)^t} = \frac{50}{(1.0608)^1} + \frac{1,050}{(1.0608)^2} = \$980.22$$

Alternatively, we can adjust the nominal cash flows to real cash flows and discount them at the real interest rate. The real cash flows have inflation stripped out. The real cash flow at times 1 and 2 years are:

$$\text{real CF}_1 = \frac{50}{(1.02)^1} = \$49.02$$

$$\text{real CF}_2 = \frac{1,050}{(1.02)^2} = \$1,009.23$$

Discounting the real cash flows at the real interest rate, we determine the present value of the real cash flows:

$$PV = \sum_{t=0}^{2} \frac{\text{real CF}_t}{(1+i_{\text{real}})^t} = \frac{49.02}{(1.04)^1} + \frac{1,009.23}{(1.04)^2} = \$980.22$$

Both approaches provide the same answer.   ◆◆

Example 5.7

Jeremy expects to retire in one year and his first pension payment at that time is $50,000. After the first pension payment, each subsequent annual pension payment is adjusted for inflation so that in real terms the pension payments remain level for the remaining 29 years of the pension payout period. The inflation rate is 2% and the annual effective interest rate is 6%.

Determine the present value of the annual pension payments.

Solution

Let's first determine the present value using real cash flows and the real interest rate. The first nominal pension payment should be adjusted for one year of inflation. The first real pension payment at time one year is:

$$\text{real CF}_1 = \frac{50,000}{1.02} = \$49,019.61$$

In real terms, the pension payments remain level over the pension payout period. Subsequent annual real pension payments of $49,019.61 are then discounted at the real interest rate to determine the present value. The real interest rate is:

$$i_{\text{real}} = \frac{(1+i)}{(1+\pi)} - 1 = \frac{1.06}{1.02} - 1 = 0.039216$$

The present value is then:

$$PV = 49,019.61 a_{\overline{30}|3.9216\%} = 49,019.61 \times \frac{1 - 1.039216^{-30}}{0.039216} = \$855,779.53$$

Note that this approach is the same as using a compound increasing annuity-immediate to determine the present value at a net interest rate of:

$$j = \frac{0.06 - 0.02}{1.02} = 3.9216\%$$

We now can recognize this net interest rate as the real interest rate. Using the compound increasing annuity-immediate formula, the present value is:

$$PV = \frac{50,000}{1.02} a_{\overline{30}|3.9216\%} = 49,019.61 \times \frac{1 - 1.039216^{-30}}{0.039216} = \$855,779.53$$

Alternatively, we can determine the present value using nominal cash flows and the nominal interest rate. The present value is determined using a geometric series:

$$PV = \frac{50,000}{1.06} + \frac{50,000(1.02)}{(1.06)^2} + \cdots + \frac{50,000(1.02)^{29}}{(1.06)^{30}}$$

$$= \frac{50,000}{1.06}\left[1 + \frac{1.02}{1.06} + \cdots + \left(\frac{1.02}{1.06}\right)^{29}\right]$$

$$= \frac{50,000}{1.06} \times \frac{1 - \left(\frac{1.02}{1.06}\right)^{30}}{1 - \left(\frac{1.02}{1.06}\right)}$$

$$= \$855,779.50$$

The slight difference is due to rounding.   ♦ ♦

5.3 Investment funds

Consider an investment fund such as a pension fund. The investment manager of the pension fund is compensated based on the performance of the fund relative to the performance of similar funds, so it is important to be able to evaluate the fund's investment performance. To evaluate the performance of the fund over a particular period, we consider:

- the initial value of the fund
- any external cash flows that take place, such as inflows from contributions and outflows to retirees, and
- the final value of the fund.

We then perform calculations to assess the investment performance. Here we look at two methods of doing this: the **dollar-weighted** interest rate and the **time-weighted** interest rate.

Let's consider each of these with an example first before we define each one in more detail. Suppose an investment manager has a 3-year track record. The investment manager earned 20% in the first year and 5% in each of the two succeeding years. So, $1,000 invested with the investment manager for three years grows to:

$$1,000(1.20)(1.05)(1.05) = \$1,323.00$$

This is equivalent to earning an annual effective interest rate over three years of 9.78%:

$$(1+i)^3 = (1.20)(1.05)^2$$
$$i = (1.323)^{1/3} - 1$$
$$i = 0.097792$$

The annual effective interest rate of 9.78% is the geometric average of 1.20 and 1.05. Since the rate of 5% was earned for two years, the 1.05 factor has an exponent of 2, giving it more weight than the 1.20 factor. Since this kind of average gives more weight to rates of return that are earned for longer periods of time, it is called a **time-weighted** interest rate.

When there are no cash flows into or out of the fund over the investment period, the time-weighted interest rate is equal to the internal rate of return.

Now let's suppose this investor deposited $5,000 at the beginning of the second year in addition to the $1,000 that was deposited at the beginning of the first year. At the end of three years, these deposits have grown to:

$$1,000(1.20)(1.05)(1.05) + 5,000(1.05)(1.05) = \$6,835.50$$

We can calculate the internal rate of return earned by this investor by solving the following equation for i:

$$1,000(1+i)^3 + 5,000(1+i)^2 - 6,835.50 = 0$$

Using trial and error, the internal rate of return that satisfies this equation is 6.19%. The internal rate of return is similar to the time-weighted rate of return, but the IRR takes into account cash flows that occur during the investment period. Since the cash flows (which are measured in dollars) affect the internal rate of return, the IRR is also known as the **dollar-weighted** interest rate.

Let's generalize the calculation of these two ways to express interest rates, beginning with the dollar-weighted rate and ending with the time-weighted rate.

If we accumulate the initial value of the fund and the cash flows (both negative and positive) at an annual interest rate i, and set this equal to the final value of the fund, we have an equation of value. The rate of interest that satisfies this equation of value is the dollar-weighted rate of return, which is the same as the fund's IRR. In words, the equation of value is:

$$\text{accumulated value of initial fund} + \text{accumulated value of cash flows} = \text{final fund value}$$

If the value of a fund is F_0 at time 0 and F_T at ending time T, and there are cash flows (deposits into or withdrawals from the fund) of $c_1, c_2, \ldots, c_n$ at times $t_1, t_2, \ldots, t_n$, we can develop the equation of value to calculate the dollar-weighted rate of interest, i, for the period from time 0 to time T. The equation of value is:

$$F_0(1+i)^T + c_1(1+i)^{T-t_1} + c_2(1+i)^{T-t_2} + \cdots + c_n(1+i)^{T-t_n} = F_T$$

The dollar-weighted interest rate is the yield i that satisfies this equation.

Dollar-weighted interest rate

The dollar-weighted rate of interest is the interest rate that equates the accumulated value of the initial fund and the accumulated value of the cash flows with the final fund value:

$$F_0(1+i)^T + \sum_{s=1}^{n} c_s(1+i)^{T-t_s} = F_T$$

The fund values used in these calculations are usually the market values of the fund. The cash flows that are used in the above equation need to be *external* to the fund, that is, they are not cash flows generated from the fund itself. This means that if the fund manager invests in bonds or stocks and earns interest or dividends, the interest or dividends do not count as cash flows.

However, payments made from the fund (*eg* benefits paid to the retirees) count as negative cash flows and deposits into the pension fund count as positive cash flows.

We generally work in annual time periods to calculate the dollar-weighted rate of interest, since performance measurements are usually quoted as effective annual rates.

Example 5.8

The value of a pension fund on 1/1/03 was $2 million. During 2003, the pension fund paid out $100,000 in benefits on June 1 and September 1 and the fund received a contribution of $20,000 on November 1. The value of the fund on 12/31/03 was $1,900,000. Set up the equation of value to calculate the dollar-weighted rate of interest for the pension fund in 2003.

Solution

The timeline diagram is:

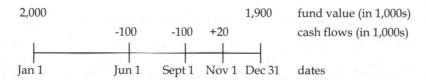

The equation of value (in 1,000s) is:

$$2,000(1+i) - 100(1+i)^{\frac{7}{12}} - 100(1+i)^{\frac{4}{12}} + 20(1+i)^{\frac{2}{12}} = 1,900 \qquad \blacklozenge\blacklozenge$$

A numerical technique is required to solve the equation in this example. An initial guess for the value of i is inserted into the equation, and the results are used to develop a better guess. This iterative process is continued until a reasonably accurate estimate is obtained. Using a spreadsheet speeds this process considerably.

There are techniques that can be used to calculate a first guess. If only an approximate answer is required, then the simple interest approximation might be close enough.

Simple interest approximation for compound interest

To find an approximate value of the dollar-weighted rate of interest, expand the equation using a first-order binomial expansion, *ie* replace $(1+i)^n$ with $(1+ni)$ and solve the resulting equation.

Let's consider the equation we obtained in the above example:

$$2,000(1+i) - 100(1+i)^{\frac{7}{12}} - 100(1+i)^{\frac{4}{12}} + 20(1+i)^{\frac{2}{12}} = 1,900$$

Dividing by 10 and using the first-order binomial expansion, we have:

$$200(1+i) - 10\left(1+\frac{7}{12}i\right) - 10\left(1+\frac{4}{12}i\right) + 2\left(1+\frac{2}{12}i\right) = 190$$

$$\Rightarrow 182 + \frac{1,147}{6}i = 190$$

$$\Rightarrow i = 4.2\%$$

The equation of value can be solved numerically to give an interest rate of about 4.18%, so the above approximation is quite accurate in this case. In fact, if the time period under consideration is around one year or less, the simple interest approximation is usually fairly accurate. But as the time period becomes much greater than 1.25 years or so, especially if the magnitude of the cash flows is large relative to the fund values, then the simple interest approximation begins to diverge significantly from the compound interest calculation. In this case, trial and error can be used to determine a more accurate solution.

Example 5.9

On January 1, 2003, the value of a pension fund was \$4 million. The pension fund received a contribution of \$1 million on June 30, 2003 and \$1.5 million on March 31, 2004. It also received dividends from its investments of \$100,000 on December 1, 2003. The fund paid out \$4,570,000 on November 1, 2004. If the value of the fund on December 31, 2004 was \$2 million, find an approximate value for the annualized dollar-weighted rate of interest for this two-year period.

Solution

The equation of value (in millions) is:

$$4(1+i)^2 + 1(1+i)^{1.5} + 1.5(1+i)^{\frac{9}{12}} - 4.57(1+i)^{\frac{2}{12}} = 2$$

Note that the dividend is not an external cash flow, so we do not include it.

To find an approximate value for the interest rate, we use the first-order binomial expansion:

$$4(1+2i) + 1(1+1.5i) + 1.5\left(1+\frac{9}{12}i\right) - 4.57\left(1+\frac{2}{12}i\right) = 2$$

$$\Rightarrow \quad i \approx 0.0071$$

So the dollar-weighted rate of interest is approximately 0.71%. In fact, the accurate figure is 0.7074%.   ◆◆

As we have seen, the value of the dollar-weighted rate of interest depends on the precise timing and amount of the cash flows. The cash flows affect the fund balances over time, and the IRR is a complex average of the rates of return earned over each time interval, with the periods of relatively large fund balances having more weight than the periods of relatively small fund balances. Since the fund balances are measured in dollars, 'dollar-weighted' is a good description for the IRR.

Usually, professional fund managers who direct investment pension funds have no control over the timing or amounts of the external cash flows. Therefore if we are comparing the performance of different fund managers, the dollar-weighted rate of interest doesn't always provide a fair comparison. So let's consider an alternative measure that doesn't depend on the size or the timing of the cash flows, namely the **time-weighted rate of interest**. The time-weighted rate of interest is also referred to as the **time-weighted rate of return**.

This measure of performance calculates an overall growth factor over the period by multiplying each of the growth factors for the sub-periods between external cash flows.

Time-weighted interest rate

Let F_0 be the initial value of the fund at time 0 and F_T be the final value of the fund at ending time T. Let the external cash flows be $c_1, c_2, \ldots, c_n$, and let the value of the fund just *before* each of these cash flows be $F_1, F_2, \ldots, F_n$.

The time-weighted rate of interest is then the value of i that satisfies the equation:

$$(1+i)^T = \frac{F_1}{F_0} \times \frac{F_2}{F_1 + c_1} \times \frac{F_3}{F_2 + c_2} \times \cdots \times \frac{F_T}{F_n + c_n}$$

Illustrating the value of the fund and the cash flows on a diagram, we have:

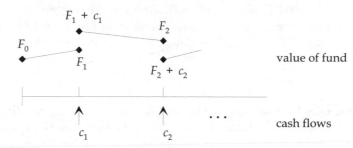

The cash flows can be positive or negative. In the above diagram, $c_1 > 0$ and $c_2 < 0$.

The right-hand side of this equation is calculated by multiplying the growth factors for the periods between cash flows. The growth factor between the start and the first cash flow is the value of the fund just before the first cash flow divided by the value of the fund at the start, F_1 / F_0. Just after the first cash flow, the fund has a value of $F_1 + c_1$. Just before the second cash flow, the value of the fund is F_2, so the growth factor over this time period is $F_2 / (F_1 + c_1)$, and so on. The growth factors can be less than one if the fund has fallen in value during the period.

Similar to the dollar-weighted rate of interest, we generally work in years to get the time-weighted interest rate since it is usually expressed as an annual effective rate.

As a reminder, the cash flows here are external cash flows, that is, cash flows that take place between the fund and an external source.

Note that the *times* of the cash flows don't enter into the calculations for the time-weighted rate of interest.

Example 5.10

The value of a pension fund on 1/1/03 was $2 million. During 2003, the pension fund paid out $100,000 in pensions on June 1 and September 1 and the fund received a contribution of $20,000 on November 1. The value of the fund on 12/31/03 was $1,900,000. On May 31, 2003 the fund was valued at $2.05 million; on August 31, 2003 its value was $2 million; and on October 31, 2003 its value was $1.99 million. Calculate the time-weighted rate of interest of the fund for 2003.

Solution

It may be helpful to draw a table showing the value of the fund at the start, the end and just before each of the cash flows, as well as the cash flows themselves. The amounts can then be put into the formula directly.

The table for the above example is:

Date	Value of the fund just before the cash flow	Cash flow
1/1/03	2.00	
6/1/03	2.05	−0.10
9/1/03	2.00	−0.10
11/1/03	1.99	0.02
12/31/03	1.90	

The equation of value is:

$$1 + i = \frac{2.05}{2.00} \times \frac{2.00}{2.05 - 0.10} \times \frac{1.99}{2.00 - 0.10} \times \frac{1.90}{1.99 + 0.02} = 1.0408$$

So the time-weighted rate of interest is 4.08%.

♦♦

Example 5.11

The value of a fund at the start of a year is $100,000. At the end of each quarter, the fund receives an injection of $10,000. Just after these cash flows, the value of the fund is initially $115,000, then $113,000, then $125,000, then finally $130,000. Calculate the time-weighted rate of interest for the fund.

Solution

Notice that the values of the fund are given just after the cash flows. To get the value of the fund before the cash flows, we need to subtract the cash flows that have just been received.

Date	Value of the fund just before the cash flow	Cash flow
1/1/xx	100,000	
3/31/xx	105,000	10,000
6/30/xx	103,000	10,000
9/30/xx	115,000	10,000
12/31/xx	120,000	10,000

The equation for the time-weighted rate of interest is:

$$1+i = \frac{105}{100} \times \frac{103}{115} \times \frac{115}{113} \times \frac{120}{125} = 0.918796$$

So the time-weighted rate of interest is −8.1%.   ◆◆

In the previous example, if the fund values halfway through each quarter had been provided instead of the fund values just before the cash flows, we would not have been able to calculate the time-weighted interest rate accurately. We need to know (or be able to calculate) the fund value just before each of the cash flows. This is one of the disadvantages of the time-weighted method. For a fund that has a lot of transactions, the assets need to be valued frequently.

So which is more appropriate: the time-weighted or the dollar-weighted interest rate? The answer depends on the purpose of the question.

To evaluate the performance of an investment manager, the time-weighted rate of return is generally the better interest rate to use. It isn't fair to penalize or reward the investment manager based on the timing of external deposits or withdrawals. Instead, the investment manager should be encouraged to earn the highest possible return in each investment period.

To evaluate the performance of a series of deposits into or withdrawals from a fund, the dollar-weighted rate of return is generally the better interest rate to use. The dollar-weighted interest rate depends partly on the investment manager's performance, but it also depends on the timing of the cash flows. The dollar-weighted return is less useful for evaluating investment managers, but it is useful to ascertain the performance of a particular series of cash flows.

Example 5.12

Elizabeth and Andrew are both investment fund managers. The balance of each of their funds is $1,000 on 1/1/2003.

On 12/31/2003, Elizabeth's fund value is $2,000. On 1/1/2004, a deposit of $20,000 is made to Elizabeth's fund, and the new fund balance is $22,000. On 12/31/2004, the fund value is $22,000.

On 12/31/2003, Andrew's fund value is $1,200. On 1/1/2004, a withdrawal of $1,000 is made from Andrew's fund, and the new fund balance is $200. On 12/31/2004, the fund value is $180.

Determine the dollar-weighted and the time-weighted returns for both Elizabeth and Andrew over this two-year period. Who had the higher return in 2003? Who had the higher return in 2004?

Solution

The equation of value to determine Elizabeth's dollar-weighted return is:

$$1,000(1+i)^2 + 20,000(1+i) = 22,000$$

Let $x = (1+i)$ and the equation can be solved using the quadratic equation:

$$1,000x^2 + 20,000x - 22,000 = 0$$

$$x = \frac{-20,000 \pm \sqrt{(20,000)^2 - 4(1,000)(-22,000)}}{2(1,000)}$$

$$\Rightarrow x = 1 + i = 1.045361$$

So Elizabeth's dollar-weighted return is 4.5%.

The equation for Elizabeth's time-weighted return is:

$$(1+i)^2 = \frac{2,000}{1,000} \times \frac{22,000}{22,000} = 2.0$$

$$\Rightarrow i = (2.0)^{0.5} - 1 = 0.414214$$

So Elizabeth's time-weighted return is 41.4%.

The equation of value to determine Andrew's dollar-weighted return is:

$$1,000(1+i)^2 - 1,000(1+i) = 180$$

Let $x = (1+i)$ and the equation can be solved using the quadratic equation:

$$1,000x^2 - 1,000x - 180 = 0$$

$$x = \frac{1,000 \pm \sqrt{(-1,000)^2 - 4(1,000)(-180)}}{2(1,000)}$$

$$\Rightarrow x = 1 + i = 1.155744$$

So Andrew's dollar-weighted return is 15.6%.

The equation for Andrew's time-weighted return is:

$$(1+i)^2 = \frac{1,200}{1,000} \times \frac{180}{200} = 1.08$$

$$\Rightarrow i = (1.08)^{0.5} - 1 = 0.039230$$

So Andrew's time-weighted return is 3.9%.

Elizabeth's fund grew from $1,000 to $2,000 in 2003, so her 2003 return is:

$$\frac{2,000}{1,000} - 1 = 100.0\%$$

Andrew's fund grew from $1,000 to $1,200 in 2003, so his 2003 return is:

$$\frac{1,200}{1,000} - 1 = 20.0\%$$

After the 1/1/2004 deposit of $20,000, Elizabeth's fund started 2004 at $22,000 and ended at $22,000, so her 2004 return is 0%.

After the 1/1/2004 withdrawal of $1,000, Andrew's fund fell from $200 to $180 in 2004, so his 2004 return is:

$$\frac{180}{200} - 1 = -10.0\%$$

Even though Andrew experienced lower returns than Elizabeth did each year, his dollar-weighted return was greater than Elizabeth's dollar-weighted return.

Elizabeth's fund received a large deposit just before the market did poorly. This affected Elizabeth's dollar-weighted return since her fund was highest just as the market did poorly.

Andrew's fund experienced a withdrawal just before the market did poorly, so his fund was at a low point at that time.   ♦ ♦

5.4 Allocating investment income

An investment fund must address the issue of allocating investment income between new deposits made in the current year and older deposits made in prior years. There are two common methods to do this: the **portfolio** method and the **investment year** method.

The portfolio method credits all of the funds in the account with an average portfolio interest rate, which reflects the average earnings on all of the assets in the account. New deposits into the account are credited with the same portfolio average interest rate as older deposits already in the account. While this method results in fairly stable interest crediting rates from year to year, it results in a lower interest rate credited to new deposits during periods of rising interest rates, since the new deposits earn the lower portfolio average rate based on all of the assets in the portfolio. Conversely, during periods of declining interest rates, the portfolio method results in a higher interest rate credited to new deposits, since the new deposits earn the higher portfolio average rate rather than the lower new money rate.

The investment year method, which is also known as the **new money** method, credits a new money rate to new deposits for a period of time, after which the portfolio average rate is credited. During periods of rising interest rates, new deposits receive the higher new money rate while older deposits earn the lower portfolio average rate. In this case, the portfolio average rate is less than the new money rate since the portfolio average rate includes the investment return made in earlier years at lower rates. During periods of declining interest rates, new deposits receive the lower new money rate while older deposits earn the higher portfolio average rate. In this case, the portfolio average rate is greater than the new money rate since the portfolio average rate includes the investment return made in earlier years at higher rates.

The following hypothetical table shows how annual effective interest rates are being credited to an investment fund by calendar year of investment. In this case, the investment year method applies for the first three years after an investment is made, after which the portfolio average rate is used. The notation i(t) refers to the investment year rate for the t-th year after a deposit.

Calendar year of investment	Investment year rates			Calendar year of portfolio rate	Portfolio rate
	i(1)	i(2)	i(3)		
1995	3.7%	3.6%	3.5%	1998	6.0%
1996	3.2%	3.1%	3.0%	1999	5.5%
1997	2.7%	2.6%	2.5%	2000	5.0%
1998	2.2%	2.1%	2.0%	2001	4.5%
1999	1.7%	1.6%	1.5%	2002	4.0%

An investment made at the beginning of 1995 would earn the investment year rate of 3.7% in 1995, the investment year rate of 3.6% in 1996, and the investment year rate of 3.5% in 1997. Starting in 1998, an investment made at the beginning of 1995 would earn the portfolio average rates. The 1995 investment would earn the portfolio rate of 6.0% in 1998, the portfolio rate of 5.5% in 1999, the portfolio rate of 5.0% in 2000, and so on.

An investment made at the beginning of 1999 would earn the investment year rate of 1.7% in 1999, the investment year rate of 1.6% in 2000, and the investment year rate of 1.5% in 2001. The 1999 investment would earn the portfolio rate of 4.0% in 2002, and it would continue to earn the subsequent portfolio rates after 2002.

Once we notice the pattern in reading this table, we see that we read across the row to determine the investment year rate for a particular calendar year of investment for each year until we get to the portfolio rate column. At that point, we start reading down the portfolio rate column to determine the portfolio rate for each year.

Let's work an example.

The previous table is repeated for convenience to show the annual effective rates credited to an investment fund by calendar year of investment. The investment year method applies for the first 3 years, after which a portfolio rate is used.

Calendar year of investment	Investment year rates			Calendar year of portfolio rate	Portfolio rate
	i(1)	i(2)	i(3)		
1995	3.7%	3.6%	3.5%	1998	6.0%
1996	3.2%	3.1%	3.0%	1999	5.5%
1997	2.7%	2.6%	2.5%	2000	5.0%
1998	2.2%	2.1%	2.0%	2001	4.5%
1999	1.7%	1.6%	1.5%	2002	4.0%

A deposit of $100 is made at the beginning of 1997. How much interest was credited during 1998 and 2000? What is the total accumulated fund value at the end of 2002?

The $100 deposit at the beginning of 1997 is credited with the investment year rates for 1997 and 1998. The amount of interest credited in 1998 is:

$$100(1.027)(0.026) = \$2.67$$

The $100 deposit is credited with the investment year rate for 1997 – 1999 and then it is credited with the portfolio rate in 2000. The amount of interest credited in 2000 is:

$$100(1.027)(1.026)(1.025)(0.05) = \$5.40$$

The $100 deposit is credited with the investment year rate for 1997 – 1999 and then it is credited with the portfolio rate from 2000 – 2002. The total fund value at the end of 2002 is:

$$100(1.027)(1.026)(1.025)(1.05)(1.045)(1.04) = \$123.25$$

Example 5.13

Using the same table as before:

(i)   How much interest is credited in the calendar years 1997 through 1999 inclusive to a deposit of $100 made at the beginning of 1995?

(ii)   What were the interest rates credited in calendar year 1999 for deposits made in 1999, 1998, 1997, and so on?

(iii) What were the new money rates credited in the first year of investment for deposits made in 1995, 1996, 1997, and so on?

Solution

Part (i)

The $100 deposit at the beginning of 1995 earns the new money rate of 3.7% in 1995 and the new money rate of 3.6% in 1996. The accumulated value of the deposit at the end of 1996 is:

$$100(1.037)(1.036) = \$107.43$$

The $100 deposit at the beginning of 1995 also earns the new money rate of 3.5% in 1997, the portfolio rate of 6% in 1998 and the portfolio rate of 5.5% in 1999. The accumulated value of the deposit at the end of 1999 is:

$$100(1.037)(1.036)(1.035)(1.06)(1.055) = \$124.35$$

The amount of interest credited during the years 1997 – 1999 inclusive equals the accumulated value of the fund at the end of 1999 less the accumulated value of the fund at the end of 1996:

$$124.35 - 107.43 = \$16.92$$

Part (ii)

In calendar year 1999, the interest rates credited were 1.7% for new deposits made in 1999, 2.1% for deposits made in 1998, 2.5% for deposits made in 1997, and 5.5% for deposits made prior to 1997. As we can see, the interest rates credited in the calendar year of 1999 appear on an upwardly sloping diagonal within the table.

Part (iii)

The new money rates credited in the first year of deposit appear in the first column of the investment year rates, $i(1)$. The new money rates credited in the first year of deposit were 3.7% in 1995, 3.2% in 1996, 2.7% in 1997, 2.2% in 1998, and 1.7% in 1999.   ♦♦

5.5 *Loans: the amortization method*

In this chapter, we consider two ways of repaying loans: the **amortization** method and the **sinking fund** method. Under the amortization method, the borrower repays the loan by making regular payments. Each payment pays the interest then due and repays some of the principal amount borrowed. Under the sinking fund method, the borrower pays interest payments throughout the loan period and then pays off the loan in full at the end of the loan period.

The key difference between these methods is that with amortization, the loan amount is gradually reduced during the term, whereas with a sinking fund, the loan amount usually remains fixed until the end.

We study the sinking fund method in the next section. But for now, let's turn our attention to the amortization method.

We first consider one key calculation in order to analyze loans, and that is calculating how much of the loan is still owed at any point in time during the loan period. Phrases such as loan outstanding, balance outstanding, and principal outstanding all refer to the loan balance. If the borrower wants to pay off the loan early, this is the amount still owed to the lender.

Once we have determined the loan balance, we can answer these questions:

- How much are the payments on a loan?
- How much interest and principal is being paid in a particular installment payment?

There are two methods for calculating the loan balance: the **prospective** method and the **retrospective** method. The prospective method considers what is going to happen in the future.

Prospective method to determine outstanding balance on a loan

Under the prospective method, the balance outstanding at any time is equal to the present value of the future loan payments:

loan balance = PV(future loan payments)

The retrospective method considers what has already happened.

Retrospective method to determine outstanding balance on a loan

Under the retrospective method, the balance outstanding at any time is equal to the accumulated value of the loan minus the accumulated value of the loan payments made to date:

loan balance = AV(loan) − AV(loan payments made to date)

These two methods can be used regardless of whether the payments are level or changing. The rate of interest used to calculate the present value and the accumulated value is the rate of interest specified in the loan (which may vary over time).

The two methods provide the same answer if the same assumptions about the amounts and timing of payments are made and the same rates of interest are used.

These formulas enable us to calculate the payments required to pay off a loan. Typically, the loan payment is level over the life of the loan, and the loan payment is usually determined at the start of the loan. Using the prospective method, we can solve for the level annual loan payment X for an n-year loan of L made at time 0 at an annual effective interest rate of i:

$$\text{loan balance} = \text{PV(future loan payments)}$$

$$\Rightarrow \quad L = X a_{\overline{n}|i}$$

$$\Rightarrow \quad X = \frac{L}{a_{\overline{n}|i}}$$

Level loan payment by prospective method

The level annual loan payment X for an n-year loan of L made at time 0 at an annual effective interest rate of i is:

$$X = \frac{L}{a_{\overline{n}|i}}$$

This formula can be modified if the loan payments are made more or less frequently than annually by using the appropriate $p$thly annuity present value factor or by using the number of periods and the periodic effective loan interest rate.

Example 5.14

A bank makes a loan of \$5,000. Level payments are made annually in arrears (that is, at the end of each year) for 5 years. The bank uses an annual effective rate of interest of 6%. Calculate the amount of each payment using the amortization method.

Solution

Using the prospective method, the annual payment X is:

$$X = \frac{5,000}{a_{\overline{5}|6\%}} = \frac{5,000}{(1 - 1.06^{-5})/0.06}$$

$$= \frac{5,000}{4.212364} = \$1,186.98$$

◆◆

Example 5.15

Using the information from Example 5.14, calculate the amount of the loan outstanding immediately after the second loan payment.

Solution

The payment is $1,186.98 as calculated in Example 5.14.

Using the prospective method, the loan balance outstanding immediately after the second payment (*ie* at the end of the second year) and with three payments left to go is:

$$B_2 = 1,186.98\, a_{\overline{3}|6\%}$$

The present value of the three remaining payments is:

$$B_2 = 1,186.98 \times \frac{1 - 1.06^{-3}}{0.06} = 1,186.98 \times 2.673012 = \$3,172.81$$

Alternatively, using the retrospective method, the loan outstanding at the end of the second year is:

$$B_2 = 5,000(1.06)^2 - 1,186.98\, s_{\overline{2}|6\%} = 5,618.00 - 1,186.98 \frac{1.06^2 - 1}{0.06} = \$3,172.82 \qquad \blacklozenge\blacklozenge$$

The slight difference has occurred because we have rounded the payment amount ($1,186.98) to 6 significant figures, so we cannot guarantee 6 significant figures of accuracy in the answer.

Notice that after $2/5 = 40\%$ of the payments have been made, only 36.5% of the loan principal has been repaid, *ie* $(5,000 - 3,172.82)/5,000$. We'll soon will see why this is the case.

In practice, use whichever method is preferred to calculate the amount of loan outstanding, but the prospective method is often quicker.

Once we know how to determine the payment amount, we can calculate the total interest that is paid on the loan. In some countries, lenders are required by law to state the total amount of interest payable and/or the total of all the payments so that borrowers can see what they are committing themselves to when they agree to a loan.

Example 5.16

Using the information from Example 5.14, calculate the total amount of interest that is paid on the loan over the 5-year period using the amortization method.

Solution

The annual payment is $1,186.98. So the total amount repaid over 5 years is:

$$1,186.98 \times 5 = 5,934.90$$

This is used to pay off the principal of $5,000. So the total amount of interest paid is:

$$5,934.90 - 5,000 = \$934.90 \qquad \blacklozenge\blacklozenge$$

We can use the prospective or retrospective method to determine the interest and principal portions of each loan payment. In other words, we can determine how much of a particular payment is allocated to pay the interest due for that period and how much (the remainder) is allocated to pay off some of the original loan principal.

Interest portion of a loan payment

The interest portion of a loan payment is determined by multiplying the effective interest rate for the payment period by the principal outstanding after the previous payment.

Assuming annual payments and an annual effective interest rate of i, the interest paid in payment t is I_t:

$$I_t = iB_{t-1}$$

where B_{t-1} is the principal balance outstanding after the previous payment.

Since the payments are only used to pay off interest and principal, we can use the interest paid in each payment to calculate the principal paid in each payment.

Principal portion of a loan payment

The principal portion of a loan payment is the payment amount less the interest paid in that payment:

$$P_t = \frac{L}{a_{\overline{n}|i}} - I_t$$

Near the start of a loan, there is a large amount of principal outstanding, so the interest forms a large proportion of each payment and the principal paid is a correspondingly small proportion. As the loan progresses, the principal outstanding drops. This means that the interest forms a decreasing proportion of the loan and the principal repaid is an increasing proportion of each payment.

Let's consider a 25-year loan of $100,000 at 6% to be repaid with annual payments at the end of each year. The level annual loan payment is:

$$X = \frac{100,000}{a_{\overline{25}|6\%}} = \frac{100,000}{12.783356} = \$7,822.67$$

The loan balance at time 0 is $100,000, so the amount of interest in the first payment is:

$$I_1 = iB_0 = 0.06 \times 100,000 = \$6,000.00$$

The amount of principal in the first payment is:

$$P_1 = 7,822.67 - 6,000 = \$1,822.67$$

Interest makes up $6,000 / 7,822.67 = 76.7\%$ of the first payment.

Under the prospective method, the loan balance at time 24 years is just the present value of the last loan payment at time 25 years:

$$B_{24} = \frac{7,822.67}{1.06} = \$7,379.88$$

So the amount of interest in the last payment is:

$$I_{25} = iB_{24} = 0.06 \times 7,379.88 = \$442.79$$

The amount of principal in the last payment is:

$$P_{25} = 7,822.67 - 442.79 = \$7,379.88$$

which is exactly enough to pay off the loan balance. Interest makes up about $442.79 / 7,822.67 = 5.7\%$ of the last payment.

The graph below shows how the split between principal and interest changes over the course of this loan.

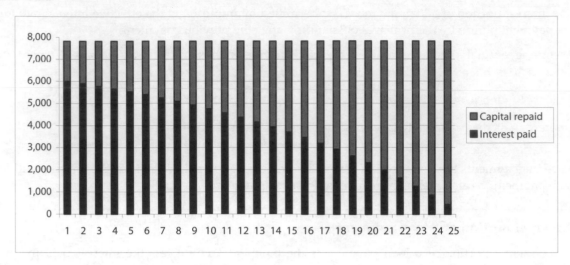

Example 5.17

Using the information from Example 5.14, calculate the interest and principal paid in the fourth payment using the amortization method.

Solution

The annual payment is \$1,186.98. In order to calculate the interest included in this payment, we need to find the principal outstanding after the 3rd payment when there are two payments remaining:

$$B_3 - 1,186.98a_{\overline{2}|6\%} = 1,186.98 \times \frac{1-1.06^{-2}}{0.06} = \$2,176.20$$

There is one year between payments, so there is one year's interest. The interest paid is:

$$I_4 = 0.06 \times 2,176.20 = \$130.57$$

So the principal paid is:

$$P_4 = 1,186.98 - 130.57 = \$1,056.41 \qquad \blacklozenge\blacklozenge$$

Example 5.18

A loan of \$15,000 is repaid using the amortization method by monthly payments at the end of each month for 8 years. The nominal rate of interest convertible quarterly is 8% a year. Find:

(i)   the monthly payment

(ii)   the principal outstanding at the end of the 4th year after the payment has been made

(iii)   the interest and principal repaid in the 49th payment.

Solution

Part (i)

Let X be the monthly payment. Then:

$$15,000 = 12Xa_{\overline{8}|}^{(12)}$$

evaluated at $i^{(4)} = 0.08$.

We need i and $i^{(12)}$, so:

$$i = \left(1 + \frac{i^{(4)}}{4}\right)^4 - 1 = \left(1 + \frac{0.08}{4}\right)^4 - 1 = 8.2432\%$$

$$i^{(12)} = 12\left((1+i)^{\frac{1}{12}} - 1\right) = 7.9473\%$$

Then:

$$X = \frac{15,000}{12 \times a_{\overline{8}|8.2432\%}^{(12)}} = \frac{15,000}{12 \times 5.906026} = \$211.65$$

An alternative approach is to work in quarters using an effective quarterly interest rate of:

$$\frac{i^{(4)}}{4} = \frac{0.08}{4} = 2\%$$

This gives the equation of value:

$$15,000 = 3 X a_{\overline{32}|2\%}^{(3)}$$

Part (ii)

After the 4th year, there are 4 years to go. Expressing the outstanding balance in months, the principal balance outstanding at 48 months is:

$$B_{48} = 12 \times 211.65 a_{\overline{4}|}^{(12)} = 12 \times 211.65 \times \frac{1 - 1.082432^{-4}}{0.079473} = \$8,678.40$$

Your answer may differ by 10 or 20 cents depending on how you have rounded your intermediate calculations.

Part (iii)

The 49th payment is made at the end of the first month of the fifth year. The principal outstanding at the start of that month is the answer to part (ii), $8,678.40.

So the interest paid in the 49th payment is the monthly effective interest rate times the balance at 48 months:

$$I_{49} = \left((1.08243216)^{\frac{1}{12}} - 1\right) \times 8,678.40 = \$57.47$$

The principal repaid in the 49th payment is:

$$P_{49} = 211.65 - 57.47 = \$154.18 \qquad \qquad \blacklozenge \blacklozenge$$

The loan payments do not need to be level amounts. The same theory is applied when the payments vary over time.

Example 5.19

A loan of $50,000 is repaid using the amortization method by annual payments at the end of each year for 10 years. Each payment is $100 higher than the one before. The annual effective rate of interest is 4%. Find:

(i)   the first payment

(ii)   the last payment

(iii)   the principal outstanding at the end of the 8th year (after the payment made at that time)

(iv)   the interest and principal repaid in the 5th payment.

Solution

Part (i)

Let the first payment be X. Then the equation of value is:

$$50,000 = Xv + (X+100)v^2 + (X+200)v^3 + \cdots + (X+900)v^{10}$$
$$= (X-100)a_{\overline{10}|} + 100(Ia)_{\overline{10}|}$$

Since $i = 4\%$:

$$a_{\overline{10}|} = \frac{1-1.04^{-10}}{0.04} = 8.110896 \qquad \ddot{a}_{\overline{10}|} = \frac{1-1.04^{-10}}{1-1.04^{-1}} = 8.435332$$

$$(Ia)_{\overline{10}|} = \frac{8.435332 - 10(1.04)^{-10}}{0.04} = 41.992248$$

So the first payment is:

$$50,000 = 8.110896X - 811.0896 + 4,199.2248$$
$$\Rightarrow \quad X = \$5,746.82$$

Part (ii)

The last payment is $X + 900$, so it is \$6,646.82.

Part (iii)

At the end of the 8th year, there are two payments left to go. The principal outstanding is:

$$B_8 = (X+800)v + (X+900)v^2$$
$$= \frac{6,546.82}{1.04} + \frac{6,646.82}{1.04^2} = \$12,440.38$$

We could also have evaluated this using annuity factors:

$$(X+700)a_{\overline{2}|} + 100(Ia)_{\overline{2}|}$$

However, since only two payment dates are involved, it is easier to perform the calculations directly.

Part (iv)

Immediately after the 4th payment, the principal outstanding is:

$$B_4 = (X+400)v + (X+500)v^2 + \cdots + (X+900)v^6 = (X+300)a_{\overline{6}|} + 100(Ia)_{\overline{6}|}$$

Since $i = 4\%$:

$$a_{\overline{6}|} = \frac{1-1.04^{-6}}{0.04} = 5.242137 \qquad \ddot{a}_{\overline{6}|} = \frac{1-1.04^{-6}}{1-1.04^{-1}} = 5.451822$$

$$(Ia)_{\overline{6}|} = \frac{5.451822 - 6(1.04)^{-6}}{0.04} = 17.748379$$

So the principal outstanding is:

$$B_4 = 31,698.26 + 1,774.84 = \$33,473.10$$

The interest in the 5th payment is:

$$I_5 = 0.04 \times 33,473.10 = \$1,338.92$$

The principal repaid in the 5th payment is:

$$P_5 = (X + 400) - 1,338.92 = \$4,807.90$$

◆◆

The progress of a loan can be seen by drawing up a **loan schedule** or **amortization schedule** showing each payment split by interest paid, principal repaid and the outstanding loan balance.

To illustrate this, let's return to Example 5.14. The information is repeated here for convenience.

A bank makes a loan of \$5,000. The payments are made yearly in arrears for 5 years. The bank uses an annual effective rate of interest of 6%.

We calculated earlier that the payment is \$1,186.98. In the first year the interest paid is:

$$I_1 = 0.06 \times 5,000 = \$300$$

This means that the principal repaid in the first year is $P_1 = 1,186.98 - 300 = \$886.98$. After the first payment, the principal outstanding is $B_1 = 5,000 - 886.98 = \$4,113.02$.

We can proceed through the loan period in this way, obtaining the following results presented in a loan schedule:

Time	Payment	Interest	Principal repaid	Principal outstanding
0				5,000.00
1	1,186.98	300.00	886.98	4,113.02
2	1,186.98	246.78	940.20	3,172.82
3	1,186.98	190.37	996.61	2,176.20
4	1,186.98	130.57	1,056.41	1,119.79
5	1,186.98	67.19	1,119.79	0.00

We suggest that you verify the rest of the values in the table until you are comfortable with the calculations.

A loan schedule is just a numerical presentation of the calculations obtained using the retrospective method. Once the initial payment has been calculated, loan schedules can be constructed very easily with a spreadsheet, using recursive formulas to calculate each row of numbers from those in the previous row. If done correctly, the loan balance outstanding at the end should be zero.

5.6 *Loans: the sinking fund method*

The sinking fund method is a method of paying off a loan in which the borrower pays interest payments throughout the loan period and then pays the loan in full at the end of the loan period. The interest payments to the lender are known as the **service payments** of the loan. The lender also requires the borrower to make deposits into a fund in order to accumulate the amount of the final payment. This fund is known as the **sinking fund**, hence the name of this method.

The rate of interest payable on the loan (usually denoted by i) and on the sinking fund (usually denoted by j) may or may not be the same.

In many cases, a sinking fund loan is set up so that each service payment exactly equals the amount of interest due on the loan in each period. The interest due on the loan is the periodic effective interest rate times the original loan amount, or iL for a loan with annual payments. If the service payment amount is not specified, the service payment is assumed to be equal to the amount of interest due on the loan.

When the service payment equals the amount of interest due, the accumulated value at time n of the periodic sinking fund payments should equal the loan amount so that the accumulated value of the sinking fund pays off the loan at maturity.

Sinking fund loan equation of value (when service payments equal interest due)

The sinking fund loan equation of value when the periodic service payments equal the interest due on the loan in each period is:

$$L = \text{AV(sinking fund payments at } j)$$
$$= \text{SFP} \times s_{\overline{n}|j}$$

where SFP is the sinking fund payment.

We don't need to include the service payments and interest due on the loan in this calculation since they cancel each other out. Using this result, we arrive at the standard sinking fund payment formula when the service payments equal the interest due on the loan.

Sinking fund loan payment (when service payments equal interest due)

The sinking fund loan payment equals the original loan amount divided by the appropriate accumulated value factor:

$$\text{SFP} = \frac{L}{s_{\overline{n}|j}}$$

When the service payment equals the amount of interest due, the total payment on the loan is the amount of the service payment, iL, plus the sinking fund payment, SFP.

We can also determine the net amount of the loan at any point in time.

Net amount of sinking fund loan (when service payments equal interest due)

The net amount of the sinking fund loan at time t is determined by subtracting the accumulated amount of the sinking fund payment at time t from the original loan amount:

$$\text{Net amount of loan}_t = L - \text{SFP} \times s_{\overline{t}|j}$$

Remember that when the service payment equals the amount of interest due on the loan, we are not paying off any of the original loan until the end. Since the net amount of the loan at the end of the loan period must be zero, this gives us a way of calculating the total payment required in each period (that is, the service plus the sinking fund contribution).

 ### *Example 5.20*

A loan of $6,000 is repaid annually over 7 years using the sinking fund method. Interest is charged at an annual effective rate of 10% on the loan. Money is invested in the sinking fund at the end of each year and this money earns interest at an annual effective rate of 8%. Find the total annual payment required.

Solution

Interest of $10\% \times 6{,}000 = \$600.00$ (the service payment) is due on the loan at the end of each year. We also need to calculate the annual payment that needs to be made into the sinking fund.

Since the accumulated value of the sinking fund must be equal to the original loan, we have:

$$\text{SFP} \times s_{\overline{7}|8\%} = 6{,}000$$

Since:

$$s_{\overline{7}|8\%} = \frac{1.08^7 - 1}{0.08} = 8.922803$$

We have:

$$\text{SFP} = \frac{6{,}000}{8.922803} = \$672.43$$

So the total annual payment is $1,272.43, consisting of a \$600.00 service payment and a $672.43 contribution into the sinking fund.   ♦♦

Example 5.21

Repeat Example 5.20 using an interest rate of 10% for the sinking fund.

Solution

The same interest of $0.1 \times 6{,}000 = 600$ is due on the loan at the end of each year. The annual payment that needs to be made into the sinking fund is determined by:

$$\text{SFP} \times s_{\overline{7}|10\%} = 6{,}000$$

We have:

$$\text{SFP} = \frac{6{,}000}{s_{\overline{7}|10\%}} = \frac{6{,}000}{9.487171} = \$632.43$$

So the total annual payment is $1,232.43, consisting of \$600.00 as a service payment on the loan and $632.43 into the sinking fund.

If we calculate the annual payment, Y, using the amortization method we get:

$$6{,}000 = Y a_{\overline{7}|10\%} \quad \Rightarrow \quad Y = \frac{6{,}000}{4.868419} = \$1{,}232.43$$ ♦♦

So if the interest rate payable on the loan is the same as the interest earned on the sinking fund, the total annual payments under the amortization and sinking fund methods are the same.

The reason that the two methods give the same answer when the two interest rates are the same is that it then makes no difference whether the payments pay off the loan directly (the amortization method) or if some of the money is set aside (into the sinking fund) where it is increasing in value at exactly the same rate as the outstanding loan.

Consider a loan of $1. The level payment using the amortization method is:

$$\frac{1}{a_{\overline{n}|i}}$$

The service payment on a loan of $1 at an interest rate of i using the sinking fund method is just i. The sinking fund payment on a loan of $1 at an interest rate of i is:

$$\frac{1}{s_{\overline{n}|i}}$$

So when the sinking fund interest rate equals the loan interest rate, we have the total payment on the loan by the amortization method equal to the total payment on the loan by the sinking fund method:

$$\frac{1}{a_{\overline{n}|i}} = i + \frac{1}{s_{\overline{n}|i}}$$

If we have a loan of $1, the left-hand side is the annual payment using the amortization method, while the right hand side is the annual service payment and the annual sinking fund contribution for the sinking fund method.

Algebraically, this relationship can be proven by:

$$\frac{1}{a_{\overline{n}|i}} - \frac{1}{s_{\overline{n}|i}} = \frac{i}{1-v^n} - \frac{i}{(1+i)^n - 1} = \frac{i}{1-v^n} - \frac{iv^n}{1-v^n} = \frac{i(1-v^n)}{1-v^n} = i$$

However, the service payment to the lender may not equal the amount of interest due on the loan. As before with a sinking fund loan, the loan is to be repaid with periodic service payments to the lender and with periodic sinking fund payments into the sinking fund. At the maturity of the loan, the accumulated amount of the loan must equal to the accumulated amount of the service payments plus the accumulated value of the sinking fund payments.

Sinking fund loan general equation of value

At time n, the accumulated value of the loan L at the loan interest rate i equals the accumulated value of the service payments (SP) to the lender at the loan interest rate i plus the accumulated value of the sinking fund payments (SFP) at the sinking fund interest rate j:

$$L(1+i)^n = \text{SP} \times s_{\overline{n}|i} + \text{SFP} \times s_{\overline{n}|j}$$

We must use this equation when the periodic service payments on the loan do not equal the amount of interest due on the loan in each period.

Example 5.22

A loan of $10,000 is repaid annually over 10 years using the sinking fund method. Interest on the loan is charged at an annual effective rate of 5%, but the lender requires a service payment of $600 at the end of each year. Determine the level annual sinking fund payment if the sinking fund credits interest at an annual effective interest rate of 4%.

Solution

In this case, the interest due on the loan is $0.5 \times 10,000 = \$500$ and the service payment is $600. Since the service payment does not equal the interest due on the loan, we need to use the general sinking fund equation of value. Setting the accumulated value of the loan at the loan interest rate equal to the accumulated value of the service payments at the loan interest rate plus the accumulated value of the sinking fund payments at the sinking fund interest rate, we have:

$$10,000(1.05)^{10} = 600s_{\overline{10}|5\%} + \text{SFP} \times s_{\overline{10}|4\%}$$

Calculating the required values:

$$s_{\overline{10}|5\%} = \frac{1.05^{10} - 1}{0.05} = 12.577893$$

$$s_{\overline{10}|4\%} = \frac{1.04^{10} - 1}{0.04} = 12.006107$$

Plugging these into the equation of value, we can solve for the sinking fund payment:

$$SFP = \frac{10,000(1.628895) - 600(12.577893)}{12.006107}$$

$$= \$728.15 \qquad \blacklozenge \blacklozenge$$

The total payment on the loan is the service payment to the lender plus the sinking fund payment. In Example 5.22, the total loan payment is $600.00 + 728.15 = \$1,328.15$.

We can determine the net amount of the loan at any point in time. This is similar to the balance outstanding using the amortization method.

Net amount of sinking fund loan

The general equation for the net amount of the sinking fund loan at time t is determined by subtracting the accumulated amount of the service payment at interest rate i and the accumulated amount of the sinking fund payment at interest rate j from the accumulated value of the original loan amount at interest rate i:

$$\text{Net amount of loan}_t = L(1+i)^t - SP \times s_{\overline{t}|i} - SFP \times s_{\overline{t}|j}$$

At the maturity of the loan, the net amount of the loan is zero.

Example 5.23

Using the information from Example 5.22, determine the net amount of the loan after 3 years.

Solution

The net amount of the loan after 3 years is:

$$10,000(1.05)^3 - 600s_{\overline{3}|5\%} - 728.15s_{\overline{3}|4\%}$$

$$= 10,000(1.157625) - 600(3.152500) - 728.15(3.121600)$$

$$= \$7,411.76 \qquad \blacklozenge \blacklozenge$$

Chapter 5 Practice Questions

Question guide

- Questions 5.1 – 5.9 test material from Sections 5.1 – 5.4.

- Questions 5.10 – 5.16 test material from Sections 5.5 – 5.6.

- Questions 5.17 – 5.20 are from the SOA/CAS Course 2 exam or the IOA/FOA 102 exam.

Question 5.1

A bank lends Elaine $5,000 now. She repays $620 at the end of each quarter for 5 years. Find the net present value for the bank using a nominal rate of interest of 4% a year convertible quarterly.

Question 5.2

A project requires an initial investment of $10,000 and it produces net cash flows of $10,000 one year from now and $2,000 two years from now. The annual effective interest rate is 11%. Determine the project's net present value and internal rate of return.

Question 5.3

A zero-coupon bond costs $85 and it will pay $100 in 5 years. Determine the internal rate of return for this bond.

Question 5.4

A project requires an initial investment of $50,000. The project will generate net cash flows of $15,000 at the end of the first year, $40,000 at the end of the second year, and $10,000 at the end of the third year. The annual effective interest rate is 13%. What is the internal rate of return for the project?

Question 5.5

$30,000 is invested at the start of each year for the next 20 years. The money invested earns interest at an annual effective rate of 4%. The interest earns interest at an effective rate of 2% a year. If all interest payments are made at the end of the year, find the value of the investment at the end of 20 years.

Question 5.6

The real interest rate is 5% and the inflation rate is 3%. Brian expects a payment of $100 in one year, and subsequent payments increase by $5 each year for 5 more years. Determine the accumulated value of these payments at time 6 years.

Question 5.7

Mr. and Mrs. Rich both decide to invest identical amounts of money in the stock of a particular corporation.

They each invested $1,000 at the start of the year when the stock price was $1.00. They also each invested an additional $1,000 on June 30. Mrs. Rich's stock purchase was processed at 1:55 p.m. on that day, while Mr. Rich's was processed at 2:05 p.m.

Unfortunately for Mrs. Rich, the stock price fell suddenly from $1.25 to $0.80 at 2:00 p.m. that day.

By first calculating the number of shares Mr. and Mrs. Rich will each have at the end of the year (when the stock price had risen again to $1.00), find the value of each spouse's fund at the end of the year, and then calculate the dollar-weighted rate of interest in each case.

Question 5.8

On 1/1/03, the value of a pension fund was $4 million. The pension fund received a contribution of $1 million on June 30, 2003 and $1.5 million on March 31, 2004. The fund paid out a large payment of $4,570,000 on November 1, 2004. The value of the fund on June 29, 2003 was $4.3 million; on March 30, 2004 it was $5.2 million; on October 31, 2004 it was $6 million; and on December 31, 2004 it was $2 million. Find the time-weighted rate of interest.

Question 5.9

The following table shows the annual effective interest rates credited to an investment fund by calendar year of investment. The investment year method applies for the first two years, after which a portfolio rate is used.

Calendar year of investment	Investment year rates		Calendar year of portfolio rate	Portfolio rate
	$i(1)$	$i(2)$		
1995	t	5.5%	1997	4.5%
1996	6.0%	6.1%	1998	5.0%
1997	7.0%	$t+2.5\%$	1999	5.5%

An investment of $100 is made at the beginning of 1995 and 1997. The total amount of interest credited by the fund during the year 1998 is $13.81. Calculate t.

Question 5.10

Payments on a $10,000 loan are made quarterly in arrears for 10 years. The annual effective rate of interest is 7%. Find the quarterly payment using the amortization method.

Question 5.11

Payments on a $10,000 loan are made quarterly in arrears for 10 years. The annual effective rate of interest is 7%. Find the principal outstanding after the 6th payment. Use the amortization method.

Question 5.12

Payments on a $10,000 loan are made quarterly in arrears for 10 years. The annual effective rate of interest is 7%. Find the total amount of interest payable on the loan, using the amortization method.

Question 5.13

Payments on a $10,000 loan are made quarterly in arrears for 10 years. The annual effective rate of interest is 7%. Find the interest and principal paid in the 10th payment. Use the amortization method.

Question 5.14

A company takes out a 10-year loan of $50,000 at an annual effective interest rate of 10% to be repaid with level payments at the end of each year. Three years later, the company refinances the loan at an annual effective interest rate of 6%, but it maintains the same maturity date. What is the new level payment after the loan is refinanced?

Question 5.15

A loan of $80,000 is repaid using the amortization method by annual payments at the end of each year for 10 years. Each payment is $1,600 higher than the one before. The annual effective rate of interest is 5%. Find:

(i)   the first payment

(ii)   the interest due in the first period.

Question 5.16

A loan of $50,000 over 15 years can be repaid using either of the following methods:

(i)   amortization method with an annual effective rate of interest of 6%

(ii)   sinking fund method where interest is charged on the loan at an annual effective rate of $i\%$ and is earned on the sinking fund at an annual effective rate of 5.5%.

The payments under both methods are constant and made at the end of each year. If the annual payments are the same under both methods, find i.

Question 5.17   *SOA/CAS (amended)*

A corporation is considering an investment in one of two potential projects. Each project requires an initial investment of $5,000. Project X will produce cash flows of $300 at the end of each 6-month period. The cash flows are expected to continue forever. The first cash flow is expected 6 months after the initial investment. Project Y will have a single cash flow of $Z, which will be received exactly 5 years after the initial investment. The IRR on both projects is the same. Calculate the net present value of Project Y, using an annual effective interest rate of 10%.

Question 5.18   *SOA/CAS*

A 20-year loan of $20,000 may be repaid under the following two methods:

i)   amortization method with equal annual payments at an annual effective rate of 6.5%

ii)   sinking fund method in which the lender receives an annual effective rate of 8% and the sinking fund earns an annual effective rate of j.

Both methods require a payment of X to be made at the end of each year for 20 years.

Calculate j.

Question 5.19   *SOA/CAS*

You are given the following information about the activity in two different investment accounts:

Account K			
	Fund value before activity	Activity	
Date		Deposit	Withdrawal
January 1, 1999	100.0		
July 1, 1999	125.0		X
October 1, 1999	110.0	2X	
December 31, 1999	125.0		

Account L			
	Fund value before activity	Activity	
Date		Deposit	Withdrawal
January 1, 1999	100.0		
July 1, 1999	125.0		X
December 31, 1999	105.8		

During 1999, the dollar-weighted return for investment account K equals the time-weighted return for investment account L, which equals i.

Calculate i.

Question 5.20   *FOA/IOA*

A loan was taken out on September 1, 1998 and was repaid with the following increasing annuity:

The first payment was made on July 1, 1999 and was $1,000. Thereafter, payments were made on November 1, March 1, and July 1 until March 1, 2004 inclusive. Each payment was 5% greater than its predecessor. The effective rate of interest throughout the period was 6% per annum.

(i)   Show the amount of the loan was $17,692 to the nearest dollar.

(ii)   Calculate the amount of principal repaid on July 1, 1999.

(iii)   Calculate both the principal component and the interest component of the seventh payment.

6

Financial instruments

Overview

Assets can be split into two categories: **real assets** and **financial assets**. Real assets are productive, such as real estate, factories and machines. Financial assets are claims on the income from real assets (or from the government).

One party's financial asset is a financial liability to the other party of the transaction, which is why financial assets and liabilities are more generally called financial instruments. Financial instruments are the focus of this chapter.

An individual or a corporation may have excess cash or may be short of cash. With excess cash, a person or a corporation can purchase an investment. When a corporation is short on cash, it may need to raise money by issuing debt or equity. Parties with excess cash provide financing to other parties that are short of cash with **financial instruments**.

Financial instruments provide financial capital and trade on financial markets. There are many types of financial instruments, such as **money market investments**, **bonds** (debt), **stocks** (equity), **mutual funds**, **guaranteed investment contracts**, and **derivative securities**. Derivative securities, such as **options**, **forwards** and **swaps**, are derived from an underlying asset or index and their values are contingent on the value of an underlying asset or index.

This chapter examines several financial instruments at a fairly high level, and then focuses on equity and debt valuation in more detail. The valuation of selected derivative securities is also discussed.

6.1 Types of financial instruments

The discussion of financial instruments in this section is not intended to present an exhaustive list of the various types of financial instruments. Rather, this discussion provides an overview of some of the most common financial instruments.

6.1.1 Money market instruments

Money market instruments are cash-like investments that consist of short-term, liquid, low-risk debt securities. A liquid asset is one that can be easily purchased and resold on a secondary market with low transaction costs. The money market is part of the fixed-income market, that is, the income generated by these investments is fixed at issue.

T-bills, certificates of deposit, and commercial paper are three examples of money market instruments.

Treasury bills (T-bills)

Treasury bills are short-term debt instruments issued by the US government. T-bills are currently issued with 4, 13, and 26 week terms. In the past, the US government issued T-bills with terms of 52 weeks, and it may choose to resume issuing these longer term T-bills in the future.

The US government promises to pay the face amount of the T-bill at the end of the term. T-bills do not pay coupons. Investors purchase T-bills at a discount to face value and earn an investment return from the difference between the purchase price and the face value. Income earned on T-bills is exempt from state and local taxes.

T-bill price

T-bills are quoted on a simple discount basis, assuming a 360-day year. The formula for calculating the price of a T-bill is:

$$\text{Price} = (\text{Face amount})\left[1 - (\text{Discount yield})\frac{n}{360}\right]$$

where:

$n =$ number of days until maturity

For example, an investor purchases a 91-day T-bill with a discount yield of 3.47% and a face amount of \$10,000. The purchase price is:

$$\text{Price} = 10,000\left[1 - (0.0347)\frac{91}{360}\right] = \$9,912.2861$$

The use of 360 in the denominator is simply a convention leftover from the days before calculators were readily available.

While T-bills are not usually quoted on an annual effective yield basis, the annual effective yield of a T-bill can still be determined. The annual effective yield on the T-bill is:

$$y = \left(\frac{\text{Face amount}}{\text{Price}}\right)^{\left(\frac{365}{n}\right)} - 1 = \left(\frac{10,000}{9,912.2861}\right)^{\frac{365}{91}} - 1 = 3.60\%$$

Certificates of deposit (CD)

A certificate of deposit is a time deposit with a bank that cannot be withdrawn on demand. The investor receives interest and principal only at the end of the fixed term. In many respects, a certificate of deposit is similar to a savings account, except that access to the deposit is restricted. CDs are called time deposits because the depositor does not have access to the deposit before the maturity date without incurring a penalty.

The interest rate credited to CDs may be fixed at outset or may vary over the term of the deposit. CDs are insured with the Federal Deposit Insurance Corporation (FDIC) up to $100,000, which provides protection against the risk of default.

Commercial paper

Commercial paper is a short-term unsecured debt note, usually issued by a large corporation. Typical terms are for one to two months, although commercial paper may be issued with a term of up to 270 days. The face amount of commercial paper is usually a multiple of $100,000.

A large company may prefer to issue commercial paper instead of borrowing money from a bank. Commercial paper is considered a relatively safe asset since the term is short, making it unlikely that the credit quality of the issuer will decline significantly in the short time until maturity.

6.1.2 Bonds

A bond is a debt instrument that requires the issuer to repay the initial principal amount plus interest. The issuer of the bond can be a government entity or a corporation. The issuer borrows the face amount from the bondholder, pays interest on the debt until the bond matures, and then repays the redemption amount at maturity. Bonds are usually issued with terms to maturity of between 1 and 30 years. A bond with a maturity of more than 1 year but less than 10 years may also be called a **note**.

Most bonds make regular interest payments to the bondholders. The interest payments are known as **coupon** payments and can be paid annually or semiannually, the latter being more common. Interest paid to bondholders is tax-deductible for the issuer. In bankruptcy, the issuer must pay off the bondholders before paying the stockholders.

If the interest rate is fixed over the life of the bond, it is a **fixed-rate bond**. If the interest rate is allowed to fluctuate, it is a **floating-rate bond**. A **zero-coupon bond** does not pay interest until the maturity of the bond, and is sold at a substantial discount to the redemption amount.

A **callable bond** gives the issuer the option to repay the principal before the maturity date. A **convertible bond** is a bond that includes an option to exchange the bond for a fixed number of shares of the common stock of the company that issued the bond.

Default risk is the risk that the bond issuer is not able to make the coupon or principal payments. Like T-bills, US government bonds have no default risk since they are backed by the full faith and credit of the US government. Rating agencies publish bond ratings for corporate bonds, which are based on an assessment of the level of default risk of the issuing corporation.

The price of a bond depends on the risk of default. The higher the default risk, the lower the bond's price will be. **Investment-grade bonds** have a low expected default rate. **High-yield bonds**, also known as **junk bonds**, have a much greater risk of default and therefore pay higher coupons than investment-grade bonds in order to compensate the lender for accepting the default risk.

Bonds that are secured with collateral have a senior claim over unsecured bonds. A mortgage can be thought of as a bond that is secured by real estate. Bonds that are not secured are called **debentures**.

Bonds are covered in more detail in Section 6.2.

6.1.3 Common stocks

A share of **common stock** represents an ownership share in the issuing company. Common stock is also referred to as **equity** or simply **stock**. The owner of a share of stock is entitled to receive a share of the company's profits in the form of **dividends**, which are paid at the discretion of the company. Common stock is a **residual** claim on the company, so shareholders only get paid after the obligations to the debt holders have been met. Dividends paid to common stockholders are not tax-deductible for the issuer.

The stockholder is also entitled to vote at the company's annual meeting on issues of corporate governance. The stockholders vote for the board of directors, to whom the power to run the company on behalf of the stockholders is delegated.

Stocks are covered in more detail in Section 6.3.

6.1.4 Preferred stocks

Preferred stock is a hybrid between equity and debt, although it is usually classified as equity. Preferred stockholders receive income in the form of fixed dividends (like bond coupons), but preferred stock dividends are paid at the company's discretion, similar to those on common stock. There is no maturity date for preferred stock, although preferred stock may be repurchased and retired by the issuer.

Preferred dividends must be paid before any common dividends are paid. If preferred dividends are suspended, preferred stock often has cumulative dividend rights, which means that the dividends accumulate during the period they are not paid, rather than being lost.

Preferred stockholders usually do not have any voting rights, but sometimes they may be granted special voting rights. A company may even issue several classes of preferred stock with different rights.

Preferred stockholders are paid after the bondholders and before the common stockholders. Dividends paid to preferred stockholders are not tax-deductible for the issuer. Corporations that own preferred stock can generally deduct a portion of the preferred dividends from their taxable income, but individuals do not receive this tax benefit.

6.1.5 Mutual funds

An individual investor may not have enough money to invest in a large bond issue. A mutual fund pools together the deposits of many investors and places those deposits under the control of a professional money manager. Each investor can then buy shares (or units) in the mutual fund and receive a pro-rata share of the fund's income and capital gains or losses. A mutual fund allows a small investor better diversification than could be achieved on his or her own.

A mutual fund can invest in many different financial instruments, such as money market instruments, bonds and stocks. There are hundreds, if not thousands, of fund choices in the US alone. A fund may specialize in one type of security or market sector, or it may invest in a wide range of securities.

If the fund manager actively tries to outperform the market, the investment strategy of the fund is called **active**. If the fund manager's goal is to match a broad market index (*eg* the S&P500), the fund is called an **index fund** and the investment strategy is said to be **passive**.

Funds that are sold by investment advisors often require the payment of a commission, or **load**, in addition to a management fee (usually expressed as a percentage of the assets under management). No-load funds do not charge a commission.

6.1.6 Guaranteed investment contracts (GICs)

GICs are offered by insurance companies and promise a guaranteed rate of return. The investor deposits funds with the insurance company, which promises to return the funds plus a guaranteed rate of interest at a certain date in the future.

The interest earned on the initial investment may be reinvested at the guaranteed rate, or it may be reinvested at some lower fixed rate, or even at a variable rate.

For example, suppose that an investor deposits $1,000,000 in a 5-year GIC with an insurance company that guarantees an annual 6% interest rate on the fund. If the GIC specifies that interest is reinvested at 6% within the GIC, then the lump sum payable to the investor at 5 years is:

$$1,000,000(1.06)^5 = \$1,338,225.58$$

A term-to-maturity of five years is common. The investor often has no access to the funds before maturity. Since the rate of return is fixed, GICs are generally viewed as conservative investments. GICs are considered illiquid since there is no established secondary market.

From a regulatory standpoint, GICs are treated as insurance contracts rather than investment contracts, because they include an option for the investor to purchase an annuity with the proceeds at the maturity of the contract. This option is rarely exercised since the annuity rates are not usually very competitive, so the investor generally receives a lump sum at maturity.

6.1.7 Derivative securities

A derivative investment derives its value from an underlying asset, such as a stock or a specified index. In this section, we'll discuss six examples of derivatives: options, forwards, futures, swaps, caps and floors.

Options

There are two main types of options: call options and put options.

A **call option** provides the buyer with the right, but not the obligation, to buy an underlying asset at a specified **exercise price**. The call buyer pays a premium to the call seller to buy the option. Call options increase in value when the price of the underlying asset value increases.

A **put option** provides the buyer with the right, but not the obligation, to sell the underlying asset at a specified price. The put buyer pays a premium to the put seller to buy the option. Put options increase in value when the price of the underlying asset value decreases.

A **European option** can only be exercised on the expiration date of the option, but an **American option** can be exercised on or before the expiration date. For example, an American call option on XYZ stock with an exercise price of $50 gives the holder of the call an option to buy a share of XYZ stock for $50 from the call writer at any time before the expiration of the option. Therefore, if the stock price rises above $50, the holder of the call option can still buy the stock for $50 by exercising the call option. A European put option on the same stock with an exercise price of $40 gives the put holder an option to sell a share of XYZ stock for $40 to the put writer at the expiration of the option. Therefore, if the stock price falls below $40, the holder of the put option can still sell the stock for $40 by exercising the put option.

With an option, the investor's loss is limited to the premium paid to purchase the option since the investor can decide to let the option expire without exercising the option.

Options are covered in more detail in Section 6.5.

Forward contracts

A **forward contract** is an agreement between two parties to buy or sell an asset at a pre-agreed price (the **forward price**) at a specified future time. One party agrees to buy and the other party agrees to sell the asset at the forward price. No cash changes hands until the maturity of the forward contract. The forward contract controls future price risk by locking in now the price at which the future transaction will occur. The forward price is an estimate of the future asset price.

For example, let's say Leonard and Larry enter into a forward contract for a share of XYZ stock. Leonard agrees to sell one share of XYZ stock to Larry in six months at the forward price of $50. Under the terms of agreement, Leonard must sell the share to Larry in six month's time for $50 and Larry must buy the share from Leonard in six month's time for $50, regardless of the actual share price at that time. If the price of the stock in six months is $55, then the forward contract produces a loss of $5 for Leonard and a profit of $5 for Larry.

Forward contracts are covered again in Section 6.5.

Futures contracts

A **futures contract** is a standardized form of a forward contract. Futures contracts differ from forward contracts in the following ways. Futures contracts are traded on an exchange – both parties to a futures contract make their agreement directly with the exchange rather than with each other. Futures contracts are only available in specified sizes, such as 1,000 shares, and on specified assets. Futures are usually settled by making a cash payment equal to the net profit or net loss instead of physically transferring the underlying asset at expiration.

With a futures contract, a trader commits to buy or sell an asset or its cash value at a specified future delivery date for a price to be paid at contract maturity. The buyer of the asset is said to have a **long position** while the seller of the asset has a **short position**. The buyer is obliged to buy the asset at the agreed upon price and the seller is obliged to sell the asset at the agreed upon price.

A futures contract generates cash flows before contract expiration since the position is **marked to market** each day. This means that at the end of each day, the new futures price is noted, and all existing futures contracts are "trued up" (*ie* reset) to that price. A cash payment is made to ensure that the long position and the short position are compensated for this change. Forward contracts, unlike futures contracts, are not marked to market.

For example, let's say that Larry takes a long futures position to buy an asset with a futures price of $50, and the closing futures price the next day is $51. Larry's contract is marked to market, so that his new position is an agreement to pay $51 for the asset. Larry didn't plan on paying more than $50 when he entered into the long position, but he is compensated for the higher futures price because $1 is credited to his broker account at the same time that the futures price is updated to $51. At the same time, $1 is deducted from the short futures position.

A more detailed example of marking to market is presented in Section 6.5.

Swaps

A **swap** is a contract between two parties in which they agree to exchange a series of payments.

An **interest rate swap** is used to convert variable floating-rate interest payments into fixed-rate interest payments, or vice versa. There are two parties to an interest rate swap: the floating-rate payer and the fixed-rate payer. The floating-rate payer pays interest based on an interest rate that can change with market conditions each period. The fixed-rate payer pays a fixed interest rate in each period.

The fixed payments can be thought of as interest payments on a deposit at a fixed rate, while the variable payments are the interest on the same deposit at a variable or floating interest rate. This deposit is called the **notional principal** since no actual exchange of principal takes place.

For example, a company that has variable-rate borrowing but would prefer to pay a fixed rate of interest can do so by entering an interest rate swap as the fixed-rate payer. The company would pay an annual fixed interest rate (*eg* 6%) into the swap, and receive a variable interest rate, which it would use to offset the cost of its variable-rate borrowing. The net result to the company is a fixed interest rate on the money it has borrowed.

In addition to the two counterparties, there usually is a dealer who arranges the swap. The dealer profits from the swap by providing a lower fixed rate to the floating-rate payer than the fixed rate paid by the fixed-rate payer. In this example, the dealer might keep 0.1% of the fixed rate and pay a 5.9% annual fixed interest rate to the floating-rate payer. The floating-rate payer pays the variable rate to the dealer who passes it on to the fixed-rate payer.

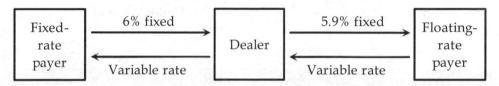

The deal is usually structured so that only the net payment is made. So, if the variable rate is 7% and the notional principal is $1,000,000, the fixed-rate payer receives an annual payment of $(0.07 - 0.06) \times 1,000,000 = \$10,000$, the floating-rate payer will make an annual payment of $(0.07 - 0.059) \times 1,000,000 = \$11,000$, and the dealer nets $(0.06 - 0.059) \times 1,000,000 = \$1,000$.

Caps

An **interest rate cap** provides protection against rising interest rates. For example, a company may have a liability that pays a variable interest rate. If the company is concerned about the interest rate rising significantly, it can use an interest rate cap to set an upper limit on the interest payment it is obliged to make.

The owner of a cap receives a payment at each payment date based on the difference between the agreed strike price and an agreed index rate. If interest is paid p times per year, the owner of the cap receives a payment on the payment date of:

$$\text{Cap payment} = \text{Max}\left[\frac{\text{Index rate} - \text{Strike rate}}{p}, 0\right] \times \text{Notional amount}$$

For example, let's say that an interest rate cap makes quarterly payments, matures in one year, and has a notional amount of $10,000,000. The strike rate is 8% and the index rate develops as shown in the next table:

Year	3-month index rate
0.25	9%
0.50	8%
0.75	7%
1.00	10%

The first cash flow from the cap after 3 months is:

$$\text{Cap payment} = \text{Max}\left[\frac{9\% - 8\%}{4}, 0\right] \times 10,000,000 = \$25,000$$

There are no cash flows from the cap at 6 months and 9 months since the index rate is below or equal to the strike rate. The cash flow from the cap after one year is:

$$\text{Cap payment} = \text{Max}\left[\frac{10\% - 8\%}{4}, 0\right] \times 10,000,000 = \$50,000$$

Floors

An **interest rate floor** is similar to an interest rate cap, but the floor protects the investor by paying only when interest rates fall below the floor. A company that receives floating-rate payments can use an interest-rate floor to set a lower limit on those payments.

The owner of an interest rate floor receives payments whenever the index rate is below the strike rate. If interest is paid p times per year, the owner of the floor receives a payment on the payment date of:

$$\text{Floor payment} = \text{Max}\left[\frac{\text{Strike rate} - \text{Index rate}}{p}, 0\right] \times \text{Notional amount}$$

6.2 *Bond valuation*

A government or a corporation may raise money by issuing debt via **bonds**. Investors can purchase these bonds, which entitle them to receive one or more future interest payments as well as a final payment when the bond matures. This final payment is made up of the last interest payment and the **redemption payment**, which is the amount to pay off (*ie* redeem) the bond at the **maturity date**. The length of time until redemption is called the **term-to-maturity** or the **term** of the bond.

The regular interest payments are called **coupons**, and they are normally paid semiannually. Bonds with coupons are called **coupon bonds**, and bonds without coupons are called **accumulation bonds** or **zero-coupon bonds**.

The coupons and redemption payment are related to the **nominal** or **par value** of the bond, which is also known as the **face amount**. This serves purely to specify the size of a particular holding and hence determine the amounts of the redemption payment and any coupons. Very often the par value is $100 or $1,000. It is generally not the price actually paid for the bond. If the redemption payment is equal to the par value, the bond is said to be *redeemed at par*. This is usually the case unless we are told otherwise.

Each bond issue has a specified **annual coupon rate**, which is usually expressed as a nominal rate convertible semiannually. For example, if a bond has a 6% annual coupon, the interest paid each year will total 6% of the nominal value or face amount, so each semiannual coupon will be 3% of the face amount.

Bond prices are set by supply and demand in the financial markets. The rate of return provided by a bond can be measured in several ways, but most commonly by its **yield-to-maturity**.

Yield-to-maturity

The **yield-to-maturity (YTM)** is the internal rate of return (IRR) on the bond.

It is the value of i that satisfies the equation of value for the bond:

Bond price = present value of coupons + present value of redemption payment

---

So, we can solve for the yield-to-maturity if we know the price of the bond and the cash flows (*ie* the coupons and the redemption payment) of the bond.

Similarly, we can calculate the price of a bond from the equation of value if we know the bond's yield-to-maturity and its cash flows. The price of a bond is usually quoted for a nominal holding (or face amount) of $100 or $1,000. This is often abbreviated to *per $100* or *per $1,000 nominal*.

The term yield-to-maturity is frequently abbreviated to yield. However, there are other yield measures associated with a bond, such as the current yield.

Current yield

The **current yield** is the annual coupon amount divided by the bond price.

Calculations relating to bonds involve the techniques that we have learned in previous chapters. However, bonds have their own specific notation, which is introduced in this section.

Example 6.1

A 10-year bond, which has just been issued, provides semiannual coupons of 6% a year in arrears. It is redeemed at par. What price is paid (per $100 nominal value) if the bond yields an annual effective rate of interest of 8%?

Solution

If we assume a $100 nominal value, the annual amount of coupon received is $0.06 \times 100 = \$6$. This is actually paid as coupons of $3 every six months. The redemption payment is $100. The timeline diagram of the bond cash flows is:

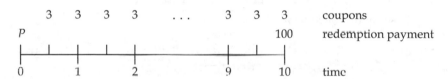

Let P denote the price of the bond:

$$P = 6a^{(2)}_{\overline{10}|8\%} + 100v^{10}_{8\%} \quad \text{or} \quad P = 3a_{\overline{2\times10}|(1.08)^{0.5}-1} + 100v^{10}_{8\%}$$

Using an 8% annual effective yield and the first of the above equations, we have:

$$P = 6\frac{1-1.08^{-10}}{2\left((1.08)^{0.5}-1\right)} + 100(1.08)^{-10} = \$87.37$$

Using the second of the above equations, we have:

$$P = 3\frac{1-1.03923^{-20}}{0.03923} + 100(1.08)^{-10} = \$87.37$$

◆◆

Note that the denominator of the semiannual annuity-immediate present value factor is the nominal yield rate, convertible semiannually, as required by the formula.

This example involves two interest rates. The annual effective *yield* of 8% is the internal rate of return achieved on the investment. When the price of this bond is $87.37, the bond is priced to yield an annual effective rate of 8%. The 6% nominal rate convertible semiannually is the *coupon* rate, which determines the amount of the coupon payments.

The following standard bond notation is useful.

Bond notation

P	Price paid
F	Face amount (or nominal value or par value)
r	Coupon rate per payment period in terms of the face amount
g	Coupon rate per payment period in terms of the redemption amount
i	Yield-to-maturity rate per payment period
C	Redemption value (equal to F unless stated otherwise)
K	Present value of redemption value: $K = C(1+i)^{-n}$
G	Base amount (amount which invested now would generate interest equal to the coupon payments indefinitely): $G = Fr / i$
n	Number of coupon payments

If the time to maturity is given in years, then the number of coupons, n, for a semiannual bond is twice the number of years to maturity.

Let's rework Example 6.1 using the standard bond notation. Using the notation given, we have:

$$F = C = 100; \quad r = g = \frac{0.06}{2} = 0.03; \quad Fr = 3.00$$

$$i = (1.08)^{0.5} - 1 = 0.039230 \quad \text{(semiannual effective yield)}$$

$$n = 2 \times 10 = 20 \text{ semiannual coupons}$$

Note that the coupon rate is 6% a year, payable semiannually. However, the definition of the symbol r relates to a single coupon period, so that $r = 0.03$.

Working in years using a semiannual annuity-immediate factor, the equation of value is:

$$P = 2Fr a_{\overline{0.5n}|}^{(2)} + Cv^{0.5n} = 6a_{\overline{10}|8\%}^{(2)} + Cv_{8\%}^{10} = \$87.37$$

Alternatively, we can work in half-year periods where the semiannual effective yield is i:

$$P = Fr a_{\overline{n}|i} + Cv_i^n = 3a_{\overline{20}|3.923\%} + Cv_{3.923\%}^{20} = \$87.37$$

Note the difference between r and g here: r is a percentage calculated by reference to the face amount; g is calculated by reference to the redemption payment. If the bond is redeemed at par, then r and g are equal. So, $Cg = Fr$, ie the redemption amount times the coupon rate per redemption amount equals the face amount times the coupon rate per face amount.

The coupon rate for a bond is normally determined from the total annual coupons, so for a bond with semiannual coupons the nominal annual coupon rate convertible semiannually would be $2r$.

If the compounding frequency of the yield is not specified, it is generally assumed to be compounded at the same frequency as the coupon payments.

The bond price formula can be re-written using the standard bond notation.

Bond price

For a semiannual bond, where n is the number of semiannual coupons, i is the *semiannual* effective yield, and r is the semiannual effective coupon rate, the price of a bond is:

$$P = Fra_{\overline{n}|i} + Cv_i^n = Fra_{\overline{n}|i} + K$$

Alternatively, the same formula can be expressed using the semiannual annuity-immediate present value factor, where i is the *annual* effective yield, but n is still the number of semiannual coupons and r is the semiannual effective coupon rate:

$$P = 2Fra_{\overline{0.5n}|i}^{(2)} + Cv_i^{0.5n} = 2Fra_{\overline{0.5n}|i}^{(2)} + K$$

where $a_{\overline{0.5n}|i}^{(2)} = \dfrac{1-(1+i)^{-0.5n}}{i^{(2)}}$.

It is important to be consistent and work either in semiannual periods or annual periods. Many students find it more convenient to work in semiannual periods.

Example 6.2

A 20-year zero-coupon bond is redeemed at par. If the price paid per $1,000 face amount is $538.76, determine the annual effective yield rate.

Solution

Using the standard bond notation, we have:

$$F = C = 1,000; \qquad P = 538.76; \qquad n = 20 \text{ years}$$

A zero-coupon bond is an accumulation bond that has no coupons. Working in years:

$$P = 538.76 = 1,000v^{20}$$

So $v^{20} = 0.53876$. This can be solved for the annual effective yield i as follows:

$$v = (1+i)^{-1} = 0.53876^{\frac{1}{20}} \quad \Rightarrow \quad i = 0.53876^{-\frac{1}{20}} - 1 = 3.14\% \qquad \blacklozenge\blacklozenge$$

Let's determine the price of the bond from Example 6.2 assuming an annual effective yield of 4%. In this case, we have:

$$P = 1,000(1.04)^{-20} = \$456.39$$

The bond's price falls from $538.76 to $456.39 when the yield increases from 3.14% to 4.0%. This illustrates an important point about bonds.

When a typical bond is issued, the coupon rate is fixed at the issue date for the life of the bond according to the prevailing bond coupon rate for a similarly risky bond with the same time to maturity. However, interest rates in the market are likely to fluctuate after the issue date, so the holder of the bond is exposed to **interest-rate risk**. That is to say, if interest rates rise after the bond is issued, the bondholder continues to receive the lower coupon rate instead of the higher prevailing market rate. As interest rates go up, the present value of the bond goes down. The bond is worth less because the present value of the future coupons and redemption amount is lower, since they are being discounted at a higher rate.

The converse is also true. As interest rates go down, the present value of the bond goes up. In this case, the coupon rate is greater than the prevailing market rate and the bondholder receives a higher coupon than could be achieved at the new lower market rate.

Bonds are also exposed to **default risk**. The borrower may default on paying the coupon if the company faces financial distress. Bondholders are creditors, so they are exposed to the risk that not all of the coupon payments will be paid by the borrower. This is one of the reasons why a creditor needs to perform detailed financial analysis on a potential borrower before agreeing to buy a bond. The coupon rate should reflect the credit risk of the borrower's potential for default. The higher the risk of default, the higher the coupon the borrower will be required to pay.

The longer the time to maturity of a bond, the greater the interest-rate risk and default risk faced by the investor. The longer maturity provides more opportunity for unexpected future events to negatively affect the borrower's ability to repay the bond. Also, the longer maturity means that the return of principal is pushed further into the future, delaying principal repayment and further discounting the present value of the principal repayment.

Example 6.3

A bond pays semiannual coupons at an annual rate of 10% of the nominal value. The annual effective yield-to-maturity is currently 4%, and the price paid per $1,000 par value is $1,404.06. If the bond is redeemed after 7 years, calculate the redemption payment.

Solution

The redemption payment is C. For a face amount of $1,000, we have:

$$P = 1,404.06$$
$$= 100 a_{\overline{7}|}^{(2)} + C v^7$$

Working in years, this can be evaluated at an annual effective yield of 4% and a nominal annual yield convertible semiannually of $2[(1.04)^{0.5} - 1] = 3.9608\%$:

$$P = 1,404.06 = 100 \frac{1 - 1.04^{-7}}{0.039608} + C(1.04)^{-7}$$
$$\Rightarrow \quad C = \$1,050.00$$

Alternatively, we could work in half-years using the semiannual effective rate of $1.04^{\frac{1}{2}} - 1 = 1.9804\%$. This would give an equation of value of:

$$P = 1,404.06$$
$$= 50 a_{\overline{14}|1.9804\%} + C v_{1.9804\%}^{14}$$

◆◆

Example 6.4

An n-year bond pays annual coupons of 5% semiannually. The annual effective yield is 8% and the price paid per $100 par value is $86. The bond is redeemed at 110%. Find n.

Solution

Per $100 face amount, we have:

$$86 = 5 a_{\overline{n}|}^{(2)} + 110 v^n$$

Working in years and using an annual effective yield of 8% and a nominal annual yield convertible semiannually of $2[(1.08)^{0.5}-1] = 7.8461\%$, where n is the number of years, we have:

$$86 = 5\frac{(1-v^n)}{0.078461}+110v^n = 63.72595(1-v^n)+110v^n = 63.72595+46.27405v^n$$

$$\Rightarrow \quad v^n = 0.48135 \quad \Rightarrow \quad n = \frac{\ln 0.48135}{\ln 1.08^{-1}} = 9.5$$

An alternative approach is to evaluate the right-hand side of the first equation for various values of n. For example, $n = 5$ gives \$95.22, $n = 10$ gives \$85.16, and $n = 9.5$ gives \$86.00.   ◆◆

The **base amount** of a bond, G, is the amount invested now that would generate interest equal to the coupons forever. It is the amount that would generate a perpetuity-immediate where the cash flows are the coupons. A formula for the price of a bond in terms of C and G is:

$$P = G+(C-G)v^n$$

The present value of a bond equals the base amount of the bond plus the present value of the redemption amount less the present value of the base amount. Logically, this makes sense. The base amount is the amount that generates the coupon amounts forever. This is added to the present value of the redemption amount, but the present value of the coupons after time n is subtracted, since the coupons do not continue forever. The coupons stop at time n.

Revisiting Example 6.1, we have:

$$P = G+(C-G)v^n = \frac{3}{0.03923}+\left(100-\frac{3}{0.03923}\right)(1.03923)^{-20} = \$87.37$$

We can derive another useful formula to determine the price of a bond. When we recognize that $v^n = 1-ia_{\overline{n|}}$, we can substitute this relationship into the bond price formula and simplify:

$$P = Fra_{\overline{n|}}+Cv^n = Fra_{\overline{n|}}+C(1-ia_{\overline{n|}}) = Fra_{\overline{n|}}+C-Cia_{\overline{n|}} = C+(Fr-Ci)a_{\overline{n|}}$$

This bond price formula retains the annuity factor, but it no longer involves the present value of the redemption amount, so it may be easier to use in some cases.

Premium and discount

Whether a bond is trading at a price above or below the redemption value is determined by the relationship between i and g. A bond that has a higher coupon rate than the market yield rate trades at a premium (*ie* at a price above the redemption value), while a bond with a lower coupon rate than the market yield rate trades at a discount (*ie* at a price below the redemption value).

A bond is called a **premium bond** when its price is greater than its redemption value.

Premium

A bond trades at a **premium** if the purchase price is greater than the redemption value, *ie* when $P > C$. The premium is the difference between the purchase price and the redemption value:

    Premium $= P-C$

A bond is a premium bond when g, the coupon rate per payment period in terms of the redemption amount, is greater than i, the yield rate per payment period. This makes sense because the bond's coupon is paying more than the bond's yield, so the bond's price will be greater than its redemption amount.

A bond is called a **discount bond** when its price is less than its redemption value.

Discount

A bond trades at a **discount** if the purchase price is less than the redemption value, *ie* when $P < C$. The discount itself is the difference between the redemption value and the purchase price:

$$\text{Discount} = C - P$$

A bond is a discount bond when g, the coupon rate per payment period in terms of the redemption amount, is less than i, the yield rate per payment period. This makes sense because the bond's coupon is paying less than the bond's yield, so the bond's price will be less than its redemption amount.

Example 6.5

For Example 6.1, Example 6.2, Example 6.3, and Example 6.4, determine the amount of premium or discount in each case.

Solution

Example 6.1: The price is $87.37. The redemption amount is $100. It is sold at a discount. The discount is $100 - 87.37 = \$12.63$.

Example 6.2: The price is $538.76. The redemption amount is $1,000. It is sold at a discount. The discount is $461.24.

Example 6.3: The price is $1,404.06. The redemption amount is $1,050. It is sold at a premium. The premium is $1,404.06 - 1,050 = \$354.06$.

Example 6.4: The price is $86. The redemption amount is $110. It is sold at a discount. The discount is $24.   ♦♦

Amortization of premium and accrual of discount: constant yield method

The value of a bond is clear at the time of purchase since its value is equal to its purchase price. Furthermore, when the bond is paid off at maturity, its value is again clear because it is equal to the redemption value. In this section, a method is introduced to assign values to the bond after the purchase and before the maturity of the bond. These values are called **book values**, and they are based on the yield at which the bond is purchased (which is known as the **book yield**). Unlike the market value of a bond, the book value does not change in response to changes in the market yield that occur after the bond is purchased.

Book value (prospective formula)

Using the prospective formula, the book value immediately after the t-th coupon is paid is equal to the present value of the future coupon payments plus the present value of the redemption amount:

$$BV_t = Fra_{\overline{n-t}|i} + Cv_i^{n-t} = Cga_{\overline{n-t}|i} + Cv_i^{n-t}$$

where:

$i = \text{book yield} = \text{yield at time of purchase (when } t = 0)$

Note that the initial book value is the purchase price of the bond, and the final book value is the redemption value of the bond:

$$BV_0 = Cga_{\overline{n}|i} + Cv_i^n = P$$
$$BV_n = C$$

The book value is therefore an accurate depiction of the value of the bond at the time of purchase and at the time the bond matures. In between those two times, the book value provides a reasonable and predictable value for the bond. Even though a bond's book value may differ from its market value between the times of purchase and maturity, the predictable nature of book values and the ease with which they can be calculated have led to the frequent use of book values in accounting statements.

A retrospective approach can also be used to determine bond book values.

Book value (retrospective formula)

Using the retrospective formula, the book value immediately after the t-th coupon is paid is equal to the accumulated value of the purchase price minus the accumulated value of the coupon payments:

$$BV_t = P(1+i)^t - Frs_{\overline{t}|i} = P(1+i)^t - Cgs_{\overline{t}|i}$$

where:

i = book yield = yield at time of purchase (when $t = 0$)

P = original purchase price

We can relate the book values from one time to the next. The book value at time t is the previous book value plus interest minus the amount of the coupon payment made at time t. We use the formula from the prospective formula to demonstrate this below:

$$BV_{t-1} = Cga_{\overline{n-t+1}|} + Cv^{n-t+1}$$
$$\Rightarrow BV_{t-1}(1+i) - Cg(1+i)a_{\overline{n-t+1}|} + Cv^{n-t} = Cg\ddot{a}_{\overline{n-t+1}|} + Cv^{n-t} = Cg(1 + a_{\overline{n-t}|}) + Cv^{n-t}$$
$$\Rightarrow BV_{t-1}(1+i) - Cg = Cga_{\overline{n-t}|} + Cv^{n-t} = BV_t$$
$$\Rightarrow BV_t = BV_{t-1}(1+i) - Cg$$

The **interest earned** in the t-th period is the periodic effective yield times the book value at the end of period $(t-1)$.

Interest earned

The interest earned in time period t is the periodic effective yield multiplied by the previous book value:

$$I_t = iBV_{t-1}$$

The book value calculation can be related to the interest earned:

$$BV_t = BV_{t-1}(1+i) - Cg$$
$$= BV_{t-1} + BV_{t-1}i - Cg$$
$$= BV_{t-1} + I_t - Cg$$

The **premium amortization** is the amount by which the book value decreases in value over the t-th time period. The premium amortization amounts are positive for bonds purchased at a premium and negative for bonds purchased at a discount:

$$PA_t = BV_{t-1} - BV_t$$

For bonds purchased at a premium, the premium amortization is equal to the amount of bond premium that is amortized in period t. For bonds purchased at a discount, the negative of the premium amortization is equal to the amount of bond discount that is accrued (or accumulated) in period t.

The premium amortization can be related to the coupon and interest earned:

$$BV_t = BV_{t-1} + I_t - Cg$$
$$\Rightarrow BV_{t-1} - BV_t = Cg - I_t$$
$$\Rightarrow PA_t = Cg - I_t$$

With a bit of algebra, we can derive another convenient expression for the premium amortization:

$$
\begin{aligned}
PA_t &= BV_{t-1} - BV_t \\
&= Cga_{\overline{n-t+1}|} + Cv^{n-t+1} - Cga_{\overline{n-t}|} - Cv^{n-t} \\
&= Cg(a_{\overline{n-t+1}|} - a_{\overline{n-t}|}) + C(v^{n-t+1} - v^{n-t}) \\
&= Cg(v^{n-t+1}) + C(v^{n-t+1} - v^{n-t}) \\
&= C(gv^{n-t+1} + v^{n-t+1} - v^{n-t}) \\
&= C[(g+1)v^{n-t+1} - v^{n-t}] \\
&= Cv^{n-t+1}[(g+1) - (1+i)] \\
&= C(g-i)v^{n-t+1}
\end{aligned}
$$

Premium amortization

The premium amortization is equal to the amount by which the book value decreases over the t-th period. We have three formulas for the premium amortization:

$$PA_t = BV_{t-1} - BV_t$$
$$PA_t = Cg - I_t$$
$$PA_t = C(g-i)v^{n-t+1}$$

For premium bonds, the amortization of premium is equal to the premium amortization:

Amortization of premium over the t-th period $= PA_t$

For discount bonds, the accumulation of discount is the negative of the premium amortization:

Accumulation of discount over the t-th period $= -PA_t$

For convenience, let's collect together the formulas for book value that we derived earlier. The formula that is best to use in practice depends on the information available.

Book value formulas

We have several equivalent expressions for book value:

$$BV_t = Cga_{\overline{n-t}|i} + Cv_i^{n-t}$$
$$BV_t = P(1+i)^t - Cgs_{\overline{t}|i}$$
$$BV_t = BV_{t-1}(1+i) - Cg$$
$$BV_t = BV_{t-1} + I_t - Cg$$
$$BV_t = BV_{t-1} - PA_t$$

For premium bonds:

$$BV_t = BV_{t-1} - \text{Amortization of premium}$$

For discount bonds:

$$BV_t = BV_{t-1} + \text{Accumulation of discount}$$

When we have two premium amortization amounts for two different periods, we can easily determine the yield rate by dividing a later premium amortization amount by an earlier premium amortization amount:

$$\frac{PA_{t+k}}{PA_t} = \frac{C(g-i)v^{n-(t+k)+1}}{C(g-i)v^{n-t+1}} = v^{-k} = (1+i)^k$$

Determining the yield from two premium amortization amounts

The periodic effective yield is related to the premium amortization amounts by the following formula:

$$\frac{PA_{t+k}}{PA_t} = (1+i)^k$$

Let's work a few problems to see how these formulas are used in practice.

Example 6.6

A 5-year bond with semiannual coupons is redeemable at par. The annual effective yield is 7% and the coupons are 5% a year. Find the price of this bond per $100 par value. Is it sold at a discount or a premium?

Solution

We have:

$$n = 10 \text{ coupons}; \quad F = C = 100; \quad r = g = \frac{0.05}{2} = 2.5\%$$

$$i = (1.07)^{0.5} - 1 = 0.03441$$

The price is:

$$P = 2.5a_{\overline{10}|} + 100v^{10} = \frac{2.5(1 - 1.03441^{-10})}{0.03441} + 100(1.03441)^{-10} = \$92.15$$

This bond is sold at a discount since $P = 92.15 < C = 100$. This is expected since $g < i$, that is $0.025 < 0.03441$. ◆◆

The following example illustrates the construction of a **bond amortization schedule**. Since the bond is at a discount, the book value *increases* each period. The amount of the increase is the accumulation of the discount, and it appears in the fourth column of the table.

 ### Example 6.7

For the bond in Example 6.6, construct the bond amortization schedule.

Solution

The complete bond amortization table is presented at the end of this solution. Let's see how to calculate each of the numbers in this table.

In each half-year, the coupon received is:

$$Fr = Cg = 100\left(\frac{0.05}{2}\right) = \$2.50$$

We next calculate the interest earned. For the first period, the interest earned is the semiannual effective yield multiplied by the price paid since the price paid is the time 0 book value:

$$I_1 = iBV_0 = (0.03441)\,92.15 = \$3.17$$

The difference between the interest earned and the coupon is the accumulation of discount:

$$\text{Accumulation of discount} = -PA_1 = I_1 - Cg = 3.17 - 2.50 = \$0.67$$

The book value at the end of the first period is:

$$BV_1 = BV_0 + \text{Accumulation of discount} = 92.15 + 0.67 = \$92.82$$

This completes the first row of the table.

In the second half-year, we have:

$$I_2 = iBV_1 = (0.03441)92.82 = \$3.19$$
$$\text{Accumulation of discount} = -PA_2 = I_2 - Cg = 3.19 - 2.50 = \$0.69$$
$$BV_2 = BV_1 + \text{Accumulation of discount} = 92.82 + 0.69 = \$93.52$$

In the third half-year, we have:

$$I_3 = iBV_2 = (0.03441)93.52 = \$3.22$$
$$\text{Accumulation of discount} = -PA_3 = I_3 - Cg = 3.22 - 2.50 = \$0.72$$
$$BV_3 = BV_2 + \text{Accumulation of discount} = 93.51 + 0.72 = \$94.23$$

In the fourth half-year, we have:

$$I_4 = iBV_3 = (0.03441)94.23 = \$3.24$$
$$\text{Accumulation of discount} = -PA_4 = I_4 - Cg = 3.24 - 2.50 = \$0.74$$
$$BV_4 = BV_3 + \text{Accumulation of discount} = 94.23 + 0.74 = \$94.98$$

Some of the values above may appear to be off by a penny, since intermediate results are shown rounded to the penny.

The entire amortization schedule is shown on the following page.

Period	Coupon	Interest earned	Accumulation of discount	Book value
0				92.15
1	2.5	3.17	0.67	92.82
2	2.5	3.19	0.69	93.52
3	2.5	3.22	0.72	94.23
4	2.5	3.24	0.74	94.98
5	2.5	3.27	0.77	95.75
6	2.5	3.29	0.79	96.54
7	2.5	3.32	0.82	97.36
8	2.5	3.35	0.85	98.21
9	2.5	3.38	0.88	99.09
10	2.5	3.41	0.91	100.00

The book value of the bond grows to the redemption amount of $100 at maturity.

You should verify the above table entries until you become comfortable with the calculations. Any line item in the above table can be calculated directly without calculating the entire table. For example, the accumulation of discount in the fifth half-year is:

$$-PA_5 = -C(g-i)v^{n-t+1} = -100(0.025-0.03441)(1.03441)^{-(10-5+1)} = \$0.77 \qquad \blacklozenge\blacklozenge$$

The amortization table for a bond sold at a premium has the same column headings except for the fourth column, which is entitled amortization of premium. This value is *subtracted* from the book value to give the next book value. In this case, we are **amortizing** or writing down the premium.

Example 6.8

For the bond in Example 6.6, suppose that the annual effective yield on the bond had been 4% instead of 7%. Determine the price paid for the bond and construct the amortization table.

Solution

The complete bond amortization schedule is presented at the end of the solution.

We have:

$$n = 10 \text{ coupons}; \quad F = C = 100; \quad r = g = \frac{0.05}{2} = 2.5\%$$

$$i = (1.04)^{0.5} - 1 = 0.01980$$

The price is:

$$P = 2.5a_{\overline{10|}} + 100v^{10} = \frac{2.5(1-1.01980^{-10})}{0.01980} + 100(1.01980)^{-10} = \$104.67$$

This bond is sold at a premium since $P = 104.67 > C = 100$. This is expected since $g > i$, that is $0.025 > 0.01980$.

The bond is purchased at a premium, so the 4th column of the amortization table is the amortization of premium that occurs in each period. The value in this column is subtracted from the preceding book value to determine the next book value.

In the first half-year, we have:

$$I_1 = iBV_0 = (0.01980)104.67 = \$2.07$$
$$\text{Amortization of premium} = PA_1 = Cg - I_1 = 2.50 - 2.07 = \$0.43$$
$$BV_1 = BV_0 - \text{Amortization of premium} = 104.67 - 0.43 = \$104.25$$

In the second half-year, we have:

$$I_2 = iBV_1 = (0.01980)104.25 = \$2.06$$
$$\text{Amortization of premium} = PA_2 = Cg - I_2 = 2.50 - 2.06 = \$0.44$$
$$BV_2 = BV_1 - \text{Amortization of premium} = 104.25 - 0.44 = \$103.81$$

In the third half-year, we have:

$$I_3 = iBV_2 = (0.01980)103.81 = \$2.06$$
$$\text{Amortization of premium} = PA_3 = Cg - I_3 = 2.50 - 2.06 = \$0.44$$
$$BV_3 = BV_2 - \text{Amortization of premium} = 103.81 - 0.44 = \$103.37$$

In the fourth half-year, we have:

$$I_4 = iBV_3 = (0.01980)103.37 = \$2.05$$
$$\text{Amortization of premium} = PA_4 = Cg - I_4 = 2.50 - 2.05 = \$0.45$$
$$BV_4 = BV_3 - \text{Amortization of premium} = 103.37 - 0.45 = \$102.91$$

Some of the values above may appear to be off by a penny due to intermediate rounding.

The entire amortization schedule is presented below.

Period	Coupon	Interest earned	Amortization of premium	Book value
0				104.67
1	2.5	2.07	0.43	104.25
2	2.5	2.06	0.44	103.81
3	2.5	2.06	0.44	103.37
4	2.5	2.05	0.45	102.91
5	2.5	2.04	0.46	102.45
6	2.5	2.03	0.47	101.98
7	2.5	2.02	0.48	101.50
8	2.5	2.01	0.49	101.01
9	2.5	2.00	0.50	100.51
10	2.5	1.99	0.51	100.00

The book value of the bond decreases to the redemption amount of $100 at maturity.

Again, you should verify the above table entries until you become comfortable with the calculations. Any line item in the above table can be calculated directly without calculating the entire table. For example, the amortization of premium in the third half-year is:

$$PA_3 = C(g-i)v^{n-t+1} = 100(0.025 - 0.01980)(1.01980)^{-(10-3+1)} = \$0.44 \qquad \blacklozenge\blacklozenge$$

Example 6.9

For the bond in Example 6.6, calculate the book value immediately after the third coupon payment using a 7% annual effective yield.

Solution

After the 3rd coupon payment, there are 7 payments left to go. The book value is:

$$BV_3 = 2.5a_{\overline{7}|3.441\%} + 100v^7_{3.441\%} = \frac{2.5(1-1.03441^{-7})}{0.03441} + 100(1.03441)^{-7} = \$94.23$$

Alternatively, after the 3rd coupon payment, there are 3.5 years left to go. The book value is:

$$BV_3 = 5a^{(2)}_{\overline{3.5}|} + 100v^{3.5} = \frac{5(1-1.07^{-3.5})}{2\left((1.07)^{\frac{1}{2}}-1\right)} + 100(1.07)^{-3.5} = \$94.23$$

This confirms the value that was calculated in Example 6.7.   ◆◆

Example 6.10

A 20-year bond, 10% coupons paid semiannually, is redeemable at par ($100). The bond's annual effective yield is 8%. Calculate the amount of premium amortized in the 11th coupon payment.

Solution

There are two ways to solve this problem. The first method provides a nice illustration of how the various values are related, but the second method is quicker.

Method 1

We determine the book value after the 10th payment when the bond has 15 years left to run. The semiannual effective yield is $(1.08)^{0.5} - 1 = 3.9230\%$. The book value after the 10th payment is:

$$BV_{10} = 0.05 \times 100a_{\overline{30}|3.9230\%} + 100(1.039230)^{-30} = \$118.80$$

The interest earned in the 11th coupon payment is then:

$$I_{11} = iBV_{10} = (0.039230)118.80 = \$4.66$$

So the amount of premium amortized is.

$$PA_{11} = Cg - I_{11} = 5.00 - 4.66 = \$0.34$$

Method 2

The amount of premium amortized in the 11th coupon can be determined directly:

$$PA_{11} = C(g-i)v^{40-11+1} = 100(0.05-0.039230)(1.039230)^{-30} = \$0.34$$ ◆◆

Amortization of premium and accrual of discount: straight-line method

The main reason for calculating a book value is to estimate the value of a bond. Although the constant yield method described in the previous section is the most common method for determining book values, there is another method known as the **straight-line** method, which can be thought of as an approximation to the constant yield method. With the straight-line method, the book value is increased for discount bonds (or reduced for premium bonds) linearly between the price paid and the redemption value over the term of the bond. The columns for the amortization of premium (or accumulation of discount) and the interest earned are then deduced from the book values.

When using the straight-line method, the prospective and retrospective formulas from the previous section no longer apply. The initial book value is still the purchase price, and the final book value is still the redemption value, but the intervening values are now driven by the fact that the premium amortization amounts are constant.

> **Straight-line method of amortizing premium and accumulating discount**
>
> The initial book value is the purchase price of the bond and the final book value is the redemption value of the bond:
>
> $$BV_0 = Cga_{\overline{n}|i} + Cv_i^n$$
> $$BV_n = C$$
>
> The premium amortization amount does not vary by period:
>
> $$PA_t = \frac{BV_0 - BV_n}{n}$$
>
> The interest earned depends on the amount of the premium amortization (which is no longer equal to the yield times the previous book value):
>
> $$I_t = Cg - PA_t$$
>
> Book values continue to depend on the preceding book value and the premium amortization:
>
> $$BV_t = BV_{t-1} - PA_t$$

 ## Example 6.11

Construct the amortization schedule using the straight-line method for determining book values for the bond in Example 6.6.

Solution

The amortization schedule is shown below.

Period	Coupon	Interest earned	Accumulation of discount	Book value
0				92.15
1	2.5	3.28	0.785	92.94
2	2.5	3.28	0.785	93.72
3	2.5	3.28	0.785	94.51
4	2.5	3.28	0.785	95.29
5	2.5	3.28	0.785	96.08
6	2.5	3.28	0.785	96.86
7	2.5	3.28	0.785	97.65
8	2.5	3.28	0.785	98.43
9	2.5	3.28	0.785	99.22
10	2.5	3.28	0.785	100.00

Making use of the formulas:

$$PA_t = \frac{92.15 - 100}{10} = -\$0.785$$

As before, the accumulation of discount is equal to $-PA_t$:

$$\text{Accumulation of discount} = -PA_t = \$0.785$$

The change in the book value from $BV_0 = \$92.15$ to $BV_{10} = \$100$ is divided into 10 equal steps of $(92.15 - 100)/10 = -\$0.785$ each, and the book value decreases by this negative amount each time. In other words, the book value increases by $0.785 each time.

The interest earned column can be determined from:

$$I_t = Cg - PA_t = 2.50 - (-0.78) = \$3.28$$

Note that the figures are actually quite similar to the prior amortization schedule. However, the book value increases slightly more quickly in the early years and slightly more slowly in the later years now. Also, the other columns are now constant throughout, whereas before, the 3rd and 4th columns increased over time. ♦♦

Callable bonds

A **callable** bond can be redeemed at the issuer's option before maturity. This makes the realized yield difficult to predict, since the realized yield will depend on when the bond is actually redeemed.

Pricing callable bonds accurately requires the use of a stochastic interest rate model, which is described in Chapter 9. In this chapter, we use a simplified model based on an assumption that the investor specifies a minimum yield that must be earned on the bond. This yield is then used to calculate multiple prices, with the prices based on each of the possible call dates of the bond. The lowest of these prices is then the maximum price that the investor can pay and still be guaranteed to receive at least the specified yield.

In order to **call** (*ie*, redeem before maturity) a callable bond, the issuer must pay a **call price** to the owner of the bond. The excess of a call price over the redemption value is known as the **call premium**.

The call prices are usually greater than the final redemption value of the bond. For example, a 5-year callable bond with a final redemption value of $100 might be callable for $103 after 2 years, $102 after 3 years, $101 after 4 years, and redeemable for $100 at the end of 5 years. In this example, the call premium is $3 after 2 years, $2 after 3 years, and $1 after 4 years, with the call prices declining to the final redemption value.

Callable bonds usually have a **call protection period** during which the bond cannot be called. In the example above, the bond has a call protection period of two years since it is not callable for the first two years.

Bonds are more likely to be called when interest rates fall because the issuer is then able to issue new debt with lower coupons. Even though the issuer might have to pay a call premium to pay off the existing debt, the benefit of replacing it with lower-coupon debt can easily outweigh the cost of the call premium to the issuer. The call option works to the detriment of the bond owner though, since when interest rates fall, the proceeds from the call must be reinvested at a lower interest rate. Callable bonds offer higher yields than similar non-callable bonds to compensate investors for this risk, which is known as **call risk**.

Fortunately, it is not always necessary to calculate prices for *all* of the call dates. There are a couple of circumstances that can reduce the number of possible call dates that must be analyzed.

First, let's consider bonds that are priced at a discount to their final redemption value.

Pricing callable discount bonds

If the following two conditions are met:

(a)   the final redemption value times the yield is greater than the coupon: $Ci > Fr$, and

(b)   each of the call prices is greater than or equal to the final redemption value of the bond,

then the highest price that guarantees a yield of at least i is calculated using the final redemption value and the maturity date of the bond.

The above rule deals with bonds that are priced at a discount to the final redemption value. The earlier a discount bond is paid off, the more valuable the bond, and therefore the lowest possible price is found by assuming that the bond is never called. This lowest possible price is the most that an investor can pay and be assured that the realized yield will be at least i.

Next, we consider bonds that are priced at a premium to their final redemption value.

Pricing callable premium bonds

If the following two conditions are met:

(a)   the final redemption value times the yield is less than the coupon: $Ci < Fr$, and

(b)   each of the call prices is greater than or equal to the final redemption value of the bond,

then the highest price that guarantees a yield of at least i is the minimum of the prices found in the steps below:

- Calculate multiple prices for the bond using each call price and its *earliest* associated call date.

- Calculate a price for the bond using the final redemption value and the maturity date of the bond.

The above rule deals with bonds that are priced at a premium to the final redemption value. When the face amount is equal to the redemption amount, a bond is priced at a premium when the coupon rate is greater than the yield. The investor is willing to pay more than the final redemption amount in order to receive the relatively high coupons. On the one hand, a call reduces the time period over which the relatively high coupons are earned and therefore brings down the value of the bond. On the other hand, a call may increase the value of the bond if the call price is larger than the final redemption value. For a given call price, the lowest price of the bond is calculated using the earliest date applicable to a call price, since using a later date would assume that more of the relatively high coupons are paid.

We could remove condition (b) from the box above and the algorithm for finding the price would remain the same, but it would then be possible for the bond to be priced at a discount instead of a premium to the final redemption value.

Consider a bond that pays annual coupons of $7, is callable for $110 any time between years 5 and 10, callable for $105 any time between years 10 and 20, and matures in 20 years for $100.

If the required yield is 9%, then we have $Ci > Fr$ since $100(0.09) > 7$. Therefore the bond is priced at a discount, and we need only calculate the price assuming that the bond matures at the end of 20 years. This price is $81.74. If the investor pays this price, then the investor is guaranteed to realize a yield of at least 9%.

If instead the required yield is 6%, then we have $Ci < Fr$ since $100(0.06) < 7$. Therefore the bond is priced at a premium, and we need to calculate 3 prices. The price of the callable bond is the lowest of the following prices calculated using a yield of 6%:

- the price assuming the bond is called for $110 at the end of 5 years, which is $111.68.
- the price assuming that the bond is called for $105 at the end of 10 years, which is $110.15.
- the price assuming that the bond matures for $100 at the end of 20 years, which is $111.47.

The minimum of the three prices is $110.15, which is found by assuming that the bond is called for $105 at the end of 10 years.

Example 6.12

An investor buys a 10-year callable bond with semiannual coupons of 6%. The bond is callable after 5 years at a call price of $102.

(i)   Determine the price of the bond to yield 7% compounded semiannually.

(ii)   Determine the price of the bond to yield 5% compounded semiannually.

Solution

Part (i)

The redemption value times the yield is greater than the coupon amount since:

$$(100)(0.035) > (100)(0.03)$$

Therefore the bond is priced at a discount and its minimum price is found as the price assuming the bond matures for its final redemption value of $100.

The bond is priced to yield 7% compounded semiannually, so the bond price is:

$$P = 3a_{\overline{20}|3.5\%} + 100(1.035)^{-20}$$
$$= \$92.89$$

Part (ii)

The redemption value times the yield is less than the coupon amount since:

$$(100)(0.025) < (100)(0.03)$$

Therefore, the bond is priced at a premium and the price must be calculated assuming that the bond is called at the earliest opportunity and again assuming that the bond is held until maturity.

If the bond is called after 5 years, then the call price of $102 is paid, and the bond price is:

$$P = 3a_{\overline{10}|2.5\%} + 102(1.025)^{-10}$$
$$= \$105.94$$

If the bond matures after 10 years, then the redemption amount of $100 is paid, and the bond price is:

$$P = 3a_{\overline{20}|2.5\%} + 100(1.025)^{-20}$$
$$= \$107.79$$

Since the price is lower if the bond is called after 5 years, the highest price that the investor can pay and still be certain of earning a yield of 5% is $105.94.   ♦ ♦

Notice that in part (ii) of this example, we only need to determine the price if the bond is called at 5 years to determine the lowest possible price and compare it to the price of the bond if it is allowed to mature. We don't need to compare the price if the bond is called at 5.5 to 9.5 years to the price if the bond is called at 5 years. The price of the bond if called at years 5.5 through 9.5 is greater than the price of the bond if called at year 5. For example, the price of the bond if called at 5.5 years is:

$$P = 3a_{\overline{11}|2.5\%} + 102(1.025)^{-11}$$
$$= \$106.28$$

We leave it to the reader to verify that the other prices from years 6 to 9.5 are greater than $105.94.

Bond price between coupon payment dates

So far, we've only considered pricing a bond on a coupon payment date. Bond coupons are generally paid every 6 months, but bonds can be sold between coupon payment dates so we need to be able to determine bond prices between coupon payment dates.

In the US, a bond price is quoted as a **clean price**. In other words, bond quotes exclude **accrued interest** between coupon payment dates. However, the buyer must pay the accrued interest to the seller, so the buyer actually pays the **full price**:

Full price = Clean price + Accrued interest

When an investor buys a bond between coupon payment dates, the buyer must compensate the seller of the bond for the **accrued interest** earned from the most recent coupon payment date to the **settlement date**. In this section, we discuss the standard method for calculating accrued interest, which is sometimes called the semi-theoretical method.

To determine accrued interest, we first need to determine the **day count**. The day count convention is used to pro-rate the interest earned over a period of time. There are two main day count conventions used with bonds: the **30-day-month/360-day-year** (30/360) and the **actual-day-month/actual-day-year** (actual/actual) methods. The former is mainly used with corporate and municipal bonds while the latter is mainly used with government bonds.

For example, let's assume that a bond purchase settles on May 10, 2004 and the bond's next coupon is on September 1, 2004. The last coupon was paid 6 months prior to September 1, on March 1. The actual number of days from March 1 to May 10 is $(31-1)+30+10=70$. The actual number of days from March 1 to September 1 is $(31-1)+30+31+30+31+31+1=184$. Under the actual/actual method, 70 days have elapsed since the last coupon was paid and there are 184 days between March 1 and September 1.

The 30/360 convention is sometimes easier to use. With the 30/360 day count convention, there are $(30-1)+30+10=69$ days from March 1 to May 10 and there are $360/2=180$ days from March 1 to September 1. As this example demonstrates, the 30/360 convention is based on an assumption that each month consists of only 30 days. However, if either the purchase date or the coupon date falls on the last or next-to-last day of the month, then the 30/360 convention becomes more complicated to apply. In that event, we use an algorithm supplied by the Securities Industry Association, which appears in Appendix B.

Once the days are counted, the accrued interest can be calculated. The accrued interest is an estimate of the coupon earned by the seller of the bond from the prior coupon payment date to the selling date, or settlement date. The buyer of the bond must pay the seller the accrued interest since the buyer will receive the next coupon in its entirety on the next coupon date.

The accrued interest is sometimes called the **accrued coupon**. Although "accrued coupon" is perhaps more descriptive than "accrued interest," the term "accrued interest" is more commonly used in practice and therefore it is the term used in this section.

Accrued interest (AI)

Accrued interest equals the coupon payment times the ratio of the number of days between the last coupon payment date and the settlement date to the total number of days between the coupon payment dates:

$$AI = \text{coupon} \times k$$

where $k = \left(\dfrac{\text{\# days between last coupon payment date and settlement date}}{\text{total \# days between coupon payment dates}} \right)$.

Returning to this example, let's say the semiannual coupon is $50. If the bond were a corporate bond, the 30/360 day count convention is used to determine the accrued interest:

$$AI = 50(69 / 180) = \$19.17$$

If the bond were a government bond, the actual/actual day count convention is used:

$$AI = 50(70 / 184) = \$19.02$$

Note that the calculation of accrued interest is somewhat arbitrary. It is simply an adjustment to the full price that is made to arrive at the clean price. As long as the market participants agree on a consistent method for calculating the accrued interest, any method will suffice. Actual bond market participants have agreed to calculate accrued interest as a linear function of k as shown in the box above. Other methods for calculating accrued interest exist, but since they are not commonly used in practice, we will not consider them here.

The **full price** of a bond between coupon payment dates is determined using the same bond price formula as before, with an adjustment for the partial period between payment dates. From before, the price of a bond is just the present value of any future coupons and redemption amount. To determine the price between coupon payment dates, the calculation is complicated a little since the present values of the coupons and the redemption amount need to be adjusted for the partial period between the purchase price and the next coupon date.

Full price of bond between coupon payment dates

The full price of a bond between coupon payment dates, P_{t+k}, is the price (based on the current yield of i) of the bond immediately after the last coupon, P_t, accumulated forward to the settlement date at the periodic effective yield i:

$$P_{t+k} = P_t(1+i)^k$$

The full price can also be calculated as the sum of the price (based on the current yield of i) of the bond immediately after the next coupon, P_{t+1}, plus the next coupon, Fr, discounted back to the settlement date at the periodic effective yield i:

$$P_{t+k} = (P_{t+1} + Fr)v_i^{1-k}$$

Let's see how these formulas are used in the next example.

Example 6.13

A corporate bond pays semiannual coupons at a coupon rate of 8%. The bond is priced to yield 6% compounded semiannually. The bond matures on 6/1/08 and is purchased with a settlement date of 10/1/03. Determine the full price of the bond as of the settlement date.

Solution

Using the first formula for the full price of a bond between settlement dates, we calculate the price of the bond as of the most recent coupon date before the settlement date. We then accumulate this value to the settlement date. The most recent coupon date before the settlement date is 6/1/03. On 6/1/03, there are 5 years until maturity, so there are 10 coupon payments remaining. Each coupon payment is $100(0.08 / 2) = \$4$. The semiannual effective yield is 3%. The price of the bond on 6/1/03 is:

$$P_t = 4a_{\overline{10}|3\%} + 100(1.03)^{-10} = \$108.530203$$

This price is then accumulated from 6/1/03 to the settlement date of 10/1/03. Since this is a corporate bond, the 30/360 day count convention is used. Under the 30/360 day count convention, there are $(30-1)+30+30+30+1=120$ days between 6/1/03 and 10/1/03. The full price of this bond at 10/1/03 is:

$$P_{t+k} = 108.530203(1.03)^{\frac{120}{180}} = \$110.69$$

Alternatively, we can find the price of the bond just after the *next* coupon payment is made when there are only 9 coupon payments remaining:

$$P_{t+1} = 4a_{\overline{9}|3\%} + 100(1.03)^{-9} = \$107.786109$$

The full price of this bond at 10/1/03 is:

$$P_{t+k} = (P_{t+1} + Fr)v_i^{1-k} = (107.786109 + 4)(1.03)^{-\left(1-\frac{120}{180}\right)} = \$110.69 \qquad \blacklozenge\blacklozenge$$

The **clean price** of a bond between coupon payment periods is the full price less the accrued interest.

Clean price of bond between coupon payment dates

The clean price of a bond between coupon payment dates is the full price P_{t+k} minus the accrued interest:

$$\text{Clean price} = P_{t+k} - AI$$

Example 6.14

Using the information from Example 6.13, determine the clean price of the bond as of 10/1/03.

Solution

The accrued interest as of 10/1/03 using the 30/360 day count convention is:

$$AI = 4(120/180) = \$2.67$$

The clean price of the bond is then:

$$\text{Clean price} = 110.69 - 2.67 = \$108.02 \qquad \blacklozenge\blacklozenge$$

6.3 *Stock valuation*

With bonds, the future expected cash flows can usually be predicted with a high degree of certainty since we know the coupon rate and the time to maturity. The uncertainties with bonds relate to interest-rate risk and credit risk. With stocks, the future expected cash flows are not nearly as certain. A stockholder receives dividends, which can vary over time with the profitability of the issuing company. Also, there is no maturity date for stocks – as long as the company remains in business, its stock can be held indefinitely and the investor continues to receive dividends. If the stock is sold at some point in the future, the investor receives the market price at that time, but the future market price of a stock is very difficult to predict with any degree of accuracy. When valuing a stock, the best we can do is to make educated assumptions using discounted cash flow (DCF) and other techniques.

The present value of a stock depends on its future dividend stream and any capital gain upon the sale of the stock. Assume that a dividend is received at time 1 year just before the stock is sold at time 1. The price at time 1 is P_1 and the dividend at time 1 is div_1. Also assume that we know the rate of return, r, required by the market for a similarly risky stock. This required return is also known as the **opportunity cost of equity capital**. The present value of the stock at time 0 is:

$$PV \text{ stock} = P_0 = \frac{div_1 + P_1}{(1+r)^1}$$

Instead of selling the stock at time 1, let's assume that we hold the stock from time 0 to time 2 years. The present value of the stock would then be equal to the present value of the dividend at time 1 plus the dividend and stock price at time 2.

$$PV \text{ stock} = P_0 = \frac{div_1}{(1+r)^1} + \frac{div_2 + P_2}{(1+r)^2}$$

As we hold the stock for longer and longer periods, the present value of the sale price becomes a smaller proportion of the present value of the dividend-paying stock since the discount factor in the denominator becomes larger as time increases. If we hold the stock indefinitely, the present value of the sale price approaches zero as the time to the sale approaches infinity. So the sale price term in the stock valuation DCF formula can be ignored if the dividend-paying stock is held indefinitely. Therefore, the present value of a dividend-paying stock is equal to the present value of the expected future dividend steam. This is called the **dividend discount model**.

General DCF stock valuation formula

The price of a share of stock is equal to the present value of the future dividend stream, discounted at the risk-adjusted required return r:

$$PV \text{ stock} = \sum_{t=1}^{\infty} \frac{div_t}{(1+r)^t}$$

Companies usually retain some of their earnings (*eg* to invest in new projects) and pay out the rest of their earnings as dividends. Dividends are used in the valuation formula for a stock since the dividends are what the shareholders actually receive. Earnings per share do not equal dividends per share unless the company pays all of its earnings out as dividends.

Several simplifying assumptions make stock valuation easier. However, when a simplifying assumption is made, we should first determine whether or not the assumption is reasonable before plowing ahead with any formula.

Level dividends

If we can reasonably assume that the dividends will remain constant over time, then the stock's present value formula can be simplified as the formula for a level perpetuity with the dividend in the numerator and the required market return rate in the denominator.

Level dividend stock valuation formula

If dividends are paid at the end of each year and are expected to remain level, then the stock price is determined by treating the level dividend as a level perpetuity-immediate:

$$PV \text{ stock} = \frac{div_1}{r}$$

This may be a reasonable assumption if the company is in a mature industry with no significant growth or investment opportunities.

Example 6.15

A stock is expected to pay dividends at a rate of $10 each year at the end of the year. Assume that the return required for similarly risky stocks is 15%. Calculate the expected stock price.

Solution

The present value of the stock is calculated as the annual dividend divided by the annual effective required return:

$$PV \text{ stock} = \frac{div_1}{r} = \frac{10}{0.15} = \$66.67$$

◆◆

Constant dividend growth

If the dividends can be reasonably expected to grow at a constant rate, then we can apply the constant growth perpetuity formula to the valuation of a stock. The sustainable dividend growth rate is denoted by g. The stock price grows at the dividend growth rate.

Let's assume that the first dividend occurs one year from now, and that each subsequent dividend grows by a factor of g each year. If the dividends are paid indefinitely:

$$\begin{aligned}
PV \text{ dividends} &= \frac{div_1}{1+r} + \frac{div_1(1+g)}{(1+r)^2} + \frac{div_1(1+g)^2}{(1+r)^3} + \cdots \\
&= \frac{div_1}{1+r}\left[1 + \frac{1+g}{1+r} + \left(\frac{1+g}{1+r}\right)^2 + \cdots\right] \\
&= \frac{div_1}{1+r}\left[\frac{1}{1-(1+g)/(1+r)}\right] \\
&= \frac{div_1}{1+r}\left[\frac{1}{(r-g)/(1+r)}\right] \\
&= \frac{div_1}{r-g}
\end{aligned}$$

Constant dividend growth stock valuation formula

If dividends are paid at the end of each year and grow at a constant annual rate of g, the stock price is determined by dividing the next dividend by the excess of the annual effective interest rate r over the annual growth rate g:

$$PV \text{ stock} = \frac{div_1}{r-g}$$

With the constant growth formula, the growth rate must be less than the required market rate, otherwise the present value of the stock will be a nonsensical negative number. Also, as the growth rate approaches the required market rate, the present value will approach infinity. When using the constant growth formula, a high stock price may be the result of using an unreasonably large dividend growth rate assumption, so be sure to check for reasonableness of all assumptions and results before reaching any conclusions.

Example 6.16

A stock is expected to pay a dividend of $10 next year. The required market return is 15% for similarly risky stocks. The dividends are expected to grow 3% per year. Calculate the expected stock price.

Solution

The present value of the dividends is:

$$PV \text{ stock} = \frac{div_1}{r-g} = \frac{10}{0.15-0.03} = \$83.33$$ ♦♦

The constant dividend growth formula can be used to solve for the required market return. If we know the dividend yield and the growth rate, then the required market rate can be calculated as the sum of those two items by rearranging the above stock present value formula. The dividend yield is simply the dividend divided by the current stock price, *ie* $(div_1)/P_0$.

We have:

$$P_0 = \frac{div_1}{r-g}$$

$$\Rightarrow r - g = \frac{div_1}{P_0}$$

$$\Rightarrow r = \frac{div_1}{P_0} + g$$

Example 6.17

A stock is currently trading at $50. It is expected to pay a dividend of $5 next year. Dividends are expected to grow by 3% each year thereafter. Calculate the required return for this stock.

Solution

The required return is:

$$r = \frac{div_1}{P_0} + g = \frac{5}{50} + 0.03 = 13\%$$ ♦♦

The growth rate can be similarly estimated. Remember that the constant dividend growth formula requires a reasonable, sustainable growth rate in order for the present value to be reasonable. If we know the dividend yield and the required market return rate, the growth rate can be calculated as the required return less the dividend yield:

$$g = r - \frac{div_1}{P_0}$$

Example 6.18

A stock is currently trading for $10. It is expected to pay a dividend of $1 per share next year. Similarly risky stocks are returning 12% on their equity. At what rate are dividends expected to grow each year?

Solution

The constant dividend growth rate is:

$$g = r - \frac{div_1}{P_0} = 0.12 - \frac{1}{10} = 2\%$$ ♦♦

Non-constant dividend growth

Sometimes a company is expected to have a high dividend growth rate for a short period of time. A high growth rate can't be assumed for very long or we run into the problem of the growth rate exceeding the required market rate, causing a huge or negative present value. But we can allow a high growth rate for a short period of time. If a company has a new product that is expected to do very well, or if it has a short-term competitive advantage, we might assume that the company has a high growth rate for a short period until its competitors are able to catch up. At that point, the growth rate should return to a lower, sustainable level.

When faced with non-constant dividend growth, split the problem into time periods where the dividends are either level or increasing at a constant rate, apply the appropriate valuation formula, and discount them back to the present. Of course, we could always apply the general DCF formula to the non-constant dividend growth case, but that may be time consuming. The trick is to break the problem into easier sub-problems, which can be solved quickly by using the simplified formulas.

Example 6.19

Company X has a short-term competitive advantage and its dividends are expected to grow at a rate of 20% for the next three years until its competition catches up. After the competition catches up, the company's dividends are expected to grow at the industry average growth rate of 5%. Assume next year's dividend is $2 and the required return is 15%. Calculate the current stock price for company X.

Solution

With a spreadsheet, we could use the general DCF formula to project the dividends out for thirty or even 100 years and sum the present value of each dividend to arrive at the present value. This is impractical without a spreadsheet. To simplify things, let's break this problem into two sub-parts so that the simple formulas can be applied.

Next year's dividend is $2. The dividend in year two will grow by 20% and the dividend in year three will grow by another 20%. Starting in year 4, the dividends grow 5% each year indefinitely. We can split this into two parts: the first 3 years and thereafter.

The present value of the first three dividends is calculated below.

Time	Dividend	Discount factor	PV of dividend
1	2.00	0.869565	1.739
2	2.40	0.756144	1.815
3	2.88	0.657516	1.894

So the present value of the first three dividends equals $1.739 + 1.815 + 1.894 = \$5.448$.

In year 4, the dividends begin to grow by 5% each year. The year 4 dividend equals the year 3 dividend times 1.05. The constant dividend growth formula is applied to the year 4 and beyond dividends to calculate the present value of those dividends at time 3.

$$P_3 = \frac{dividend_4}{r-g} = \frac{dividend_3\,(1+0.05)}{r-g} = \frac{2.88\,(1.05)}{0.15-0.05} = \$30.24$$

But we need the current value for the dividends in year 4 and beyond, not the time 3 present value. Since we calculated the value at time 3, we need to discount P_3 by 3 years, and then add it to the present value of the first 3 dividends from above to get the present value of the stock.

$$P_0 = 5.448 + \frac{30.24}{(1.15)^3} = \$25.33$$

◆◆

Using the price-to-earnings ratio to value stocks

The **price-to-earnings (P/E) ratio** is easy to remember because its name indicates how the ratio is calculated. The P/E ratio is the current stock price divided by company's earnings per share (EPS). Earnings per share is often referred to as net income per share. Net income is an accounting measure of the company's profits for the year. Dividends are paid from a company's earnings.

Price-to-earnings (P/E) ratio

The P/E ratio tells us how much investors are willing to pay for each dollar of earnings:

$$\text{P/E ratio} = \frac{\text{stock price per share}}{\text{earnings per share}} = \frac{P_0}{\text{EPS}}$$

where $\text{earnings per share} = \dfrac{\text{net income}}{\text{number of outstanding shares}}$.

A high P/E ratio indicates that the stock price is high relative to the company's current earnings. This usually means that investors expect the company to grow and are therefore willing to pay more for the stock.

The P/E ratio becomes nonsensical as the company's earnings approach zero or if the earnings are negative. Since earnings are in the denominator of the P/E ratio, the P/E ratio approaches infinity as earnings approach zero. So, a high P/E ratio does not necessarily imply that investors expect high growth from the stock.

The current price of a stock can be determined using the P/E ratio if the company's EPS and the P/E ratio are known. Rearranging the P/E ratio formula, we have:

$$PV \text{ stock} = P_0 = \left(\text{P/E ratio}\right)\left(\text{net income per share}\right)$$

The denominator of the P/E ratio is earnings per share, which is the same as net income per share. In this case, the stock price depends on earnings per share only because earnings are part of the P/E formula. But let's not forget one of our basic principles: a stock's value is the present value of the cash flows the shareholders are expected to receive. Shareholders receive dividends, which are paid from earnings.

Caution should be exercised when using earnings to value stocks. Earnings can be highly volatile and can be difficult to compare between firms because of accounting and other differences between companies. A high P/E ratio by itself does not indicate that a company is doing well. It could mean that earnings are depressed or near zero which creates an inflated P/E ratio. We should always check for reasonableness.

Still, the P/E ratio can be a valuable valuation tool when other information is not available. For example, it can be very difficult to estimate the value of a non-traded company. In this case, the market does not determine a market price of a private company since it is not traded. But if we know the P/E ratio of a similar company and the earnings of the non-traded company, we can still estimate the non-traded company's value by taking the similar company's P/E and multiplying it by the non-traded company's earnings per share.

Example 6.20

Company X is a closely held, private company, so its shares are not traded on any exchange. Company X has reported earnings of $25 million over the last 12 months. Company Y is a publicly traded competitor of company X. Company Y earned $100 million over the last 12 months and its stock price is currently $30. Company Y has ten million shares outstanding. Estimate the total market value of company X.

Solution

The total market value of a company is known as its **market capitalization**. Market capitalization equals the per share stock price times the number of shares outstanding. In this case, we need to determine the total value of company X, not the per share price.

For company Y, the EPS is used to determine the P/E ratio:

$$EPS = \frac{100,000,000}{10,000,000} = 10.0$$

$$P/E \text{ ratio} = \frac{30}{10} = 3.0$$

For company X, the total market value can be determined by multiplying the total earnings of company X by the P/E ratio of company Y:

$$Market \text{ capitalization} = (\text{total earnings})(P/E \text{ ratio}) = 25 \times 3 = \$75 \text{ million} \qquad \blacklozenge\blacklozenge$$

6.4 Short sales

When an investor sells an asset that is not currently owned by the investor, it is called a **short sale**. So, a short sale is where an asset is sold before it is purchased. This results in what is effectively a *negative* holding of the asset. This is also described as a *short holding*. An investor who sells stock short borrows the stock from a broker and immediately sells it. To close out the short sale, the investor must buy the stock back and return it to the broker. Consequently, the short seller benefits from a decline in the stock price between the sale date and the repurchase date.

The investor who sells a stock short is bearish on the stock (*ie* the investor believes that the share price of the stock will fall) and wants to benefit from the expected decline in the stock's price.

Gain on short sale

The gain on the short sale is calculated by subtracting the selling price from the purchase price for each share of stock.

Gain on short sale (in dollars)

The gain on the short sale is:

$$Short \text{ sale gain} = (\# \text{ shares})(\text{sale price} - \text{purchase price})$$

Suppose the initial stock price is $50 and the investor would like to sell 40 shares short. If the investor is able to buy the stock at the end of one year for $45, the gain on the short sale is $40(50 - 45) = \$200$.

Until the short sale is closed out, the proceeds from the short sale are kept on deposit with the broker. These proceeds do not earn interest and they cannot be withdrawn until the short position is closed out.

Margin deposit

The broker requires that the investor provide some collateral in the form of a **margin deposit** to protect against the risk of default by the investor. The broker is at risk if the stock price increases and the investor is unable to afford replacing the stock. Usually the margin deposit is expressed as a percentage of the initial share price.

For example, let's say the broker requires 50% as the margin deposit. The investor is selling 40 shares for $50 each. The margin deposit is then $0.5 \times 40 \times 50 = \$1,000$. The margin deposit represents the net investment. So, with an investment of $1,000, the investor can sell $(1,000 / 0.50) / 50 = 40$ shares short.

The margin deposit may earn interest for the investor. If the annual effective interest rate on the margin deposit is 4%, then the investor receives $0.04 \times 1,000 = \$40$ at the end of the year on the margin deposit.

Dividends

Along with the obligation to replace the borrowed shares, the short seller must also pay the broker for any dividends paid on the stock during the period of the short sale.

In this example, let's say each share of stock paid a dividend of $0.50 at the end of the year. The total dividends are $40 \times 0.50 = \$20$.

Short sale profit

Putting the pieces together, the profit to the investor over the short sale period is the gain on the short sale plus any interest earned on the margin deposit less any dividends paid by the stock over the short sale period.

Profit on short sale (in dollars)

The profit on the short sale is:

$$\text{Short sale profit} = (\text{\# shares})(\text{sale price} - \text{purchase price}) + \text{margin interest} - \text{dividends}$$

In this example, the short sale profit is $200 + 40 - 20 = \$220$.

Short sale yield

The short sale yield is expressed as an annual effective rate. As long as the short sale period is one year, the yield on the short sale is the short sale profit divided by the margin deposit.

Short sale yield

The short sale yield is:

$$\text{Short sale yield} = (\text{short sale profit}) / (\text{margin deposit})$$

In this example, the short sale yield is $220 / 1,000 = 22\%$.

Example 6.21

Fred sells a share of ABC stock short. It is worth $3.50 at that time. He pays a margin of 50% of the price of the share. He buys a share of ABC stock a year later when the price has fallen to $2.90. The margin deposit does not earn interest. What is Fred's yield on this transaction, assuming that the share pays no dividends in the year?

Solution

Fred's margin deposit is $0.5 \times 3.50 = 1.75$.

Fred's gain on this transaction is $3.50 - 2.90 = \$0.60$.

The yield on his deposit is $0.60 / 1.75 = 34.3\%$.   ♦♦

Example 6.22

Continuing with the information from Example 6.21, what is Fred's yield if the share pays a dividend of $0.50 at the end of the year and the margin payment earns interest at an annual effective rate of 4%?

Solution

The deposit is still $1.75. Fred's gain is now $0.60 + 0.04 \times 1.75 - 0.50 = \$0.17$.

The yield is $0.17 / 1.75 = 9.7\%$.   ◆ ◆

6.5 Derivative valuation

In this section, we examine some of the techniques for valuing derivative instruments.

Option valuation

An option is an agreement that one party will provide a benefit to another party under a contingent set of circumstances. The party receiving the benefit is the option buyer, who owns the option and is said to be **long** the option. The party providing the benefit is said to be **short** the option. After the expiration of an option, the option ceases to exist.

There are two main types of options: puts and calls. Each of these can be either an American or a European option. An American option allows the option holder to exercise the option on or before the expiration date. A European option only allows the option holder to exercise the option on the expiration date. American options are always worth at least as much as European options, because American options allow for early exercise. This section focuses on European options.

Call option

The owner of a call option has the right, but not the obligation, to *purchase* an asset for a specified price.

The specified price is called the **exercise price** or **strike price**. Exercising the option means making use of the call option to buy the underlying asset for the exercise price. Once the option is exercised, the option ceases to exist.

When the underlying asset is common stock, options on the stock are referred to as stock options. Let's consider a European call option on General Electric stock. Assume that the current price of General Electric stock is $30. The call option expires in 6 months and has an exercise price of $30.

> Years until expiration: $t = 0.5$
>
> Exercise price: $X = 30$

Because it is a European call, its payoff occurs upon expiration of the option in 6 months.

The table below shows how the payoff of the option depends on the price of GE stock in 6 months.

Price of GE in 6 months	Call option payoff
20	0
25	0
30	0
35	5
40	10

If GE stock can be purchased on the open market for $20 in 6 months, then the option to buy it for $30 has no value. If the option holder wants to acquire GE stock, it is cheaper to buy it on the open market for $20 than it is to buy it for $30 with the option. Therefore, if GE stock trades for $30 or less when the option expires, the option holder allows it to expire unused.

However, if GE trades for $35 when the option expires, then the call option is worth $5. The owner of the call option can use the option to purchase GE stock for $30 and sell it on the open market for $35, netting $5. As can be seen from the table, once the stock price reaches the exercise price, an increase in the stock price of $1 increases the payoff of the call option by $1.

Call option payoff

The call option payoff is the maximum of the stock price minus the exercise price and zero:

$$\text{Call option payoff} = \text{Max}(S_t - X, 0)$$

where S_t = Stock price at time t.

The graph on the following page contains two lines. The 45-degree line that runs through the origin is the payoff of the stock position. Let's take a moment here to note that the horizontal axis is *not* time. These kinds of graphs can be very helpful for envisioning option payoffs, but they have the potential to create confusion if one expects them to show how the option value changes over time. The graph below is used to show how the option payoff depends on the final value of the underlying stock, so it depicts the value of the option at only one point in time, namely upon expiration of the option.

The horizontal axis is the value of GE stock in 6 months, which is denoted by $S_{0.5}$.

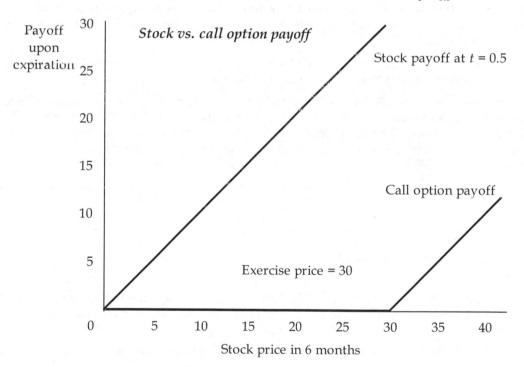

Once the stock price reaches the exercise price of 30, the call option payoff increases along with the value of the stock.

When the stock price is higher than the exercise price, the call option is said to be **in the money**. In this example, the call option is in the money when the stock price is greater than 30. If an option is in the money upon expiration, then the option is exercised at expiration.

When the stock price is less than the exercise price, the call option is said to be **out of the money**. In this example, the call option is out of the money when the stock price is less than 30. If an option is out of the money upon expiration, then the option expires unused at expiration.

Now let's turn our attention to put options.

Put option

The owner of a put option has the right, but not the obligation, to *sell* an asset for the exercise or strike price.

Let's consider a European put option on General Electric stock with the following characteristics:

> Exercise price: $X = 30$
>
> Years until expiration: $t = 0.5$

Because it is a European put, its payoff occurs upon expiration of the option in 6 months.

The table below shows how the option payoff depends on the price of GE stock in 6 months.

Price of GE in 6 months	Put option payoff
20	10
25	5
30	0
35	0
40	0

If GE stock can be sold on the open market for $40 in 6 months, then an option to sell it for $30 has no value. If the option holder wants to sell GE stock, a better deal can be obtained by selling it for $40 in the open market.

As can be seen in the table above, if GE stock trades for $30 or more when the option expires, then the put option has no value, and the option holder allows it to expire unused.

However, if GE trades for $25 when the option expires, then the put option is worth $5. The owner of the put option can use it to sell GE for $30 and then repurchase the GE stock in the open market for $25, netting $5 in the process. As can be seen from the table, once the stock price decreases to the exercise price, a one dollar decrease in the stock price increases the payoff of the put option by one dollar.

Put option payoff

The put option payoff is the maximum of the exercise price minus the stock price and zero:

> Put option payoff $= \text{Max}(X - S_t, 0)$

As can be seen in the following graph, the lower the stock price, the higher the option payoff. The maximum possible payoff of the put option is its exercise price, and it reaches this maximum only if the stock price is zero when the option matures.

If the stock price reaches the exercise price of 30 or goes higher, the put option payoff falls to zero.

When the stock price is lower than the exercise price, the put option is said to be in the money. In this example, the put option is in the money when the stock price is less than 30. If an option is in the money upon expiration, then the option is exercised at expiration.

When the stock price is greater than the exercise price, the put option is said to be out of the money. In this example, the put option is out of the money when the stock price is more than 30. If an option is out of the money upon expiration, then the option expires unused at expiration.

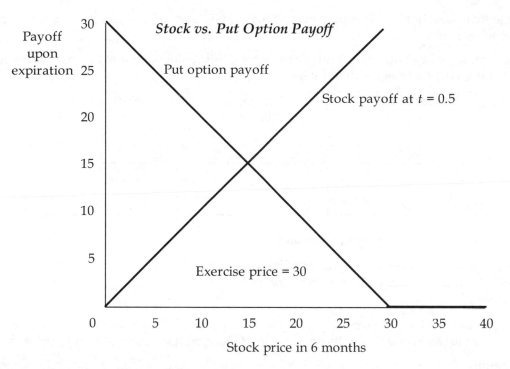

Put-call parity

Owning a put and the underlying stock produces the same payoff as owning a call and a risk-free savings account in which the only deposit was the present value of the exercise price. Since the two positions produce the same payoff, their current prices must be equivalent.

Assume that Jack holds a European call option on a stock and also puts aside enough money to purchase the stock upon expiration of the option. If the exercise price is X, and the money can be invested at an annual effective risk-free interest rate of r_f, then the amount of money to be set aside is the present value of X:

$$PV(X) = \frac{X}{(1+r_f)^t}$$

where t is the time, measured in years, until expiration of the option.

Because $X/(1+r_f)^t$ is invested in a risk-free asset, its payoff at time t is certain to be X.

Let's continue with our example above using GE stock. Assume that Jack's call option is a European option to purchase GE stock for $30, and it expires in 6 months. The table below shows how the payoff of the new position (the combination of the call option and the present value of the exercise price) depends on the final value of GE stock.

Price of GE in 6 months	Call Option Payoff	Exercise Price (X)	Jack's Total Position Payoff
20	0	30	30
25	0	30	30
30	0	30	30
35	5	30	35
40	10	30	40

We can also produce this payoff pattern with a European put option and a long position in the underlying stock.

Assume that Suzy holds a European put option on GE, and the exercise price is $30. She also owns one share of GE stock.

The next table shows how the payoff of the position (the combination of the put option and the stock holding) depends on the final value of GE stock.

Price of GE in 6 months	Put Option Payoff	Suzy's Total Position Payoff
20	10	30
25	5	30
30	0	30
35	0	35
40	0	40

Suzy's payoff pattern is exactly the same as Jack's.

Jack's position of a call plus the present value of $30 guarantees that he will have at least $30 at the end of six months, and he also participates in the upside potential of the stock if its price exceeds $30.

Suzy's position of a share of stock plus a put option also gives her participation in the upside potential of the stock, and it guarantees her at least $30 even if the stock price falls below $30.

If we assume that GE does not pay any dividends prior to the expiration of the options, then Jack and Suzy's positions must have the same initial cost since their payoffs are equal:

Cost of establishing Jack's position = Cost of establishing Suzy's position

$$C_0 + \frac{X}{(1+r_f)^t} = P_0 + S_0$$

where:

C_0 = Current value of call option

P_0 = Current value of put option

S_0 = Current value of stock

This relationship is known as put-call parity.

Put-call parity

The price of a call option plus the present value of the exercise price is equal to the price of a put option plus the current stock price:

$$C_0 + PV(X) = P_0 + S_0$$

This put-call parity relationship holds when the following three statements are true:

1. Both the call and put options are European options.

2. Both the call and put options have the same exercise price, X.

3. The underlying stock does not pay dividends prior to expiration of the option.

Example 6.23

Consider a European call option on GE stock. The exercise price is $30 and the time until expiration of the option is 6 months. The annual effective risk-free interest rate is 6%. A share of GE stock currently sells for $30. Assume that the GE stock does not pay dividends during the next 6 months.

If a European put option on GE stock with an exercise price of $30 and 6 months until expiration is currently priced at $4.14, then what is the current price of the call option?

Solution

Using put-call parity, we have:

$$C_0 + PV(X) = P_0 + S_0$$

$$\Rightarrow C_0 + \frac{30}{(1.06)^{0.5}} = 4.14 + 30$$

$$\Rightarrow C_0 = 4.14 + 30 - \frac{30}{(1.06)^{0.5}} = \$5.00 \qquad \blacklozenge\blacklozenge$$

Black-Scholes option valuation

In 1973, Fischer Black and Myron Scholes developed an option valuation formula that is still used as a standard model to value options.

Black-Scholes call option pricing formula

The value of a call option on a stock that does not pay dividends is:

$$C_0 = S_0 N(d_1) - PV(X) N(d_2)$$

where:

$$d_1 = \frac{\ln\left(\dfrac{S_0}{PV(X)}\right)}{\sigma\sqrt{t}} + \frac{\sigma\sqrt{t}}{2}$$

$$d_2 = d_1 - \sigma\sqrt{t}$$

$N(d) =$ probability that a standard normal random variable is less than d

$\sigma =$ standard deviation of the continuously compounded annual rate of return of the stock (often called stock price volatility)

$PV(X)$ is calculated using the risk-free interest rate, r_f

$t =$ time until the option matures, in years.

The formula looks intimidating, but it isn't difficult to use. We do, however, need a standard normal distribution table to find the values of $N(d_1)$ and $N(d_2)$. A standard normal distribution table is presented in Appendix A.

Example 6.24

The current price of a stock is $75. The standard deviation of its continuously compounded returns is 0.5. The stock does not pay any dividends. The annual effective risk-free interest rate is 12%.

Determine the value of a 6-month European call on this stock with an exercise price of $62.

Solution

Plugging the values into the Black-Scholes equation, we have:

$$S_0 = 75; \quad \sigma = 0.5; \quad t = 0.5; \quad X = 62; \quad r_f = 12\% \text{ (annual effective rate)}$$

$$PV(X) = \frac{62}{(1.12)^{0.5}} = 58.58449$$

$$d_1 = \frac{\ln\left(\dfrac{S_0}{PV(X)}\right)}{\sigma\sqrt{t}} + \frac{\sigma\sqrt{t}}{2} = \frac{\ln\left(\dfrac{75}{58.58449}\right)}{0.5\sqrt{0.5}} + \frac{0.5\sqrt{0.5}}{2} = 0.875449$$

$$d_2 = d_1 - \sigma\sqrt{t} = 0.521896$$

$$N(d_1) = N(0.875449) = 0.809335 \quad \text{(from a normal distribution table)}$$

$$N(d_2) = N(0.521896) = 0.699129 \quad \text{(from a normal distribution table)}$$

$$\begin{aligned}
C_0 &= S_0 N(d_1) - PV(X)N(d_2) \\
&= 75(0.809335) - 58.58449(0.699129) \\
&= 19.74205
\end{aligned}$$

The current value of the call option is $19.74.   ◆◆

The Black-Scholes model assumes that the stock price is log-normally distributed, which is the same as assuming that the continuous rate of return on the stock is normally distributed.

Example 6.25

Assume a stock's current price is $150. The standard deviation of its continuously compounded annual returns is 0.4. The stock pays no dividends. The risk-free rate of return is 5%, compounded semiannually.

If a European call option on the stock expires in one year and has an exercise price of $100, what is its current value?

Solution

Plugging the values into the Black-Scholes equation, we have:

$$S_0 = 150; \quad \sigma = 0.4; \quad t = 1; \quad X = 100; \quad r_f = (1.025)^2 - 1 \text{ (annual effective rate)}$$

$$PV(X) = \frac{100}{(1.025)^2} = 95.18144$$

$$d_1 = \frac{\ln\left(\dfrac{S_0}{PV(X)}\right)}{\sigma\sqrt{t}} + \frac{\sigma\sqrt{t}}{2} = \frac{\ln\left(\dfrac{150}{95.18}\right)}{0.4\sqrt{1}} + \frac{0.4\sqrt{1}}{2} = 1.337126$$

$$d_2 = d_1 - \sigma\sqrt{t} = 0.937126$$

$$N(d_1) = N(1.337126) = 0.909409$$

$$N(d_2) = N(0.937126) = 0.825653$$

$$C_0 = S_0 N(d_1) - PV(X)N(d_2) = 150(0.909409) - 95.18144(0.825653) = 57.82452$$

The current value of the call option is $57.82.   ◆◆

The Black-Scholes call option pricing formula does not directly calculate the value of a put, but if we use it to calculate the value of a European call option, then we can use put-call parity to find the value of the corresponding European put option.

Example 6.26

Assume a stock's current price is $150. The standard deviation of its continuously compounded annual returns is 0.4. The stock pays no dividends. The risk-free rate of return is 5%, compounded semiannually.

If a European put option on the stock expires in one year and has an exercise price of $100, what is its current value?

Solution

From the previous example, the value of the corresponding call option is $57.82. Put-call parity can then be used to find the value of the put option:

$$C_0 + PV(X) = P_0 + S_0$$

$$57.82452 + \frac{100}{(1.025)^2} = P_0 + 150$$

$$P_0 = 57.82452 + \frac{100}{(1.025)^2} - 150 = 3.005962 \quad \Rightarrow \$3.01 \qquad \blacklozenge\blacklozenge$$

Forward contract valuation

As we recall, a forward contract is an agreement between two parties to buy or sell an asset at a specified future time at the forward price.

The following notation is used to value forward contracts:

t	Time now (when the forward contract is agreed upon)
T	Future time when the transaction will occur
S_t	Asset price now, also known as the **spot price**
$F(t,T)$	Forward price agreed now
S_T	Future asset price at time T
r_f	Annual effective risk-free interest rate.

For an asset that does not produce income between times t and T, the forward price and the spot price are related as follows:

Forward price

The forward price $F(t,T)$ is equal to:

$$F(t,T) = S_t (1 + r_f)^{(T-t)}$$

To see why this result holds, let's consider the two ways in which we can be sure of holding one unit of this asset at time T.

Method 1   We can purchase the asset now (at time t) at a price of S_t and hold it until time T. This method has an initial cost of S_t.

Method 2 We can enter into a forward contract to buy one unit of the asset at time T at a forward price of $F(t,T)$. Since the risk-free interest rate is r_f, this method has an initial cost of:

$$F(t,T)(1+r_f)^{-(T-t)}$$

Since both methods are worth S_T at time T, they must have the same initial cost:

$$S_t = F(t,T)(1+r_f)^{-(T-t)}$$
$$\Rightarrow F(t,T) = S_t(1+r_f)^{(T-t)}$$

Example 6.27

A stock that pays no dividends has a current price of $50. The annual effective risk-free rate of return is 5%. Calculate the forward price for purchasing the stock in one year.

Solution

The forward price is:

$$F(0,1) = S_0(1+r_f)^{(1-0)} = 50(1.05) = \$52.50 \qquad \blacklozenge\blacklozenge$$

This result only applies to assets that do not produce income, *eg* stocks that pay no dividends.

A stock that pays dividends has a lower forward price than an otherwise equivalent stock that does not pay dividends. This is because an investor who purchases the stock through a forward contract misses out on the dividends paid during the term of the contract, which the investor would otherwise receive if the investor bought the stock in the spot market.

Let's consider the case when the amount and timing of the dividend payments are known. We need to define one more term for an income-producing asset.

Let $D(t,T)$ be the value of all net cash flows to the owner of the asset, accumulated to time T. For a stock, $D(t,T)$ can be understood as the accumulated value of the dividends.

If we know the amount and timing of the dividends, then the formula for the forward price is:

$$F(t,T) = S_t(1+r_f)^{(T-t)} - D(t,T)$$

Example 6.28

A stock has a current price of $50 and pays a dividend of $2 one year from now. If the annal effective risk-free rate of return is 5%, then what is the forward price for purchasing the stock in one year (just after the dividend is paid)?

Solution

Applying the formula, we have:

$$F(t,T) = S_t(1+r_f)^{(T-t)} - D(t,T) = 50(1.05) - 2 = \$50.50 \qquad \blacklozenge\blacklozenge$$

Futures contract valuation

Futures contracts are similar to forward contracts in that both are agreements to provide an asset in the future in exchange for a future payment (the **futures price**). Again, there is no cost to enter a futures contract.

The futures market is an active market, and new futures prices are constantly generated. At the end of each day, the final futures price is noted, and all open futures positions are trued up to that price. This means that the delivery price for an open futures contract changes each day. This is very different from a forward contract, because once a forward contract is agreed upon, the forward price for that contract does not change.

The next example illustrates the mark to market adjustments as the futures price changes over 5 days.

Example 6.29

Bob opens a long futures position for an asset, and Sam simultaneously opens a short futures position in the same asset. The contract calls for delivery of 100 units of the asset. The current futures price is $20, and Bob and Sam each have $1,000 deposited with their broker.

Calculate the contract price, Bob's account value and Sam's account value as the futures price changes to $22, $18, $24 and $26 over the next four trading days.

Solution

When the futures price changes to $22, the contract value (of 100 shares) changes to:

$$\$22 \times 100 = \$2,200$$

This is an increase of $200 from the original contract value.

Since Bob has the long futures position (he will buy the shares), his account his credited with $200 to compensate him for the increase in the contract value. And since Sam has the short futures position (he will sell the shares), his account is reduced by $200 to offset the increase in the contract value.

The table below illustrates how the mark-to-market process affects Bob's and Sam's account value as the futures price changes.

Day	Futures price	Contract value	Bob's account value	Sam's account value
1	20	2,000	1,000	1,000
2	22	2,200	1,200	800
3	18	1,800	800	1,200
4	24	2,400	1,400	600
5	26	2,600	1,600	400

◆◆

The futures market is a zero sum game. Any gain on a long futures contract is equal to the loss on a short futures contract, and any loss on a long futures contract is equal to the gain on a short futures contract. Since the number of long positions is always equal to the number of short positions, the exchange is insulated from changes in the futures price.

Chapter 6 Practice Questions

Question guide

- Questions 6.1 – 6.14 test material from Sections 6.1 – 6.3.

- Questions 6.15 – 6.17 test material from Sections 6.4 – 6.5.

- Questions 6.18 – 6.20 are from the SOA/CAS Course 2 exam or the IOA/FOA 102 exam.

Question 6.1

An investor buys a $1,000, 13-week T-bill for X and earns an annual effective yield of 6.5%. Determine X.

Question 6.2

An investor deposits $1,000,000 at the beginning of each year for 5 years in a 5-year GIC with an insurance company that guarantees an annual 6% interest rate on the fund. Determine the lump sum payable to the investor at 5 years if the interest that is generated each year is reinvested at 6%, and then determine the lump sum payable to the investor at 5 years if the interest that is generated each year is reinvested at 4%.

Question 6.3

Company A enters into a 4-year swap as a fixed-rate payer, paying 6.8% and receiving 1-year LIBOR (London InterBank Offered Rate). Company B enters into a 4-year swap as a floating-rate payer, receiving 6.7% and paying 1-year LIBOR.

The floating rate payments are determined by 1-year LIBOR on each payment date. The notional amount is $1,000,000. 1-year LIBOR develops as shown in the table below:

Time	1-year LIBOR
1	7.0%
2	8.0%
3	6.7%
4	6.0%

Identify the cash flows to/from each party during the 4-year term of the swap.

Question 6.4

An interest-rate floor maturing in 2 years makes semiannual payments and has a notional amount of $1,000,000. The strike rate is 4% and the variable rate develops as shown in the table below:

Time	6-month index rate
0.50	4.50%
1.00	4.00%
1.50	3.50%
2.00	2.75%

Determine the cash flows from the floor.

Question 6.5

A 15-year bond with a face amount of $100 pays semiannual coupons of 4% per year and is to be redeemed for $105. The bond is priced to yield 5% per year, convertible semiannually. Determine the price of the bond.

Question 6.6

Using the information from Question 6.5, determine the book value of the bond immediately after the 10th coupon is paid.

Question 6.7

Using the information from Question 6.5, determine the amount of discount accumulated in the 11th coupon payment.

Question 6.8

For a certain bond that pays semiannual coupons, it has been determined that the amount of premium amortized in the 10th payment is $0.305135 and the amount of premium amortized in the 15th coupon payment is $0.345233. Determine the bond's annual effective yield.

Question 6.9

A bond that has just been issued pays coupons of 10% a year payable semiannually. The yield expressed as a nominal rate compounded semiannually is 6% and the price paid per $1,000 par value is $1,235. The bond is to be redeemed after 10 years. By first finding the redemption value, find the interest earned in the 9th coupon payment.

Question 6.10

A bond with a $1,000 face amount pays semiannual coupons at a rate of X% per year. The bond has 20 years to maturity and is priced to yield 6% compounded semiannually. The bond's price is $884.426140. Determine the bond's semiannual coupon payment.

Question 6.11

A stock pays expected dividends of $10 at the end of each year indefinitely. The current stock price is $200. Determine the investor's required yield.

Question 6.12

A stock's next expected dividend is $10 one year from now. After that, its dividends are expected to grow by X% per year indefinitely. The current stock price is $333.33. The investor's required return is 5%. Determine X.

Question 6.13

A stock is expected to pay quarterly dividends of $0.50 at the end of each quarter. Five years from now, the investor is expected to sell the stock for $15. The investor's annual effective required return is 15%. Determine the current price of the stock.

Question 6.14

A company's net income is $25,000,000. It has 1.5 million shares outstanding and its price-to-earnings ratio is 12.1. Calculate the current price of the stock.

Question 6.15

Jack sells 100 shares of a certain stock short for $60 and buys it back one year later for $50. Just before he buys it back, a per share dividend of X is paid. Jack is required to make a margin deposit of 50% and the margin interest rate is 5%. Jack's short sale yield is 31.6667%.

Jill sells 100 shares of a certain stock short for $65 and buys it back one year later for B. Just before she buys it back, a per share dividend of X is paid. Jill is also required to make a margin deposit of 50% and the margin interest rate is 5%. Jill's short sale yield is half of Jack's.

Determine B.

Question 6.16

You are given the following information:

- Price of 6-month European call option with strike price of X is $3.33.

- Price of 6-month European put option with strike price of X is $10.31.

- $N(d_1) = 0.366172$

- $N(d_2) = 0.289741$

- The annual effective risk-free rate of return is 8%.

Use the Black-Scholes formula to find the strike price X.

Question 6.17

A T-bill maturing in 150 days for $1,000,000 has a current price of $979,167. A T-bill maturing in 60 days for $1,000,000 has a current price of $993,333.

Calculate the futures price of a 90-day T-bill to be delivered in 60 days.

Question 6.18   *SOA/CAS*

You are interested in purchasing a call option on a common stock that is currently trading at a price of $100 per share. You are given the following information:

(i)   the standard deviation of the continuously compounded annual rate of return on the stock is 0.4;

(ii)   the time to maturity of the call is 3 months (0.25 years); and

(iii) $\ln\left(\dfrac{\text{Current Share Price}}{\text{Present Value of the Exercise Price}}\right) = -0.08$, at the risk-free rate.

Calculate the price of each call option using Black-Scholes.

Question 6.19   *SOA/CAS*

You have decided to invest in two bonds. Bond X is an n-year bond with semiannual coupons, while bond Y is an accumulation bond redeemable in $\frac{n}{2}$ years. The desired yield rate is the same for both bonds. You also have the following information:

Bond X

- Par value is $1,000.

- The ratio of the semiannual bond rate to the desired semiannual yield rate, $\frac{r}{i}$, is 1.03125.

- The present value of the redemption value is $381.50.

Bond Y

- Redemption value is the same as the redemption value of bond X.

- Price to yield is $647.80.

What is the price of bond X?

Question 6.20   *FOA/IOA*

A share of common stock pays annual dividends. The next dividend is expected to be $5.00 per share and is due in exactly 3 months. Subsequent dividends are expected to grow at a rate of 4% per year and inflation will be 1.5% per year. The price per share is $125 and dividends are expected to continue forever.

Calculate the annual effective real rate of return for an investor who purchases this stock.

7

Duration, convexity, and immunization

Overview

If we are given a series of fixed cash flows (*eg* a bond) and a yield at which to discount the cash flows, then we can determine the present value—or price—of the cash flows. In this chapter, we study how a bond's price changes when its yield changes.

We study two common measures of bond price sensitivity: **duration** and **convexity**. There are three types of duration and convexity (**modified**, **Macaulay**, and **effective**). The appropriate type to use depends on the compounding frequency of the yield and whether the bond's cash flows vary with changes in its yield.

A company's **surplus** is equal to the present value of its assets minus the present value of its liabilities. If the yield used to calculate those present values changes, then both present values change, and therefore, so does the surplus. This chapter introduces a process called **immunization**, in which the assets and the liabilities are structured so that the surplus is protected against interest rate risk, *ie* the surplus does not decrease as a result of yield changes. We can also protect the surplus against the potentially adverse effects of yield changes by matching the asset cash flows exactly to the liability cash flows, a process known as **dedication.**

Finally, a comment about notation in this chapter. In previous chapters, we've used the variable p to indicate the compounding frequency of a nominal interest rate. In this chapter, we use P to indicate the price of a financial instrument and so to avoid confusion we use m instead of p to indicate compounding frequency.

7.1 Price as a function of yield

We begin by estimating how the price of a bond changes in response to changes in its yield. We do this by re-examining the bond price formula. In this chapter, we use y for yield instead of the variable i that was used in Chapter 6.

The price of an asset with fixed cash flows depends on its cash flows and on its yield:

$$P = \sum_{t>0} CF_t \left(1 + \frac{y}{m}\right)^{-mt}$$

where:

P = asset price

y = yield (nominal rate compounded m times per year)

CF_t = cash flow at time t years

The price curve graph below illustrates the relationship between the price of a bond and its yield. Notice that the price falls as the yield increases and that the curve has a convex shape:

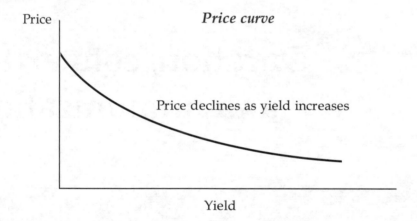

Using the Taylor Series, the price resulting from a change in the yield (Δy) is:

$$P(y + \Delta y) = P(y) + (\Delta y)P'(y) + \frac{(\Delta y)^2 P''(y)}{2} + \cdots + \frac{(\Delta y)^n P^{(n)}(y)}{n!} + \cdots$$

If we use just the first two terms of the Taylor Series, then we have:

$$P(y + \Delta y) \approx P(y) + (\Delta y)P'(y)$$

Thus, if we are given the current price of a bond and the slope of the bond's price curve, we can *estimate* the new bond price resulting from the change in the yield by using the tangent line to the price curve.

As the price curve graph on the following page illustrates, the estimate provides an approximation for $P(y + \Delta y)$.

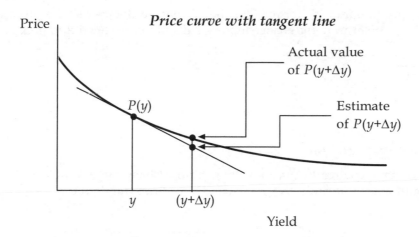

We can rearrange the partial Taylor Series in order to find a formula for the estimated percentage change in a bond's price ($\%\Delta P$) that results from a change in the bond's yield:

$$P(y + \Delta y) \approx P(y) + (\Delta y)P'(y)$$

$$\Rightarrow \frac{P(y + \Delta y) - P(y)}{P(y)} \approx (\Delta y)\frac{P'(y)}{P(y)}$$

$$\Rightarrow \%\Delta P \approx (\Delta y)\frac{P'(y)}{P(y)}$$

The final equation tells us that the percentage change in a bond's price resulting from a change in its yield is approximately equal to the change in yield multiplied by the derivative of the bond's price with respect to yield, divided by price.

7.2 Modified duration

Modified duration is defined as the negative of the derivative of the price function with respect to the yield, divided by the current price. Modified duration is the *negative* of the derivative because a bond's price has an inverse relationship with its yield. When the yield of a bond goes down, the price of the bond goes up. The negative sign in the formula below makes modified duration conveniently positive for bonds with fixed cash flows.

Modified duration

Modified duration is the negative of the derivative of the price function with respect to yield, divided by the current price:

$$ModD = -\frac{P'(y)}{P(y)}$$

Substituting modified duration into the formula for the percentage change in price gives us the percentage change in price in terms of the change in the yield and the modified duration:

$$\%\Delta P \approx (\Delta y)\frac{P'(y)}{P(y)}$$

$$\Rightarrow \%\Delta P \approx -(\Delta y)(ModD)$$

Relationship between price and modified duration

The approximate percentage change in price resulting from a change in a bond's yield is the change in the yield multiplied by the negative of the bond's modified duration:

$$\%\Delta P \approx -(\Delta y)(ModD)$$

When discussing duration, it is frequently convenient to refer to changes in the yield in terms of **basis points** (bp). One basis point is equal to 0.01%, and 100 basis points is equal to 1%. If, for example, the yield increases from 5% to 6%, we say that the yield has increased by 100 basis points. This is more precise than saying that the yield increased by 1%, which might leave one wondering if the new yield is $5\% \times 1.01 = 5.05\%$ or $5\% + 1\% = 6\%$. If a 5% yield increases by 100 basis points, then the new yield is unambiguously 6%.

Modified duration is sometimes described as the approximate percentage increase in price resulting from a 100 basis point decrease in yield. For example, if a bond's modified duration is 4, and if its yield falls by 100 bp, then the price increases by approximately 4%:

$$\%\Delta P \approx -(\Delta y)(ModD)$$

$$\%\Delta P \approx -(-0.01)(4) = 0.04 \quad \Rightarrow \quad 4\% \text{ increase in price}$$

Example 7.1

The current price of a bond is $110 and its yield is 7%. The modified duration is 5. Estimate the price of the bond if its yield falls to 6%.

Solution

First, we find the approximate percentage change in the price:

$$\%\Delta P \approx -(\Delta y)(ModD) = -(-0.01)(5) = 0.05 = 5\%$$

The bond price increases by approximately 5%, so the new bond price is approximately $115.50:

$$110 \times 1.05 = \$115.50 \qquad\qquad\qquad\qquad\qquad\qquad\qquad \blacklozenge\blacklozenge$$

If we are given a bond's cash flows and its current yield, then we can calculate the bond's price and its derivative:

$$P = \sum CF_t \left(1 + \frac{y}{m}\right)^{-mt}$$

$$\frac{dP}{dy} = \sum -tCF_t \left(1 + \frac{y}{m}\right)^{-mt-1} = \frac{\sum -tCF_t \left(1 + \frac{y}{m}\right)^{-mt}}{\left(1 + \frac{y}{m}\right)}$$

Dividing the derivative by the price gives us another formula for modified duration:

$$ModD = -\dfrac{\dfrac{dP}{dy}}{P} = \dfrac{\sum tCF_t \left(1+\dfrac{y}{m}\right)^{-mt}}{P\left(1+\dfrac{y}{m}\right)}$$

Modified duration

The modified duration of a bond can be expressed in terms of its cash flows and its yield:

$$ModD = \dfrac{\sum\limits_{t>0} tCF_t \left(1+\dfrac{y}{m}\right)^{-mt}}{P\left(1+\dfrac{y}{m}\right)}$$

Substituting for P, modified duration can also be written as:

$$ModD = \dfrac{\sum tCF_t \left(1+\dfrac{y}{m}\right)^{-mt}}{\left[\sum CF_t \left(1+\dfrac{y}{m}\right)^{-mt}\right]\left(1+\dfrac{y}{m}\right)}$$

A bond's cash flows are multiples of its par value, so the par value acts as a scaling factor for both the numerator and the denominator. Consequently, a bond's duration does not depend on its par value.

Example 7.2

A 5-year bond pays annual coupons of 5% and is priced at par. Calculate the modified duration of the bond with respect to the annual effective yield of the bond.

Solution

Any value we choose to assume for the par value will produce the same duration. It is standard practice to assume that the par value is 100 (unless we are told otherwise).

Since the bond is priced at par, its annual effective yield is 5%.

Hence, the modified duration is:

$$ModD = \dfrac{\sum tCF_t \left(1+\dfrac{y}{m}\right)^{-mt}}{P\left(1+\dfrac{y}{m}\right)}$$

$$= \dfrac{\dfrac{1\times5}{1.05}+\dfrac{2\times5}{1.05^2}+\dfrac{3\times5}{1.05^3}+\dfrac{4\times5}{1.05^4}+\dfrac{5\times105}{1.05^5}}{100(1.05)}$$

$$= \dfrac{454.595}{105}$$

$$= 4.329$$

◆◆

The modified duration depends on the frequency with which the yield is compounded. The previous example is repeated below, but this time we calculate the modified duration that is appropriate for determining the impact of a change in the semiannual yield of the bond.

Example 7.3

A 5-year bond pays annual coupons of 5% and is priced at par. Calculate the modified duration with respect to the semiannually compounded yield of the bond.

Solution

Since the bond is priced at par, its annual effective yield is 5%. Its semiannually compounded yield is therefore 4.939%:

$$2 \times \left[(1.05)^{0.5} - 1 \right] = 4.939\%$$

Using 4.939% as the semiannually compounded yield and setting $m = 2$:

$$ModD = \frac{\sum tCF_t \left(1 + \dfrac{y}{m} \right)^{-mt}}{P \left(1 + \dfrac{y}{m} \right)}$$

$$= \frac{\dfrac{1 \times 5}{1.024695^2} + \dfrac{2 \times 5}{1.024695^4} + \dfrac{3 \times 5}{1.024695^6} + \dfrac{4 \times 5}{1.024695^8} + \dfrac{5 \times 105}{1.024695^{10}}}{100(1.024695)}$$

$$= \frac{454.5951}{102.4695}$$

$$= 4.436 \qquad\qquad\qquad \blacklozenge\,\blacklozenge$$

Notice that the duration with respect to the semiannually compounded yield is a little larger than the duration with respect to the annual yield. This is because changing a yield that is compounded more frequently has a bigger impact on price than changing a yield that is compounded less frequently.

This can be illustrated using the numbers from the examples above. The semiannually compounded yield of 4.939% is equivalent to an annual effective yield of 5.000%. If we increase the semiannually compounded yield by 100 basis points to 5.939%, then we have a yield that is equivalent to an annual effective yield of 6.027%:

$$\left(1 + \frac{0.04939}{2} \right)^2 - 1 = 0.05000 \quad \text{and} \quad \left(1 + \frac{0.05939}{2} \right)^2 - 1 = 0.06027$$

So increasing the semiannually compounded yield by 100 basis points (from 4.939% to 5.939%) increases the annual effective yield by 102.7 basis points (from 5.000% to 6.027%). A 100 basis point increase in the semiannually compounded yield therefore has more impact on the price than a 100 basis point increase in the annual effective yield. Consequently, the modified duration with respect to the semiannually compounded yield is larger than the modified duration with respect to the annual effective yield.

7.3 *Macaulay duration*

The modified duration with respect to the bond's *continuously compounded* yield is known as the **Macaulay duration**. So Macaulay duration is a special case of modified duration. Some texts refer to Macaulay duration as simply "duration," leaving off the descriptive "Macaulay." Other texts use the term "duration" to refer generally to all types of duration. We take the latter approach.

Macaulay duration

Macaulay duration is the modified duration with respect to the bond's continuously compounded yield:

$$MacD = -\frac{P'(\delta)}{P(\delta)} = -\left(\frac{dP}{d\delta}\right)\frac{1}{P}$$

where:

δ = continuously compounded yield

If a bond has fixed cash flows, then the price of the bond is:

$$P = \sum CF_t e^{-\delta t}$$

The derivative of the price with respect to the bond's continuously compounded yield is:

$$\frac{dP}{d\delta} = \sum -t CF_t e^{-\delta t}$$

If we divide the derivative of the price by the price and multiply by -1, then we have a formula for Macaulay duration:

$$MacD = -\left(\frac{dP}{d\delta}\right)\frac{1}{P} = \frac{\sum t CF_t e^{-\delta t}}{\sum CF_t e^{-\delta t}}$$

From this formula, we see that Macaulay duration is the weighted average of the times that the cash flows occur, weighted by the present value of each cash flow. If there is only one cash flow, as in the case of a zero-coupon bond, then the Macaulay duration is equal to the length of time until that cash flow occurs.

Since Macaulay duration is the weighted average of the times that the cash flows occur, we can make the following observations about duration:

1.   A bond with higher coupons has a shorter duration, since the higher coupons place more weight on the earlier times relative to the weighting placed on the time of final principal cash flow.

2.   A bond with a higher yield has a shorter duration, since the higher yield has a stronger discounting effect on the present values of the more distant cash flows than it does on the present values of the near-term cash flows.

If y is the yield of the bond compounded m times per year, then:

$$e^{\delta} = \left(1 + \frac{y}{m}\right)^m$$

Therefore Macaulay duration can also be written in terms of the yield compounded m times per year:

$$MacD = \frac{\sum tCF_t e^{-\delta t}}{P} = \frac{\sum tCF_t \left(1+\dfrac{y}{m}\right)^{-mt}}{P}$$

Macaulay duration calculation

The Macaulay duration of a bond with fixed cash flows is:

$$MacD = \frac{\sum\limits_{t>0} tCF_t e^{-\delta t}}{P} = \frac{\sum\limits_{t>0} tCF_t \left(1+\dfrac{y}{m}\right)^{-mt}}{P}$$

Macaulay duration provides the approximate percentage change in price for a 100 basis point change in the bond's continuously compounded yield. If we wish to use Macaulay duration to determine the approximate price change for a percentage change in a yield that is not continuously compounded, then we must modify the calculation.

Recall that:

$$-\frac{P'(y)}{P(y)} = \frac{\sum tCF_t \left(1+\dfrac{y}{m}\right)^{-mt}}{P\left(1+\dfrac{y}{m}\right)}$$

Therefore:

$$-\frac{P'(y)}{P(y)} = \frac{MacD}{\left(1+\dfrac{y}{m}\right)}$$

From the previous section, we recall that $-\dfrac{P'(y)}{P(y)}$ is modified duration.

Relationship between Macaulay duration and modified duration

Macaulay duration can be modified by dividing it by $(1+y/m)$ to obtain modified duration:

$$ModD = \frac{MacD}{\left(1+\dfrac{y}{m}\right)}$$

This is how modified duration gained the descriptor "modified." If we begin with Macaulay duration, then it must be modified by dividing it by $(1+y/m)$ in order to obtain the modified duration that is useful for analyzing a shift in the yield y that is compounded m times per year.

Macaulay duration is the limit of modified duration as $m \to \infty$. Therefore, Macaulay duration is equal to modified duration if y is a continuously compounded yield.

Macaulay duration is only appropriate for analyzing the effect of a shift in the continuously compounded yield. Modified duration is appropriate for analyzing the effect of a shift in y, where y is the nominal annual yield compounded m times per year.

Example 7.4

A 5-year bond pays annual coupons of 5% and is priced at par. Calculate the Macaulay duration and use it to determine the modified duration with respect to the annual effective yield of the bond.

Solution

The Macaulay duration is the weighted average timing of the cash flows, weighted by the present value of each cash flow:

$$
\begin{aligned}
MacD &= \frac{\sum tCF_t\left(1+\dfrac{y}{m}\right)^{-mt}}{P} \\[4pt]
&= \frac{\dfrac{1\times 5}{1.05} + \dfrac{2\times 5}{1.05^2} + \dfrac{3\times 5}{1.05^3} + \dfrac{4\times 5}{1.05^4} + \dfrac{5\times 105}{1.05^5}}{100} \\[4pt]
&= 4.54595
\end{aligned}
$$

The modified duration is:

$$
ModD = \frac{MacD}{\left(1+\dfrac{y}{m}\right)} = \frac{4.54595}{1.05} = 4.329
$$

◆◆

Example 7.5

A 3-year bond pays semiannual coupons at an annual rate of 8% and has a semiannually compounded yield of 9%. Calculate the Macaulay duration and use it to determine the modified duration with respect to the semiannually compounded yield of the bond.

Solution

The bond pays semiannual coupons of $4 and the semiannual yield is 4.5%.

The price of the bond is $97.421:

$$
\begin{aligned}
P &= \sum CF_t\left(1+\frac{y}{m}\right)^{-mt} \\[4pt]
&= \frac{4}{1.045} + \frac{4}{(1.045)^2} + \frac{4}{(1.045)^3} + \frac{4}{(1.045)^4} + \frac{4}{(1.045)^5} + \frac{104}{(1.045)^6} \\[4pt]
&= 97.421
\end{aligned}
$$

The Macaulay duration is:

$$
\frac{\sum tCF_t\left(1+\dfrac{y}{m}\right)^{-mt}}{P} = \frac{\dfrac{0.5\times 4}{1.045} + \dfrac{1\times 4}{(1.045)^2} + \dfrac{1.5\times 4}{(1.045)^3} + \dfrac{2\times 4}{(1.045)^4} + \dfrac{2.5\times 4}{(1.045)^5} + \dfrac{3\times 104}{(1.045)^6}}{97.421}
$$

When there are a lot of terms in the numerator, it is convenient to use an increasing annuity-immediate to calculate the duration of a bond.

Recall that the formula for an increasing annuity-immediate is:

$$(Ia)_{\overline{n}|} = v + 2v^2 + 3v^3 + \cdots + nv^n = \frac{\ddot{a}_{\overline{n}|} - nv^n}{i}$$

Pulling out the factor (0.5×4) from the six terms, we have an increasing annuity-immediate:

$$MacD = \frac{0.5 \times 4 \times (Ia)_{\overline{6}|4.5\%} + \dfrac{3 \times 100}{(1.045)^6}}{97.421}$$

$$= \frac{0.5 \times 4 \times \dfrac{5.38998 - 4.60737}{0.045} + \dfrac{3 \times 100}{(1.045)^6}}{97.421}$$

$$= \frac{2 \times 17.3912 + 230.3687}{97.421}$$

$$= 2.7217$$

The modified duration is therefore:

$$ModD = \frac{MacD}{\left(1 + \dfrac{y}{m}\right)} = \frac{2.7217}{1.045} = 2.6045$$

◆◆

If an n-year bond is priced at par and pays coupons m times per year, then we can derive a shortcut to calculate the Macaulay duration. Since the bond is priced at par, its yield compounded m times per year is the same as its nominal coupon rate compounded m times per year:

$$\text{Yield} = \text{Annual coupon rate} = y^{(m)}$$

In the demonstration below, we use the formula for an annuity that increases in each $m$thly period, and therefore, for clarity, we label the yield as $y^{(m)}$. Also, the amount of principal does not affect the duration calculation, so we can assume that the principal is \$1. Since the bond is assumed to be priced at par, this implies that $P = 1$.

Hence, the Macaulay duration is:

$$\frac{1}{P} \sum tCF_t \left(1 + \frac{y^{(m)}}{m}\right)^{-mt} = \left[\sum t \left(\frac{y^{(m)}}{m}\right)\left(1 + \frac{y^{(m)}}{m}\right)^{-mt}\right] + n\left(1 + \frac{y^{(m)}}{m}\right)^{-nm}$$

The coupon payments of $\dfrac{y^{(m)}}{m}$ occur at the following times:

$$\left\{ \frac{1}{m}, \frac{2}{m}, \cdots, \frac{nm-1}{m}, n \right\}$$

So we have:

$$MacD = y^{(m)}\left[\frac{1}{m^2}v^{\frac{1}{m}} + \frac{2}{m^2}v^{\frac{2}{m}} + \frac{3}{m^2}v^{\frac{3}{m}} + \cdots + \frac{nm-1}{m^2}v^{\frac{nm-1}{m}} + \frac{nm}{m^2}v^{\frac{nm}{m}}\right] + nv^n$$

$$= y^{(m)}\left(I^{(m)}a\right)_{\overline{n}|}^{(m)} + nv^n$$

$$= y^{(m)}\left(\frac{\ddot{a}_{\overline{n}|}^{(m)} - nv^n}{y^{(m)}}\right) + nv^n$$

$$= \ddot{a}_{\overline{n}|}^{(m)} - nv^n + nv^n$$

$$= \ddot{a}_{\overline{n}|}^{(m)}$$

Macaulay duration for bonds priced at par

If a n-year bond is priced at par and its coupon rate is paid in m installments per year, then the Macaulay duration of the bond is equal to the present value of an annuity-due that pays \$1 per year in $m$thly installments for n years:

$$MacD = \ddot{a}_{\overline{n}|}^{(m)}$$

Looking back to Example 7.4, we calculated the Macaulay duration of a 5-year bond that pays annual coupons of 5% and is priced at par. Since the bond stands at par, we could have calculated the Macaulay duration using the result above, with $m=1$, $n=5$, and an interest rate of 5%:

$$MacD = \ddot{a}_{\overline{5}|5\%} = \frac{1-1.05^{-5}}{0.05/1.05} = 4.54595$$

 ### Example 7.6

A 10-year bond pays semiannual coupons of 7.4% and is priced at par. Calculate the Macaulay duration of the bond.

Solution

The bond stands at par, so we have:

$$MacD = \ddot{a}_{\overline{10}|}^{(2)} = \frac{1-(1+i)^{-10}}{d^{(2)}}$$

Since $i^{(2)} = 0.074$, we have:

$$\left(1 - \frac{d^{(2)}}{2}\right)^{-2} = \left(1 + \frac{0.074}{2}\right)^2 \quad \Rightarrow \quad d^{(2)} = 0.071360$$

Hence, the Macaulay duration is:

$$\frac{1-(1+i)^{-10}}{d^{(2)}} = \frac{1-1.037^{-20}}{0.071360} = 7.23754$$

◆◆

7.4 *Effective duration*

Macaulay and modified duration are appropriate for bonds with fixed cash flows, but some financial instruments, such as callable bonds, have **interest-sensitive cash flows**. The cash flows from callable bonds depend on future interest rates. If interest rates fall, then callable bonds are likely to be paid off early. For callable bonds and other bonds that do not have fixed cash flows, we use another kind of duration, known as **effective duration**.

We use the following notation when calculating effective duration:

P_0 is the current price of a bond

P_+ is the bond price if interest rates shift up by Δy

P_- is the bond price if the interest rates shift down by Δy

If a bond does not have fixed cash flows, then these prices are calculated by valuing the interest-sensitive cash flows associated with the new interest rates. Such valuations, of course, require that we know how the cash flows change as interest rates change. That is, we need to know the functional relationship between a bond's cash flows and the level of interest rates in order to calculate P_0, P_+, and P_-. We do not explicitly calculate P_0, P_+, and P_- in this chapter, but we need to be aware that the cash flows underlying these prices may vary depending on the level of interest rates.

When we calculated modified duration and Macaulay duration, we assumed that the bond's cash flows were fixed and did not change as interest rates changed. Based on this assumption, we were able to determine an expression for $P'(y)$. When calculating effective duration, we must consider the possibility that the bond's cash flows are not fixed, that is, that they are interest sensitive. Therefore, we cannot directly calculate a value for $P'(y)$.

Consequently, when calculating effective duration, we estimate the derivative of a bond's price with respect to yield as the "rise over run" from the price points we have available:

$$\text{Estimate for } P'(y) \ = \frac{P_+ - P_-}{2\Delta y}$$

The graph below illustrates that we are using the slope of the secant to estimate the slope of the price function:

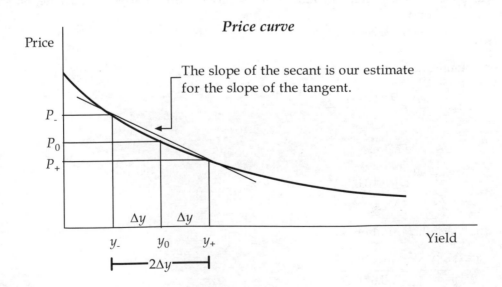

Effective duration (*EffD*) is similar to modified duration, but it uses the estimate for $P'(y)$ instead of the actual value:

$$EffD = -\frac{\text{Estimate for } P'(y)}{P(y)} = -\frac{\dfrac{P_+ - P_-}{2\Delta y}}{P_o} = \frac{P_- - P_+}{P_0(2\Delta y)}$$

Effective duration

Effective duration is calculated with the following formula:

$$EffD = \frac{P_- - P_+}{P_0(2\Delta y)}$$

If the cash flows of a bond are fixed, then the effective duration calculation produces a result that is quite close to the bond's modified duration if we use a small value of Δy. However, if the cash flows are interest sensitive (*ie* if the cash flows change as yields change), then effective duration provides a better measure than modified duration of the bond's sensitivity to interest rate changes.

In the example below, we calculate the effective duration for a bond with fixed cash flows.

Example 7.7

A 3-year bond paying 8% coupons semiannually has a current price of $97.4211 and a current yield of 9% compounded semiannually. If the bond's yield increases by 100 basis points, then the price will be $94.9243. If the bond's yield decreases by 100 basis points, then the price will be $100.00. Calculate the effective duration of the bond.

Solution

The effective duration is 2.6050:

$$EffD = \frac{P_- - P_+}{P_0(2\Delta y)} = \frac{100.0000 - 94.9243}{97.4211(2)(0.01)} = 2.6050$$

◆ ◆

Looking back to Example 7.5, the modified duration of a 3-year bond that pays semiannual coupons of 8% and has a semiannually compounded yield of 9% is 2.6045. Since we calculated the effective duration to be 2.6050, we see that the effective duration and the modified duration are almost the same. As this example illustrates, when a bond has fixed cash flows, its effective duration is quite close to its modified duration.

In the next example, we examine a callable bond.

Example 7.8

A 5-year callable bond has a current price of $100.00. If the yield increases by 50 basis points, then the price falls to $97.90. If the yield decreases by 50 basis points, then the price increases to $101.80. Calculate the effective duration of the bond.

Solution

The effective duration is 3.900:

$$EffD = \frac{P_- - P_+}{P_0(2\Delta y)} = \frac{101.80 - 97.90}{100.00(2)(0.005)} = 3.900$$

◆ ◆

Effective duration can be used in the same way as modified duration to estimate price changes resulting from changes in the yield:

$$\%\Delta P \approx (\Delta y)\frac{P'(y)}{P(y)}$$

$$\Rightarrow \%\Delta P \approx -(\Delta y)(EffD)$$

Relationship between price and effective duration

The percentage change in a bond's price resulting from a change in its yield is approximately equal to the change in the yield multiplied by the negative of the bond's effective duration:

$$\%\Delta P \approx -(\Delta y)(EffD)$$

Example 7.9

Use the effective duration from Example 7.8 to estimate the change in price resulting from a 100 basis point increase in the bond's yield.

Solution

The effective duration is 3.900, so the price change when the yield increases by 100 basis points is:

$$\%\Delta P \approx -(\Delta y)(EffD)$$
$$\%\Delta P \approx -(0.01)(3.900)$$
$$\%\Delta P \approx -3.900\%$$

The price resulting from a 100 basis point increase in the bond's yield is $96.100:

$$100.000(1 - 0.03900) = 96.100 \qquad \blacklozenge\blacklozenge$$

Note that the value of Δy used in the above formula for the relationship between price and effective duration is not necessarily the same as the value of Δy used to calculate the effective duration. This is illustrated in Example 7.8 and Example 7.9. We set $\Delta y = 0.005$ to calculate the effective duration in Example 7.8, but when considering the impact of a 100 basis point shift in Example 7.9, we used $\Delta y = 0.01$.

7.5 Convexity

Duration provides a reasonable estimate for the percentage change in price for a very small change in yield, but when the yield change is large, duration does not account for the curvature (also called **convexity**) of the price curve.

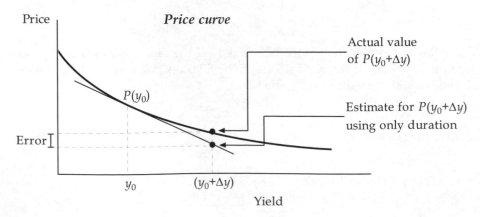

Notice that the prices produced by duration alone (those on the straight tangent line above) are below the actual prices for a shift in the yield in either direction away from y_0. This means that using duration alone *underestimates* the prices resulting from both increases and decreases in the yield. To fix this problem, a positive adjustment is needed. This positive adjustment is called the convexity adjustment.

We can derive the convexity adjustment by incorporating another term from the Taylor series:

$$P(y + \Delta y) \approx P(y) + (\Delta y)P'(y) + \frac{(\Delta y)^2 P''(y)}{2}$$

Once again, we solve for the percentage change in price resulting from a change in yield:

$$P(y + \Delta y) \approx P(y) + (\Delta y)P'(y) + \frac{(\Delta y)^2 P''(y)}{2}$$

$$\Rightarrow \frac{P(y + \Delta y) - P(y)}{P(y)} \approx (\Delta y)\frac{P'(y)}{P(y)} + \frac{(\Delta y)^2}{2}\frac{P''(y)}{P(y)}$$

$$\Rightarrow \%\Delta P \approx (\Delta y)\frac{P'(y)}{P(y)} + \frac{(\Delta y)^2}{2}\frac{P''(y)}{P(y)}$$

The final term contains the value for convexity:

$$\text{Convexity} = \frac{P''(y)}{P(y)}$$

Convexity

Convexity is defined as the second derivative of price with respect to yield, divided by the current price.

$$\text{Convexity} = \frac{P''(y)}{P(y)}$$

We can express the percentage change in price resulting from a change in yield in terms of duration and convexity.

Relationship between price, duration, and convexity

Duration and convexity can be used to estimate the percentage change in a bond's price resulting from a change in the bond's yield:

$$\%\Delta P \approx -(\Delta y)(\text{Duration}) + \frac{(\Delta y)^2}{2}(\text{Convexity})$$

Since $(\Delta y)^2$ is always positive, adding this additional term to the formula for $\%\Delta P$ increases the estimate for the percentage increase in price as long as the convexity is positive. For bonds with fixed cash flows, convexity is always positive.

The equation above is suitable for use with modified duration or effective duration. Macaulay duration can also be used in the equation if Δy represents the change in the continuously compounded yield.

As with duration, the calculation of convexity depends on the compounding frequency of the yield. If the yield is compounded m times per year, then:

$$P = \sum CF_t \left(1 + \frac{y}{m}\right)^{-mt}$$

$$\frac{dP}{dy} = \sum -tCF_t \left(1 + \frac{y}{m}\right)^{-mt-1}$$

$$\frac{d^2P}{dy^2} = \sum t\left(t + \frac{1}{m}\right)CF_t \left(1 + \frac{y}{m}\right)^{-mt-2}$$

$$\text{Convexity} = \frac{\dfrac{d^2P}{dy^2}}{P} = \frac{\sum t\left(t + \frac{1}{m}\right)CF_t \left(1 + \frac{y}{m}\right)^{-mt-2}}{P}$$

The convexity formula above is analogous to the formula for modified duration and so it is sometimes called **modified convexity**. However, because it is not easily obtained by modifying another formula it is often just called convexity. Unfortunately, this formula for convexity isn't especially convenient to memorize or use.

7.5.1 Macaulay convexity

In practice, Macaulay convexity $(MacC)$, which has a much simpler formula, is more commonly used. Macaulay convexity is based on the continuously compounded yield δ, and therefore Macaulay convexity applies when the continuously compounded yield is shifted:

$$P = \sum CF_t e^{-\delta t}$$

$$\frac{dP}{d\delta} = \sum -tCF_t e^{-\delta t}$$

$$\frac{d^2P}{d\delta^2} = \sum t^2 CF_t e^{-\delta t}$$

$$MacC = \frac{\dfrac{d^2P}{d\delta^2}}{P} = \frac{\sum t^2 CF_t e^{-\delta t}}{P}$$

Macaulay convexity

If a bond with fixed cash flows has a continuously compounded yield of δ, then its Macaulay convexity is:

$$MacC = \frac{\sum\limits_{t>0} t^2 CF_t e^{-\delta t}}{P} = \frac{\sum\limits_{t>0} t^2 CF_t \left(1 + \frac{y}{m}\right)^{-mt}}{P} \text{ since } e^{-\delta} = \left(1 + \frac{y}{m}\right)^{-m}$$

Notice that Macaulay convexity is the limit of the general convexity formula as $m \to \infty$.

Macaulay convexity is related to the extent to which the cash flows are spread out around the duration of the bond. Earlier, we noted that Macaulay duration is the weighted average of the times that the cash flows occur, weighted by the present value of each cash flow.

We define **dispersion** as the weighted average of the squares of the differences between the times that the cash flows occur and the Macaulay duration of the bond, weighted by the present value of each cash flow:

$$\text{Dispersion} = \frac{\sum (t - MacD)^2 CF_t e^{-\delta t}}{\sum CF_t e^{-\delta t}}$$

$$= \frac{\sum (t^2 - 2tMacD + MacD^2) CF_t e^{-\delta t}}{\sum CF_t e^{-\delta t}}$$

$$= \frac{\sum t^2 CF_t e^{-\delta t} - 2MacD \sum t CF_t e^{-\delta t} + MacD^2 \sum CF_t e^{-\delta t}}{\sum CF_t e^{-\delta t}}$$

$$= MacC - 2MacD^2 + MacD^2$$

$$= MacC - MacD^2$$

So, the dispersion of a bond is equal to its Macaulay convexity minus the square of its Macaulay duration. Rearranging the formula, we see that convexity increases as dispersion increases:

$$MacC = \text{Dispersion} + MacD^2$$

Dispersion

If a bond with fixed cash flows has a continuously compounded yield of δ, then its Macaulay convexity is the sum of its dispersion and the square of its Macaulay duration:

$$MacC = \text{Dispersion} + MacD^2$$

where:

$$\text{Dispersion} = \frac{\sum (t - MacD)^2 CF_t e^{-\delta t}}{\sum CF_t e^{-\delta t}}$$

Since a zero-coupon bond has a dispersion of zero, a zero-coupon bond's Macaulay convexity is equal to the square of its Macaulay duration. For example, the Macaulay convexity of a 5-year zero coupon bond is 25.

Dispersion measures the degree to which the cash flows of a bond are spread out around its duration, so if the cash flows are more spread out, the dispersion is higher, and consequently the Macaulay convexity is higher.

7.5.2 Effective convexity

Another type of convexity is estimated from a given set of observed prices and their corresponding yields. This estimated convexity is called **effective convexity** (*EffC*). Using the same notation as in Section 7.4, we can estimate the second derivative of price with respect to yield by finding the difference between the first differences:

$$EffC \approx \left(\frac{d^2 P}{dy^2} \right) \frac{1}{P} \approx \left(\frac{\Delta(\Delta P)}{(\Delta y)^2} \right) \frac{1}{P} = \frac{(P_+ - P_0) - (P_0 - P_-)}{(\Delta y)^2 P_0} = \frac{(P_+ + P_- - 2P_0)}{(\Delta y)^2 P_0}$$

Effective convexity

$$EffC = \frac{(P_+ + P_- - 2P_0)}{(\Delta y)^2 P_0}$$

Let's revisit Example 7.7 in which we calculated effective duration. This time, we calculate effective convexity.

Example 7.10

A 3-year bond paying 8% coupons semiannually has a current price of $97.4211 and a current yield of 9% compounded semiannually. If the bond's yield increases by 100 basis points, then the price will be $94.9243. If the bond's yield decreases by 100 basis points, then the price will be $100.00. Calculate the effective convexity of the bond.

Solution

The effective convexity is 8.4273:

$$EffC = \frac{(P_+ + P_- - 2P_0)}{(\Delta y)^2 P_0} = \frac{94.9243 + 100 - 2 \times 97.4211}{(0.01)^2 \times 97.4211} = 8.4273$$

                                                            ◆ ◆

Example 7.11

For the bond described in Example 7.7 and Example 7.10, calculate two estimates for the new price resulting from a 150 basis point increase in the bond's yield. For the first estimate, use only the previously calculated effective duration of 2.6050. For the second estimate, use both the effective duration and the effective convexity.

Solution

First, using just duration, the estimated change in the price is:

$$\%\Delta P \approx -(0.015)(2.6050) = -0.039075$$

The price falls by 3.9075%:

$$(1 - 0.039075)(97.4211) = 93.614$$

So using duration alone, the estimate for the new price is $93.614.

Second, using both duration and convexity, the change in price is:

$$\%\Delta P \approx -(0.015)(2.6050) + \frac{(0.015)^2}{2}(8.4273) = -0.038127$$

The price therefore falls by 3.8127%:

$$(1 - 0.038127)(97.4211) = 93.707$$

Using both duration and convexity, the estimate for the new price is $93.707.   ◆ ◆

In the example above, when we estimated the price change based on duration alone, we estimated that the price would fall to $93.614. Making use of convexity as well as duration, we have a better estimate of $93.707. The actual price of the bond out to three decimal places is 93.706 when the yield is 10.50%, so the estimate based on both duration and convexity is much more accurate than the estimate based on duration alone.

7.6 Duration, convexity, and prices: putting it all together

7.6.1 Revisiting the percentage change in price

As we saw earlier, the general formula for the percentage change in price resulting from a change in yield is:

$$\%\Delta P \approx -(\Delta y)(\text{Duration}) + \frac{(\Delta y)^2}{2}(\text{Convexity})$$

Since there are several types of duration and convexity, let's review how to use them in the formula above. The key idea is that the duration, convexity, and change in yield (Δy) should all be based on the same compounding frequency. That is, they should all be consistent with each other.

1. Modified duration and convexity are appropriate for calculating $\%\Delta P$ provided that the yield used to calculate them is compounded at the same frequency as the yield that is shifted. Furthermore, modified duration and convexity are appropriate only if the bond's cash flows are fixed.

2. Macaulay duration and Macaulay convexity are appropriate for calculating $\%\Delta P$ only if the yield change being examined is a change in the continuously compounded yield. Furthermore, Macaulay duration and Macaulay convexity are only appropriate if the bond's cash flows are fixed.

3. Effective duration and effective convexity are appropriate for calculating $\%\Delta P$ provided that the effective duration, effective convexity, and Δy are all based on the same compounding frequency, which should also be the same frequency as the yield that is shifted. Effective duration and effective convexity are appropriate even if the bond's cash flows are not fixed.

Macaulay duration and Macaulay convexity can be viewed as a subset of modified duration and convexity because they are the limit of modified duration and convexity as $m \to \infty$.

In practice, effective duration and effective convexity are used most frequently. For a bond with fixed cash flows, effective duration and effective convexity produce results that are close to those produced by modified duration and convexity. For bonds with interest-sensitive cash flows (such as callable bonds), effective duration and effective convexity produce more accurate results than modified duration and convexity.

7.6.2 The passage of time and duration

The passage of time has two effects on the duration of a bond with a fixed maturity:

1. The time until the occurrence of each cash flow becomes shorter. Thus as time passes, the duration tends to decrease.

2. The earliest cash flows are paid out and drop out of the equation. Thus as time passes, more weight is given to the more distant cash flows, causing duration to increase.

These two effects tend to cause duration to decrease until a cash flow occurs, at which time duration spikes upward. In the end, however, once there is only one cash flow left, Macaulay duration becomes equal to the time until the final cash flow. Ultimately, the overall trend is for duration to decrease over time.

7.6.3 Portfolio duration and convexity

If a portfolio contains more than one bond, the duration of the portfolio can be calculated as the weighted average of the bonds' durations, using the market values of the bonds as the weights.

If there are n bonds in a portfolio and bond k has price P_k and duration D_k, then the market value of the portfolio is:

$$P_1 + P_2 + \cdots + P_n = MV_{Port}$$

The duration of the portfolio is:

$$-\frac{\dfrac{d}{dy}MV_{Port}}{MV_{Port}} = -\frac{\dfrac{d}{dy}(P_1 + P_2 + \cdots + P_n)}{MV_{Port}}$$

$$= \frac{-\dfrac{dP_1}{dy}}{MV_{Port}} + \frac{-\dfrac{dP_2}{dy}}{MV_{Port}} + \cdots + \frac{-\dfrac{dP_n}{dy}}{MV_{Port}}$$

$$= \left(\frac{P_1}{P_1}\right)\frac{-\dfrac{dP_1}{dy}}{MV_{Port}} + \left(\frac{P_2}{P_2}\right)\frac{-\dfrac{dP_2}{dy}}{MV_{Port}} + \cdots + \left(\frac{P_n}{P_n}\right)\frac{-\dfrac{dP_n}{dy}}{MV_{Port}}$$

$$= \left(\frac{P_1}{MV_{Port}}\right)\frac{-\dfrac{dP_1}{dy}}{P_1} + \left(\frac{P_2}{MV_{Port}}\right)\frac{-\dfrac{dP_2}{dy}}{P_2} + \cdots + \left(\frac{P_n}{MV_{Port}}\right)\frac{-\dfrac{dP_n}{dy}}{P_n}$$

$$= \frac{P_1}{MV_{Port}}D_1 + \frac{P_2}{MV_{Port}}D_2 + \cdots + \frac{P_n}{MV_{Port}}D_n$$

Likewise, the convexity of a portfolio is the weighted average of the convexity of each bond. If each bond's convexity is denoted by C_k, then:

$$\text{Convexity of portfolio} = \frac{P_1}{MV_{Port}}C_1 + \frac{P_2}{MV_{Port}}C_2 + \cdots + \frac{P_n}{MV_{Port}}C_n$$

Example 7.12

A portfolio contains two bonds, each with a par value of $1,000. The first bond matures in 2 years, has an annual effective yield of 4%, and pays annual coupons of 5%. The second bond matures in 5 years, has an annual effective yield of 4%, and is a zero coupon bond.

Calculate the modified duration of the portfolio.

Solution

The market value of the first bond is:

$$MV_1 = \frac{50}{1.04} + \frac{1,050}{1.04^2} = 1,018.86$$

The modified duration of the first bond is:

$$ModD_1 = \frac{\dfrac{50}{1.04} + \dfrac{(2)1,050}{1.04^2}}{1,018.86(1.04)} = 1.878$$

The market value of the second bond is:

$$MV_2 = \frac{1,000}{1.04^5} = 821.93$$

The modified duration of the second bond is:

$$ModD_2 = \frac{\dfrac{5(1,000)}{1.04^5}}{\dfrac{1,000}{1.04^5}(1.04)} = \frac{5}{1.04} = 4.808$$

The market value of the portfolio is:

$$1018.86 + 821.93 = 1,840.79$$

The modified duration of the portfolio is:

$$ModD_{Port} = \frac{1,018.86}{1,840.79}1.878 + \frac{821.93}{1,840.79}4.808 = 3.186$$

◆◆

7.7 *Immunization*

In the normal course of business, financial institutions often accept payment in exchange for taking on liabilities. When a bank, for example, sells a certificate of deposit, it is accepting payment now in exchange for an agreement to pay a specified amount in the future. Payments that a company is required to make are called **liability cash flows**. The cash flows emanating from the company's investments are called **asset cash flows**. Of course, companies try to manage their affairs so that their asset cash flows exceed their liability cash flows.

If a company is sound, then the present value of its assets (PV_A) is greater than or equal to the present value of its liabilities (PV_L):

$$PV_A \geq PV_L$$

Let's define **surplus** as the present value of the assets minus the present value of the liabilities.

Surplus

Surplus, $S(y)$, is the amount by which the present value of the assets exceeds the present value of the liabilities when the interest rate used to calculate the present values is y:

$$S(y) = PV_A - PV_L$$

Since both PV_A and PV_L are the discounted value of future cash flows, both are sensitive to changes in the interest rate. If the rate of interest falls, both present values increase. If the rate of interest increases, then both present values fall.

Our main concern is that if the rate of interest falls, then the present value of the assets might increase by less than the present value of the liabilities. Or if the rate of interest increases, then the present value of the assets might fall by more than the present value of the liabilities. In both cases, the surplus would decrease.

Immunization is the act of protecting (*ie*, immunizing) a surplus position from changes in the rate of interest. The key characteristic of an immunized position is that a change in the rate of interest does not decrease the surplus.

If we assume that the yield curve is flat and that the only possible change in the yield curve is a small parallel shift, then we can determine the conditions necessary for an immunized portfolio. We'll learn more about yield curves in the next chapter. For now, let's just say that a flat yield curve is one in which the yields do not vary by maturity. Furthermore, a parallel shift in the yield curve means that the yields all change by the same amount, regardless of maturity. A parallel shift in a flat yield curve results in a new flat yield curve, above or below the previous yield curve.

Based on this assumption that the yields do not vary by maturity, there are three conditions that must be met for a portfolio to be immunized. Frank Redington, a British actuary, derived these conditions in the 1950s. **Redington immunization** protects the surplus from *small* changes in the interest rate used to discount the assets and liabilities. Redington immunization is frequently referred to simply as immunization, and we follow this convention for the remainder of this chapter.

The first condition is that the present value of the assets must be equal to the present value of the liabilities.

Immunization condition #1

Present value of assets = Present value of liabilities

Some authors prefer to express this condition as requiring that the present value of the assets be *greater than or equal to* the present value of the liabilities. Although there is nothing wrong with having more assets than liabilities, we use the more traditional requirement that the present value of the assets be *equal to* the present value of the liabilities.

The second immunization condition is that the duration of the assets must be equal to the duration of the liabilities.

Immunization condition #2

Duration of assets = Duration of liabilities

Earlier in this chapter, we learned that duration is approximately the percentage increase in the value of an asset that occurs when the yield on the asset shifts down by 100 basis points. We can calculate the duration of a liability in the same way that we calculate the duration of an asset. The same formula is used, but the cash flows are liability cash flows instead of asset cash flows.

If we select the assets so that the duration of the assets is equal to the duration of the liabilities, then when the yield changes, each should change in value by approximately the same amount.

When both the assets and the liabilities consist of fixed cash flows, it is common to use Macaulay duration as the duration measure, but matching modified duration is equivalent to matching Macaulay duration, so either one can be used. If the cash flows are not fixed, then effective duration should be used.

The third immunization condition is that the convexity of the assets must be greater than the convexity of the liabilities.

Immunization condition #3

Convexity of assets > Convexity of liabilities

Recall that a financial instrument with positive convexity has a higher value after an interest rate shift than indicated by duration alone. It is desirable that the value of the assets be higher than the value of the liabilities after an interest rate change, and this can be accomplished by making sure that the convexity of the assets is greater than the convexity of the liabilities.

As with duration, any of the versions of convexity can be used if the cash flows are fixed, but effective convexity must be used if the cash flows are interest sensitive.

Conditions for immunization

1.   Present value of assets = Present value of liabilities

2.   Duration of assets = Duration of liabilities

3.   Convexity of assets > Convexity of liabilities

Our definition of surplus is:

$$S(y) = PV_A - PV_L$$

Taking the first and second derivatives, we have:

$$S'(y) = \frac{dPV_A}{dy} - \frac{dPV_L}{dy} \qquad S''(y) = \frac{d^2PV_A}{dy^2} - \frac{d^2PV_L}{dy^2}$$

Modified duration is the negative of the first derivative of the present value divided by the present value:

$$ModD = -\frac{P'(y)}{P(y)}$$

$$P'(y) = -ModD \times P(y)$$

Substituting, we can write the first derivative of surplus in terms of the duration of the assets and liabilities:

$$S'(y) = \frac{dPV_A}{dy} - \frac{dPV_L}{dy}$$

$$S'(y) = -ModD_A \times PV_A + ModD_L \times PV_L$$

Convexity is the second derivative of the present value divided by the present value:

$$C = \frac{P''(y)}{P(y)}$$

$$P''(y) = C \times P(y)$$

Substituting, we write the second derivative in terms of the convexity of the assets and liabilities:

$$S''(y) = \frac{d^2PV_A}{dy^2} - \frac{d^2PV_L}{dy^2}$$

$$S''(y) = C_A \times PV_A - C_L \times PV_L$$

We now have the following formulas for surplus, its first derivative, and its second derivative:

$$S(y) = PV_A - PV_L$$
$$S'(y) = -ModD_A \times PV_A + ModD_L \times PV_L$$
$$S''(y) = C_A \times PV_A - C_L \times PV_L$$

If we assume that the three conditions for immunization are satisfied, then we can make some observations about the surplus, its first derivative, and its second derivative.

From immunization condition #1, we have $PV_A = PV_L$, so:

$$S(y) = PV_A - PV_L$$
$$S(y) = 0$$

Immunization condition #2 tells us that $ModD_A = ModD_L$. Making use of immunization conditions #1 and #2, we have:

$$S'(y) = -ModD_A \times PV_A + ModD_L \times PV_L$$
$$S'(y) = 0$$

Immunization condition #3 tells us that $C_A > C_L$. Making use of immunization conditions #1 and #3, we have:

$$S''(y) = C_A \times PV_A - C_L \times PV_L$$
$$S''(y) > 0$$

So if immunization conditions #1, #2, and #3 are satisfied, we have:

$$S(y) = 0 \quad S'(y) = 0 \quad S''(y) > 0$$

Suppose the yield changes by a small amount, Δy. Using the Taylor Series, the new level of surplus is:

$$S(y + \Delta y) \approx S(y) + \Delta y S'(y) + \frac{(\Delta y)^2 S''(y)}{2}$$

If the first two immunization conditions are satisfied, then $S(y) = 0$ and $S'(y) = 0$, so:

$$S(y + \Delta y) \approx 0 + 0 + \frac{(\Delta y)^2 S''(y)}{2}$$
$$S(y + \Delta y) \approx \frac{(\Delta y)^2 S''(y)}{2}$$

And the third immunization condition implies that $S''(y) > 0$, so:

$$S(y + \Delta y) > 0$$

for small yield changes. Regardless of the direction of the yield change, the surplus increases from zero to a value greater than zero.

We have demonstrated that if the three immunization conditions are satisfied, then surplus increases when the yield changes.

The following graph illustrates the price curves for an immunized position consisting of a portfolio of assets and a portfolio of liabilities.

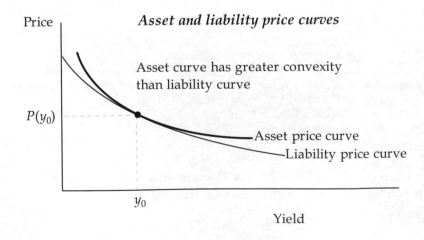

If the current yield is y_0, then the assets and the liabilities have the same value and duration, but the convexity of the assets is higher than the convexity of the liabilities. This means that if the yield shifts up or down, then the value of the assets will be greater than the value of the liabilities.

Example 7.13

A bank has issued a certificate of deposit obligating it to pay $1,000 in 3 years. The bank can fund this liability only through the purchase of 2-year bonds and 10-year bonds. The 2-year bonds have annual coupons of 10%. The 10-year bonds are zero-coupon bonds. Both bonds have a par value of $100. The current annual effective yield is 10%.

Determine how much the bank should invest in each bond in order to meet the first two immunization conditions. Does this allocation also meet the third immunization condition?

Solution

We use Macaulay duration and Macaulay convexity to solve this problem, but an equivalent result could be obtained with modified duration and convexity.

The present value and duration of the liability are:

$$PV_L = \frac{1,000}{1.10^3} = 751.31 \qquad MacD_L = \frac{3(1,000)(1.1)^{-3}}{751.31} = 3.00$$

Since the present value of the liability is $751.31, the present value of the assets must also be $751.31 to satisfy the first immunization condition.

The 2-year bond is priced at par since its coupon rate and yield are both 10%. Therefore, its duration is equal to the value of a 2-year annuity-due. The Macaulay durations of the two bonds are:

$$\text{Duration of 2-year bond} = \ddot{a}_{\overline{2}|10\%} = \frac{1-(1.10)^{-2}}{0.10/1.10} - 1.909$$

$$\text{Duration of 10-year zero-coupon bond} = \frac{(10)CF_{10}(1.10)^{10}}{CF_{10}(1.10)^{-10}} = 10.000$$

If $x\%$ of the $751.31 is invested in the two-year bond and $(1-x\%)$ is invested in the 10-year bond, then we can solve for the value of $x\%$ that satisfies the second immunization condition that the duration of the assets be equal to the duration of the liabilities:

$$MacD_A = MacD_L$$

$$\Rightarrow (x\%)(1.909) + (1-x\%)(10.000) = 3.000$$

$$\Rightarrow x\% = 86.5\%$$

So 86.5% of $751.31 is invested in the 2-year bond, and 13.5% is invested in the 10-year bond:

$$\text{Investment in 2-year bond} = 86.5\% \times 751.31 = 649.88$$
$$\text{Investment in 10-year bond} = 13.5\% \times 751.31 = 101.43$$

We check to see if the Macaulay convexity of the assets is greater than the Macaulay convexity of the liabilities. The Macaulay convexity of the liabilities is 9.00:

$$MacC_L = \frac{\sum t^2 CF_t e^{-\delta t}}{P} = \frac{\sum t^2 CF_t \left(1+\frac{y}{m}\right)^{-mt}}{P} = \frac{9(1,000)(1.10)^{-3}}{751.31} = 9.00$$

The Macaulay convexities of the bonds are:

$$\text{Convexity of 2-year bond} = \frac{1^2(10)(1.10)^{-1} + 2^2(110)(1.10)^{-2}}{100} = 3.727$$

$$\text{Convexity of 10-year bond} = \frac{10^2(100)(1.10)^{-10}}{100(1.10)^{-10}} = 100.000$$

Therefore, the Macaulay convexity of the asset portfolio is 16.724:

$$MacC_A = 0.865 \times 3.727 + 0.135 \times 100.000 = 16.724$$

Since the convexity of the asset portfolio is greater than the convexity of the liability, the company has immunized its position.   ♦♦

The three conditions for immunization may be satisfied at a specific point in time, but as time passes, the duration and convexity of the assets do not necessarily change at the same rate as the duration and convexity of the liabilities. Also, changes in the yield affect the durations and convexities of the assets and the liabilities differently. Therefore, an immunized portfolio must be **rebalanced** periodically to bring it back into compliance with the three conditions. Rebalancing can be accomplished on the asset side or on the liability side, but it is frequently easier to adjust the asset portfolio than it is to adjust the liability portfolio. By periodically selling some assets and buying others, a portfolio manager can maintain a position that satisfies the three immunization conditions.

Frequent rebalancing provides better protection than infrequent rebalancing, but it also brings increased transactions costs. The frequency with which the portfolio is rebalanced depends on the objectives and opportunities of the portfolio manager.

Immunization protects the surplus from interest rate shifts. In fact, since the convexity of the assets is greater than the convexity of the liabilities, an immunized position actually benefits from changes in the interest rates. So, every company should immunize and obtain as much convexity as possible for their assets, right? Not quite. Remember that we began our discussion of immunization with the assumption that yields do not vary by maturity. In reality, yields usually do vary by maturity (*ie* the yield curve is not usually flat), and changes to the yields can also vary by maturity (*ie* the yield curve shifts may not be parallel).

Let's see what happens in the previous example if the yields on the bonds increase but the yield for the liability stays the same.

Example 7.14

A bank has issued a certificate of deposit obligating it to pay $1,000 in 3 years. As described in the previous example, the bank funds this liability by investing $649.88 in the 2-year bonds and $101.43 in the 10-year bonds. Immediately after the bank purchases the bonds, the yields on the bonds rise to 11% while the yield on the liability remains 10%. Find the bank's new surplus.

Solution

Let's assume that the par value of the bonds is $100.

The price of the 2-year bond is $100.00 since it is priced at par, and the bank purchased 6.4988 2-year bonds:

$$\text{Price of 2-year bond} = 100.00$$

$$\text{Number of 2-year bonds} = \frac{649.88}{100.00} = 6.4988$$

The price of the 10-year bond is $38.5543, and the bank purchased 2.6308 10-year bonds:

$$\text{Price of 10-year bond} = \frac{100.00}{1.10^{10}} = 38.5543$$

$$\text{Number of 10-year bonds} = \frac{101.43}{38.5543} = 2.6308$$

When the interest rate increases from 10% to 11%, the present value of the assets falls to $731.40:

$$PV_A = 6.4988\left[10a_{\overline{2}|11\%} + 100(1.11)^{-2}\right] + 2.6308\left[100(1.11)^{-10}\right]$$
$$= 638.75 + 92.65 = 731.40$$

But the present value of the liabilities remains at $751.31:

$$PV_L = \frac{1,000}{1.10^3} = 751.31$$

The surplus is now negative:

$$\text{Surplus} = PV_A - PV_L = 731.40 - 751.31 = -\$19.91 \qquad \blacklozenge\blacklozenge$$

The example above illustrates that immunization may not protect the surplus from a nonparallel shift in the yield curve. There are a couple of approaches to dealing with the problem of nonparallel shifts in the yield curve. Both involve bringing the asset cash flows closer to the liability cash flows.

The first approach is to create a revised immunization condition #3.

Revised immunization condition #3

The convexity of the assets should be *just slightly greater* than the convexity of the liabilities.

This new immunization condition still keeps the convexity of the assets larger than the convexity of the liabilities, but it now specifies that the convexity of the assets should be "just slightly" larger than the convexity of the liabilities.

Convexity is related to the degree to which the cash flows are dispersed around the duration. If we keep the duration of a portfolio fixed while spreading out the cash flows of the portfolio, the convexity increases. As in the example above, though, spreading the asset cash flows out so much that their timing is significantly different from the timing of the liability cash flows can lead to problems if the yield curve changes in a nonparallel fashion.

This revised condition could be loosely paraphrased as, "Keep the asset cash flows more spread out than the liability cash flows, but not too much more spread out."

7.8 Full immunization

The previous section showed that Redington immunization protects the surplus for *small* shifts in a flat yield curve. Under certain circumstances, the surplus is also protected for *large* shifts in a flat yield curve. Under these circumstances, the position is **fully immunized**, which means that the surplus is protected for interest rate changes of any size.

Consider a position consisting of a single liability payable at time T and two asset cash flows payable at times $T-q$ and $T+r$, where T, q, and r are greater than zero and $(T-q) \geq 0$. The amount of the liability cash flow is L, the amount of the first asset cash flow is Q, and the amount of the second asset cash flow is R. The position is illustrated on the timeline below.

Cash Flow		Q	L	R	
Time	0	$(T-q)$	T	$(T+r)$	

The position is fully immunized if it meets the following conditions:

Conditions for full immunization of a single liability cash flow

1.   Present value of assets = Present value of liability

2.   Duration of assets = Duration of liability

3.   The asset cash flows occur before and after the liability cash flow. That is:

         $(T-q) < T < (T+r)$

A fully immunized position also satisfies the conditions for Redington immunization described in the previous section. The first two conditions for a fully immunized position are the same as for Redington immunization. Below, we show that these two conditions, combined with the condition that $(T-q) \leq T \leq (T+r)$, imply that the third condition of Redington immunization, which requires that the convexity of the asset portfolio exceed the convexity of the liability portfolio, is also satisfied.

If a position is fully immunized, then by condition #2, the Macaulay duration of the liability is equal to the Macaulay duration of the assets. Since the liability consists of a single cash flow occurring at time T, the Macaulay duration of both the liability and the assets is equal to T:

     $MacD_L = MacD_A = T$

Since there is just one liability cash flow, the dispersion of the liability is zero:

     $\text{Dispersion}_L = \dfrac{[T-T]^2 \, Le^{-\delta T}}{Le^{-\delta T}} = 0$

The dispersion of the assets, however, is positive since q, r, Q, and R are nonzero:

$$\text{Dispersion}_A = \frac{[(T-q)-T]^2 \, Qe^{-\delta(T-q)} + [(T+r)-T]^2 \, Re^{-\delta(T+r)}}{Qe^{-\delta(T-q)} + Re^{-\delta(T+r)}}$$

$$= \frac{q^2 Qe^{-\delta(T-q)} + r^2 Re^{-\delta(T+r)}}{Qe^{-\delta(T-q)} + Re^{-\delta(T+r)}}$$

Hence:

     $\text{Dispersion}_A > 0$

Macaulay convexity is equal to the sum of dispersion and the square of Macaulay duration. Therefore, the Macaulay convexity of the liability is:

     $MacC_L = 0 + T^2 = T^2$

The Macaulay convexity of the assets is:

$$MacC_A = \text{Dispersion}_A + T^2$$

Since $\text{Dispersion}_A > 0$, the Macaulay convexity of the assets exceeds that of the liability:

$$MacC_A > MacC_L$$

Thus, a fully immunized portfolio satisfies condition #3 of Redington immunization. This tells us that a fully immunized portfolio has positive surplus for any small change in the interest rate.

In fact, a fully immunized position has positive surplus regardless of the magnitude of the interest rate change. A proof of this broader statement is provided at the end of this section.

Example 7.15

An insurance company has an obligation to pay $1,000,000 at the end of 10 years. It has a zero-coupon bond that matures for $413,947.55 in 5 years, and it has a zero-coupon bond that matures for $864,580.82 in 20 years. The current annual effective yield is 10%.

(i)   Is the company's position fully immunized?
(ii)   Does the company's position satisfy the conditions for Redington immunization?
(iii)   What is the new level of surplus if the interest rate falls to 0%?
(iv)   What is the new level of surplus if the interest rate rises to 80%?

Solution

Part (i)

The present value of the liability is:

$$PV_L = \frac{1,000,000}{1.10^{10}} = \$385,543.29$$

The present value of the assets is:

$$PV_A = \frac{413,947.55}{1.10^5} + \frac{864,580.82}{1.10^{20}} = \$385,543.29$$

Therefore $PV_L = PV_A$, so the first condition for full immunization is satisfied.

The Macaulay duration of the liability is 10 since there is just one cash flow, and it occurs at time 10:

$$MacD_L = 10$$

The Macaulay duration of the assets is:

$$MacD_A = \frac{413,947.55(1.10)^{-5}(5) + 864,580.82(1.10)^{-20}(20)}{385,543.29} = 10.0$$

Therefore $MacD_L = MacD_A$, so the second condition for full immunization is satisfied.

The final condition for full immunization is also satisfied since:

$$5 < 10 < 20$$

Therefore the company's position is fully immunized.

Part (ii)

The company's position also satisfies the conditions for Redington immunization. A fully immunized portfolio always satisfies the conditions for Redington immunization.

Part (iii)

If the interest rate falls to 0%, then surplus is:

$$\text{Surplus} = PV_A - PV_L = \frac{413,947.55}{1.00^5} + \frac{864,580.82}{1.00^{20}} - \frac{1,000,000}{1.00^{10}} = \$278,528.37$$

Part (iv)

If the interest rate increases to 80%, then the surplus is:

$$\text{Surplus} = PV_A - PV_L = \frac{413,947.55}{1.80^5} + \frac{864,580.82}{1.80^{20}} - \frac{1,000,000}{1.80^{10}} = \$19,113.02$$

◆◆

Since the position is fully immunized, it is no surprise that the surplus is positive for Parts (iii) and (iv). In fact, the surplus is positive for any interest rate.

The conditions for full immunization apply when there is just one liability cash flow. If a company wants to fully immunize a position consisting of multiple liability cash flows, it can do so by allocating the assets (or portions of the assets) to each liability, so that the conditions for full immunization are satisfied for each liability cash flow and its designated assets.

Just as with Redington immunization, full immunization is based on an assumption that the yield curve is flat and the only possible shift in the yield curve is a parallel shift. Full immunization is also similar to Redington immunization in that a fully immunized position must be rebalanced periodically.

Full immunization proof

This section proves that a position meeting the three conditions for full immunization has positive surplus when the interest rate changes, regardless of the size of the change.

The continuously compounded yield δ is used in this proof to make the notation convenient, but the proof could also be written in terms of a non-continuously compounded yield. The current yield is δ_0. As stated earlier, a liability payment of L is due at time T. An asset cash flow of Q occurs at time $T-q$, and an asset cash flow of R occurs at time $T+r$.

First, condition #1 is used to derive L in terms of δ_0, q, r, Q, and R:

Present value of assets = Present value of liability

$$Qe^{-(T-q)\delta_0} + Re^{-(T+r)\delta_0} = Le^{-T\delta_0}$$

$$L = Qe^{q\delta_0} + Re^{-r\delta_0}$$

Recall from the previous section that conditions #1 and #2 imply that the first derivative of the surplus is zero at the current yield. Below, an expression for the first derivative of surplus is determined:

$$S(\delta) = Qe^{-(T-q)\delta} + Re^{-(T+r)\delta} - Le^{-T\delta}$$

$$S'(\delta) = -Q(T-q)e^{-(T-q)\delta} - R(T+r)e^{-(T+r)\delta} + LTe^{-T\delta}$$

Setting the first derivative equal to zero at the current interest rate, we have:

$$S'(\delta_0) = 0$$

$$-Q(T-q)e^{-(T-q)\delta_0} - R(T+r)e^{-(T+r)\delta_0} + LTe^{-T\delta_0} = 0$$

$$-QTe^{-(T-q)\delta_0} + Qqe^{-(T-q)\delta_0} - RTe^{-(T+r)\delta_0} - Rre^{-(T+r)\delta_0} + LTe^{-T\delta_0} = 0$$

$$-T\left[Qe^{-(T-q)\delta_0} + Re^{-(T+r)\delta_0} - Le^{-T\delta_0} \right] + \left[Qqe^{-(T-q)\delta_0} - Rre^{-(T+r)\delta_0} \right] = 0$$

From condition #1, the quantity in the first set of brackets is equal to zero since the present value of the assets equals the present value of the liabilities. Therefore, the expression in the second set of brackets must equal zero also, and this provides us with an expression that can be used to find R in terms of δ_0, q, r, and Q:

$$Qqe^{-(T-q)\delta_0} - Rre^{-(T+r)\delta_0} = 0$$

$$R = \frac{Qqe^{-(T-q)\delta_0}}{re^{-(T+r)\delta_0}}$$

$$R = Q\left(\frac{q}{r}\right)e^{(q+r)\delta_0}$$

The value of the surplus at some interest rate δ is:

$$S(\delta) = Qe^{-(T-q)\delta} + Re^{-(T+r)\delta} - Le^{-T\delta}$$

Earlier, we determined an expression for L in terms of δ_0, q, r, Q, and R. Substituting in this expression for L:

$$S(\delta) = Qe^{-(T-q)\delta} + Re^{-(T+r)\delta} - (Qe^{q\delta_0} + Re^{-r\delta_0})e^{-T\delta}$$

$$= e^{-T\delta}\left[Qe^{q\delta} + Re^{-r\delta} - (Qe^{q\delta_0} + Re^{-r\delta_0})\right]$$

Earlier, we determined an expression for R in terms of δ_0, q, r, and Q. Substituting in this expression for R:

$$S(\delta) = e^{-T\delta}\left[Qe^{q\delta} + Q\left(\frac{q}{r}\right)e^{(q+r)\delta_0}e^{-r\delta} - \left(Qe^{q\delta_0} + Q\left(\frac{q}{r}\right)e^{(q+r)\delta_0}e^{-r\delta_0}\right)\right]$$

$$= e^{-T\delta}Qe^{q\delta_0}\left[e^{q(\delta-\delta_0)} + \frac{q}{r}e^{-r(\delta-\delta_0)} - \left(1+\frac{q}{r}\right)\right]$$

Let's write $S(\delta)$ as the product of two functions:

$$S(\delta) = g(\delta) \times h(\delta)$$

where:

$$g(\delta) = e^{-T\delta}Qe^{q\delta_0}$$

$$h(\delta) = e^{q(\delta-\delta_0)} + \frac{q}{r}e^{-r(\delta-\delta_0)} - \left(1+\frac{q}{r}\right)$$

We now show that both $g(\delta)$ and $h(\delta)$ must be positive when $\delta \neq \delta_0$.

Since Q is positive, $g(\delta)$ has a lower bound of zero, which it approaches as δ approaches infinity. Therefore $g(\delta)$ is positive for all δ.

We can demonstrate that $h(\delta)$ has a lower bound of zero by taking its derivative:

$$h(\delta) = e^{q(\delta-\delta_0)} + \frac{q}{r}e^{-r(\delta-\delta_0)} - \left(1+\frac{q}{r}\right)$$

$$h'(\delta) = qe^{q(\delta-\delta_0)} - qe^{-r(\delta-\delta_0)}$$

Since q and r are both positive:

$$h'(\delta) \begin{cases} = 0 & \text{for } \delta = \delta_0 \\ > 0 & \text{for } \delta > \delta_0 \\ < 0 & \text{for } \delta < \delta_0 \end{cases}$$

Therefore, the slope of $h(\delta)$ is negative when $\delta < \delta_0$, zero when $\delta = \delta_0$, and positive when $\delta > \delta_0$. This indicates that the minimum value of $h(\delta)$ occurs when $\delta = \delta_0$. The graph on the following page is one possible illustration of $h(\delta)$.

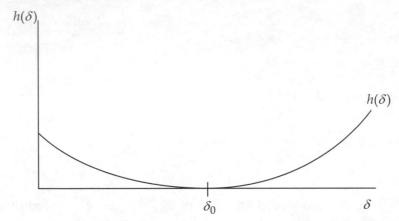

Since the minimum of $h(\delta)$ occurs at δ_0, the minimum of $h(\delta)$ is zero:

$$h(\delta_0) = e^{q(\delta_0 - \delta_0)} + \frac{q}{r} e^{-r(\delta_0 - \delta_0)} - \left(1 + \frac{q}{r}\right) = 0$$

Therefore, for all values of δ other than δ_0, $h(\delta)$ is positive.

We have shown that both $g(\delta)$ and $h(\delta)$ are positive when $\delta \neq \delta_0$. Therefore, their product must also be positive when $\delta \neq \delta_0$. This means that:

$$S(\delta) > 0 \text{ for } \delta \neq \delta_0$$

Since the surplus is positive for any change in the interest rate from δ_0, the position is fully immunized.

7.9 *Dedication*

Dedication, which is also known as **cash flow matching**, calls for matching the asset and liability cash flows exactly. For each liability payment there is an equal asset payment made at the same time.

A dedicated portfolio of assets can be constructed to fund a set of known liabilities. Large pension plans, for example, are often able to predict their liability payments with a great deal of accuracy. Once the liability payments are known, the portfolio manager selects assets that provide cash flows to match the liability payments.

An advantage to dedication is that rebalancing is not necessary. A disadvantage of dedication is that it limits the universe of bonds that can be purchased. A bond might be attractively priced, but if its cash flows do not match up with the liability cash flows, then the portfolio manager is unable to buy the bond under a dedication strategy. Because the universe of bonds from which the portfolio manager can choose is limited, the portfolio's yield may not be as high as would be the case under immunization.

Example 7.16

A bank has an obligation to pay $1,000 in one year and $4,000 in 4 years. The bank has decided to pursue a dedication strategy. The annual effective yield on a 1-year zero coupon bond is 8%, and the annual effective yield on a 4-year zero coupon bond is 9%.

Calculate the cost of establishing the asset portfolio.

Solution

In order to match the liability cash flow of $1,000 in one year, the bank must purchase a zero-coupon bond that matures in one year for $1,000. The cost of this bond is $925.93:

$$\frac{1,000}{1.08} = 925.93$$

In order to match the liability cash flow of $4,000 in four years, the bank must purchase a zero-coupon bond that matures in four years for $4,000. The cost of this bond is $2,833.70:

$$\frac{4,000}{1.09^4} = 2,833.70$$

In total, the bank pays $3,759.63 to establish the asset portfolio:

$$925.93 + 2,833.70 = 3,759.63 \qquad \blacklozenge\blacklozenge$$

The preceding example illustrates that cash flow matching is a fairly simple process when zero-coupon bonds are used.

If coupon-paying bonds are used, then cash flow matching calls for matching the longest liability first and working backwards to the shortest liability. We begin by purchasing an asset that has a final cash flow that is equal to the final liability cash flow. The net liability cash flows remaining are those cash flows that are not offset by the asset cash flows. The new final net liability cash flow is identified and another asset is then purchased to offset it. This process is continued until all of the liability cash flows are exactly offset by asset cash flows.

Example 7.17

A company has the following projected liability cash flows:

Year	1	2	3	4	5
Liability cash flow	179	679	144	3,144	824

There are three assets available for investment:

- 2-year bond with annual coupons of 7%
- 4-year bond with annual coupons of 4%
- 5-year bond with annual coupons of 3%

Each bond has a par value of $100. The annual effective yield on all three bonds is 5%.

The company has decided to pursue a dedication strategy. Determine the amount of each bond to be purchased, and calculate the cost of establishing the asset portfolio.

Solution

The final liability cash flow is $824. The final cash flow from the 5-year bond is its principal payment plus its coupon payment:

$$\text{Final cash flow of 5-year bond} = 100 + 3 = 103$$

We can determine the number of 5-year bonds that provides an asset cash flow of $824 in 5 years:

$$\text{Number of 5-year bonds to purchase} = \frac{824}{103} = 8.0$$

Subtracting the cash flows produced by the eight 5-year bonds from the liability cash flows gives us the net liability cash flows remaining:

Year	1	2	3	4	5
Liability cash flow	179	679	144	3,144	824
Cash flow from 8 5-year bonds	24	24	24	24	824
Net liability cash flow remaining	155	655	120	3,120	0

The new final net liability cash flow is $3,120 at the end of year 4. This is offset by purchasing thirty of the 4-year bonds:

$$\text{Number of 4-year bonds to purchase} = \frac{3,120}{104} = 30.0$$

Subtracting the cash flows produced by the thirty 4-year bonds from the net liability cash flows gives us the new net liability cash flows remaining in the bottom row of the table below:

Year	1	2	3	4	5
Liability cash flow	179	679	144	3,144	824
Cash flow from 8 5-year bonds	24	24	24	24	824
Net liability cash flow remaining	155	655	120	3,120	0
Cash flow from 30 4-year bonds	120	120	120	3,120	0
Net liability cash flow remaining	35	535	0	0	0

The new final net liability cash flow is $535 at the end of year 2. This is offset by purchasing five of the 2-year bonds:

$$\text{Number of 2-year bonds to purchase} = \frac{535}{107} = 5.0$$

Subtracting the cash flows produced by the five 2-year bonds from the net liability cash flows gives us the new net liability cash flows remaining in the bottom row of the table below:

Year	1	2	3	4	5
Liability cash flow	179	679	144	3,144	824
Cash flow from 8 5-year bonds	24	24	24	24	824
Net liability cash flow remaining	155	655	120	3,120	0
Cash flow from 30 4-year bonds	120	120	120	3,120	0
Net liability cash flow remaining	35	535	0	0	0
Cash flow from 5 2-year bonds	35	535	0	0	0
Net liability cash flow remaining	0	0	0	0	0

The net liability cash flows are now all zero, so the purchase of eight 5-year bonds, thirty 4-year bonds, and five 2-year bonds results in a cash-matched portfolio.

In order to determine the cost of the asset portfolio, we determine the price of each asset:

$$\text{Price of 2-year bond} = 7a_{\overline{2}|5\%} + \frac{100}{1.05^2} = 103.7188$$

$$\text{Price of 4-year bond} = 4a_{\overline{4}|5\%} + \frac{100}{1.05^4} = 96.4540$$

$$\text{Price of 5-year bond} = 3a_{\overline{5}|5\%} + \frac{100}{1.05^5} = 91.3410$$

To find the cost of establishing the portfolio, we sum the cost of purchasing five 2-year bonds, 30 4-year bonds, and eight 5-year bonds:

$$\text{Cost to establish asset portfolio} = 5 \times 103.7188 + 30 \times 96.4540 + 8 \times 91.3410 = 4,142.94$$

The cost to establish the asset portfolio is \$4,142.94.   ◆◆

Chapter 7 Practice Questions

Question guide

- Questions 7.1 – 7.11 test material from Sections 7.1 – 7.4

- Questions 7.12 – 7.18 test material from Sections 7.5 – 7.8

- Questions 7.19 – 7.20 are from the SOA Course 6 exam

Question 7.1

A 4-year bond pays annual coupons of 8%. The annual effective yield on the bond is 5%. Calculate the modified duration of the bond.

Question 7.2

The current price of a bond is $114.72 and the current yield is 6.00%. The modified duration of the bond is 7.02. Use the modified duration to estimate the price of the bond if the yield increases to 6.10%.

Question 7.3

A zero-coupon bond matures in 20 years for $1,500. The bond's yield is 4% compounded semiannually. Calculate the modified duration of the bond.

Question 7.4

A two-year bond has 8% annual coupons payable semiannually. The bond's yield is 10% compounded semiannually. Calculate the modified duration of the bond.

Question 7.5

A zero-coupon bond matures in 15 years for $2,000. The bond's yield is 7% compounded monthly. Calculate the Macaulay duration of the bond.

Question 7.6

Determine the modified duration of the zero-coupon bond in the preceding question.

Question 7.7

A 22-year bond pays 7% annual coupons and has a current price of $81.12. The annual effective yield on the bond is 9%. The Macaulay duration of the bond is 10.774. Estimate the new price if the yield falls to 8.95%.

Question 7.8

A 30-year bond pays 6% annual coupons payable semiannually. The bond's yield is 6% compounded semiannually. Calculate the modified duration of the bond.

Question 7.9

A 15-year mortgage is repaid with level monthly payments. The yield is 12% compounded monthly. Calculate the Macaulay duration of the mortgage.

Question 7.10

A 20-year bond yielding 9% has a price of $127.79. If the bond's yield falls to 8.75%, then the price of the bond will increase to $130.65. If bond's yield increases to 9.25%, then the price of the bond will fall to $125.02. Calculate the effective duration of the bond.

Question 7.11

A five-year bond with a coupon of 6.7% pays coupons semiannually. It is currently yielding 6.4%. Its current price is $101.2666. If the bond's yield increases by 10 basis points, then its price falls to $100.8422. If the bond's yield falls by 10 basis points, then its price rises to $101.6931.

Calculate the bond's effective duration.

Question 7.12

Calculate the effective convexity of the bond in Question 7.11.

Question 7.13

Use the effective duration calculated in Question 7.11 and effective convexity calculated in Question 7.12 to estimate the new price of the bond if its yield increases by 75 basis points.

Question 7.14

A perpetuity pays $1 at the end of each year. The annual effective yield is 5%. Calculate the price, modified duration, and convexity of the perpetuity.

Question 7.15

A zero-coupon bond matures in 5 years. Calculate the Macaulay duration and Macaulay convexity for the bond.

Question 7.16

The modified duration of an 8-year bond is 5.35 and its convexity is 39.19. Estimate the percentage change in the price of the bond if its yield increases by 63 basis points.

Question 7.17

An insurance company has committed to make a payment of $100,000 in 10 years. In order to fund this liability, the company has invested $27,919.74 in a 5-year zero-coupon bond and $27,919.74 in a 15-year zero-coupon bond. The annual effective yield on all assets and liabilities is 6%. Determine whether the company's position is immunized.

Question 7.18

An insurance company has committed to make a payment of $100,000 in 5 years. The insurance company can fund this liability only through the purchase of 4-year zero-coupon bonds and 10-year zero-coupon bonds. The annual effective yield for all assets and liabilities is 12%. Determine how much the bank should invest in each bond in order to immunize its position.

Question 7.19   *SOA*

You are given the following information with respect to a callable bond:

Time	Expected Cash Flows at a 7% Annual Yield
1	8.00
2	7.90
3	107.80

Annual Yield	Bond Price
6%	104.33
7%	102.37
8%	99.76

The current yield is 7%.

Calculate the ratio of the modified duration to the effective duration of this bond.

Question 7.20   *SOA*

The current price of a bond is 100. The derivative of the price with respect to the yield to maturity is -700. The yield to maturity is 8%.

Calculate the Macaulay duration.

8

The term structure
of interest rates

Overview

Up to this point, we have generally assumed that only one interest rate applies to all investments, but in reality interest rates vary with the length of time for which an investment is made. For example, the yield on a 3-year bond may be 4.8%, but the yield on a 10-year bond with the same coupon rate may be 6.7%.

The relationship between interest rates and their associated terms until maturity is called the **term structure of interest rates**. The previous chapters have been based upon yields. In this chapter, we introduce two additional types of interest rates that can be used to describe the term structure: **spot rates** and **forward rates**.

Like yields, spot rates and forward rates are derived from the market prices of assets traded in the financial markets. Spot rates and forward rates allow us to identify whether an asset is priced consistently with other assets. If we identify an asset that is undervalued or overvalued according to the term structure of interest rates, then we may be able to exploit the situation to make a risk-free profit. This situation is called an **arbitrage** opportunity.

To keep things simple, most of this chapter is based on annual effective compounding. Later in the chapter, we generalize to non-annual compounding and non-annual time periods.

8.1 Yield-to-maturity

As we saw in Chapter 6, an asset's **yield-to-maturity** (or **yield** for short) is equal to its internal rate of return, which is the interest rate that equates the present value of the asset's cash flows with its price.

So, if the asset price is P, and the cash flow at time t is CF_t, then the annual effective yield y satisfies the following relationship:

$$P = \sum_{t>0} \frac{CF_t}{\left(1+y\right)^t}$$

The hypothetical table of yields below (Table 8.1) was constructed from ten bonds of different maturities, each paying annual coupons:

Table 8.1

Maturity	Annual coupon rate	Annual effective yield
1	2.000%	5.000%
2	5.500%	5.487%
3	5.961%	5.961%
4	11.000%	6.293%
5	3.000%	6.651%
6	14.000%	6.776%
7	0.000%	7.250%
8	7.500%	7.276%
9	4.000%	7.536%
10	8.000%	7.582%

The price of an asset is determined by supply and demand in the financial markets. The resulting yield is unique to that asset, and it cannot be used to find the present value of a different cash flow pattern.

So the yields in Table 8.1 apply only to the bonds with the coupons described by the second column of this table. For example, we can calculate the price of a 2-year bond with an annual coupon of 5.5% by discounting its cash flows at a yield of 5.487%. But if a different 2-year bond has a coupon rate other than 5.5%, then it would not be appropriate to find its price using a yield of 5.487%, because the bond has a different cash flow pattern, and hence a different internal rate of return.

Example 8.1

Using the yields in Table 8.1, calculate the price of:

(i)   a 1-year bond paying 2% annual coupons

(ii)   a 2-year bond paying 5.5% annual coupons

(iii)   a 3-year bond paying 10% annual coupons.

Assume that the principal amount of each bond is $100.

Solution

Part (i)

The 1-year bond's cash flow is discounted using a yield of 5.000%:

$$P = \sum CF_t \left(1+y\right)^{-t} = \frac{102}{1.05} = 97.1429$$

The price of the 1-year bond is $97.14.

Part (ii)

The 2-year bond's cash flows are discounted using a yield of 5.487%:

$$P = \sum CF_t \left(1+y\right)^{-t} = \frac{5.5}{1.05487} + \frac{105.5}{1.05487^2} = 100.0240$$

The price of the 2-year bond is $100.02.

Part (iii)

The price of the 3-year bond cannot be directly calculated from Table 8.1. We are given the yield on a 3-year bond with an annual coupon of 5.961%. A 3-year bond with an annual coupon of 10% will have a different yield-to-maturity.   ◆◆

The graph of a bond's yield against the bond's time until maturity is called a **yield curve**. The yield curve for our 10 hypothetical bonds is shown below:

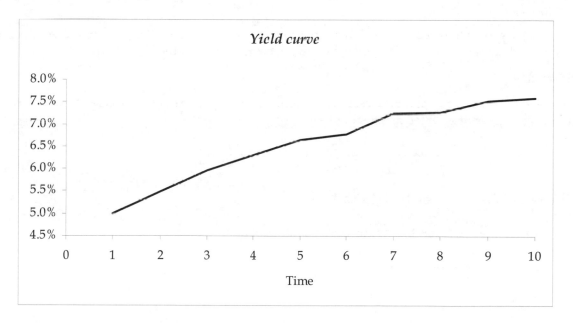

The yield curve shown here is upward sloping. This is often the case in reality, but the yield curve can also be flat or downward sloping, or it can even have a peak or valley.

Yield curves are often constructed using the yields on the most recently issued US government securities. This is known as an **on-the-run yield curve**. These securities are actively traded and free of default risk.

A **par yield curve** is a theoretical construction, in which each bond's coupon rate is assumed to be equal to the bond's yield. Remember that when a bond's coupon is equal to its yield, the price of the bond is equal to the bond's par value, and the bond is said to be priced at par. Of course, we should not actually expect to see bonds of all maturities trading for their par value. The par yield curve tells us the hypothetical coupons that would cause each bond to trade at par.

8.2 Spot rates

Given a well-defined yield curve, we can calculate the interest rate that can be earned on a deposit made now and left to accumulate for a specified period of time. This kind of interest rate is called a **spot rate**. The spot rate is also the rate that is used to discount a single cash flow occurring at a particular point in time.

Spot rates

The t-year spot rate, s_t, is the annual interest rate that can be earned on an investment made now, to be repaid as a lump sum with interest at time t years.

Spot rates can be used to calculate the price of a security using the formula below:

$$P = \sum_{t>0} \frac{CF_t}{\left(1+s_t\right)^t}$$

where s_t is the annual effective spot rate applicable to a cash flow occurring at time t.

When we use a bond's yield to calculate its price, we use just one yield. But when we use spot rates to calculate a bond's price, the formula above calls for multiple spot rates, one for each cash flow.

Example 8.2

The 1-year spot rate is 6.2%. The 2-year spot rate is 6.5%. Calculate the price of a 2-year bond paying 15% annual coupons. Assume that the principal amount of the bond is $100.

Solution

The cash flow occurring at time 1 year is discounted at 6.2% per year, and the cash flow occurring at time 2 years is discounted at 6.5% per year:

$$P = \sum \frac{CF_t}{\left(1+s_t\right)^t} = \frac{15}{\left(1+s_1\right)} + \frac{115}{\left(1+s_2\right)^2} = \frac{15}{1.062} + \frac{115}{1.065^2} = 115.5151$$

The price of the 2-year bond is $115.52.   ◆◆

We can also use spot rates to find the present values of annuities:

$$a_{\overline{n}|} = \frac{1}{\left(1+s_1\right)} + \frac{1}{\left(1+s_2\right)^2} + \cdots + \frac{1}{\left(1+s_n\right)^n}$$

$$\ddot{a}_{\overline{n}|} = 1 + \frac{1}{\left(1+s_1\right)} + \frac{1}{\left(1+s_2\right)^2} + \cdots + \frac{1}{\left(1+s_{n-1}\right)^{n-1}}$$

Example 8.3

Given the following annual effective spot rates, find the present value of an annuity that pays $100 at the end of each year for 3 years:

Time	Annual effective spot
1	5.000%
2	6.000%
3	8.000%

Solution

The cash flow occurring at the end of each year is discounted by the appropriate spot rate:

$$100a_{\overline{3}|} = 100\left(\frac{1}{1.05^1} + \frac{1}{1.06^2} + \frac{1}{1.08^3}\right) = 100(2.63621) = 263.62$$

The present value of the annuity is \$263.62.   ◆◆

Spot rates can be derived from observed bond prices in a couple of different ways. First, we can observe the prices of zero-coupon bonds in the market. Since an n-year zero-coupon bond has just one cash flow at time n, the n-year spot rate (s_n) is the internal rate of return on an n-year zero-coupon bond. If there are zero-coupon bonds at each maturity, then we can calculate a complete set of spot rates in this way.

A second method is to derive the spot rates from the prices of a set of coupon bonds, using a method known as **bootstrapping**. Under the bootstrapping method, we calculate the 1-year spot rate from the price of a 1-year bond and then use this information to calculate the 2-year spot rate from the price of a 2-year bond, and so on.

Bootstrapping is based on the fact that the yields and the spot rates must produce the same prices. Otherwise, **arbitrage** (risk-free profit) is possible. Suppose, for example, that the present value of a bond based on its yield is higher than the present value of the bond based on the spot rates. In that case, we could buy the bond from someone that is using the spot rates to price the bond and sell it to someone that is using the yield to price the bond. We would have an immediate risk-free profit equal to the difference in the prices.

Arbitrage is covered further in Section 8.4, but for now it is enough to know that well functioning markets do not allow arbitrage. Our bootstrapping methodology is based on the assumption that arbitrage is not possible, and therefore yields and spot rates must produce the same prices.

Let's use the bootstrapping method to calculate the spot rates for the bonds in Table 8.1.

In Example 8.1, we calculated the price of a 1-year bond paying 2% annual coupons to be \$97.1429, so we can calculate the 1-year spot rate as follows:

Price using yield = Price using spot rates

$$\Rightarrow \sum \frac{CF_t}{(1+y)^t} = \sum \frac{CF_t}{(1+s_t)^t}$$

$$\Rightarrow 97.1429 = \frac{102}{1+s_1} \qquad \Rightarrow s_1 = 5.000\%$$

Notice that the 1-year spot rate of 5.000% is equal to the 1-year yield. The spot rate is equal to the yield only because the 1-year bond produces just one cash flow. Therefore, the yield and the spot rate are both equal to the interest rate that discounts \$102 payable in one year to \$97.1429 now.

In Example 8.1, we also calculated the price of a 2-year bond paying 5.5% annual coupons to be \$100.0240. We can use this price and the fact that $s_1 = 5.000\%$ to determine the 2-year spot rate:

Price using yield = Price using spot rates

$$\sum \frac{CF_t}{(1+y)^t} = \sum \frac{CF_t}{(1+s_t)^t}$$

$$\Rightarrow 100.0240 = \frac{5.5}{1+s_1} + \frac{105.5}{(1+s_2)^2} = \frac{5.5}{1.05} + \frac{105.5}{(1+s_2)^2}$$

$$\Rightarrow s_2 = 5.500\%$$

Example 8.4

Using the bonds in Table 8.1, calculate the 3-year spot rate, s_3.

Solution

Since the annual coupon is equal to the yield-to-maturity, the bond stands at par, *ie* it has a price of $100. Hence, we calculate the 3-year spot rate as follows (using $s_1 = 5.000\%$ and $s_2 = 5.500\%$):

$$\sum \frac{CF_t}{(1+y)^t} = \sum \frac{CF_t}{(1+s_t)^t}$$

$$\Rightarrow 100.0000 = \frac{5.961}{1+s_1} + \frac{5.961}{(1+s_2)^2} + \frac{105.961}{(1+s_3)^3} = \frac{5.961}{1.05} + \frac{5.961}{(1.055)^2} + \frac{105.961}{(1+s_3)^3}$$

$$\Rightarrow s_3 = 6.000\%$$ ◆◆

This bootstrapping process can be continued until a spot rate for each year is determined.

The steps in the bootstrapping process are:

1. Calculate the prices of the bonds that were used to construct the yield curve.

2. Set s_1 equal to the yield of the bond paying a single cash flow at time 1.

3. Find s_2, based on the price of the bond maturing at time 2 and the previously determined value of s_1.

4. Find s_3, based on the price of the bond maturing at time 3 and the previously determined values of s_1 and s_2.

5. And so on ...

The process is continued until the desired number of spot rates has been calculated.

The completed spot rate table for our hypothetical set of bonds is shown below.

Table 8.2

Maturity	Annual effective spot rate
1	5.000%
2	5.500%
3	6.000%
4	6.400%
5	6.700%
6	7.001%
7	7.250%
8	7.499%
9	7.700%
10	7.901%

The graph of the spot rates against their maturities is known as the **spot rate curve**. The spot curve derived from our hypothetical set of bonds is shown below.

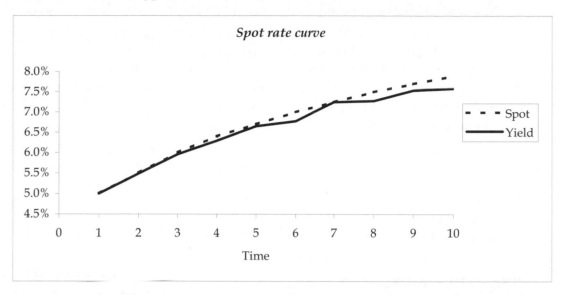

Spot rate curve

Notice that the spot rates in this example are generally higher than the yields. This is because a bond's yield-to-maturity can be viewed as a weighted average of the spot rates associated with each of the bond's cash flows. Since the yield curve is increasing, the spot rates in this term structure also increase over time and tend to be higher than the yields.

With just two exceptions, the yield is less than the spot rate. The two exceptions occur where the bond has just one cash flow, and at those points, the yield is equal to the spot rate. This occurs at time 1 year because the bond maturing in 1 year has only one cash flow, which is equal to its coupon plus its principal. It also occurs at time 7 years, because the 7-year bond used to construct the yield curve is a zero-coupon bond.

Although the yield appears to be equal to the spot rate at times 2, 3, and 5, it is actually a little bit less than the spot rate. At time 2, for example, the yield is 5.487%, and the spot rate is 5.500%.

8.3 Forward rates

A forward rate is a rate of interest that can be locked in now and that applies from one specified time to another specified time in the future. A set of spot rates implies a set of forward rates.

Forward rates

The forward rate beginning at time t years is an interest rate specified now for an investment beginning at time t and lasting until time $(t+1)$. It is called the t-year forward rate, and it is denoted by f_t.

Forward rates can be used to calculate the price of a security as follows:

$$P = \sum_{t>0} \frac{CF_t}{(1+f_0)(1+f_1)\cdots(1+f_{t-1})}$$

where f_t is the annual effective forward rate applicable from time t to time $(t+1)$.

The notation for forward rates is a little different from the notation for spot rates. The subscript t for a *spot* rate denotes the *end* point of the t-year time interval to which the spot rate applies. The beginning of the time interval to which the spot rate applies is time 0.

The subscript t for a *forward* rate denotes the *beginning* of the time interval to which the forward rate applies. We could add a second subscript to denote the end point of the time interval, but if we assume that the intervals are all the same size, we can dispense with the second subscript. In this section, we assume that the time intervals are all 1 year, so f_t denotes an interest rate that applies to a time interval beginning at time t and ending at time $(t+1)$, where the time interval is measured in years.

There is more than one way to refer to the value of f_t. Below are six common ways of describing f_t:

1.   the t-year forward rate
2.   the forward rate applicable from time t to time $(t+1)$
3.   the forward rate applicable to the $(t+1)$th year
4. t-year deferred one-year forward rate
5.   one-year forward rate for year t
6. t-year forward one-year rate

We'll primarily refer to the first three ways in this text since they are more frequently used, but the others are provided for completeness.

Example 8.5

The annual effective forward rate of interest applicable from time 0 to time 1 is 4.8%. The 1-year annual effective forward rate is 5.1%. The 2-year annual effective forward rate is 5.3%. Calculate the price of a 3-year bond paying 8% annual coupons. Assume that the principal amount of the bond is $100.

Solution

The price of the bond is:

$$P = \sum \frac{CF_t}{\left(1+f_0\right)\left(1+f_1\right)\cdots\left(1+f_{t-1}\right)}$$

$$= \frac{8}{1.048} + \frac{8}{(1.048)(1.051)} + \frac{108}{(1.048)(1.051)(1.053)} = 108.0143$$

The price of the bond is $108.01.   ◆◆

Forward rates can be calculated from the yield curve in a manner that is similar to the bootstrapping methodology employed to calculate the spot rates. Let's calculate the forward rates implied by the bonds in Table 8.1.

The 1-year bond has just one cash flow, so we can use our formula for price in terms of the forward rates to find f_0, the forward rate at time 0:

Price using yield = Price using forward rates

$$\Rightarrow 97.1429 = \frac{102}{1+f_0} \qquad \Rightarrow \qquad f_0 = 5.000\%$$

Notice that the forward rate beginning at time 0 is 5.000%, which the same as the 1-year yield, which is the same as the 1-year spot rate. The initial forward rate is equal to the 1-year yield and the 1-year spot rate, because there is just one cash flow at the end of one year. The yield, spot, and forward rate must all be equal to the interest rate that discounts $102 to $97.1429 over 1 year.

Now that we have the forward rate applicable to the first year, we can use the 2-year bond (with a price of $100.0240) to determine f_1, the forward rate applicable from time 1 to time 2:

$$100.0240 = \frac{5.5}{1+f_0} + \frac{105.5}{(1+f_0)(1+f_1)}$$

$$\Rightarrow 100.0240 = \frac{5.5}{1.05} + \frac{105.5}{(1.05)(1+f_1)} \qquad \Rightarrow f_1 = 6.003\%$$

Example 8.6

Using the bonds in Table 8.1, calculate f_2, the 2-year forward rate.

Solution

We can use the values for f_0 and f_1 in the formula for the price of the 3-year bond in order to find the forward rate applicable to the third year, f_2:

$$100.0000 = \frac{5.961}{1+f_0} + \frac{5.961}{(1+f_0)(1+f_1)} + \frac{105.961}{(1+f_0)(1+f_1)(1+f_2)}$$

$$\Rightarrow 100.0000 = \frac{5.961}{1.05} + \frac{5.961}{(1.05)(1.06003)} + \frac{105.961}{(1.05)(1.06003)(1+f_2)}$$

$$\Rightarrow f_2 = 7.006\% \qquad\qquad\qquad\qquad\qquad\qquad\qquad \blacklozenge\blacklozenge$$

This process can be continued until we have a full set of forward rates for our example as follows:

Table 8.3

t	Annual effective forward rate (f_t)
0	5.000%
1	6.003%
2	7.006%
3	7.611%
4	7.905%
5	8.519%
6	8.758%
7	9.262%
8	9.318%
9	9.723%

The **forward rate curve** is shown below. In this case, the forward rates happen to be greater than the corresponding spot rates and yields, but it is also possible for the forward rates to dip below the spot rates and yields.

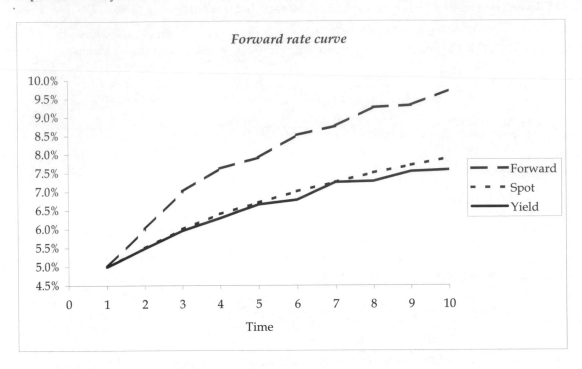

Example 8.7

Making use of the following yield curve, calculate the forward rates applicable to the first, second, and third years.

Maturity	Annual coupon	Annual effective yield
1	2.000%	15.000%
2	5.500%	15.000%
3	5.961%	15.000%

Solution

We can determine the forward rate applicable to the first year based on the fact that the price of the 1-year bond must be the same whether it is calculated with the yield or the first forward rate:

Price using yield = Price using forward rates

$$\Rightarrow \frac{102}{(1.15)} = \frac{102}{1+f_0} \qquad \Rightarrow \qquad f_0 = 0.1500$$

The price of the 2-year bond must also be the same whether it is calculated with the yield or the forward rates:

Price using yield = Price using forward rates

$$\Rightarrow \frac{5.50}{1.15} + \frac{105.5}{(1.15)^2} = \frac{5.50}{1.15} + \frac{105.50}{(1.15)(1+f_1)} \qquad \Rightarrow \qquad f_1 = 0.1500$$

The price of the 3-year bond must also be the same whether it is calculated with the yield or the forward rates:

$$\text{Price using yield} = \text{Price using forward rates}$$

$$\Rightarrow \frac{5.961}{1.15} + \frac{5.961}{(1.15)^2} + \frac{105.961}{(1.15)^3} = \frac{5.961}{1.15} + \frac{5.961}{(1.15)(1.15)} + \frac{105.961}{(1.15)(1.15)(1+f_2)}$$

$$\Rightarrow f_2 = 0.1500$$

Thus the forward rates applicable to the first, second, and third years are 15%, 15%, and 15%. ◆◆

This example is a special case known as a **flat yield curve** because the yields are the same for each maturity, making the graph of the yield curve a flat line. If any one of the yield curve, the spot curve, or the forward curve is flat, then the other two curves must also be flat, and the yields, spot rates and forward rates are all equal to the same rate.

Let's consider the relationship between the forward rates and the spot rates in the general case (*ie* the curves may or may not be flat).

The present value of a cash flow occurring at time t years can be calculated using spot rates as:

$$\frac{CF_t}{(1+s_t)^t}$$

The present value of the same cash flow calculated using forward rates is:

$$\frac{CF_t}{(1+f_0)(1+f_1)\cdots(1+f_{t-1})}$$

Since the two present values must be equal, this leads to the following general relationship:

$$(1+s_t)^t = (1+f_0)(1+f_1)\cdots(1+f_{t-1})$$

or:

$$s_t = \sqrt[t]{(1+f_0)(1+f_1)\cdots(1+f_{t-1})} - 1$$

So, the value $(1+s_t)$ is a geometric average of the values $(1+f_0)$, $(1+f_1)$, ..., $(1+f_{t-1})$. Further, we have:

$$(1+s_{t-1})^{t-1} = (1+f_0)(1+f_1)\cdots(1+f_{t-2})$$

$$(1+s_{t-1})^{t-1} = \frac{(1+s_t)^t}{(1+f_{t-1})}$$

$$\Rightarrow f_{t-1} = \frac{(1+s_t)^t}{(1+s_{t-1})^{t-1}} - 1$$

Relationships between forward rates and spot rates

$$(1+s_t)^t = (1+f_0)(1+f_1)\cdots(1+f_{t-1})$$

$$s_t = \sqrt[t]{(1+f_0)(1+f_1)\cdots(1+f_{t-1})} - 1$$

$$f_{t-1} = \frac{(1+s_t)^t}{(1+s_{t-1})^{t-1}} - 1$$

Example 8.8

The 1-year spot rate is 5.0%, the 2-year spot rate is 5.5%, and the 3-year spot rate is 6.0%. Calculate the forward rates applicable to the first, second, and third years.

Solution

The first forward rate is equal to the first spot rate:

$$(1+s_1) = (1+f_0)$$
$$(1.05) = (1+f_0) \quad \Rightarrow \quad f_0 = 5.000\%$$

We can use either the first formula or the third formula from the above box to find the forward rate applicable to the second year. Using the first formula:

$$(1+s_2)^2 = (1+f_0)(1+f_1)$$
$$(1.055)^2 = (1.05)(1+f_1) \quad \Rightarrow \quad f_1 = 6.002\%$$

Again, we can use either the first formula or the third formula from the above box to find the forward rate applicable to the third year. Using the third formula:

$$f_{t-1} = \frac{(1+s_t)^t}{(1+s_{t-1})^{t-1}} - 1$$

$$f_2 = \frac{1.06^3}{1.055^2} - 1 = 7.007\%$$

◆◆

The forward rates calculated above match (with some slight differences due to rounding) the forward rates in Table 8.3. This is because the spot rates provided in the example are the same as the spot rates in Table 8.2, which are based on the yields in Table 8.1. Since the spot rates are consistent with the yields, they produce the same forward rates as the yields.

Example 8.9

You are given the following annual effective forward rates of interest:

t	Annual effective forward rate (f_t)
0	3.8%
1	4.5%
2	4.1%

Calculate the 2-year and 3-year spot rates.

Solution

Using the relationship:

$$s_t = \sqrt[t]{(1+f_0)(1+f_1)\cdots(1+f_{t-1})} - 1$$

We have:

$$s_2 = \sqrt[2]{(1+f_0)(1+f_1)} - 1 = \sqrt[2]{(1.038)(1.045)} - 1 = 4.149\%$$
$$s_3 = \sqrt[3]{(1+f_0)(1+f_1)(1+f_2)} - 1 = \sqrt[3]{(1.038)(1.045)(1.041)} - 1 = 4.133\%$$

◆◆

8.4 Arbitrage

8.4.1 Opportunity for arbitrage

When assets are not priced consistently, there may be an **arbitrage** opportunity.

Arbitrage

An arbitrage opportunity exists when an investor is able to lock in a risk-free profit with no net outlay of funds. This is accomplished through the simultaneous purchase and sale of assets.

In this section, we apply our knowledge of yields, spot rates, and forward rates to identify potential arbitrage opportunities arising from inconsistent bond prices.

The term **arbitrage** is sometimes prefaced by the word "risk-free" implying that there is such a thing as **risky arbitrage**. Some texts regard the buying and selling of assets in a manner that is very likely to produce profits but still has a small chance of producing losses to be risky arbitrage. We, however, use the strict definition of arbitrage presented above, in which an arbitrage opportunity precludes the possibility of losses, and therefore arbitrage is risk-free.

In reality, arbitrage opportunities may exist briefly due to short-term inconsistencies between asset prices, but they are not likely to persist for long. By exploiting these short-term inconsistencies, market participants are able to make risk-free profits. The process of taking advantage of these opportunities requires the participants to purchase the assets that are priced too low and to sell the assets that are priced too high, thereby exerting natural market pressures to bring the prices back into line (*ie* increasing demand for the assets that are priced too low, and increasing supply of the assets that are priced too high).

In this section, several simplifying assumptions are made to support the contention that arbitrage opportunities are anomalies and cannot persist for long. Although these assumptions are not completely realistic, they provide a reasonable approximation of reality for a significant portion of the investment community.

- There are no transaction costs to buying or selling financial instruments.
- There are no margin requirements for short selling.
- Market participants can buy or sell the bonds represented by the yield curve.
- Market participants can buy or sell zero-coupon bonds at prices indicated by the spot rates.
- Market participants can lock in the current forward rates now for the purpose of lending or borrowing over a future time interval.

The key principle in this section is that an arbitrage opportunity exists if the relationships between yields, spot rates, and forward rates that were established in the previous sections fail to hold. This means that the asset prices produce an arbitrage opportunity.

Example 8.10

A 2-year bond paying annual coupons of 5.5% is priced at $101 per $100 of par. The 1-year spot rate is 5.0% and the 2-year spot rate is 5.5%. Determine whether an arbitrage opportunity exists.

Solution

The price of the bond that is consistent with the spot rates is $100.0248. This price is inconsistent with the market price, and therefore arbitrage is possible.

$$P = \sum \frac{CF_t}{\left(1+s_t\right)^t} = \frac{5.5}{1.05} + \frac{105.5}{1.055^2} = 100.0248 \qquad \blacklozenge\blacklozenge$$

8.4.2 Arbitrage profits

Students may initially find it difficult to know where to begin when creating a position that produces arbitrage profits. In order to understand how to create arbitrage profits, it is helpful to know the difference between taking a **long position** and a **short position** in an asset.

- An investor with a long position in an asset benefits if the asset's price goes up. A common way to take a long position in an asset is to purchase it.

- An investor with a short position in an asset benefits if the asset's price goes down. A common way to take a short position in an asset is to sell it.

An arbitrageur seeking to exploit an arbitrage opportunity must first identify an asset that is incorrectly priced relative to the rest of the market. If the asset price is too high relative to the rest of the market, then it is **overvalued**. If the asset price is too low relative to the rest of the market, then it is **undervalued**.

If the asset is overvalued, then the arbitrageur takes a short position in the asset. If the asset is undervalued, then the arbitrageur takes a long position in the asset.

In order to make the position risk-free, the arbitrageur must also take an offsetting position in other assets in such a way as to replicate the cash flows of the mispriced asset.

Let's illustrate this by considering how to exploit the arbitrage opportunity identified in Example 8.10 in which the 2-year bond has a market price of $101, but the price that is consistent with the spot rates is $100.0248. The bond is overvalued, so we should take a short position in the asset (*ie* we should sell the bond).

An arbitrageur can take advantage of this discrepancy with the following strategy:

1. Sell short the 5.5% bond in order to receive $101.

2. Buy a zero-coupon bond paying $5.50 in one year and a zero-coupon bond paying $105.50 in two years. The purchase price of these two bonds is:

$$P = \frac{5.5}{1.05} + \frac{105.5}{1.055^2} = \$100.0248$$

After completing these two steps, the arbitrageur achieves a net profit at time 0 of:

$$101 - 100.0248 = \$0.9752$$

At time 1 year, the arbitrageur must provide the cash flow of $5.50 that is required by the 5.50% bond that was sold short. But the 1-year zero-coupon bond that the arbitrageur purchased provides $5.50 at time 1 year. Thus the arbitrageur has no net cash flows at time 1.

At time 2 years, the arbitrageur must provide the cash flow of $105.50 that is required by the 5.50% bond that was sold short. But the 2-year zero-coupon bond that the arbitrageur purchased provides $105.50 at time 2 years. Thus the arbitrageur has no net cash flow at time 2.

Let's take a look at the cash flows at the end of each year that result from this position.

Time	Cash flow from short position	Cash flow from long position	Net cash flow
0	101.0000	−100.0248	0.9752
1	−5.5000	5.5000	0.0000
2	−105.5000	105.5000	0.0000

Since the net cash flows at times 1 and 2 are zero, the only net cash flow that the arbitrageur experiences is the net receipt of $0.9752 at time 0.

In general, an arbitrage profit can be made by taking a short position in an asset that is overvalued, and by creating a long position consisting of assets that will produce the same cash flows as the overvalued asset that is shorted. Alternatively, an arbitrageur can take a long position in an asset that is undervalued, and create a short position consisting of assets that will produce the same cash flows as the undervalued asset that is bought long.

The arbitrageur establishes a position that produces a positive cash flow now (equal to the difference between the cost of the long position and the proceeds from the short position) and requires no future payments.

The next example considers the case of a bond that is undervalued.

Example 8.11

A 2-year bond paying annual coupons of 5.5% is priced at $99 per $100 of par. The 1-year spot rate is 5.0% and the 2-year spot rate is 5.5%. Determine whether an arbitrage opportunity exists. If an arbitrage opportunity exists, develop a strategy that a produces a risk-free profit with no net cash outlay.

Solution

From Example 8.10, the price of the bond that is consistent with the spot rates is $100.0248.

Since the market price of the bond is $99, the bond is undervalued relative to the price that is consistent with the spot rates, and an arbitrage opportunity exists.

An arbitrageur can take advantage of this arbitrage opportunity with the following strategy:

1. Buy the 5.5% bond for $99.

2. Sell short a zero-coupon bond paying $5.50 in one year and a zero-coupon bond paying $105.50 in two years. The sale price of these two bonds is:

$$P = \frac{5.5}{1.05} + \frac{105.5}{1.055^2} = 5.2381 + 94.7867 = \$100.0248$$

After completing those two steps, the arbitrageur is left with a risk-free profit at time 0 of:

$$100.0248 - 99.0000 = \$1.0248$$

At time 1, the arbitrageur receives $5.50 from the 5.50% bond that was purchased. But the 1-year zero-coupon bond that the arbitrageur sold requires a payment of $5.50 at time 1 year. Thus the arbitrageur has a net cash flow of zero at time 1.

At time 2, the arbitrageur receives $105.50 from the 5.50% bond that was purchased. But the 2-year zero-coupon bond that the arbitrageur sold requires a payment of $105.50 at time 2 years. Thus the arbitrageur has a net cash flow of zero at time 2.

Let's take a look at the cash flows at the end of each year that result from this position.

Time	Cash flow from short position	Cash flow from long position	Net cash flow
0	100.0248	-99.0000	1.0248
1	-5.5000	5.5000	0.0000
2	-105.5000	105.5000	0.0000

Since the net cash flows occurring at times 1 and 2 are zero, the only net cash flow that the arbitrageur experiences is the net receipt of $1.0248 at time 0.   ♦♦

In the preceding example, a profit of $1.0248 could be earned immediately with no risk or capital outlay. What do you suppose will happen when investors learn of this opportunity? Arbitrageurs will want to take advantage of this opportunity. This means that arbitrageurs will be clamoring to buy the 5.50% bond, and they will want to sell the 1-year and 2-year zero-coupon bonds. This will drive up the price of the 5.50% bond, and it will decrease the prices of the zero-coupon bonds. The price adjustments will continue until the arbitrage opportunity no longer exists. The pursuit of arbitrage profits leads to the disappearance of arbitrage opportunities.

Let's consider an example involving forward rates.

Example 8.12

A 3-year bond paying annual coupons of 5.961% is priced at par. The forward rates are $f_0 = 5.000\%$, $f_1 = 6.002\%$, and $f_2 = 8.000\%$.

Develop a strategy that a produces a risk-free profit with no net cash outlay.

Solution

The price of the bond that is consistent with the forward rates is:

$$P = \frac{5.961}{1 + f_0} + \frac{5.961}{(1 + f_0)(1 + f_1)} + \frac{105.961}{(1 + f_0)(1 + f_1)(1 + f_2)}$$

$$= \frac{5.961}{1.05} + \frac{5.961}{(1.05)(1.06002)} + \frac{105.961}{(1.05)(1.06002)(1.08)}$$

$$= \$99.1822$$

The market price of $100 is higher than the price of $99.1822 that was calculated with the forward rates. Since the bond is overvalued with respect to the price calculated with the forward rates, an arbitrage opportunity exists.

An arbitrageur can sell the 5.961% bond short for $100 and replicate its cash flow for only $99.1822.

In order to determine a replication strategy, the arbitrageur begins by investing the cost of the strategy, $99.1822, for one year at 5%. At the end of the year, $5.961 must be paid out to cover the coupon due on the bond sold short, and the remainder is then invested from time 1 year to time 2 years:

$$99.1822(1.05) - 5.961 = \$98.1803$$

At the end of the second year, $5.961 is again paid out to cover the coupon due on the bond sold short, and the remainder is then invested from time 2 years to time 3 years:

$$98.1803(1.06002) - 5.961 = \$98.1121$$

Summarizing, an investor can take advantage of this arbitrage opportunity with the following strategy:

1. Sell the 5.961% bond for $100.

2. Lock in the forward rates over the next three years by making the following agreements now:
   - Agree to invest $99.1822 now at 5.000% for one year.
   - Agree to invest $98.1803 in one year at 6.002% for one year.
   - Agree to invest $98.1121 in two years at 8.000% for one year.

After completing these steps, the investor is left with a net profit at time 0 of:

$$100.0000 - 99.1822 = \$0.8178$$

Let's take a look at the cash flows at the end of each year that result from this position.

Time	Cash flow from short position	Cash flow from long position	Net cash flow
0	100.0000	− 99.1822	0.8178
1	− 5.9610	5.9610	0.0000
2	− 5.9610	5.9610	0.0000
3	− 105.9610	105.9610	0.0000

The cash flow from the long position is initially negative since the $99.1822 that is invested at time 0 is an outflow for the investor.

At time 1, the $99.1822 has grown to:

$$99.1822(1 + f_0) = 99.1822(1.05) = 104.1413$$

Of this amount, $98.1803 is invested at 6.002%, leaving positive cash flow of $5.961 at time 1:

$$104.1413 - 98.1803 = 5.961$$

At time 2, the $98.1803 has grown to:

$$98.1803(1 + f_1) = 98.1803(1.06002) = 104.0731$$

Of this amount, $98.1121 is invested at 8.000%, leaving positive cash flow of 5.961 at time 2:

$$104.0731 - 98.1121 = 5.961$$

At time 3, the $98.1121 has grown to $105.961:

$$98.1121(1 + f_2) = 98.1121(1.08) = 105.961$$

Since there are no net cash flows occurring at times 1, 2, and 3, the only net cash flow that the investor experiences is the net receipt of $0.8178 at time 0.   ◆ ◆

8.5   *Non-annual compounding*

Thus far, we have worked with yields, spots, and forwards that are compounded once per year (*ie* annual effective rates). Bond prices can also be calculated based on yields, spots, and forwards that are compounded at other frequencies.

Yield-to-maturity compounded m times per year

The yield of an asset is the interest rate that equates the present value of the asset's cash flows with its price:

$$P = \sum_{t>0} \frac{CF_t}{\left(1 + \dfrac{y^{(m)}}{m}\right)^{mt}}$$

where $y^{(m)}$ is the yield, compounded m times per year.

Spot rates compounded m times per year

The t-year spot rates compounded m times per year satisfy the relationship:

$$P = \sum_{t>0} \frac{CF_t}{\left(1 + \dfrac{s_t^{(m)}}{m}\right)^{mt}}$$

where $s_t^{(m)}$ is the spot rate, compounded m times per year, applicable to a cash flow occurring at time t.

Forward rates compounded m times per year

The forward rates compounded m times per year, satisfy the relationship:

$$P = \sum_{t>0} \frac{CF_t}{\left(1 + \dfrac{f_0^{(m)}}{m}\right)^{m}\left(1 + \dfrac{f_1^{(m)}}{m}\right)^{m} \cdots \left(1 + \dfrac{f_{t-1}^{(m)}}{m}\right)^{m}}$$

where $f_{t-1}^{(m)}$ is the annual forward rate, compounded m times per year, applicable from time $(t-1)$ to time t.

We can also express the relationship between spot rates and forward rates in terms of rates that are compounded at non-annual frequencies.

Forward rates and spot rates under non-annual compounding

If the spot rates are compounded m times per year and the forward rates are compounded p times per year, then:

$$\left(1 + \frac{s_t^{(m)}}{m}\right)^{mt} = \left(1 + \frac{f_0^{(p)}}{p}\right)^{p}\left(1 + \frac{f_1^{(p)}}{p}\right)^{p} \cdots \left(1 + \frac{f_{t-1}^{(p)}}{p}\right)^{p}$$

and:

$$\left(1 + \frac{f_{t-1}^{(p)}}{p}\right)^{p} = \frac{\left(1 + \dfrac{s_t^{(m)}}{m}\right)^{mt}}{\left(1 + \dfrac{s_{t-1}^{(m)}}{m}\right)^{m(t-1)}}$$

Example 8.13

A 2-year bond pays coupons of 10% annually. Its annual effective yield is 12%. The 1-year spot rate, compounded 12 times per year is 11%.

Find the value of $f_1^{(4)}$, the forward rate applicable in the second year, expressed as a rate that is compounded quarterly.

Solution

The price of the 2-year bond, per $100 of par value is:

$$\frac{10}{1.12} + \frac{110}{1.12^2} = \$96.6199$$

The annual effective 1-year spot rate is:

$$s_1 = \left(1 + \frac{s_1^{(12)}}{12}\right)^{12} - 1 = \left(1 + \frac{0.11}{12}\right)^{12} - 1 = 0.11572$$

Solving for the 2-year annual effective spot rate:

$$96.6199 = \frac{10}{1.11572} + \frac{110}{(1+s_2)^2} \quad \Rightarrow \quad s_2 = 12.022\%$$

Setting $t = 2$ and $m = 1$ in the second formula from the box above, we have:

$$\left(1 + \frac{f_{t-1}^{(p)}}{p}\right)^p = \frac{\left(1 + \dfrac{s_t^{(m)}}{m}\right)^{mt}}{\left(1 + \dfrac{s_{t-1}^{(m)}}{m}\right)^{m(t-1)}}$$

$$\left(1 + \frac{f_1^{(p)}}{p}\right)^p = \frac{(1+s_2)^2}{(1+s_1)}$$

We can use the 1-year spot rate and the 2-year spot rate to find the forward rate applicable to the second year, expressed as a rate that is compounded quarterly:

$$\left(1 + \frac{f_1^{(4)}}{4}\right)^4 = \frac{(1+0.12022)^2}{(1+0.11572)^1}$$

$$\left(1 + \frac{f_1^{(4)}}{4}\right)^4 = 1.12474$$

$$\Rightarrow f_1^{(4)} = 11.929\% \qquad\qquad\qquad\qquad\qquad\qquad ◆◆$$

8.6   *Non-annual forward rates*

Thus far, we have examined only cash flows that occur at yearly intervals. The definition of spot rates, however, allows us to price cash flows that occur at any point in time. Recall that:

$$P = \sum \frac{CF_t}{(1+s_t)^t}$$

where s_t is the annual effective spot rate applicable to a cash flow occurring at time t.

Example 8.14

The annual effective 6-month spot rate is 7%, and the annual effective 1-year spot rate is 8%. Calculate the price of a 1-year bond that pays semiannual coupons, has an annual coupon rate of 9%, and has $100 of par value.

Solution

The bond pays a coupon of $4.50 in 6 months and in 1 year it pays the coupon of $4.50 and the par value of $100.

The spot rates provided are:

$$s_{0.5} = 7\%$$
$$s_{1.0} = 8\%$$

The price of the 2-year bond, per $100 of par value is $101.1096:

$$\frac{4.5}{1.07^{0.5}} + \frac{104.5}{1.08} = 101.1096$$

◆◆

Forward rates can also apply for periods of time other than one year.

Non-annual forward rates

Forward rates applicable to time periods of length h can be used to calculate the price of a security using the following formula:

$$P = \sum_{t>0} \frac{CF_t}{\left(1 + f_{0,h}\right)^h \left(1 + f_{h,2h}\right)^h \cdots \left(1 + f_{t-h,t}\right)^h}$$

where $f_{a,b}$ is the annual effective forward rate applicable from time a to time b.

Example 8.15

The annual effective forward rate applicable from time 0 to time 0.5 is 7%. The annual effective forward rate applicable from time 0.5 to 1 is 9.0093%:

$$f_{0,0.5} = 7.000\%$$
$$f_{0.5,1} = 9.0093\%$$

Calculate the value of a 1-year bond that pays semiannual coupons, has an annual coupon rate of 9%, and has $100 of par value.

Solution

The price of the 1-year bond, per $100 of par value is:

$$P = \frac{4.5}{\left(1 + f_{0,0.5}\right)^{0.5}} + \frac{104.5}{\left(1 + f_{0,0.5}\right)^{0.5} \left(1 + f_{0.5,1.0}\right)^{0.5}}$$

$$= \frac{4.5}{1.07^{0.5}} + \frac{104.5}{(1.07)^{0.5} (1.090093)^{0.5}}$$

$$= \$101.1096$$

◆◆

The relationship between non-annual forward rates and spot rates is similar to the relationship derived earlier between annual forward rates and spot rates. The relationships derived earlier in Section 8.3 are the special cases of the relationships described below, with $h = 1$.

Relationship between spot rates and non-annual forward rates

$$(1+s_t)^t = \left(1+f_{0,h}\right)^h \left(1+f_{h,2h}\right)^h \cdots \left(1+f_{t-h,t}\right)^h$$

$$f_{t-h,t} = \left(\frac{(1+s_t)^t}{(1+s_{t-h})^{t-h}} \right)^{\frac{1}{h}} - 1$$

Example 8.16

Using the information in Example 8.15, calculate the 1-year annual effective spot rate.

Solution

The 1-year annual effective spot rate is calculated as:

$$(1+s_1) = (1.07)^{0.5}(1.090093)^{0.5} = 1.080000$$
$$\Rightarrow s_1 = 8.000\%$$

◆◆

Example 8.17

Based on the following spot rate curve, find the annual effective forward rate applicable from time 2 years to time 5 years.

Time	Annual effective spot
1	7.000%
2	6.000%
3	8.000%
4	9.000%
5	10.000%

Solution

In this case, we seek to find $f_{2,5}$. We note that $h = 3$:

$$f_{t-h,t} = \left(\frac{(1+s_t)^t}{(1+s_{t-h})^{t-h}} \right)^{\frac{1}{h}} - 1$$

$$f_{2,5} = \left(\frac{(1+s_5)^5}{(1+s_2)^2} \right)^{\frac{1}{3}} - 1 = \left(\frac{1.10^5}{1.06^2} \right)^{\frac{1}{3}} - 1 = 12.75\%$$

The annual effective forward rate applicable over the 3-year period from time 2 years to time 5 years is 12.75%.

This rate may also be referred to as the 2-year deferred 3-year forward rate.

◆◆

Forward rates can also be expressed as rates that are effective for time periods other than one year. In fact, it is common to express the forward rates as rates that are effective for a period of length h.

Recall from Chapter 4 that the effective interest rate for a period of length $1/p$ is:

$$\frac{i^{(p)}}{p} = (1+i)^{\frac{1}{p}} - 1$$

where i is the annual effective interest rate.

The above formula applies to all three kinds of interest rates: yields, spots, and forwards. Substituting h for $1/p$ and expressing the interest rates as forward rates, we have:

$$\frac{f_{t-h,t}^{\left(\frac{1}{h}\right)}}{\frac{1}{h}} = \left(1 + f_{t-h,t}\right)^{h} - 1$$

Example 8.18

Using the information in Example 8.15, convert the annual effective forward rates into forward rates that are effective over six months.

Use the calculated forward rates to calculate the price of a bond that pays semiannual coupons, has an annual coupon rate of 9%, and has $100 of par value.

Solution

The question requires that we find $\dfrac{f_{0,0.5}^{(2)}}{2}$ and $\dfrac{f_{0.5,1.0}^{(2)}}{2}$:

$$\frac{f_{0,0.5}^{(2)}}{2} = (1.07)^{0.5} - 1 = 0.034408$$

$$\frac{f_{0.5,1.0}^{(2)}}{2} = (1.090093)^{0.5} - 1 = 0.044075$$

The effective forward rate over the first six months is 3.4408%, and the effective forward rate over the second six months is 4.4075%.

The price of the bond is:

$$\frac{4.50}{1.034408} + \frac{104.50}{(1.034408)(1.044075)} = \$101.1096$$

◆◆

8.7 Key information when using interest rates

This chapter has presented three kinds of interest rates (yields, spots, and forwards) and has shown how these rates can apply over different time periods and how they can be compounded at different frequencies. Let's take a moment to identify the key pieces of information needed to use an interest rate correctly.

In this section, we consider three questions that must be answered before we can use an interest rate. For forward rates, one additional question must be answered.

Frequently, we are presented with problems that do not explicitly provide answers to all of these questions. When this occurs, we must be ready to answer some or all of the questions based on the context of the problem.

Key questions when using interest rates

To use an interest rate appropriately, we must first answer the following questions:

1.   What type of interest rate is being used: a yield, a spot rate, or a forward rate?

2.   Is the interest rate an annual rate, or is it expressed as a rate over some other interval?

3.   What is the compounding frequency of the interest rate?

And for forward rates, we must also know:

4.   When does the period covered by the forward rate begin and end?

Question 1 from the box above asks what type of interest rate is being used. This chapter has shown that the methodology for valuing a set of cash flows depends on whether yields, spot rates or forward rates are being used.

Question 2 deals with the possibility that the interest rate is not an annual rate. If we are given an interest rate of $X\%$, then we must determine whether the interest rate is $X\%$ per year, per month, per quarter, or per some other time interval. If the time interval is not specified, it is generally assumed to be one year.

Question 3 reminds us that an interest rate can be compounded at different frequencies. If the rate is not an annual rate, then the compounding frequency is usually one, but it is theoretically possible for the compounding frequency to be other than one. Usually, however, if the compounding frequency differs from one, then we are dealing with an annual rate of interest. When valuing bonds that make semiannual coupon payments, for example, it is common for investment professionals to express the yields as annual rates that are compounded twice per year.

Question 4 relates to forward rates only. We must know the beginning and the end of the period to which the forward rate is applicable. Most texts use notation similar to that used in this text:

f_t indicates that the period begins at time t and ends at time $(t+1)$

$f_{a,b}$ indicates that the period begins at time a and ends at time b

Be aware though, that other texts sometimes use the second subscript to indicate the length of the time interval, *ie* in some texts $f_{a,h}$ indicates that the period ends at time $(a+h)$.

Also, other texts might assume a time interval other than one year for the length of the period to which f_t applies. The assumed length can usually be determined from the context of the information presented.

Although we can provide no universal answers to the questions in the box above, knowing which questions to ask about interest rates is sometimes half the battle to successfully using them!

Chapter 8 Practice Questions

Question 8.1

Given the following yields and coupons for bonds with $100 of par value, determine the price for each bond.

Maturity	Annual coupon	Annual effective yield
1	10.000%	8.000%
2	4.000%	8.979%
3	20.000%	9.782%

Question 8.2

Given the following annual effective spot rates, find the present value of a 3-year bond paying 15% annual coupons and having a par value of $100.

Time	Annual effective spot
1	7.000%
2	6.000%
3	8.000%

Question 8.3

Given the yield curve from Question 8.1, calculate the 1-year, 2-year, and 3-year annual effective spot rates.

Question 8.4

We are given the following table of yields for bonds that pay annual coupons:

Maturity	Annual coupon	Annual effective yield
1	8.000%	4.000%
2	7.000%	4.967%
3	10.000%	5.424%
4	6.000%	6.600%
5	7.500%	7.664%

The 5-year spot rate is $s_5 = 8\%$.

Find the present value of an annuity-immediate that pays $40 per year for 5 years.

Hint: A shortcut allows us to avoid calculating the spot rates for years 1 through 4.

Question 8.5

Given the following table of forward rates, find the present value of a 3-year bond paying 15% annual coupons and having a par value of $100.

t	f_t
0	7.000%
1	5.009%
2	12.114%

Question 8.6

Using the spot rates calculated for Question 8.3, calculate the annual forward rates applicable to the first, second and third years: f_0, f_1, and f_2.

Question 8.7

Use the par yield curve described by the table below to determine the annual forward rates applicable to the first, second, and third years: f_0, f_1, and f_2.

Maturity	Annual coupon	Annual effective yield
1	5.000%	5.000%
2	6.500%	6.500%
3	8.500%	8.500%

Question 8.8

Given the following forward rates, calculate the 1-year, 2-year, and 3-year spot rates:

t	f_t
0	7.000%
1	5.009%
2	12.114%

Question 8.9

We are given the yields on three bonds that pay annual coupons, but their coupons are unknown.

Maturity	Annual coupon	Annual effective yield
1	X	10.000%
2	Y	10.000%
3	Z	10.000%

Find the 1-year, 2-year, and 3-year spot rates.

Question 8.10

Using the information from Question 8.9, find the forward rates applicable to the first, second, and third years: f_0, f_1, and f_2.

Question 8.11

We are given the following prices for bonds paying annual coupons:

Maturity	Annual coupon	Price per $100 of par
1	10.000%	106.7961
2	2.000%	94.4588
3	8.000%	100.7571

Find the price of a 3-year bond with annual coupons of 12% and $100 of par value.

Question 8.12

The table below provides the prices of 5 zero-coupon bonds:

Maturity	Price per $100 of par
1	97.0874
2	90.7029
3	81.6298
4	73.5030
5	64.2529

Determine the value of f_3, the annual effective forward rate applicable from time 3 to time 4.

Question 8.13

The 1-year spot rate is 5%. The forward rate applicable to the time interval beginning at time 1 and ending at time 2 is 7%. The annual effective yield on a 3-year bond priced at par and having annual coupons is 8%.

Find the 3-year spot rate.

Question 8.14

A 2-year bond pays annual coupons of 5.50%, has an annual effective yield of 9.3%, and has a par value of $100. The 1-year spot rate is 7.0%, and the 2-year spot rate is 9.0%.

Describe a strategy that requires the sale or purchase of exactly one of the 5.50% 2-year bonds and produces arbitrage profits of $0.59.

Question 8.15

A 1-year bond paying annual coupons of 12% has an annual effective yield of 12%. A 2-year bond paying annual coupons of 10% has an annual effective yield of 14.847%. The bonds have $100 of par value.

(i)   Calculate the value of the implied 2-year spot rate, s_2.

(ii)   An investor wants to invest $1,000 for two years at the spot rate calculated in Part (i). Suppose the investor is unable to find an institution willing to accept a 2-year deposit. Describe how the investor's objective can be accomplished through purchase and sale of the 1-year 12% bond and the 2-year 10% bond.

Question 8.16

Suppose the investor described in Question 8.15 finds an institution willing to accept a $1,000 deposit for two years. To the surprise of the investor, the institution is willing to pay 17% interest on the 2-year deposit. Based on the 2-year spot rate calculated in Question 8.15, the investor realizes that there is an opportunity to earn an arbitrage profit. The investor is unable to find an institution willing to lend at the 2-year spot rate calculated in Question 8.15, but the investor is able to buy and/or sell the 1-year 12% bond and the 2-year 10% bond.

Describe a strategy that allows the investor to earn an arbitrage profit of $35.08.

Question 8.17

The following spot rates are expressed as rates compounded twice per year:

$$s_1^{(2)} = 10\% \qquad s_2^{(2)} = 15\% \qquad s_3^{(2)} = 20\%$$

Find the present value of a 3-year bond paying annual coupons of 4%.

Question 8.18

The following forward rates are expressed as rates compounded twice per year:

$$f_0^{(2)} = 6\% \qquad f_1^{(2)} = 5\% \qquad f_2^{(2)} = 7\%$$

Find the 1-year, 2-year, and 3-year spot rates, expressed as rates compounded four times per year.

Question 8.19

The forward rates in the table below are expressed as monthly effective rates:

t	0	$\dfrac{1}{12}$	$\dfrac{2}{12}$	$\dfrac{3}{12}$	$\dfrac{4}{12}$	$\dfrac{5}{12}$	$\dfrac{6}{12}$	$\dfrac{7}{12}$	$\dfrac{8}{12}$	$\dfrac{9}{12}$	$\dfrac{10}{12}$	$\dfrac{11}{12}$
$\dfrac{f_{t,t+\frac{1}{12}}^{(12)}}{12}$	1.0%	1.5%	0.8%	2.0%	0.5%	1.3%	1.0%	1.1%	1.2%	0.6%	0.2%	0.9%

Find the following semiannually compounded spot rates: $s_{0.5}^{(2)}$ and $s_{1.0}^{(2)}$.

Question 8.20   *SOA (modified)*

You are given the following spot rates:

$$s_{0.5}^{(2)} = 12.00\%$$

$$s_{1.0}^{(2)} = 13.50\%$$

$$s_{1.5}^{(2)} = 14.66\%$$

$$s_{2.0}^{(2)} = 16.00\%$$

Calculate the 1-year implied forward rate for the second year, expressed as a rate that is effective over six months.

9

Stochastic interest rates

Overview

In most of this text, an implicit assumption has been made that the future interest rates are known in advance. That is, the interest rates are not random, but **deterministic**.

In this chapter, we consider the interest rates to be **stochastic**, which means that the future interest rates are random variables. We cannot say now what the interest rates will be in the future, but if we make an assumption about the statistical distribution of the future interest rates, then we can draw some conclusions about the future interest rates and the financial cash flows associated with them.

9.1 Interest rates as random variables

In this chapter, future interest rates are assumed to be unknown, and are regarded as random variables.

Let's define the random variable i_t to be the interest rate applicable from time $(t-1)$ to time t.

Accumulated values

If an investment of \$1 is made now, it accumulates at time n years to AV_n where:

$$AV_n = (1+i_1)(1+i_2)\cdots(1+i_n)$$

279

So, AV_n is itself a random variable, with the following properties.

Accumulated values as random variables

The expected accumulated value at time n of $1 invested now is:

$$E[AV_n] = E[(1+i_1)(1+i_2)\cdots(1+i_n)]$$

The variance of the accumulated value at time n of $1 invested now is:

$$Var[AV_n] = E[AV_n^2] - (E[AV_n])^2$$

These formulas can be used to find the expected value and variance of the accumulated value when the probability distribution of the values of i_t is known.

Let's consider a simple model known as the **fixed interest rate model**. In this model, the initial interest rate is determined in the first year and the subsequent interest rates are then fixed at that initial interest rate. Therefore, the future interest rates in this model are perfectly correlated.

Example 9.1

The interest rates for the next two years follow the fixed interest rate model.

The annual effective interest rate during the next two years will be one of 6%, 8% or 10% with the following distribution:

$$i_t = \begin{cases} 0.06 \text{ with probability } 0.3 \\ 0.08 \text{ with probability } 0.4 \\ 0.10 \text{ with probability } 0.3 \end{cases}$$

Once the interest rate is determined, it remains constant throughout the next two years.

(i)   Find the expected accumulated value of $1 invested now for a period of two years.

(ii)   Find the variance of the accumulated value of $1 invested now for a period of two years.

Solution

The complete distribution of AV_2 is given below:

i_1 , i_2	Probability	AV_2	$(AV_2)^2$
0.06	0.3	$(1.06)(1.06) = 1.1236$	$1.1236^2 = 1.262477$
0.08	0.4	$(1.08)(1.08) = 1.1664$	$1.1664^2 = 1.360489$
0.10	0.3	$(1.10)(1.10) = 1.2100$	$1.2100^2 = 1.464100$

Part (i)

The expected accumulated value at the end of two years is:

$$\begin{aligned} E[AV_n] &= E[(1+i_1)(1+i_2)] \\ &= (1.1236)(0.3) + (1.1664)(0.4) + (1.2100)(0.3) \\ &= \$1.16664 \end{aligned}$$

Part (ii)

The expected value of the square of the accumulated value is:

$$E[(AV_n)^2] = E\left[\left((1+i_1)(1+i_2)\right)^2\right]$$
$$= (1.262477)(0.3) + (1.360489)(0.4) + (1.464100)(0.3)$$
$$= 1.36217$$

The variance of the accumulated value is:

$$Var[AV_n] = E[AV_n^2] - \left(E[AV_n]\right)^2 = 1.36217 - 1.16664^2 = 0.00112 \qquad \blacklozenge\blacklozenge$$

Another interest rate model, known as the **varying interest rate model**, allows the interest rate to change each year. In this model, the interest rate in each year is independent of the interest rates in the other years.

 ### Example 9.2

The interest rates for the next two years follow the varying interest rate model.

The annual effective interest rate during the next year will be 6%, 8% or 10%. The following year the annual effective interest rate will again be 6%, 8% or 10%. In each year, the distribution is:

$$i_t = \begin{cases} 0.06 \text{ with probability } 0.3 \\ 0.08 \text{ with probability } 0.4 \\ 0.10 \text{ with probability } 0.3 \end{cases}$$

(i)   Find the expected accumulated value of $1 invested now for a period of two years.

(ii)   Find the variance of the accumulated value of $1 invested now for a period of two years.

Solution

The complete distribution of AV_2 is given below:

(i_1, i_2)	Probability	AV_2	$(AV_2)^2$
(0.06, 0.06)	(0.3)(0.3) = 0.09	(1.06)(1.06) = 1.1236	$1.1236^2 = 1.262477$
(0.08, 0.08)	(0.4)(0.4) = 0.16	(1.08)(1.08) = 1.1664	$1.1664^2 = 1.360489$
(0.10, 0.10)	(0.3)(0.3) = 0.09	(1.10)(1.10) = 1.2100	$1.2100^2 = 1.464100$
(0.06, 0.08) or (0.08, 0.06)	2(0.3)(0.4) = 0.24	(1.06)(1.08) = 1.1448	$1.1448^2 = 1.310567$
(0.06, 0.10) or (0.10, 0.06)	2(0.3)(0.3) = 0.18	(1.06)(1.10) = 1.1660	$1.1660^2 = 1.359556$
(0.08, 0.10) or (0.10, 0.08)	2(0.4)(0.3) = 0.24	(1.08)(1.10) = 1.1880	$1.1880^2 = 1.411344$

Part (i)

The expected accumulated value is calculated as the sum of the possible ending values times their associated probabilities:

$$\begin{aligned}
E[AV_n] &= E[(1+i_1)(1+i_2)] \\
&= (1.1236)(0.09) + (1.1664)(0.16) + (1.2100)(0.09) \\
&\quad + (1.1448)(0.24) + (1.1660)(0.18) + (1.1880)(0.24) \\
&= \$1.16640
\end{aligned}$$

Part (ii)

The expected value of the square of the accumulated value is:

$$\begin{aligned}
E[(AV_n)^2] &= E\left[\left((1+i_1)(1+i_2)\right)^2\right] \\
&= (1.262477)(0.09) + (1.360489)(0.16) + (1.464100)(0.09) \\
&\quad + (1.310567)(0.24) + (1.359556)(0.18) + (1.411344)(0.24) \\
&= 1.36105
\end{aligned}$$

The variance of the accumulated value is:

$$Var[AV_n] = E[AV_n^2] - \left(E[AV_n]\right)^2 = 1.36105 - 1.16640^2 = 0.00056 \qquad \blacklozenge\blacklozenge$$

In the examples above, the fixed interest rate model has a higher expected accumulated value (\$1.16664) than the varying interest rate model (\$1.16640). Under the fixed interest rate model, in the second year, the highest interest rate of 10% is applied to the account only when the highest interest rate is applied in the first year. This can be considered an efficient allocation of the interest rates in the second year, because the higher the fund value at the end of the first year, the higher the interest rate the fund earns in the second year. That is, the highest interest rate is applied when the fund value is highest.

Present values

The present value at time 0 of \$1 payable at time n years is:

$$PV_n = \left(\frac{1}{1+i_1}\right)\left(\frac{1}{1+i_2}\right)\cdots\left(\frac{1}{1+i_n}\right)$$

Present values as a random variables

The expected present value of \$1 payable at time n is:

$$E[PV_n] = E\left[\frac{1}{(1+i_1)(1+i_2)\cdots(1+i_n)}\right]$$

The variance of the present value of \$1 payable at time n is:

$$Var[PV_n] = E[PV_n^2] - \left(E[PV_n]\right)^2$$

The *actual* present value at time 0 is not known until all n of the interest rates are revealed, but the *expected* present value can be calculated at time 0 if the distribution of the interest rates is known.

Notice that:

$$PV_n \times AV_n = 1$$

But this does not imply an analogous relationship for $E[PV_n]$ and $E[AV_n]$. In general:

$$E[PV_n] \times E[AV_n] \neq 1$$

Let's illustrate this using a numerical example.

Example 9.3

Using the fixed interest rate model in Example 9.1, find the expected present value at time 0 of $1 payable at time 2.

Solution

The expected present value can be calculated as the sum of the possible present values times their associated probabilities:

$$E[PV_n] = E\left[\frac{1}{(1+i_1)(1+i_2)}\right] = \left(\frac{1}{1.06^2}\right)(0.3) + \left(\frac{1}{1.08^2}\right)(0.4) + \left(\frac{1}{1.10^2}\right)(0.3)$$

$$= \$0.857868 \qquad \qquad \blacklozenge\blacklozenge$$

We calculated the accumulated value in Example 9.1 to be 1.166640. Notice that:

$$E[PV_n] \times E[AV_n] = 0.857868 \times 1.166640 = 1.000824$$

so:

$$E[PV_n] \times E[AV_n] \neq 1$$

The expected present value times the expected accumulated value is not equal to 1.

9.2 Independent and identically distributed interest rates

As we have seen, if an investment of $1 is made now, it accumulates at time n years to:

$$AV_n = (1+i_1)(1+i_2)\cdots(1+i_n)$$

and the expected accumulated value is:

$$E[AV_n] = E[(1+i_1)(1+i_2)\cdots(1+i_n)]$$

If $i_1, i_2, \cdots, i_n$ are **independent** random variables, then the expected value of the product is equal to the product of the expected values:

$$E[AV_n] = E[(1+i_1)]E[(1+i_2)]\cdots E[(1+i_n)]$$
$$= (1+E[i_1])(1+E[i_2])\cdots(1+E[i_n])$$

Furthermore, if the interest rates are identically distributed, then:

$$E[AV_n] = (1+E[i_t])^n = (1+\bar{i})^n$$

where $\bar{i} = E(i_t)$ for $t = 1, \cdots, n$.

Expected accumulated values under independent and identical distributions

If the future interest rates are independent and identically distributed, then the expected accumulated value at time n years of $1 invested now is:

$$E[AV_n] = (1 + \bar{i})^n$$

where $\bar{i}$ is the expected value of each of the future interest rates.

The formula above does not hold if the interest rates are not independent. In Example 9.1, the expected value of the future interest rates is 8%:

$$E(i_t) = 0.3 \times 0.06 + 0.4 \times 0.08 + 0.3 \times 0.10 = 0.08$$

But the expected accumulated value is $1.16664, which is not equal to the square of the quantity "1 plus the expected interest rate:"

$$1.16664 \neq (1.08)^2$$

since

$$(1.08)^2 = 1.16640$$

In Example 9.2, however, the interest rates are independent and identically distributed, so the expected accumulated value is therefore equal to the square of the quantity "1 plus the expected interest rate." Let's rework Example 9.2 making use of the expected value of the future interest rate.

Example 9.4

The interest rates for the next two years follow the varying interest rate model.

The annual effective interest rate during the next year will be 6%, 8% or 10%. The following year the annual effective interest rate will again be 6%, 8% or 10%. In each year, the probabilities are:

$$i_t = \begin{cases} 0.06 \text{ with probability } 0.3 \\ 0.08 \text{ with probability } 0.4 \\ 0.10 \text{ with probability } 0.3 \end{cases}$$

Find the expected accumulated value at time 2 of $1 invested now.

Solution

The future interest rates are independent of each other, and they are identically distributed. The expected value of each future interest rate is:

$$\bar{i} = E(i_t) = 0.3 \times 0.06 + 0.4 \times 0.08 + 0.3 \times 0.10 = 0.08$$

The expected value of the accumulated value at time 2 is:

$$E[AV_2] = (1 + \bar{i})^2 = (1.08)^2 = 1.1664 \qquad \blacklozenge\blacklozenge$$

As expected, the solution is the same. Making use of $\bar{i}$ is more convenient than determining the entire probability distribution of AV_n as we did in Example 9.2.

Let s^2 be the variance of each i_t:

$$Var(i_t) = s^2$$

We can derive an expression for the variance of AV_n in terms of $\bar{i}$ and s^2:

$$E[AV_n^2] = E[(1+i_1)^2(1+i_2)^2\cdots(1+i_n)^2]$$

$$= E[(1+i_1)^2]E[(1+i_2)^2]\cdots E[(1+i_n)^2]$$

$$= \prod_{t=1}^{n} E[(1+i_t)^2] = \prod_{t=1}^{n} E[1+2i_t+i_t^2]$$

$$= \prod_{t=1}^{n}\Big[E[1]+E[2i_t]+E[i_t^2]\Big] = \prod_{t=1}^{n}\Big[1+2\bar{i}+E[i_t^2]\Big]$$

Since the variance of i_t is s^2, we have:

$$s^2 = E[i_t^2]-(E[i_t])^2 = E[i_t^2]-\bar{i}^2$$

$$\Rightarrow E[i_t^2] = s^2+\bar{i}^2$$

Substituting the value for $E[i_t^2]$ into the equation for $E[AV_n^2]$:

$$E[AV_n^2] = \prod_{t=1}^{n}\Big[1+2\bar{i}+E[i_t^2]\Big]$$

$$= \prod_{t=1}^{n}\Big[1+2\bar{i}+s^2+\bar{i}^2\Big]$$

$$= (1+2\bar{i}+s^2+\bar{i}^2)^n$$

$$-[(1+\bar{i})^2+s^2]^n$$

The variance of AV_n can be written as:

$$Var(AV_n) = E[AV_n^2]-(E[AV_n])^2$$

$$= E[AV_n^2]-[(1+\bar{i})^n]^2$$

$$= [(1+\bar{i})^2+s^2]^n-(1+\bar{i})^{2n}$$

Variance of accumulated values under independent and identical distributions

If the future interest rates are independent and identically distributed, then the variance of the accumulated value at time n years of \$1 invested now is:

$$Var(AV_n) = [(1+\bar{i})^2+s^2]^n-(1+\bar{i})^{2n}$$

where s^2 is the variance of each of the future interest rates.

Next, we derive an expression for the expected present value of \$1 payable at time n years.

Recall that the expected present value is:

$$E[PV_n] = E\left[\frac{1}{(1+i_1)(1+i_2)\cdots(1+i_n)}\right]$$

If the interest rates are independent, then:

$$E[PV_n] = E\left[\frac{1}{(1+i_1)}\right]E\left[\frac{1}{(1+i_2)}\right]\cdots E\left[\frac{1}{(1+i_n)}\right]$$

If the interest rates are also identically distributed, then:

$$E[PV_n] = \left(E\left[\frac{1}{1+i_t} \right] \right)^n = \overline{v}^n$$

where:

$$\overline{v} = E\left[\frac{1}{1+i_t} \right] \quad \text{for } t = 1, \cdots, n$$

Expected present values under independent and identical distributions

If the future interest rates are independent and identically distributed, then the expected value of the present value of $1 payable at time n years is:

$$E[PV_n] = \overline{v}^n$$

where $\overline{v}$ is the expected value of the 1-year discount factor:

$$\overline{v} = E\left[\frac{1}{1+i_t} \right] \quad \text{for } t = 1, \cdots, n$$

In general:

$$E\left[\frac{1}{1+i_t} \right] \neq \frac{1}{1+E[i_t]}$$

Therefore:

$$\overline{v} \neq \frac{1}{1+\overline{i}}$$

Attempts to interpret the expected present value of $1 payable at time n can give rise to confusion. The expected present value is *not* equal to the amount that must be invested now in order to have an expected accumulated value of $1 at the end of n years. The following example uses the varying interest rate model we saw earlier to demonstrate this fact.

Example 9.5

The interest rates for the next two years follow the varying interest rate model.

The annual effective interest rate during the next year will be 6%, 8% or 10%. The following year the annual effective interest rate will again be 6%, 8% or 10%. In each year, the probabilities are:

$$i_t = \begin{cases} 0.06 \text{ with probability } 0.3 \\ 0.08 \text{ with probability } 0.4 \\ 0.10 \text{ with probability } 0.3 \end{cases}$$

(i)   How much must be invested now in order for the expected accumulated value in two years to be $1?

(ii)   What is the expected present value of $1 payable at time 2?

Solution

(i)   If X is invested now, then the expected accumulated value in two years is:

$$(X)E[AV_2] = X(1+\overline{i})^2 = X(1.08)^2$$

Setting the expected accumulated value in two years equal to 1, we then solve for X:

$$X(1.08)^2 = 1$$
$$\Rightarrow X = 0.857339$$

Thus if \$0.857339 is invested today, the expected value of the investment at time 2 is \$1.

(ii)   To calculate the expected present value of \$1 payable at time 2, we first find $\bar{v}$:

$$\bar{v} = E\left[\frac{1}{1+i_t}\right] = 0.3\left(\frac{1}{1.06}\right) + 0.4\left(\frac{1}{1.08}\right) + 0.3\left(\frac{1}{1.10}\right) = 0.926117$$

It is then a simple matter to find $E[PV_2]$:

$$E[PV_2] = \bar{v}^2 = 0.857692 \qquad\qquad \blacklozenge\blacklozenge$$

Knowledge of the variance s^2 is not sufficient to allow us to find a convenient expression for the variance of PV_n. If it is necessary to calculate it, the calculation can often be performed based on first principles.

9.3 Log-normal interest rate model

It is common to assume that the one-year accumulation factors follow a lognormal distribution. In a lognormal interest rate model, we assume that $\ln(1+i_t)$ is distributed normally. This is equivalent to saying that the continuous interest rate $\tilde{\delta}_t$ has a normal distribution, where:

$$e^{\tilde{\delta}_t} = 1+i_t$$
$$\tilde{\delta}_t = \ln(1+i_t)$$

The random variable $\tilde{\delta}_t$ is the force of interest that applies from time $(t-1)$ to time t. Note that $\tilde{\delta}_t$ differs from δ_t of Chapter 1. In Chapter 1, we defined δ_t as the force of interest applicable for an infinitesimally small time period at time t. The tilde ~ (pronounced TILL-duh) differentiates the random variable $\tilde{\delta}_t$ (which is applicable for one entire period) from δ_t (which is the instantaneous force of interest).

Before applying the lognormal distribution to interest rates, let's describe it in general terms.

Lognormal distribution

The random variable Y has a lognormal distribution with parameters μ and σ^2 if $X = \ln(Y)$ is a normal random variable with mean μ and variance σ^2:

$$E[X] = E[\ln(Y)] = \mu$$
$$Var[X] = Var[\ln(Y)] = \sigma^2$$

The mean and variance of Y are then:

$$E[Y] = e^{\mu + \sigma^2/2}$$
$$Var[Y] = e^{2\mu + \sigma^2}(e^{\sigma^2} - 1)$$

Assume that $(1+i_t)$ has a lognormal distribution and $\ln(1+i_t)$ has the following mean and variance:

$$E[\ln(1+i_t)] = E[\tilde{\delta}_t] = \mu$$
$$Var[\ln(1+i_t)] = Var[\tilde{\delta}_t] = \sigma^2$$

If we know the expected value and variance of the natural log of the one-year accumulation factor, then we can determine the expected value and variance of the one-year accumulation factor itself.

One-year accumulation factors under the lognormal distribution

If $(1+i_t)$ is has a lognormal distribution with parameters μ and σ^2, then the mean and the variance of $(1+i_t)$ are:

$$E[1+i_t] = e^{\mu+\sigma^2/2}$$

$$Var[1+i_t] = e^{2\mu+\sigma^2}(e^{\sigma^2}-1)$$

The natural log of the accumulated value at time n years of \$1 deposited now can be expressed as the sum of the forces of interest applicable in each year:

$$AV_n = (1+i_1)(1+i_2)\cdots(1+i_n)$$

$$\Rightarrow \ln(AV_n) = \ln(1+i_1) + \ln(1+i_2) + \cdots + \ln(1+i_n)$$

$$\Rightarrow \ln(AV_n) = \tilde{\delta}_1 + \tilde{\delta}_2 + \cdots + \tilde{\delta}_n$$

If the values of i_t are independent and identically distributed, then so are the values of $\tilde{\delta}_t$, so the expected value of the natural log of the accumulated value is:

$$E[\ln(AV_n)] = E[\tilde{\delta}_1 + \tilde{\delta}_2 + \cdots + \tilde{\delta}_n]$$

$$= n\mu$$

If all values of i_t are independent and identically distributed, then we can also find the variance of the natural log of AV_n:

$$Var[\ln(AV_n)] = Var[\tilde{\delta}_1 + \tilde{\delta}_2 + \cdots + \tilde{\delta}_n]$$

$$= n\sigma^2$$

Since $\ln(AV_n)$ is the sum of independent and identically distributed normal variables, $\ln(AV_n)$ is itself normally distributed with mean $n\mu$ and variance $n\sigma^2$. This implies that AV_n has a lognormal distribution with parameters $n\mu$ and $n\sigma^2$.

Accumulated values under independent and identical lognormal distributions

If $(1+i_1)$, $(1+i_2)$, $\cdots$, $(1+i_n)$ have independent and identical lognormal distributions, such that each lognormal distribution has mean μ and variance σ^2, then AV_n, the accumulated value at time n years of \$1 deposited now, has a lognormal distribution with the parameters $n\mu$ and $n\sigma^2$. Therefore:

$$E[AV_n] = e^{n\mu+n\sigma^2/2}$$

$$Var[AV_n] = e^{2n\mu+n\sigma^2}(e^{n\sigma^2}-1)$$

Example 9.6

Suppose $(1+i_t)$ follows a lognormal distribution with $\mu = 0.05$ and $\sigma^2 = 0.02$. Find the expected accumulated value of \$10,000 left on deposit for 8 years.

Solution

We can use the general result:

$$E[AV_n] = e^{n\mu + n\sigma^2/2}$$

Hence, the expected accumulated value is:

$$10,000 \times E[AV_8] = 10,000e^{8(0.05)+8(0.02)/2} = 10,000(1.616074) = \$16,160.74 \qquad \blacklozenge\blacklozenge$$

We can also derive a convenient expression for the expected value and variance of the present value of \$1 payable at time n. The natural log of the present value can be expressed as the negative of the sum of the forces of interest applicable in each year:

$$PV_n = \left(\frac{1}{1+i_1}\right)\left(\frac{1}{1+i_2}\right)\cdots\left(\frac{1}{1+i_n}\right)$$

$$\ln(PV_n) = \ln\left(\frac{1}{1+i_1}\right) + \ln\left(\frac{1}{1+i_2}\right) + \cdots + \ln\left(\frac{1}{1+i_n}\right)$$

$$= -\ln(1+i_1) - \ln(1+i_2) - \cdots - \ln(1+i_n)$$

$$= -\tilde{\delta}_1 - \tilde{\delta}_2 - \cdots - \tilde{\delta}_n$$

Once again, if we assume that i_1, i_2, $\cdots$, i_n are independent and identically distributed, then we can determine the expected value of the natural log of PV_n:

$$E[\ln(PV_n)] = E[-\tilde{\delta}_1 - \tilde{\delta}_2 - \cdots - \tilde{\delta}_n]$$

$$= -n\mu$$

The assumption that the values of i_t are independent and identically distributed also allows us to find the variance of the natural log of PV_n:

$$Var[\ln(PV_n)] = Var[-\tilde{\delta}_1 - \tilde{\delta}_2 - \cdots - \tilde{\delta}_n]$$

$$= n\sigma^2$$

Since $\ln(PV_n)$ is the sum of independent and identically distributed normal variables, $\ln(PV_n)$ is itself normally distributed with mean $-n\mu$ and variance $n\sigma^2$. This implies that PV_n has a lognormal distribution with parameters $-n\mu$ and $n\sigma^2$.

Present values under independent and identical lognormal distributions

If $(1+i_1)$, $(1+i_2)$, $\cdots$, $(1+i_n)$ have independent and identical lognormal distributions, such that each lognormal distribution has mean μ and variance σ^2, then the present value of \$1 that is payable at time n has a lognormal distribution with the parameters $-n\mu$ and $n\sigma^2$:

$$E[PV_n] = e^{-n\mu + n\sigma^2/2}$$

$$Var[PV_n] = e^{-2n\mu + n\sigma^2}(e^{n\sigma^2} - 1)$$

Example 9.7

Suppose $(1+i_t)$ follows a lognormal distribution with $\mu = 0.05$ and $\sigma^2 = 0.02$. Find the expected present value of a payment of $10,000 that will be made in 8 years.

Solution

The expected present value is:

$$10,000 \times E[PV_n] = 10,000e^{-8(0.05)+8(0.02)/2} = 10,000 \times 0.726149 = \$7,261.49 \qquad \blacklozenge\blacklozenge$$

We have found that if $(1+i_1)$, $(1+i_2)$, $\cdots$, $(1+i_n)$ have independent and identical lognormal distributions, then AV_n and PV_n have lognormal distributions.

But even if i_t does not have a lognormal distribution, as long as the distributions of i_t are independent and identical for all t, the distributions of AV_n and PV_n approach lognormal distributions as n increases. This is a result of the Central Limit Theorem.

Central Limit Theorem

Suppose X_1, X_2, $\cdots$, X_n are independent and identically distributed random variables with mean μ and variance σ^2, and Y is the sum of the random variables:

$$Y = X_1 + X_2 + \cdots + X_n$$

where:

$$E[X_t] = \mu \quad \text{and} \quad Var[X_t] = \sigma^2 \quad \text{for } t = 1, \cdots, n$$

As n becomes large, the distribution of Y approaches a normal distribution with mean $n\mu$ and variance $n\sigma^2$. That is, as n increases:

$$Y \rightarrow N(n\mu, n\sigma^2)$$

Suppose that i_1, i_2, $\cdots$, i_n are independent and identically distributed. Regardless of the form of their probability distribution, there is a mean and standard deviation for $\ln(1+i_t)$. We denote the mean by μ and the standard deviation by σ:

$$E[\ln(1+i_t)] = E[\tilde{\delta}_t] = \mu$$
$$Var[\ln(1+i_t)] = Var[\tilde{\delta}_t] = \sigma^2$$

Notice that we have not specified the type of distribution (*ie* the following results hold regardless of whether the distribution for i_t or $(1+i_t)$ is uniform, binomial, normal, or some other distribution). As before:

$$AV_n = (1+i_1)(1+i_2)\cdots(1+i_n)$$
$$\Rightarrow \ln(AV_n) = \ln(1+i_1) + \ln(1+i_2) + \cdots + \ln(1+i_n)$$
$$\Rightarrow \ln(AV_n) = \tilde{\delta}_1 + \tilde{\delta}_2 + \cdots + \tilde{\delta}_n$$

At this point, we see that $\ln(AV_n)$ is the sum of n independent and identically distributed random variables. Therefore, according to the Central Limit Theorem, as n becomes large, the distribution of $\ln(AV_n)$ approaches a normal distribution with mean $n\mu$ and variance $n\sigma^2$. In a similar fashion, it can be shown that the distribution of $\ln(PV_n)$ approaches a normal distribution with mean $-n\mu$ and variance $n\sigma^2$.

Implications of the Central Limit Theorem for accumulated values and present values

Suppose i_1, i_2, $\cdots$, i_n are independent and identically distributed, and:

$$E[\ln(1+i_t)] = \mu$$

$$Var[\ln(1+i_t)] = \sigma^2$$

Then, regardless of the type of distribution underlying the random variables denoted by i_t, as n increases, the distribution of AV_n approaches a lognormal distribution with parameters $n\mu$ and $n\sigma^2$:

$$\ln(AV_n) \rightarrow N(n\mu, n\sigma^2)$$

Likewise, as n increases, the distribution of PV_n approaches a lognormal distribution with parameters $-n\mu$ and $n\sigma^2$:

$$\ln(PV_n) \rightarrow N(-n\mu, n\sigma^2)$$

Due to this result from the Central Limit Theorem, the normal distribution can be used to find confidence intervals for AV_n or PV_n even when $(1+i_t)$ does not have a lognormal distribution.

Suppose $\ln(1+i_1)$, $\ln(1+i_2)$, ..., $\ln(1+i_n)$ are independent and identically distributed with mean μ and standard deviation σ, and we wish to determine the probability that AV_n is less than X. Then for large n, we have:

$$P(AV_n < X) = P\left[\ln(AV_n) < \ln(X)\right]$$

$$= P\left[\frac{\ln(AV_n)-n\mu}{\sigma\sqrt{n}} < \frac{\ln(X)-n\mu}{\sigma\sqrt{n}}\right]$$

$$= P\left[Z < \frac{\ln(X)-n\mu}{\sigma\sqrt{n}}\right]$$

where Z is the standard normal variable:

$$Z \sim N(0,1)$$

In the same manner, we can determine the probability that PV_n is less than X:

$$P(PV_n < X) = P\left[\ln(PV) < \ln(X)\right]$$

$$= P\left[\frac{\ln(PV_n)-(-n\mu)}{\sigma\sqrt{n}} < \frac{\ln(X)-(-n\mu)}{\sigma\sqrt{n}}\right]$$

$$= P\left[Z < \frac{\ln(X)+n\mu}{\sigma\sqrt{n}}\right]$$

Confidence intervals and the lognormal distribution

If $(1+i_t)$ has independent and identical lognormal distributions for all t, such that $\ln(1+i_t)$ is normally distributed with mean μ and variance σ^2, then the probability that the accumulated value of \$1 invested now is less than X at time n years is:

$$P(AV_n < X) = P\left[Z < \frac{\ln(X) - n\mu}{\sigma\sqrt{n}}\right]$$

The probability that the present value of \$1 payable at time n is less than X is:

$$P(PV_n < X) = P\left[Z < \frac{\ln(X) + n\mu}{\sigma\sqrt{n}}\right]$$

where Z is the standard normal variable, *ie* $Z \sim N(0,1)$.

The following example uses the varying interest rate model from Example 9.2 and extends it for 20 years. The interest rates are independent and identically distributed.

Example 9.8

The interest rates for the next twenty years follow the varying interest rate model.

The annual effective interest rate during each year will be 6%, 8% or 10. In each year, the probabilities are:

$$i_t = \begin{cases} 0.06 \text{ with probability } 0.3 \\ 0.08 \text{ with probability } 0.4 \\ 0.10 \text{ with probability } 0.3 \end{cases}$$

Use the lognormal approximation to estimate the probability that the accumulated value at the end of 20 years of \$1 deposited now is less than \$5.

Solution

The table below provides the expected values of $\ln(1+i_t)$ and $\left[\ln(1+i_t)\right]^2$.

Probability	$1+i_t$	$\ln(1+i_t)$	$\left[\ln(1+i_t)\right]^2$
0.3	1.06	0.058269	0.003395
0.4	1.08	0.076961	0.005923
0.3	1.10	0.095310	0.009084
Expected value	**1.08**	**0.076858**	**0.006113**

The expected value of $\ln(1+i_t)$ is:

$$\mu = 0.076858$$

The variance of $\ln(1+i_t)$ is:

$$\sigma^2 = 0.006113 - (0.076858)^2 = 0.0002058$$

Therefore we have:

$$E[\ln(AV_{20})] = 20\mu = 20(0.076858)$$

$$Var[\ln(AV_{20})] = 20\sigma^2 = 20(0.0002058)$$

The probability that AV_{20} is less than 5 is:

$$P(AV_{20} < 5) = P\left[\ln(AV_{20}) < \ln(5)\right]$$

$$= P\left[\frac{\ln(AV_{20}) - 20\mu}{\sigma\sqrt{20}} < \frac{\ln(5) - 20(0.076858)}{\sqrt{0.0002058} \times \sqrt{20}}\right]$$

$$= P[Z < 1.127]$$

From a standard normal table, we can find the probability that a standard normal random variable is less than 1.127:

$$P[Z < 1.127] = 0.87$$

Therefore:

$$P(AV_{20} < 5) = 0.87$$

The probability that the accumulated value is less than \$5 at the end of 20 years is 87%.   ◆◆

9.4   Binomial interest rate trees

In the two previous sections, we assumed that the interest rates in each period are independent of the interest rates in the other periods. Although this assumption is computationally convenient, it isn't necessarily realistic. Experience suggests that interest rates tend to unfold as adjustments to previous interest rates rather than as rates that are completely unrelated to the previous interest rates. If the interest rate today is 5% for example, experience suggests that the interest rate tomorrow will likely be relatively close to 5%.

One way to address this concern is to develop an **interest rate tree** to describe the possible paths that interest rates can take in the future. An interest rate tree consists of a lattice of possible future interest rates known as **short rates**. The short rates are single-period spot rates that might occur in the future.

When building interest rate trees, the initial interest rate for the first full period, i_1, is assumed to be known. It is the current one-period interest rate available in the market. With a **binomial interest rate tree**, the next period's interest rate can take one of two values. And each of those two values then transitions into one of two other possible interest rates in the subsequent period.

If the interest rates **recombine**, then an upward movement followed by a downward movement results in the same interest rate as a downward movement followed by an upward movement. The binomial interest rate trees described in this section are recombining trees.

In this section, we use an interest rate model known as the **multiplicative binomial model**. In this model, each interest rate in the tree is assumed to be a multiple of the interest rate that preceded it:

$$i_{t+1} = i_t(1+\gamma) \quad \text{or} \quad i_{t+1} = i_t/(1+\gamma)$$

where γ (gamma) is the volatility parameter of the model.

The lattice shown in Figure 9.1 is based on the assumption that the interest rate in the first year is 4% and γ is 0.3. The interest rate for the next period can either increase or decrease by 30%. The probability of an upward movement in the interest rate is denoted by p and the probability of a downward movement in the interest rate is therefore $(1-p)$.

Figure 9.1

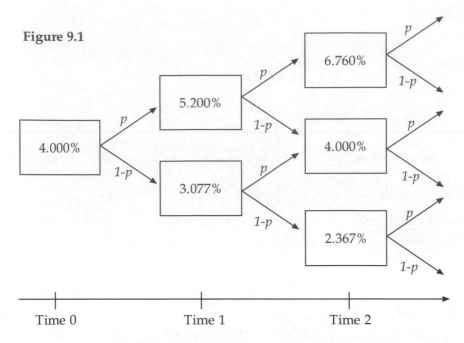

At time 0, the interest rate that applies from time 0 to time 1 is 4%. At time 1, the interest rate that applies from time 1 to time 2 is either 5.200% or 3.077%:

$$i_2 = 4.000(1.3) = 5.200\% \quad \text{or} \quad i_2 = 4.000/(1.3) = 3.077\%$$

The model is recombining because an upward movement followed by a downward movement leads to the same interest rate as a downward movement followed by an upward movement. For example, beginning at time zero, an upward movement followed by a downward movement leads to the same interest rate in time 2 (4.000%) as a downward movement followed by an upward movement.

We can use the interest rate tree to calculate the expected value of future cash flows. The probabilities used with interest rate trees are called **risk-neutral probabilities**. The advantage to using risk-neutral probabilities is that the expected present value based on these probabilities is equal to the current price of the cash flows being valued. We do not explore further the development of risk-neutral probabilities in this textbook. Instead, we focus on how to use them in a lattice to find the current value of future cash flows.

The valuation process is a recursive process, beginning with the rightmost nodes and working to the left. At each node, the value is calculated as the present value of the expected value in the subsequent period:

$$V = \frac{p(V_U + CF_U) + (1-p)(V_D + CF_D)}{(1+i_t)}$$

where:

CF_U = cash flow occurring at the up node to the right

CF_D = cash flow occurring at the down node to the right

V_U = value of future cash flows at the up node

V_D = value of future cash flows at the down node

The values of V_U and V_D exclude the value of the cash flows occurring at that node. That is, V_U and V_D are the values of *future* cash flows only.

Example 9.9

Use the interest-rate tree in Figure 9.1 with $p = 0.75$ to value a 1-year zero coupon bond with $1,000 par value.

Solution

Using the terminology above, we have:

$i_1 = 4\%$

$V_U = 0$

$V_D = 0$

$CF_U = 1,000$

$CF_D = 1,000$

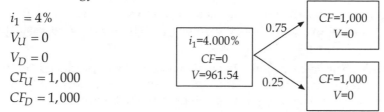

Hence, the value of the bond is:

$$V = \frac{p(V_U + CF_U) + (1-p)(V_D + CF_D)}{(1 + i_t)}$$

$$= \frac{0.75(0 + 1,000) + (0.25)(0 + 1,000)}{1.04} = 961.54$$

◆◆

The solution to Example 9.9 could also have been calculated by discounting the cash flow maturity in one year's time ($1000) by the interest rate over the next year (4%):

$$V = \frac{1,000}{1.04} = 961.54$$

Let's look at how to use the interest rate tree to value a 2-year bond.

Example 9.10

Use the interest-rate tree in Figure 9.1 with $p = 0.75$ to value a 2-year bond with $1,000 par value and annual coupons of 3.5%.

Solution

The cash flows and values at the nodes are shown below. Notice that the interest rates at time 2 (which apply from time 2 to time 3) are not relevant here, since the last cash flow occurs at time 2.

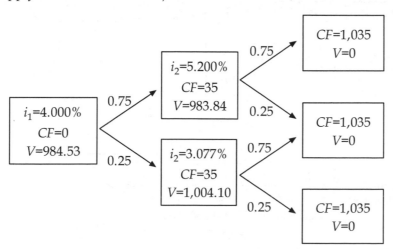

Upper node at time 1: $\quad V = \dfrac{0.75(0 + 1,035) + (0.25)(0 + 1,035)}{1.052} = \$983.84$

295

Lower node at time 1: $V = \dfrac{0.75(0+1,035)+(0.25)(0+1,035)}{1.0377} = \$1,004.10$

Value at time 0: $V = \dfrac{0.75(35+983.84)+(0.25)(35+1,004.10)}{1.04} = \$984.53$

Hence, the value of the bond is \$984.53.   ◆◆

In the two examples above, we found the value of fixed cash flows, but the primary benefit of interest rate lattices is that they allow us to find the value of **interest-sensitive** cash flows, *eg* callable bonds.

Callable bonds have interest-sensitive cash flows because the cash flows produced by the bond depend on the actual interest rates that emerge. If the bond is called, it is redeemed by the issuer before the stated maturity date by paying the specified call price to the bondholder.

The bond is more likely to be called as interest rates fall (when the issuer is able to borrow more cheaply) and less likely to be called as interest rates rise (when the cost of borrowing is higher).

The valuation of callable bonds using an interest rate tree is similar to the valuation of noncallable bonds, but for callable bonds we assume that the value of a callable bond at any node cannot exceed the call price. After all, if the value of the future cash flows exceeds the call price at any time, then the issuer can save money by calling the bond.

In terms of the formula, this means that V_U and V_D are constrained such that they cannot exceed the call price.

Example 9.11

Use the interest-rate tree from Example 9.10 with $p = 0.75$ to calculate the value of a 2-year \$1,000 callable bond with annual coupons of 3.5%, callable any time after one year. The call price is \$1,000.

Solution

The cash flows and values at the nodes are shown below.

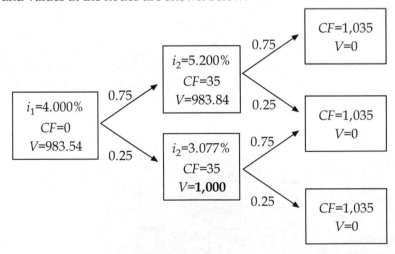

Upper node at time 1: $V = \dfrac{0.75(0+1,035)+0.25(0+1,035)}{1.052} = \$983.84$

Lower node at time 1: $V = \dfrac{0.75(0+1,035)+0.25(0+1,035)}{1.03077} = \$1,004.10$

but this value cannot exceed the call price of \$1,000, so:

$V = \$1,000$

Value at time 0: $$V = \frac{0.75(35 + 983.84) + 0.25(35 + 1{,}000)}{1.04} = \$983.54$$

Hence, the value of the callable bond is $983.54.   ◆◆

Notice that the value of the callable bond ($983.54) is lower than the value of the otherwise equivalent noncallable bond ($984.53). In general:

Price of noncallable bond > Price of callable bond

This is because the callable bond does not experience as much price appreciation if interest rates fall. The value of the callable bond at time 1 cannot exceed $1,000.

In Chapter 7, we studied how the price of a bond changes as interest rates vary. In the context of an interest rate tree, a shift in the interest rates consists of adding or subtracting a constant number of basis points to or from every interest rate in the lattice. If we shift the entire interest rate tree, then we obtain a new price. By shifting the tree up and down and calculating the corresponding prices of the callable bond, we can calculate the effective duration with respect to a shift in all of the possible future interest rates.

The formula for effective duration in this context is:

$$EffD = \frac{P_- - P_+}{P_0 (2\Delta i)}$$

where Δi is the amount added and subtracted to the interest rates to produce P_+ and P_- respectively.

The following examples show how a new price is computed after the interest rate tree is shifted up or down.

Example 9.12

Calculate the new price of the bond in Example 9.11 if the interest rate tree is shifted up by 50 basis points.

Solution

The new interest rate tree consists of the original interest rate tree with 50 basis points added to each interest rate.

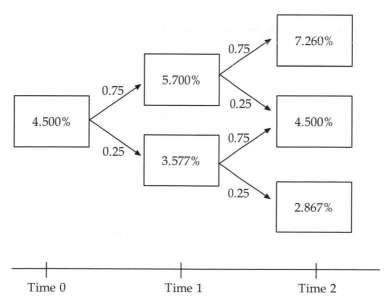

The cash flows and values at the nodes are shown below.

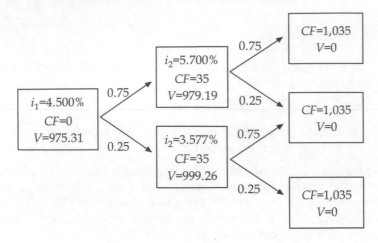

Upper node at time 1: $V = \dfrac{0.75(0+1,035)+(0.25)(0+1,035)}{1.057} = \$979.19$

Lower node at time 1: $V = \dfrac{0.75(0+1,035)+(0.25)(0+1,035)}{1.03577} = \$999.26$

Value at time 0: $V = \dfrac{0.75(35+979.19)+(0.25)(35+999.26)}{1.045} = \$975.31$

The new value of the callable bond is \$975.31.   ♦♦

The next example illustrates how to compute a new price when the interest rate tree is shifted down.

Example 9.13

Calculate the new price of the bond in Example 9.11 if the interest rate tree is shifted down by 50 basis points.

Solution

The new interest rate tree consists of the original interest rate tree with 50 basis points subtracted from each interest rate.

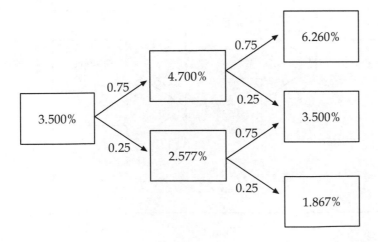

The cash flows and values at the nodes are shown below.

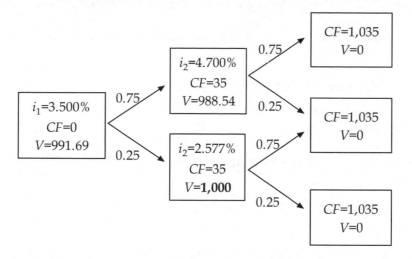

Upper node at time 1: $V = \dfrac{0.75(0+1,035)+(0.25)(0+1,035)}{1.047} = \$988.54$

Lower node at time 1: $V = \dfrac{0.75(0+1,035)+(0.25)(0+1,035)}{1.02577} = \$1,009.00$

but this value cannot exceed the call price of $1,000, so:

$V = \$1,000$

Value at time 0: $V = \dfrac{0.75(35+988.54)+(0.25)(35+1,000)}{1.035} = \$991.69$

The new value of the callable bond is $991.69.   ◆◆

We now have the current price from Example 9.11, the price resulting from an upward shift from Example 9.12, and the price resulting from a downward shift from Example 9.13. Therefore, we have enough information to calculate the effective duration of the bond.

Example 9.14

Calculate the effective duration of the bond in Example 9.11 using an interest rate shift of 50 basis points.

Solution

We calculated P_+ and P_- in the two previous examples. Putting those values into the equation for effective duration produces:

$$EffD = \frac{P_- - P_+}{P_0(2\Delta i)} = \frac{991.69 - 975.31}{983.54(2)(0.005)} = 1.665$$

◆◆

Attempts to value interest-sensitive cash flows with deterministic interest rates are problematic because a deterministic model discounts a fixed set of cash flows. Stochastic models take into account the fact that the cash flows depend on the future interest rates. Interest rate trees allow us to use stochastic interest rates to value such cash flows and to determine the price sensitivity to changes in the possible future interest rates.

Chapter 9 Practice Questions

Question 9.1

A stochastic interest rate model is based on the assumption that the annual interest rate during the next year will be 5% and that the interest rate in subsequent years will be at a fixed but unknown level with the probabilities described by the following probability distribution:

$$i_t = \begin{cases} 0.05 \text{ with probability } 0.25 \\ 0.07 \text{ with probability } 0.40 \\ 0.10 \text{ with probability } 0.35 \end{cases}$$

What is the expected accumulated amount at the end of the tenth year of an initial investment of $1,000?

Question 9.2

Use the information in Question 9.1 to find the standard deviation of the accumulated amount at the end of the tenth year.

Question 9.3

The yield obtained by an investor each year is expected to be 10%, 12%, or 15% with the probabilities 0.2, 0.5, and 0.3 respectively. Find the mean and standard deviation of the accumulated value of an initial sum of $5,000 invested for 6 years if the yields in different years are independent.

Question 9.4

A stochastic interest rate model is based on an assumption that the interest rates in different years are independent and identically distributed with a normal distribution having a mean of 14% and a standard deviation of 3%. What is the mean of the accumulated value of $100,000 at the end of three years?

Question 9.5

Consider the following formulas for calculating the mean value of the accumulated amount of $1 using a stochastic interest rate model in which the interest rates in different years are assumed to be independent and identically distributed with the same distribution as i.

I. $E[AV_n] = E\left[1 + i^n\right]$

II. $E[AV_n] = E\left[(1+i)^n\right]$

III. $E[AV_n] = \left(E[1+i]\right)^n$

IV. $E[AV_n] = \left(1 + E[i]\right)^n$

Which of these formulas are correct expressions for the mean of the accumulated value?

Question 9.6

An investor intends to make deposits into an investment account at the start of each of the next three years. The amounts of the deposits are shown in the table below. Assume that interest rates follow the varying rate model in which the mean and standard deviation of the rate of return in each year are as shown in the table.

Year	Deposit	Mean rate of return	Standard deviation of rate of return
1	10,000	4%	1%
2	8,000	10%	4%
3	32,000	7%	1%

Calculate the mean of the accumulated value at the end of three years.

Question 9.7

The accumulated value of an annuity immediate depends on the future interest rates:

$$s_{\overline{n}|} = \left[(1+i_2)(1+i_3)\cdots(1+i_n)\right] + \left[(1+i_3)(1+i_4)\cdots(1+i_n)\right] + \cdots + \left[(1+i_n)\right] + [1]$$

Assuming the interest rates in each year are independent and identically distributed, derive an expression for the expected accumulated value of an annuity immediate.

Question 9.8

Assume that $E[i_t] = 0.05$ and $Var[i_t] = 0.0002$ for $t = 1, 2$. Further assume that the interest rates in each year are independent and identically distributed.

(i)   Find the expected accumulated value at the end of two years of $1 deposited now.

(ii)   Find the variance of the accumulated value at the end of two years of $1 deposited now.

Question 9.9

Assume that $E[i_t] = 0.05$ and $Var[i_t] = 0.0002$ for $t = 1, 2$. Further assume that the interest rates in each year are independent and identically distributed and that $(1+i_t)$ has a lognormal distribution. Find the parameters μ and σ^2 of the lognormal distribution.

Question 9.10

Using the values of μ and σ^2 that were calculated for Question 9.9 to answer the following questions about the distribution in Question 9.9.

(i) Use μ and σ^2 to find the expected accumulated value at the end of two years of $1 deposited now.

(ii) Use μ and σ^2 to find the variance of the accumulated value at the end of two years of $1 deposited now.

Question 9.11

A stochastic interest rate model is based on the assumption that the accumulation factors in different years are independent and identically distributed with a lognormal distribution having a mean of 1.10 and a standard deviation of 0.025.

Which of the following statements about the statistical distribution of the accumulation factor for a 2-year period are correct?

I. The mean of the distribution is 1.21.

II. The standard deviation of the distribution is 0.05.

III. The distribution is lognormal.

Question 9.12

Over the next 40 years the annual effective interest rates are independent random variables with the probability distribution for each interest rate being:

$$i_t = \begin{cases} 0.08 \text{ with probability } 0.50 \\ 0.12 \text{ with probability } 0.50 \end{cases}$$

(i) Find the expected value and variance of $\ln(1+i_t)$.

(ii) An investment of $10,000 is deposited into a fund. Use the lognormal approximation to estimate the probability that the fund grows to at least $400,000 by the end of 40 years.

Question 9.13

Interest rates from year to year are independent random variables. Assume that $(1+i_t)$ follows a lognormal distribution with parameters $\mu = 0.076911$ and $\sigma^2 = 0.0001$. Find a 95% confidence interval for the accumulated value at the end of three years of $100 invested now.

Question 9.14

A stochastic interest rate model is based on the assumption that the annual growth factors for each future year are independently distributed with a lognormal distribution with parameters $\mu = 0.06$ and $\sigma^2 = 0.001$.

Calculate the mean and standard deviation of the annual effective rate of return.

Question 9.15

Using the information provided in Question 9.14, calculate the median of the annual effective rate of return.

Question 9.16

A single payment of $10,000 must be made at the end of 5 years. Using the information provided in Question 9.14, calculate the probability that an initial investment of $7,000 will be sufficient to meet the liability for this payment.

Question 9.17

State whether the probability calculated in Question 9.16 becomes greater or smaller if the interest rate model is based on an unknown interest rate that is constant in all future years instead of the assumption that the rates for each year are independent. Assume that the basic distribution for the interest rates remains the same. Explain your reasoning.

Question 9.18

Create an interest rate tree based on the following information describing a multiplicative binomial model:

$$\gamma = 0.4$$
$$p = 0.5$$
$$i_1 = 7.5\%$$

Using the model, find the value of a callable bond that pays 8% annual coupons. The bond matures in two years, and it is callable beginning in one year for its par value of $100.

Question 9.19   SOA

You are given the following with respect to a multiplicative binomial model:

- The current short rate is 4%.
- Rates are twice as likely to rise as they are to fall.
- The volatility parameter is 20%.

Determine the expected short rate two periods from now.

Question 9.20   SOA

You are given the following multiplicative binomial branching model where the value of the short rate one year from now is either:

- $$r_1^u = r_0(1+\gamma) \quad \text{or} \quad r_1^d = \frac{r_0}{(1+\gamma)} \quad \text{with equal probability.}$$
- The volatility is 25%.
- The current value of the short rate is 4%.

Calculate the value of a 2-year interest rate floor with a 3.5% strike level and a notional amount of $100.

Review questions

Question 1

Dick and Bruce each open up a new bank account at time 0. Dick deposits $500 into his account and Bruce deposits $711.05 into his account. Each account earns the same annual effective interest rate.

The amount of interest earned by Dick during his account's 15th year equals the amount of interest earned by Bruce during his account's 7th year. Determine the annual effective interest rate.

(A)   4.5%
(B)   5.0%
(C)   5.5%
(D)   6.0%
(E)   6.5%

Question 2

Sheryl receives cash flows of $500 at time 0, $1,000 at time 3 years, and $1,500 at time 6 years. The present value of these cash flows is $2,276.90 at an annual effective interest rate i.

Determine i.

(A)   5.0%
(B)   7.5%
(C)   10.0%
(D)   12.5%
(E)   15.0%

Question 3

Rebecca will receive $500 at time 0, $750 at time 5 years, $1,500 at time 10 years, and $12,131.33 at time n years. The accumulated value of this payment stream at time n years is $24,262.66 and the annual effective interest rate is 12%.

Determine n.

(A)   15
(B)   16
(C)   17
(D)   18
(E)   19

Question 4

A bank account accumulates at a force of interest of:

$$\delta_t = \begin{cases} 0.025t \text{ for } 0 \le t \le 4 \\ 0.10 \text{ for } t > 4 \end{cases}$$

Determine the annual effective interest rate earned over the first five-year period.

(A) 5.0%
(B) 6.2%
(C) 7.4%
(D) 8.6%
(E) 9.8%

Question 5

Which of the following expressions does not represent a definition for $a_{\overline{n}|}$?

(A) $1/i - v^n / i$

(B) $\ddot{a}_{\overline{n+1}|} - 1$

(C) $(1+i)^{-(n+1)} \ddot{s}_{\overline{n}|}$

(D) $(i / \delta) \bar{a}_{\overline{n}|}$

(E) $_{m|} a_{\overline{n}|} v^{-m}$

Question 6

A perpetuity that pays \$25,000 at the end of each year has a present value of \$416,666.67. Mike receives the first 10 payments. Ann receives the next 25 payments. Liz receives the remaining payments.

Determine which of the following inequalities correctly describes the relationship between the present value of payments received by Mike, Ann and Liz.

(A) Liz > Ann > Mike
(B) Liz > Mike > Ann
(C) Ann > Mike > Liz
(D) Mike > Ann > Liz
(E) Mike > Liz > Ann

Question 7

Cindy has exactly ten years before she retires. She would like to make ten level annual deposits of X at the beginning of each year starting today into a retirement account so that she will receive 25 level annual payments of $50,000 each year, with the first retirement payment occurring ten years from today. The annual effective interest rate earned by the account is 4%.

Determine X.

(A)   60,558.89
(B)   62,058.89
(C)   63,558.89
(D)   65,058.89
(E)   66,558.89

Question 8

A perpetuity that pays $100 at the beginning of each year has a present value of $1,250. An annuity that pays $152.30 at the end of each year for n years has the same present value assuming the same interest rate.

Determine n.

(A)   13
(B)   14
(C)   15
(D)   16
(E)   17

Question 9

Wally receives payments of $10 at time 0, $20 at time 1 year, $30 at time 2 years, and so on, forever. The present value of Wally's payment stream is $2,684.56.

Ron receives payments of $9 paid continuously over the first year, $18 paid continuously over the second year, $27 paid continuously over the third year, and so on, forever. The present value of Ron's payment stream is X.

The same rate of interest is used in the calculation of both of their present values. Calculate X.

(A)   2,230.49
(B)   2,341.60
(C)   2,452.71
(D)   2,563.82
(E)   2,674.93

Question 10

Kirby receives a payment stream over 10 years of $100 paid continuously over the first year, $95 paid continuously over the second year, $90 paid continuously over the third year, and so on, down to $55 paid continuously over the tenth year.

The annual effective interest rate is 4.5%. Determine the accumulated value of these payments at time 15 years.

(A)   980.57
(B)   1,036.12
(C)   1,091.67
(D)   1,147.22
(E)   1,241.62

Question 11

The present value of a series of 25 payments starting at $50 at the beginning of the first year and increasing by $5 each year thereafter is equal to $X.

The annual effective interest rate is 4%. Calculate X.

(A)   1,596.82
(B)   1,605.91
(C)   1,615.00
(D)   1,624.09
(E)   1,633.18

Question 12

Dan would like to have $1,000,000 in his bank account in exactly 30 years to fund his retirement in Florida. Dan opens his account today with a deposit of $X, and each subsequent annual deposit will increase by 5%. Dan plans to make a total of 30 annual deposits.

The annual effective interest rate is 4%. Determine X.

(A)   8,900.00
(B)   8,915.15
(C)   8,930.30
(D)   8,945.45
(E)   8,960.60

Question 13

Calculate the nominal rate of interest convertible quarterly that is equivalent to a nominal rate of discount of 15% per year convertible semiannually.

(A)   14.1%
(B)   14.5%
(C)   15.0%
(D)   15.4%
(E)   15.9%

Question 14

Determine an expression for the present value of an annuity that pays $15 at the end of every 5 years for 50 years.

(A) $15a_{\overline{50}|} / a_{\overline{5}|}$

(B) $15s_{\overline{50}|} / a_{\overline{5}|}$

(C) $15a_{\overline{50}|} / s_{\overline{5}|}$

(D) $15s_{\overline{50}|} / s_{\overline{5}|}$

(E) $(15/50)a_{\overline{50}|}$

Question 15

An annuity pays $5 at the end of each quarter during the first year, $10 at the end of each quarter during the second year, $15 at the end of each quarter during the third year, and so on, until the last four payments of $75 are made at the end of each quarter during the 15th year. The annual effective interest rate is 8%.

Determine the accumulated value at time 15 years.

(A)   3,620.12
(B)   3,642.34
(C)   3,664.56
(D)   3,686.78
(E)   3,709.00

Question 16

At a nominal interest rate of j convertible every other year, an investment of $500 now and an investment of $1,000 at the end of four years will accumulate to $2,041.16 at the end of the 8th year.

Calculate j.

(A)   6%
(B)   9%
(C)   12%
(D)   15%
(E)   18%

Question 17

Reggie buys a 5-year decreasing annuity for $X. Reggie will receive $500 today, $490 three months from now, $480 six months from now, and for each quarter thereafter the payment decreases by $10 for the remaining part of the 5-year period.

The nominal interest rate is 9% convertible monthly. Determine X.

(A)   6,528
(B)   6,625
(C)   6,722
(D)   6,819
(E)   6,916

Question 18

Shirley takes out a loan of $4,000 with a 12% nominal interest rate convertible monthly. Shirley makes payments of $100 at the end of each month.

Calculate the amount of interest due in the tenth payment.

(A)　34.38
(B)　35.18
(C)　35.98
(D)　36.78
(E)　37.58

Question 19

An investor makes level deposits of $250 at the end of each year into a fund for 10 years. The deposits earn a 15% annual effective rate of interest which is paid at the end of each year. The interest is immediately reinvested into the same fund at an annual effective interest rate of 11%.

Determine the accumulated value of the fund at the end of 10 years.

(A)　4,766.34
(B)　4,791.59
(C)　4,816.84
(D)　4,842.09
(E)　4,867.34

Question 20

At the beginning of the year, an investment fund was established. The time (in months), deposits, withdrawals, and the fund values (immediately before any cash flows) are recorded in the following table:

Time	Deposit	Withdrawal	Fund value
0	200	0	0.00
3	0	100	203.89
8	400	0	108.10
11	0	300	526.16
12	0	0	227.79

The dollar-weighted yield and the time-weighted yield earned by the fund during the year are x and y, respectively. Determine $x - y$.

(A)　−1.4%
(B)　−0.7%
(C)　0.0%
(D)　0.7%
(E)　1.4%

Question 21

A car loan is being repaid with 48 monthly payments of $300 each. With the 24th payment, the borrower pays an extra $500, and then repays the balance over three more years with a revised monthly payment. The annual effective interest rate is 6%.

Calculate the amount of the revised monthly payment.

(A)   181.18
(B)   190.59
(C)   200.00
(D)   209.41
(E)   218.82

Question 22

Lynn borrows $15,000 for 5 years at an annual effective interest rate of 6%. At the end of each year, she pays the lender $1,000 and deposits a level amount necessary to repay the loan in full after 5 years into a sinking fund that earns an annual effective interest rate of 4%.

Determine the total annual payment that Lynn makes.

(A)   2,665
(B)   2,915
(C)   3,165
(D)   3,415
(E)   3,665

Question 23

An *n*-year, $1,000 par value bond with an unknown redemption amount pays 8% nominal semiannual coupons. The bond is purchased to yield an annual effective rate of 10.25%. Given that the book value of the bond is $900 at the end of 4 years, determine the book value of the bond at the end of 8 years.

(A)   867.68
(B)   894.37
(C)   921.06
(D)   947.75
(E)   974.44

Question 24

Marsha can buy a $1,000 par value bond with coupons of 8% payable semiannually that will mature for $1,050 at the end of 20 years. The price of this bond is $835.51.

Instead, she buys a zero-coupon bond that will pay $1,000 at the end of 10 years. If she pays $X, she will earn the same annual effective yield as the coupon bond. Determine X.

(A)   376.89
(B)   388.00
(C)   399.11
(D)   410.22
(E)   421.33

Question 25

A $100 par value bond pays coupons semiannually at an annual rate of $x\%$ and has exactly 2.5 years left until it matures at par. The current price of the bond is $106.87 and the next semiannual coupon occurs six months from today.

The bond's semiannual effective coupon rate is 150 basis points greater than the bond's semiannual effective yield. Determine x.

(A)   3.0
(B)   4.5
(C)   6.0
(D)   7.5
(E)   9.0

Question 26

A $1,000 par value bond pays annual coupons of $70. The bond is redeemable in 20 years but is callable any time from the end of 10th year at $1,050.

Based on her desired yield, an investor calculates the following potential purchase prices, P:

- Assuming the bond is called at the end of the 10th year: $P = \$1,101.52$
- Assuming the bond is held until maturity: $P = \$1,114.70$

The investor buys the bonds at the highest price that guarantees she will receive at least her desired yield rate regardless of when the bond is called.

The investor holds the bond for 15 years, after which time the bond is called.

Calculate the yield rate that the investor earns.

(A)   5.84%
(B)   6.00%
(C)   6.03%
(D)   6.16%
(E)   7.07%

Question 27

On January 1, 2005, Roger sold stock A for $80 with a margin requirement of 75%. On December 31, 2005, the stock paid a dividend of $3, and an interest amount of $5 was credited to the margin account. On January 1, 2006, Roger covered the short sale at a price of X, earning a 22% return.

Calculate X.

(A)   63.8
(B)   65.6
(C)   68.8
(D)   71.8
(E)   95.2

Question 28

The stock of Company X sells for $58 per share assuming an annual effective interest rate of i. Annual dividends will be paid at the end of each year forever.

The first dividend is $5, with each subsequent dividend 2.5% greater than the previous year's dividend. Determine i.

(A)   6.12%
(B)   6.55%
(C)   7.62%
(D)   8.62%
(E)   11.12%

Question 29

A 20-year bond pays annual coupons of 10%, matures for its par value of $100, and is purchased to yield 15%.

Determine the amount of the accumulation of discount in the 20th year.

(A)   1.57
(B)   2.09
(C)   3.78
(D)   4.35
(E)   4.55

Question 30

A bond pays semiannual coupons of 7% per year, has a par value of $1,000, and matures in 22 years. The bond is purchased to yield an annual effective rate of 4%.

Determine the premium at which the bond is purchased.

(A)   417.13
(B)   419.89
(C)   436.20
(D)   437.14
(E)   443.55

Question 31

Consider the following three bonds:

- A 30-year bond pays 5% annual coupons and is priced to yield 4% annual effective. Its Macaulay duration is X.
- A 30-year bond pays 2% annual coupons and is priced to yield 4% annual effective. Its Macaulay duration is Y.
- A 30-year bond pays 5% annual coupons and is priced to yield 6% annual effective. Its Macaulay duration is Z.

Determine which of the following inequalities correctly describes the relationship between X, Y and Z.

(A) $X < Y < Z$
(B) $Y < X < Z$
(C) $Y < Z < X$
(D) $Z < Y < X$
(E) $Z < X < Y$

Question 32

A bond will pay a coupon of $50 at the end of each 6 months until it matures for its face value of $1,000 at the end of two years. The bond's Macaulay duration when valued using an annual interest rate of 20% compounded semiannually is X.

Calculate X.

(A)   1.70
(B)   1.74
(C)   1.85
(D)   1.90
(E)   1.92

Question 33

Jason has purchased 3 bonds to establish the following portfolio:

- Bond A has semiannual coupons of 6%, a Macaulay duration of 18.71 years, and was purchased for $1,182.56
- Bond B is a 15-year bond with a Macaulay duration of 11.34 years and was purchased for $896.20
- Bond C is a zero-coupon bond maturing in 12 years and was purchased for $556.84.

Calculate the Macaulay duration of the portfolio at the time of purchase.

(A)   14.79
(B)   14.85
(C)   14.92
(D)   14.99
(E)   15.07

Question 34

An insurance company accepts an obligation to pay $100,000 at the end of each year for two years. The insurance company creates a portfolio from the following bonds at a total cost of X in order to exactly match its obligation:

- one-year 8% annual coupon bond with an annual yield rate of 6%
- two-year 3% annual coupon bond with an annual yield rate of 6%
- three-year 6% annual coupon bond with an annual yield rate of 6%

Calculate X.

(A)   181,400
(B)   183,339
(C)   184,983
(D)   186,983
(E)   196,379

Question 35

An insurance company has accepted an obligation to pay $10,000 at the end of three years. The insurance company immunizes its portfolio by purchasing the following two bonds:

- two-year zero-coupon bond with a face value of $1,000
- five-year bond with annual coupons of 10% and a face value of $1,000

The yield curve is level at 10%. The number of five-year bonds purchased is X.

Determine X.

(A)   3.09
(B)   3.46
(C)   3.83
(D)   4.20
(E)   4.57

Question 36

Yield rates to maturity for zero-coupon bonds are currently quoted at 8% for one-year maturity, 9% for two-year maturity, and 10% for three-year maturity. Let i be the one-year forward rate (*ie* the rate applicable from the end of the first year until the end of the second year) implied by the current yields of these bonds.

Calculate i.

(A)   7.0%
(B)   8.0%
(C)   9.0%
(D)   10.0%
(E)   15.1%

Question 37

A 10-year bond with 7% annual coupons is priced to yield 8%. A 10-year bond with 8% coupons is priced to yield 8.3%.

Find the 10-year spot rate.

(A)   5.2%
(B)   6.0%
(C)   9.0%
(D)   16.6%
(E)   19.7%

Question 38

The one-year spot rate is 15%, the two-year spot rate is 20%, and the three-year spot rate is 23%.

Sadie will receive $500 in 2 years. She arranges now to deposit the $500 when she receives it in 2 years, and she locks in the 2-year forward rate as the rate of interest to be earned.

Determine the value of the investment at the end of three years.

(A)   544.61
(B)   571.09
(C)   626.09
(D)   630.38
(E)   646.13

Question 39

The one-year spot rate is 5%, the two-year spot rate is 10%, the three-year spot rate is 13%, the 4-year spot rate is 15%, and the 5-year spot rate is 19%.

A 4-year bond pays annual coupons of 15% and has a par value of $1,000.

Find the present value of the bond.

(A)   924
(B)   938
(C)   1,000
(D)   1,028
(E)   1,064

Question 40

Each of the following bonds pays annual coupons and has a par value of $1,000.

- Bond A is a 1-year bond with a coupon rate of 6%, and its price is $990.65.

- Bond B is a 2-year bond with a coupon rate of 4%, and its price is $929.02.

- Bond C is a 3-year bond with a coupon rate of 23%, and its price is $1,444.87.

Calculate the 3-year spot rate.

(A)   5%
(B)   6%
(C)   7%
(D)   8%
(E)   9%

Appendix A – The normal distribution

The standard normal distribution function has a mean of zero and a standard deviation of one. This table is used with the Black-Scholes option valuation model (Chapter 6) and the log-normal stochastic interest rate model (Chapter 9). The normal distribution function is graphed below:

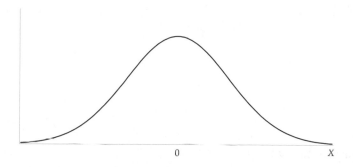

The table below gives the value of the cumulative normal distribution function $\Phi(x)$ for certain values of x where:

$$\Phi(x) = \Pr\left(X \le x\right) = \frac{1}{\sqrt{2\pi}} \int_{-\infty}^{x} e^{-w^2/2} \, dw$$

The integer of x is given in the top row, and the first decimal place of x is given in the left column. Since the density function of x is symmetric, the value of the cumulative distribution function for negative x can be obtained by subtracting from unity the value of the cumulative distribution function for x.

x	0	1	2	3
0.0	0.5000	0.8413	0.9772	0.9987
0.1	0.5398	0.8643	0.9821	0.9990
0.2	0.5793	0.8849	0.9861	0.9993
0.3	0.6179	0.9032	0.9893	0.9995
0.4	0.6554	0.9192	0.9918	0.9997
0.5	0.6915	0.9332	0.9938	0.9998
0.6	0.7257	0.9452	0.9953	0.9998
0.7	0.7580	0.9554	0.9965	0.9999
0.8	0.7881	0.9641	0.9974	0.9999
0.9	0.8159	0.9713	0.9981	1.0000

For example:

$$\Phi(0.5) = 0.6915$$
$$\Phi(1.2) = 0.8849$$
$$\Phi(-1.2) = 1 - \Phi(1.2) = 1 - 0.8849 = 0.1151$$

Appendix B – The 30/360 day count method

The 30/360 day count method is used to determine the number of days between two dates based on an assumption that each month has 30 days.

Let the variables below describe the earlier of the two dates:

$M1$ = month of the earlier date

$D1$ = day of the earlier date

$Y1$ = year of the earlier date

Let the variables below describe the later of the two dates:

$M2$ = month of the later date

$D2$ = day of the later date

$Y2$ = year of the later date

The following rules should be applied in the order presented:

1. If $D1$ is the last day of February, and $D2$ is the last day of February, then change $D2$ to 30.

2. If $D1$ is the last day of February, then change $D1$ to 30.

3. If $D1$ is 30 or 31, and $D2$ is 31, then change $D2$ to 30.

4. If $D1$ is 31, then change $D1$ to 30.

The number of days between the two dates is then:

$$\text{Number of days} = 360(Y2 - Y1) + 30(M2 - M1) + (D2 - D1)$$

Solutions to practice questions

Free online solutions manual

Detailed worked solutions to every practice question in this book be downloaded free of charge from the BPP Professional Education website at **www.bpptraining.com** (go to any page and look for Text Question Solutions in the "About our Products" menu). Other useful study resources can also be found in our online store.

Chapter 1:   Interest rates

Q1.1: $363.00

Q1.2:   0.253%

Q1.3: $1,723.54

Q1.4:   0.529%

Q1.5: $1,884.45

Q1.6:   The accumulated value is $5,030.78 at 5% and $1,894,817.37 at 10%.

Q1.7: $1,573.08

Q1.8: $13,947.55

Q1.9: $4,950.00

Q1.10: 6.542%

Q1.11: $224.66

Q1.12: $886.92

Q1.13: $40.50

Q1.14: $380.87

Q1.15: $164.87

Q1.16: $319.48

Q1.17: $38.90

Q1.18: $784.60

Q1.19: $3.511%

Q1.20: $6.45

Chapter 2:   Level annuities

Q2.1: $9,089.89

Q2.2: $560.69

Q2.3: $77.76

Q2.4: $49,839.51

Q2.5: $22.97

Q2.6: $2,249.60

Q2.7: $942.79

Q2.8: $1,438.90

Q2.9: $350.22

Q2.10: $161.05

Q2.11: $36,781.74

Q2.12: $5,139.79

Q2.13: 17

Q2.14: 21.5%

Q2.15: 9.15%

Q2.16: 15

Q2.17: $17,193.27

Q2.18: 0.36

Q2.19: 30

Q2.20: 12.25%

Chapter 3:   Varying annuities

Q3.1: $4,647.00

Q3.2: $7,440.00

Q3.3: $8,831.22

Q3.4: $22,788.32

Q3.5: $4,448.74

Q3.6: $9,747.74

Q3.7: $241.14

Q3.8: $77,284.41

Q3.9: $43,099.50

Q3.10: $68,292.28

Q3.11: $1,711.49

Q3.12: $1,615.40

Q3.13: $179,451.76

Q3.14: $179,451.76

Q3.15: $92.57

Q3.16: $549.07

Q3.17: 2.0305

Q3.18: 0.04

Q3.19: 111.11

Q3.20: $1,314.39

Chapter 4:   Non-level interest rates and annuities

Q4.1: $46,236.14

Q4.2:   8.16%

Q4.3: $6,170.17

Q4.4: $1,557.76

Q4.5:   6.23%

Q4.6: $3,714.26

Q4.7: $9,138.00

Q4.8: $24,939.80

Q4.9: $240,390.22

Q4.10: $3,671.76

Q4.11: $1,959,000.90

Q4.12: $3,162.86

Q4.13: $34,972.92

Q4.14: $251.97

Q4.15: $2,191.59

Q4.16: $5,549.27

Q4.17: $39.83

Q4.18: $1,952.75

Q4.19: $2,729.21

Q4.20: $116.19

Chapter 5:   Project appraisal and loans

Q5.1: $6,188.24

Q5.2:   17.08%

Q5.3:   3.3038%

Q5.4:   14.83%

Q5.5: $886,999.03

Q5.6: $820.04

Q5.7:   Mrs. Rich's dollar-weighted interest rate is –13.2% and Mr. Rich's dollar-weighted interest rate is 16.9%.

Q5.8:   14.9%

Q5.9:   0.05

Q5.10: $346.96

Q5.11: $8,895.44

Q5.12: $3,878.40

Q5.13: The interest paid in the 10th payment is $141.58 and the principal paid in the 10th payment is $205.38.

Q5.14: $7,096.55

Q5.15:   (i) $3,801.83
       (ii) $4,000.00

Q5.16:   5.83%

Q5.17: $559.88

Q5.18:   14.18%

Q5.19:   15%

Q5.20:   (i) $17,691.77
       (ii) $119.73
       (iii) The interest component of the 7th payment is $261.67 and the principal component of the 7th payment is $1,078.43.

Chapter 6:   Financial instruments

Q6.1: $984.38

Q6.2:   If the interest is reinvested at 6%, the lump sum at 5 years is $5,975,318.54.
If the interest is reinvested at 4%, the amount payable at 5 years is $5,949,463.19.

Q6.3:   The net payments received by each party are as follows:

Time	1-year LIBOR	Net Payment Received by A	Net Payment Received by B	Dealer Receives
1	7.0%	2,000	-3,000	1,000
2	8.0%	12,000	-13,000	1,000
3	6.7%	-1,000	0	1,000
4	6.0%	-8,000	7,000	1,000

Q6.4:   There are no cash flows at 6 months nor at 1 year.
The cash flow at 18 months is $2,500.00 and the cash flow at 2 years is $6,250.00.

Q6.5: $91.92

Q6.6: $95.26

Q6.7: $0.38

Q6.8:   5.06%

Q6.9: $33.60

Q6.10: $25.00

Q6.11:   0.05

Q6.12:   0.02

Q6.13: $14.53

Q6.14: $201.67

Q6.15: $59.48

Q6.16: $80.03

Q6.17: $985,739

Q6.18: $4.79

Q6.19: $1,055.09

Q6.20: 6.7%

Chapter 7:   Duration, convexity and immunization

Q7.1:   3.428

Q7.2: $113.915

Q7.3:   19.608

Q7.4:   1.7955

Q7.5:   15

Q7.6:   14.913

Q7.7: $81.52

Q7.8:   13.8378

Q7.9:   5.414

Q7.10: 8.81

Q7.11: 4.20

Q7.12: 20.74

Q7.13: $98.14

Q7.14: The price is $20.0, the modified duration is 20.0, and the convexity is 800.0.

Q7.15: The Macaulay duration is 5, and the Macaulay convexity is 25.

Q7.16: –3.29%

Q7.17: The company's position is immunized.

Q7.18: The company invests $47,285.58 in the 4-year bond and $9,457.12 in the 10 year bond.

Q7.19   1.167

Q7.20: 7.56

Chapter 8:   The term structure of interest rates

Q8.1:   The price of the 1-year bond is $101.8519.
        The price of the 2-year bond is $91.2389.
        The price of the 3-year bond is $125.5085.

Q8.2: $118.66

Q8.3:   The 1-year annual effective spot rate is 8.0%.
        The 2-year annual effective spot rate is 9.0%.
        The 3-year annual effective spot rate is 10.0%.

Q8.4: $166.83

Q8.5: $118.66

Q8.6:   The annual forward rate applicable for the first year is 8.0%.
        The annual forward rate applicable for the second year is 10.009%.
        The annual forward rate applicable for the third year is 12.028%.

Q8.7:　The annual forward rate applicable for the first year is 5.0%.
　　　　The annual forward rate applicable for the second year is 8.122%.
　　　　The annual forward rate applicable for the third year is 13.212%.

Q8.8:　The 1-year spot rate is 7.0%.
　　　　The 2-year spot rate is 6.0%.
　　　　The 3-year spot rate is 8.0%.

Q8.9:　The 1-year spot rate is 10.0%.
　　　　The 2-year spot rate is 10.0%.
　　　　The 3-year spot rate is 10.0%.

Q8.10:　The forward rate applicable for the first year is 10.0%.
　　　　The forward rate applicable for the second year is 10.0%.
　　　　The forward rate applicable for the third year is 10.0%.

Q8.11:　$111.44

Q8.12:　11.0564%

Q8.13:　8.1996%

Q8.14:　The bond is undervalued, so we buy the bond for $93.3425. We also borrow $5.1402 at the 1-year spot rate and $88.7972 at the 2-year spot rate.

Q8.15:　(i) 15.0%
　　　　(ii) The investor should purchase 12.0227 2-year bonds and sell 1.0735 1-year bonds.

Q8.16:　The investor sells 12.4445 2-year bonds and purchases 1.1111 1-year bonds. The investor also deposits $1,000 at 17% for two years.

Q8.17:　$65.33

Q8.18:　The nominal 1-year spot rate compounded quarterly is 5.9557%.
　　　　The nominal 2-year spot rate compounded quarterly is 5.4621%.
　　　　The nominal 3-year spot rate compounded quarterly is 5.9541%.

Q8.19:　The nominal half-year spot rate compounded semiannually is 14.612%.
　　　　The nominal 1-year spot rate compounded semiannually is 12.396%.

Q8.20:　9.2646%

Chapter 9:　　Stochastic interest rates

Q9.1:　$2.045.92

Q9.2:　$336.91

Q9.3:　The mean is $10,136.43 and the standard deviation is $398.01.

Q9.4:　$148,154.40

Q9.5:　Statements III and IV are correct.

Q9.6:　$55,896.80

Q9.7:　If the interest rates are independent and identically distributed, then the expected accumulated value of an annuity-immediate is equal to the accumulated value of an annuity-immediate calculated at the mean interest rate.

Q9.8:　(i) $1.1025
　　　　(ii) 0.000441

Q9.9:　The mean is 0.0486995 and the variance is 0.0001814.

Q9.10:   (i) 1.1025
        (ii) 0.000441

Q9.11:   Statements I and III are correct.

Q9.12:   (i) The expected value is 0.0093832 and the variance is 0.00033065.
        (ii) 84.5%

Q9.13:   ($121.75, $130.30)

Q9.14:   The mean is 0.0623676 and the variance is 0.0011292.

Q9.15:   6.1837%

Q9.16:   21.1%

Q9.17:   Under the constant model, the probability is 36.0%.

Q9.18: $99.41

Q9.19:   4.65%

Q9.20: $0.363

Review questions

Q1:   A

Q2:   B

Q3:   E

Q4:   B

Q5:   D

Q6:   D

Q7:   D

Q8:   C

Q9:   B

Q10:   E

Q11:   D

Q12:   B

Q13:   E

Q14:   C

Q15:   D

Q16:   A

Q17:   C

Q18:   A

Q19:   B

Q20:   E

Q21:   B

Q22:   E

Q23:   D

Q24:   A

Q25:   E

Q26:   D

Q27:   C

Q28:   E

Q29:   D

Q30:   E

Q31:   E

Q32:   C

Q33:   A

Q34:   B

Q35:   B

Q36:   D

Q37:   A

Q38:   E

Q39:   D

Q40:   B

Free online solutions manual

Detailed worked solutions to every practice question in this book be downloaded free of charge from the BPP Professional Education website at **www.bpptraining.com** (go to any page and look for Text Question Solutions in the "About our Products" menu). Other useful study resources can also be found in our online store.

Bibliography

Babbel, David and Craig Merrill. "Valuation of Interest-Sensitive Financial Instruments." Society of Actuaries, Monograph M-FI96-1, 1996.

Black, Fisher and Myron Scholes. "The Pricing of Options and Corporate Liabilities." Journal of Political Economy, Volume 81, 1973.

Brealey, Richard, and Stewart Myers. "Principles of Corporate Finance." McGraw-Hill/Irwin, 7th edition, 2003.

Broverman, Samuel. "Mathematics of Investment and Credit." Actex, 2nd edition, 1996.

Copeland, Thomas and J. Fred Weston. "Financial Theory and Corporate Policy." Addison-Wesley, 3rd edition, 1992.

Fabozzi, Frank, editor. "The Handbook of Fixed Income Securities." McGraw-Hill, 6th edition, 2001.

Hull, John. "Options, Futures, and other Derivatives." Prentice Hall, 3rd edition, 1997.

Kellison, Stephen. "The Theory of Interest." Irwin/McGraw-Hill, 2nd edition, 1991.

Mayle, Jan. "Standard Securities Calculation Methods." Securities Industry Association, 2nd printing, 1996.

Mizrahi, Abe and Michael Sullivan. "Calculus and Analytic Geometry." Wadsworth Publishing Company, 1982.

Redington, Frank. "Review of the Principles of Life-Office Valuations." Journal of the Institute of Actuaries, Volume 78, 1952.

Ross, Sheldon. "An Introduction to Mathematical Finance." Cambridge University Press, 1st edition, 1999.

Zima, Petr and Robert Brown. "Mathematics of Finance." McGraw-Hill, 2nd edition, 1996.

Index